IN WHICH THEY SERVED

The Royal Navy Officer Experience
in the Second World War

BRIAN LAVERY

CONWAY

A Conway Maritime book

© Brian Lavery, 2008

First published in hardback in Great Britain
in 2008 by Conway,
an imprint of Anova Books,
10 Southcombe Street,
London W14 0RA
www.anovabooks.com
www.conwaypublishing.com

This paperback edition first published in 2009

British Library Cataloguing in Publication Data:
A catalogue record for this book is available
from the British Library.

ISBN: 9781844860975

Edited and designed by DAG Publications Ltd.

Printed and bound in the UK by CPI Mackays, Chatham ME5 8TD

To receive regular email updates on forthcoming
Conway titles, email conway@anovabooks.com
with 'Conway Update' in the subject field.

CONTENTS

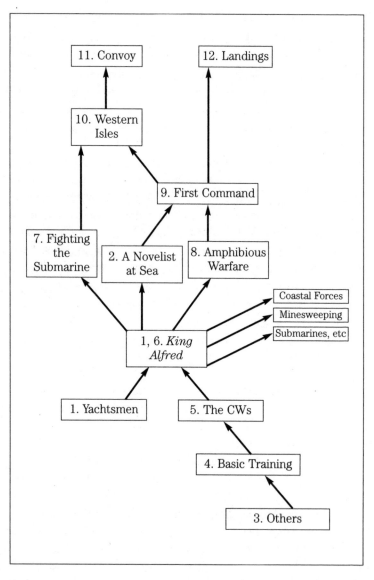

11. Convoy

12. Landings

10. Western Isles

9. First Command

7. Fighting the Submarine

2. A Novelist at Sea

8. Amphibious Warfare

1, 6. *King Alfred*

Coastal Forces

Minesweeping

Submarines, etc

1. Yachtsmen

5. The CWs

4. Basic Training

3. Others

INTRODUCTION

This book tells the story of the temporary naval officers who enabled the Royal Navy to expand around sevenfold during the Second World War. It recounts the experiences of the young men, mostly without any sailing or military experience, who had to learn very quickly to cope in the dangerous and unforgiving environment of the sea. It outlines how they were selected and trained in the techniques and skills they had to learn, and how they responded to the training.

The navy had no plans to expand on such a scale and did not see the necessity until the war was well under way. It had to learn new techniques such as the use of radar, and open up new areas such as amphibious operations. Most of the training went against the grain for traditional naval officers, who tended to believe that a boy had to start about the age of 13 as they did in Nelson's day, and have long years of naval education before taking charge. There were many difficulties along the way, but in the end the improvised system worked. The blend of naval discipline and individual initiative produced a highly effective force.

Temporary naval officers fought on all fronts and in all types of ship – battleships, submarines, minesweepers, coastal craft and many others. For the sake of space and in order to allow it to remain reasonably focused, this book tends to concentrate on two particular areas, convoy escort and amphibious warfare, which took up a large proportion of temporary officers and arguably had the most direct effect on winning the war.

I have tried to tell the story through the eyes of the individuals concerned, particularly those who had to go from almost no knowledge of naval affairs to taking charge of a watch or even a small ship in less than a year. Their training divides quite naturally into different stages, as shown in the diagram. I am grateful to all those who wrote memoirs of the period, and particularly to Geoffrey Ball who has added much to his papers in the Imperial War Museum through correspondence.

Thanks are also due to the staffs of the Imperial War Museum, National Maritime Museum, London Library and National Archives, and especially those in Hove Library who maintain a small but very important collection of *King Alfred* papers, collected by Judy Middleton when writing a book on the base.

I

THE YACHTSMEN GO TO WAR

It was a glittering occasion on 23 October 1936, two days after Trafalgar Day, when the Auxiliary Patrol Club held its annual dinner. Its members had distinguished themselves in small boats in the last war, and there was silence when the new First Sea Lord and professional head of the Royal Navy, Admiral of the Fleet Sir Ernle Chatfield, stood up to address them. He was perhaps the finest naval officer of his day, a veteran of the Battle of Jutland in 1916 and of long struggles to keep up the navy's strength and to regain control of the Fleet Air Arm from the RAF. He was a small, rather distinguished-looking man. Lacking any humour, but noted for his great strength of mind, he looked nothing like the traditional image of a British admiral. Everyone knew that another war was now possible, as Nazi Germany, Fascist Italy and Imperial Japan all pursued aggressive and expansionist policies. Chatfield's message was tailored to his audience. Recognizing their services in the past, he announced the formation of a new naval reserve, of yachtsmen who would be called up to train as officers on the outbreak of war.

It was advertised in the press next day, and there was an instant response. Within a few days 300 men had written to HMS *President*, the headquarters of the London Division of the Royal Naval Volunteer Reserve, and a similar number had applied to the Admiral Commanding Reserves. The Admiralty had anticipated the possibility that the scheme might prove very popular, in which case, 'steps will have to be taken to restrict the numbers to estimated requirements'. But it did not anticipate the response. Ewen Montague was one of those who were attracted.

To my joy, the Admiralty formed the R.N.V.(S.)R. – the supplementary reserve. This was simply a list of people who had some knowledge of seamanship, boat handling and navigation, and who were ready to be called up on the outbreak of war and who the Navy felt, with training, might make officers. There were no drills or periods of annual training, a factor of importance to me with a busy junior practice at the Bar.[1]

Though it was not nearly as widespread as it later became, yachting was a thriving sport in 1936. Yachtsmen might be divided into three main categories according to the size of their boats. At the top end were the millionaires' private yachts, as big as small ships and manned by professional crews. One advertised for sale in the same week as the Supplementary Reserve scheme was announced boasted an 'owner's suite comprising large stateroom, bathroom and valet's cabin', while for guests there were 'six splendid cabins, two bathrooms and maid's cabin'.[2] The Admiralty was more interested in the boats in this case – the crews might prove useful in wartime as ordinary members of the Merchant Navy or the Royal Naval Reserve, but not in the Supplementary Reserve. The yachts, on the other hand, could often be adapted for anti-submarine, patrol or training purposes. The navy had used them in large numbers in the last war as part of the Auxiliary Patrol, and currently it kept a list of those that might be suitable in the next. At the top of the tree was the Royal Yacht *Victoria and Albert* of 1901, and the Admiralty's own yacht *Enchantress*. These were already listed among His Majesty's Ships, and the *Enchantress* would serve as a convoy escort in wartime. Among the private ones was T. O. M. Sopwith's *Philante*, which was then under construction by Camper & Nicholson at Gosport and was destined to become the largest private yacht in Britain; and the *Lady Shahrazad*, which was currently owned by M. S. Myers in the City of London. She was nearly 200 feet long, had a cruising range of nearly 3,000 miles and was lying at Greenock. She had already served as a hospital ship in the last war and had crossed the Atlantic several times.

The lower end of yachting consisted of small, open boats, mostly used for inshore racing but occasionally for cruising by some hardy souls who did not mind sleeping afloat and under canvas. They were the forerunner of the modern dinghy, and there were many 'one design' classes adapted to conditions in the waters round local clubs. The International 14-foot dinghy was in more general use and was the most popular boat type. It could be taken to races around the country, for its hull was the largest that could be transported by rail for six shillings, and the mast was the longest that could be accommodated on a standard goods wagon. Boats like these needed crews with athletic qualities and a good deal of sailing skill, but they did not necessarily foster the techniques of navigation and crew organization that the Admiralty was looking for. Many young men used them as a stepping-stone to larger boats. The novelist Nicholas Monsarrat wrote, 'I had raced a 14-foot dinghy from the age of fifteen, and crewed in boats as big as four tons ... Once I crewed in the Mersey Race, which started in the Menai Straits, took us across to Dublin, then back to Holyhead. We lost our way – it was enough to say that I was still learning navigation – and fetched up, miles and even days astern of the fleet, on an unknown coast which just had to be somewhere in Ireland.'[3] That, he considered, was a reasonable amount of yachting to enter the navy as an RNVR officer.[4] Monsarrat also eked out his income by writing humorous articles for the yachting magazines. In 1937 he suggested that every yacht needed a crew of at least nine, including 'A man handy with fender, boathook and above all, with his tongue. Nine times out of ten it's the man who gets his insult in first who wins an apology for the collision.' He concluded, 'They'd look well in a four tonner, wouldn't they?'[5]

This was part of the middle range, of decked boats with cabins, which could be used either for racing or for long-distance cruising. The majority of them were sailing boats, with deep ballast keels so that they could not capsize except in the most extreme circumstances. Smaller boats might be fitted with cabins, but it was generally felt that 'at the yachting ports 6-tonners and motor cruisers of about 30 ft form the greater part of the pleasure fleet'.[6] Yachting at this level was a fairly exclusive sport, because the factors that later opened it up to a mass market were not yet present. Hulls could not yet be moulded in fibreglass, each having to be individually constructed, usually in wood, occasionally in steel. A six-tonner might cost about £400 new, a 28-foot motor cruiser about £600, about the same as a small suburban house.[7] There were no electronic aids to navigation, so sailing was highly skilled work, especially with a deep keel underneath – there was a high penalty for going aground, particularly if the tide fell and the boat was left lying on its side for several hours, with the risk of discomfort and damage and the certainty of loss of prestige in the yacht club. Such yachts were generally owned by businessmen and the professional middle classes, and crewed by their friends and family. This was an ideal recruiting ground for reserve officers.

Most were also members of yacht clubs, some of which were rather exclusive organizations. Membership could be used as a measure of one's place on the social scale, which appealed to the Admiralty. There were more than 200 of them in Britain in 1936. At the top was the Royal Yacht Squadron of Cowes, which already had strong links with the navy. Its members were entitled to fly the white ensign, and a number of places were reserved for naval officers – for others, membership was very expensive and the entrance fee was 100 guineas (£105), far in excess of any other club, and there was a long waiting list. The Royal London Yacht Club was not far behind, with its clubhouse in Cowes. Its commodore from 1936 was Sir Richard Fairey the aircraft designer, and its members included Sopwith.[8] Some clubs had a specialist membership, such as barristers, graduates of Oxford and Cambridge or certain public schools, or particular branches of the armed forces. Clubs with 'Royal' in the title were generally socially superior and more expensive. 'Yacht' clubs were higher in the scale than 'sailing' clubs, which tended to concentrate more on dinghies. All clubs had balls and dinners outside the sailing season, when etiquette was often on a level with that demanded in the naval wardroom, and sometimes modelled on naval tradition.

A Scottish powerboat builder, Silver of Roseneath, outlined what could be done with different types of craft in peacetime. Thirty-foot boats were ideal for estuaries such as the Clyde; a 40-foot boat could range from there to the south coast of England; and a 50- or 60-foot boat could go as far afield as the Mediterranean.[9] Sailing yachtsmen tended to look down on powerboat owners, even if most sailing yachts had a small auxiliary engine of their own. But powerboat techniques were obviously useful to the navy. Many ship's boats were now powered by motor rather than sail or steam. Small powerboats had proved their use for inshore work in the last war. And foreign navies, including the Germans and Italians, were working hard to develop fast motor boats that could launch torpedoes against much larger ships. There was plenty of scope for the motor yachtsman in the new reserve.

Both sailing yachts and powerboats could be raced, and again there was a hierarchy. At the top of the sailing tree, until very recently, was the King's own racing yacht *Britannia*, which had won many races since she was built in 1893. Recently she had been ceremoniously sunk on the death of King George V. Next was the J-class, huge racing yachts, 127 feet long but with only a single mast. Yachting opinion was agreed that they were expensive toys for the very rich, except that they supported national prestige in the America's Cup races. Otherwise, they preferred smaller and more accessible racing yachts.

Cowes Week every August was one of the great events of the social season, but in 1936 it was blighted by the death of the King, the absence of *Britannia*, and an unusually high number of dismastings. Other glamorous races included the America's Cup, in which the latest British challengers were financed by Sopwith. Another contest that tested the mettle was the Fastnet race of 608 miles from Plymouth out to the rock of that name and back again. P. Guingand sailed in it in 1939 as navigator of the yacht *Thalassa*, owned by Alan B. Baker, and was happy with the result: '1000. All hands on deck. Customs aboard. Just heard we've got a second in one class, having been beaten only by Rose (45 ton). We are 16 ton so feel quite elated.'[10] Many more yachts raced locally, often within their clubs. In powerboat racing, the doyen was Hubert Scott-Paine of the British Power Boat Company. His *Miss Britain III* was the

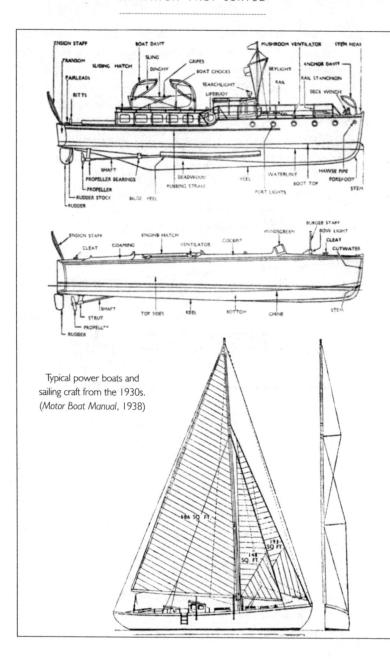

Typical power boats and sailing craft from the 1930s.
(*Motor Boat Manual*, 1938)

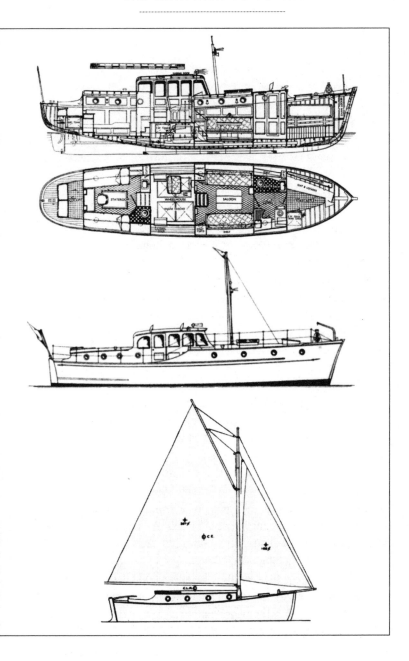

first boat to exceed 100mph, and he was a strong advocate of fast motor boats for the navy.

Yachting was recovering slowly from the effects of the great depression. Eight thousand tons of yachts over 100 tons each had been built in the last boom year of 1930; this dipped to less than a thousand tons, then rose to 4,000 tons by 1937. By the time the boatyards of the Clyde, Solent and east coast of England were no longer as silent as they had been, and powerboat builders were preparing for a boom. The yachting community, like everyone else, had a shock in December when King Edward VIII ended his short reign by abdication to marry an American divorcee; but it felt rather happier with the new King, George VI. He was a naval officer like his father before him, and patron of several yacht clubs. He was seen as a safe pair of hands or, as the yachting press put it, an old-fashioned traditional rig. They looked forward to his Coronation Review in May 1937, when the Royal Navy would be out in force and yachts of all shapes and sizes would be allocated spaces to watch the festivities. They also looked forward to the next America's Cup race, when *Endeavour II*, sponsored by Sopwith, would take on the Americans.

The idea of a yachtsman reserve was not completely new, and it had long been recognized that skills acquired during play or leisure might be useful in work or in warfare – as late as the 1920s it was claimed that fox-hunting was essential in training the army's future cavalry officers. In 1831 an article in the *United Services Journal* claimed, 'In time of war also, the advantage of commanding the services of a well-disciplined and orderly body of seamen, such as is employed in the [yacht] clubs, must be allowed to be incalculable by all who understand the machinery of naval governments.'[11] The idea was dormant for seventy years, until in 1903 Erskine Childers published his bestselling novel *The Riddle of the Sands*, in which yachtsmen expose a planned German invasion of England. This led to political pressure to form a reserve of part-time officers and seaman. Since 1859 the navy had supported the Royal Naval Reserve, made up of merchant officers and seamen, but it had no wish to allow amateurs on the decks of its warships. Nevertheless the new Royal Naval Volunteer Reserve was formed in 1903 and flourished across the country. At the start of the war in 1914, Winston Churchill (then First Lord of the Admiralty) believed that the ships of the navy were fully manned already and sent most of the RNVR off to the Western Front, where many of them fought and died as part of the Royal Naval Division. There was cause to regret this later on, as the submarine menace threatened to bring Britain to its knees, and the skills of amateurs, such as the members of the Auxiliary Patrol that Chatfield addressed in 1936, were needed to fight against the U-boats in coastal waters.

The navy took the RNVR a little more seriously after 1918, but it had its limits as a reserve. It actually used very few yachtsmen, for as D. A. Rayner of the Liverpool Division put it, 'To join the RNVR meant giving up so much leisure that it was almost impossible to combine the two.'[12] It remained quite small, with a maximum of 809 officers and 5,371 men on the eve of war in 1939.[13] This was not nearly enough to cover any planned expansion. Moreover, the army and the RAF were already earmarking suitable people for commissions and might pick up the best candidates in this way.

The idea of a yachtsman reserve was revived in June 1936 when the secretary of the Royal Cruising Club wrote to the Admiralty pointing out that it had many members with 'very considerable cruising experience in control of their own yachts' who would make ideal officers for a new auxiliary patrol. The Admiralty replied that 'a scheme for earmarking suitable gentlemen in peace time for service … in war' was already under consideration. Inside the Admiralty there was much debate about what was needed. There was no obvious requirement for a 'small craft reserve' as such, and to form one out of the blue would be an insult to established RNVR officers who had given up so much spare time to train. On the other hand, there was much interest in Parliament and the press, and there was the need to do something with the 'many who are too old, unable to spare time for all the necessary drills, or who live too far from any R.N.V.R. headquarters'. Therefore the scheme was devised to 'satisfy the requirements of this class of volunteer without in any way cutting across the present R.N.V.R. organization ...'

The scheme was quickly drawn up and approved by the Board of Admiralty eight days before Chatfield's speech. Treasury officials noted with satisfaction that 'it is not proposed to issue any pay, retainer, or allowances in time of peace'. It was established by Order in Council early in November and was to be called the Royal Naval Volunteer (Supplementary) Reserve or RNV(S)R. It was open to 'gentlemen who are interested in yachting and similar pursuits' aged from 18 to 39 who were resident in the United Kingdom and 'of pure European descent, and the son of either natural-born or naturalised British parents'. They would have to be of a high physical standard, equal to that of executive officers in the Royal Navy, though the eyesight requirements were relaxed slightly. Men were invited to apply to the nearest of eight RNVR divisions throughout the country.[14]

Each would fill in a form giving his 'Special Qualifications (Knowledge of Navigation, Practical Seamanship, etc.)' and agree that

> in the event of my enrollment in the Royal Naval Supplementary Reserve I undertake to serve subject to the provisions of the 'Naval Forces Act 1903,' and the acts incorporated therein and of the Admiralty Regulations made in pursuance thereof, and to the Rules of the Division for the time being, and to the customs and usages of His Majesty's Naval Service should my services be required on mobilisation.[15]

It was stressed to them that they would receive no payments or retainers in peacetime, but they were encouraged to undertake training at their own expense.[16]

The RNVR divisions were overwhelmed with the rush of applicants, especially in London, which contained a prosperous middle class and was within easy reach of the yachting areas of the Solent and the east coast rivers. Lord Runciman, the shipping magnate, now in his 90th year, wrote to *The Times* to volunteer his services – he could still 'handle a big or small sailing vessel, mend or fake a sail, and handle a marlinspike ...'[17] The First Lord of the Admiralty kept him happy by making him honorary commodore of the new reserve, but he died soon afterwards.

The yachting press was cautious about the scheme at first. *Yachting Monthly* considered it 'a step in the right direction' but deplored the lack of any formal training. It did not expect the new reservists to feature largely in any war.

> The day of the 18 knot patrol launch and the amateur 'mosquito fleet' is long past. We anticipate that home coastal patrol would be carried on by seaplanes, assisted in thick weather, by a fleet of 40 knot hydroplanes in the hands of specially trained naval men. What is almost certain is that the volunteers will not be put in charge of such small craft but will be given other work of a less specialized nature on shore and in larger units afloat.[18]

The weekly *Yachting World* was more positive. The scheme was 'heartening indeed', for there was 'a keenness among amateur yachtsmen' that had been 'in danger of being neglected'.[19] But by November it was beginning to sense a certain amount of criticism. 'In yacht clubs, at dinners, in all sorts of places, views have been aired, alternative schemes mooted. Voluntary training should have been included, a uniform should have been designed, etc., etc. ...' The magazine defended the authorities: 'The scheme must be based on actual naval requirements and not on what yachtsmen might find amusing.'[20]

There was a slight dip in interest after the first excitement. At the end of February 1937, *Yachting World* reported, 'the zeal of the newly enrolled members of the Royal Naval Volunteer Supplementary Reserve has outrun not discretion but the scope of the reserve as it now exists'. More training was suggested, following the example of the Little Ship Club of central London. It had 1,200 members and claimed to be the largest in the world, and it had the resources to introduce classes for the reservists. Other yachtsmen founded the London Flotilla to support their training. They persuaded shipping companies to provide facilities and some voyaged as far as the Baltic and Mediterranean. They bought two old naval picket boats, known as the *Response* (to the call for volunteers) and the *Reply*.[21] R. J. B. Walker had no yachting experience as such, but he joined a group operating from the small, picturesque port of Pin Mill on the east coast of England, led by a member of a wealthy family.

> We sailed out into the North Sea, altered course together in formation, practiced abandoning ship, Morse and semaphore, and became skilled in signaling with the International Code. August Courtauld, though a highly competent yachtsman, was a terrifying skipper. He would go out in all weathers, crowd on the maximum of sail and, with the Courtauld millions behind him, did not mind in the least if his sails were torn to shreds – he just ordered a new set.[22]

Yachting Monthly remained sceptical about the scheme and reported, 'We understand that the Royal Naval Supplementary Reserve is still wanting capable men. Applications have not been slow in coming in, but it is learned that the majority are rejected on account of unsuitability, physical unfitness and inferior eyesight.'[23] There was a further influx during the Munich Crisis two years after the scheme was announced, and the prospect of war seemed very real. New entrants included K. Adlard Coles, who had cruised extensively in the Baltic, and Peter Scott, the naturalist and son of the tragic Antarctic hero, who was a champion in 14-footers.[24] By that time 1,300 candidates had been examined and enrolled but a further 1,090 were still awaiting their interviews, of whom 911 were in the London Division area.[25]

In 1938, in order to assist in the selection of Supplementary Reserve candidates and encourage their training, the Marine Department of the Board of Trade set up the Yacht Master's Certificate (Coastal). This was less demanding than the full Yacht

Master's Certificate of Competency, which demanded 'a thoroughly sound knowledge of fore-and-aft seamanship'. Non-members of the RNVSR were allowed to sit for it, but there was a strict eyesight test to meet naval needs, and it had to be taken without glasses. Examinations were held in various centres, rather obscurely on the fifth Monday of a month. There was a two-hour written paper on the compass, two hours on meteorology and three on chartwork, including a sample passage posing such questions as,

> The weather clearing up, the vessel's speed was increased to 10 knots, and a S.W. by W. compass course steered. Rinrawos Pt. Lt.-Ho. bore S. 9 degrees by compass, and after continuing on this course for 1 hour, it bore abeam by compass.
>
> Find the vessel's position at time of taking second bearing.

This was followed by oral examination on tides, general navigation and pilotage (including the all-important Regulations for Preventing Collisions at Sea), seamanship, rigging and the management of boats. The examination on signals could be taken at a later date and demanded a knowledge of Morse code, semaphore and flag signals.[26] The scheme came too late to have much effect, and less than 150 members of the reserve had passed it, or higher qualifications, by June 1939.[27]

Everyone knew that the navy would have to expand its officer corps in wartime, but the questions were by how much, and from what sources. In March 1939 it was reasonably confident of finding enough officers, for 'the increase of requirements of officers in the Navy is nothing like so big as that in the Army'. It intended to continue with the normal training of regular officers with a view to the future and the entry of trainee regular officers, through either Dartmouth College at about the age of thirteen or the Special Entry Scheme at eighteen, was to continue throughout the war.

> Owing to the fact that naval cadets enter the Navy before the usual school leaving age and to the length of time required to

train naval officers, it will be desirable to continue entries at the normal level in order to avoid dislocation after the war. By a normal level is meant the numbers required to give the flow likely to be needed after the war.[28]

As First Lord of the Admiralty from the first day of the conflict, Winston Churchill suggested,

We have at the present time to face the possibility of a war for which all the national resources are required. The Manpower Sub-Committee of the [Committee of Imperial Defence] are drawing up arrangements for the full utilization of the manpower of the country. They have not however dealt with the question of the supply of officers except for an arrangement for the allocation of University personnel. The Merchant Marine is expected to supply a proportion of the officers whom the Navy will require in time of war and the above-mentioned University scheme will doubtless supply a good many more. It is to be expected however that there will be requirements beyond what can be supplied from these sources.[29]

Promotions from lower deck regulars were to be considered, but only reluctantly and on a small scale. The head of the Commission and Warrant Branch at the Admiralty wrote, 'It will hardly be possible to keep these down to the peacetime level. There will therefore be a risk that there might be a surplus of this type of officer after the war.'[30] Officers might come from the Merchant Navy, but many of the most suitable ones had already been taken up through the Royal Naval Reserve, and it was obvious that merchant shipping would need all the officers it could find to fight a war against the U-boat blockade. Eventually the navy would have to turn to educated men of the general, non-seafaring population to officer its ships, but that would take time. For now, the yachtsmen of the Supplementary Reserve provided a ready supply as the navy expanded.

War was declared on 3 September 1939, and mobilization of the Royal Navy began immediately. The regular force (excluding Royal Marines) stood at 9,762 officers and 109,170 men in January 1939. That was supplemented by calling up retired officers and ratings, the merchant seamen of the Royal Naval Reserve, and amateurs of the RNVR. In general the mobilization worked reasonably well. The administrative side had been tested many times, and there had been a practical exercise during the Munich Crisis of 1938. The Admiralty was less used to dealing with the Supplementary Reservists, and there was some confusion about their call-up, but it was soon agreed to take them in batches for short naval training. By the end of the first week of war, the initial group of direct entrants to the Royal Navy commissions was on its way to an improvized training base on the south coast of England.

The Admiralty chose Hove, near Brighton, as the centre for training the supplementaries. It was already the headquarters of the Sussex Division of the RNVR, the only one out of eight that was based on shore rather than in an antiquated training ship, so it allowed some room for expansion. There was a partly completed municipal swimming pool and leisure centre next door, which could be adapted for training purposes. The peacetime members of the RNVR would be quickly mobilized in the event of war, so the space would be available. Most of the other divisions were in great cities like London, Bristol, Glasgow and Hull, which could expect heavy bombing, whereas Hove was a small, non-industrial town. As a holiday resort it had good passenger transport links, particularly with London, where a large number of the supplementaries lived. As the war was expected to develop in 1939, it was well away from enemy action but had access to the English Channel for training. Of course, the last condition soon altered with the fall of France in 1940.

The training base was to be commissioned as a ship, in well established naval tradition. The name of King Alfred was already attached to the leisure centre. It was very acceptable to the navy, for he had founded the first English navy in AD 875. It had been used for an armoured cruiser earlier in the century, but there was no ship of that name in the navy now. The fiction of being a ship was maintained in several ways. Technically the name of HMS *King Alfred* was borne by *Motor Launch 1649*, formerly used by the Sussex Division of the RNVR, and the whole school of several hundred officers and men was attached to it. Staff and trainees in the buildings were expected to use nautical terms 'on board', almost to the point of pedantry. One trainee officer complained, 'The constant talk of houses as 'hookers', the floors as 'decks', and upstairs as 'up-top' not only depressed me, but had the effect of making me think that my contemporaries were all experts, which was, in fact, very far from the case.' Some of his colleagues even referred to one end of the building as 'the bow'.[31]

There was a rush of new enrolments in the training scheme as soon as war was declared. After the first batches, not all the new officers under training were members of the peacetime Supplementary Reserve. Sub-Lieutenant P. de Guingand had sailed in the Fastnet race of 1939, but his name did not appear on the Supplementaries list, nor did that of Geoffrey Willans, who was interviewed in the Admiralty Building in November 1939:

I understand, Mr. Willans, that you have done some yachting? Yes – guardedly. Cruised round Brest and the Bay of Biscay? Yes – still more guardedly.

Then came the real questions.

What, for instance, were those funny little numbers on the chart? Fathoms, I suggested brightly. ... then, goodness, what was an occulting light? Two ships, one here, one over there, which one would keep out of the way of the other?[32]

Not all were yachtsmen, for the scheme included provision for others who might be suitable. Broadcaster and writer Ludovic Kennedy entered by a rather circuitous route. At first he got no reply from the Admiralty and was told he was on a waiting list long after he had actually been commissioned. Meanwhile he found a way in through the universities scheme. A naval background was a great aid at this stage: Kennedy's father was a naval captain who had been retired compulsorily in 1922 and was now commanding the armed merchant cruiser *Rawalpindi*, in which he would shortly lose his life. His group included Bill Richmond, son of a rear-admiral and naval historian, and Peter Beatty, the son of the commander of the battlecruisers at Jutland and the most famous admiral of his day. Even if these men had no great sailing skills, they were at least steeped in naval culture and tradition, and were less likely to be disorientated than many later candidates were.

One of the staff describes the rush to get things ready for the new officers:

Headquarters of the Sussex Division R.N.V.R. at Victoria Terrace were in the last throes of mobilization, and we newcomers had to step warily among their household goods, glad of an option on the left-hand corner of somebody else's mantelpiece to find stowage for our paperwork. The offices buzzed with activity, and in the Mess Sir Cooper Rawson, in shirt sleeves, strove gallantly to pack books and pictures, amid the flying feet of messengers and boy scouts.

Our job was to rig a fair sized Officers' Training Establishment, as it were, on the beach. There was a syllabus of training to be chopped into periods of instruction, into time-tables and into Routine. ... There were lectures to be written, class rooms to find and furnish, billets to arrange and the Paymaster Captain alone knows what problems of administration to be solved by *leger-de-main* in the small hours of the morning.[33]

HMS *King Alfred* was commanded throughout the war by Captain John Pelly, a regular naval officer who had first entered Dartmouth in 1903 at the age of fourteen. He served in battleships during the First World War and in training ships in the 1920s. He commanded a sloop on the China Station but retired in 1934 to farm in Essex and was recalled at the start of the war. He was a tall man with a large face, but he was rather retiring and was not often seen about the 'decks' of his new ship. He was a dominant personality in setting up the training programmes and maintaining standards, and according to *The Times* he was 'ideally fitted by temperament for this onerous task, being gifted with a genial and strong personality and a constant thoughtfulness for the welfare of others ...'[34]

'ALL MY OWN UNAIDED WORK'

Lieutenant-Commander
Edward Crick. (*KA Magazine*)

Commander F. P. Frai had served as a radio operator in the First World War and afterwards joined the Sussex Division of the RNVR. He was commissioned in 1927. As maintenance commander at the start of the war, he provided the local knowledge for setting up *King Alfred*, until he was transferred to Leith in 1940. There were two wings to the teaching staff. There were nine instructor officers in mid-1940, under Instructor-Commander C. D. Howell. They were graduates with good degrees, employed to teach general subjects like mathematics and science and wore light blue cloth between their rank stripes to distinguish them from generalist officers of the

Captain Pelly. (*KA Magazine*)

executive branch of the navy. These were represented in the Training Branch, headed by Commander J. S. Head, who was also the Chief of Staff. Barrister Ewen Montague was outraged when Head banned the carrying of pipes by officers in uniform, and put a newspaper photograph of the First Sea Lord carrying one on the ship's notice board. Head replied with a notice that read:

Special arrangements have now been made whereby any officer at present under training at H.M.S. *King Alfred* may smoke a pipe on shore when in uniform and in public, in spite of K.R and A.I. No. so-and-so ... when he become[s] First Sea Lord.[35]

Under Head were nine lieutenant-commanders of the regular navy, one of whom was a specialist in gunnery and another in torpedoes. There were four RNVR lieutenants, one as liaison officer and another in charge of physical training. There were also four sub-lieutenants RNVR to act as officers of the watch, to take charge of the ship on a minute to minute basis.

Lieutenant-Commander Edward A. Crick was one of the first instructors at the base, and he too would remain throughout the war. He was educated at Lancing College, which would soon become part of the *King Alfred* complex, and joined the navy via the Special Entry scheme for naval officers in 1915 at the age of eighteen. His performance was mediocre (he was 40th out of a class of 62), but he was commissioned and served in the destroyer *Viceroy* and the cruiser *Caradoc* before retiring under the Geddes Axe (the post-First World War drive for economies) in 1922, to be recalled at the outbreak of war. He had a knack of producing clear blackboard drawings, including 'The whole naval might of Britain', according to the *King Alfred Magazine*.[36] He was genial and popular, and in 1943 his drawing and writing skills were used to produce *The Seaman's Pocket-Book*, a simplified and much more readable version of the old *Manual of Seamanship* which was issued to new entrants to the navy. The staff of *King Alfred* also included a medical branch of four, headed by a surgeon-commander, six accountant officers including the captain's secretary, and a chaplain.[37]

There was also a large staff of petty officers, mostly ageing regulars recalled from retirement, like the officers. Petty Officer E. G. Hardy, for example, had served in the last *King Alfred*, a four-funnelled cruiser, on the China Station in 1908–10. Technically the new temporary sub-lieutenants were senior to the petty officers, but it was accepted in training bases that such men could take charge of

Dress before and after entry to *King Alfred*. (*KA Magazine*)

parades, and they could be just as fearsome as any sergeant-major in the army. Ludovic Kennedy was one of the first to make the acquaintance of Chief Petty Officer Vass – 'a tubby little chief gunner's mate'.[38] Like Crick, he featured regularly in the Magazine – under the heading, 'Things one seldom hears', the first item was 'Who is C.P.O. Vass?'[39] His prominent nose and receding chin were caricatured more than once.

The base was formally commissioned on 11 September 1939, and the first 210 officers arrived that day. 'They came in taxis, on foot, and some even in limousines driven by liveried chauffeurs. They sported top hats, bowlers, trilbies, and golf caps, and they wore morning suits, tweeds, grey flannels, and shorts.'[40] They had been told to be prepared for a stay of up to three months and according to one of the staff, 'their baggage looked so formidable that we sent them straight off to their billets to unload.' They were examined by the medical team, and overall about ten per cent were rejected. The others were led into a reception party hosted by the captain. The trainees then 'cruised about in tow of C.P.O. instructors' while spectators watched them through the railings. There was no room to parade inside the headquarters, but fortunately the autumn weather was good enough to work outside. The first formal parade (known to the navy as 'Divisions') was a moment of extreme emotion for Ewen Montagu. He stood fast when the order 'Fall out the Roman Catholics' was given – as a Jew, he expected another order to cover the other religions. Instead he found himself in a Church of England service, including the naval prayer.

'O Eternal Lord God, who alone spreadest out the heavens and rulest the raging of the sea; who hast compassed the waters with bounds until day and night come to an end. Be pleased to receive into thy most Almighty and most gracious protection the persons of thy servants, and the fleet in which we serve.'

He found it completely appropriate: 'at that moment, with a group of us dedicating ourselves together to a common effort in anticipation of unknown dangers, saying *that* prayer together was exactly right and a most moving experience.'[41]

There was still some disorder a week after the commissioning when the officers' mess was opened 'amidst dirt and foul noises … in the space that was intended to be an underground car park. We sat upon green Corporation chairs (which left marked, almost indelible impressions on us) and at Contractor's tables that seemed to be supported by more legs than a centipede.'[42]

The navy was very careful to distinguish its temporary officers from the regulars, unlike the other services – in the army, Territorials no longer had to wear a 'T' on their shoulders or lapels. The officers of the regular navy wore straight stripes. Most had trained for about 6½ years before being commissioned. The merchant seamen of the Royal Naval Reserve wore a complex pattern of intertwined braid, and those of the RNVR, regarded as vastly inferior to 'real' officers of the regular Royal Navy, had wavy stripes and hence were known as the 'wavy navy'. According to the popular saying, the RNR were sailors trying to be gentlemen, the RNVR were gentlemen trying to be sailors, and the RN were neither, or both, according to who one was talking to.

There was little uniformity in the early days of the course, when officers had had no chance to provide themselves with the proper clothing. According to Ludovic Kennedy, they were 'dressed (for uniforms took time to be made) in an odd assortment of sports jackets, casual trousers, Trilby hats and caps'.[43] Dress was important, nevertheless. 'The standard to be reached by a Sub-Lieutenant R.N.V.R. in September 1939 was the possession of a full uniform. An additional pair of trousers would almost certainly have led to accelerated promotion.'[44] The leaflet issued at the beginning of 1941 detailed what an officer had to provide for himself out of a £40 grant. He needed an 'undress' coat, the eight-button double-breasted blue jacket, also known as the monkey jacket, that was the characteristic part of a naval officers' dress. He also needed a pair of blue trousers, a cap with badge, brown tan gloves, white shirts with linen collars, a black tie, dark blue or black socks, black leather boots or shoes without toecaps and a blue overcoat. Full uniform was worn in the evening, but for daytime instruction he wore only the monkey jacket and cap, with grey flannel trousers and green gaiters, a cricket or tennis shirt, white cashmere scarf and a blue or white sweater.[45]

The trainee officers over the age of twenty had the rank of 'Probationary Temporary Acting Sub-Lieutenant.' As a lawyer, Ewen Montagu 'couldn't but admire the cautious way in which the Admiralty kept its options open – three ways of getting rid of one!'[46] Ludovic Kennedy fell foul of the regulations when he was asked how old he was:

'Nineteen, sir,' I said. 'I shall be twenty in two weeks time.'
'In that case,' he said,' I shall have to disrate you to midshipman. You were born two weeks too late.'[47]

Officers under training were billeted out to local landladies and hotels, which were numerous in a seaside resort like Hove. They were instructed to 'take care to do no damage in their Billets, and not to disturb any "blackout" arrangements'. They were to remember they were still under naval discipline and to report any 'reasonable' complaints to the Billeting Officer, Shipwright-Lieutenant H. S. Brice.

Ludovic Kennedy was allocated to one of 'Hove's numerous genteel hotels where the residents were mostly retired service people and old ladies'. At first he shared a room with 'a rather dreary man who claimed he was kept awake by my flow of language during the night'. At 7.30 each morning he and his comrades walked a few hundred yards to *King Alfred*.[48]

One officer was far less satisfied and wrote a poem for the *King Alfred Magazine*.

> I've stood for the stains on the wall,
>   Mrs. Randall,
> I've stood for the stains on the wall ...
> The tea-pot with just half a spout,
>   Mrs. Randall ...
> The bath where the water leaks out,
>   Mrs. Randall ...
> That slowly decaying stuffed trout,
>   Mrs. Randall,
> That leers from the case in the hall ...
> The way that your family shout,
>   Mrs. Randall ...
> Oh hell ... that's the worst of them all![49]

Officers under training were members of the wardroom mess and usually dined there unless they had permission to eat 'ashore'. They had to pay a shilling (5p) a day to supplement the basic naval ration. The comforts of the mess began to improve. 'Now we have lino on the floors, soft seats to sit upon, and an Ante-Room bathed in fresh air and sunshine.' The base had taken over the whole of the Hove leisure centre by the spring of 1940. 'The major bath is now the Great Hall. Here we have Church, cinema shows, and general lectures. The minor bath is the Cadet Ratings' Recreational Room and Library and the Restaurant is used as the Officers' Ante-Room.'[50] There were guest nights on Thursdays, to which any officer under training was entitled to invite male friends. In the early days Ludovic

Kennedy put on 'a superb burlesque of a political speech', and Edward Benbow, a concert pianist, played and accompanied songs.[51] The tradition of an entertainment put on by the trainees soon became established.

A regular routine began to emerge at *King Alfred*. New arrivals for each course reported to the headquarters to be assigned to their accommodation, and each was sent off to 'sling his hammock' (that is, to settle into his billet). He was medically examined and then interviewed by the captain, who would tell him finally whether he was accepted or not. Officers under training were organized in classes of 20 to 25, each taking it in turn to serve as class captain, taking command when mustered as a class and holding responsibility for its good order. According to a joke in the magazine, 'The *Class Captain* is the member of the class whose name comes next on the class list. In theory, he is in command: in practice, he is in the minority.'[52] He was assisted by a class regulating officer, mainly responsible for seeing that information was passed on.[53]

The course lasted about ten days for the early entrants, but gradually became longer. In July 1940 Commander Head wrote,

Self-help should be the Keynote of all training and this is particularly true here where we try to put ten weeks' work into half that period. Hours of instruction and syllabuses have been arranged with the object of avoiding specialisation, and thus prepare the trainee for the general needs of the fleet. Therefore when officers are drafted they should be able to feel confident that they are capable of carrying out the duties assigned to them.[54]

Nicholas Monsarrat was rather dismissive of the training, which consisted of 'learning how to salute and how to respond in a seamanlike manner to the Loyal Toast (don't stand up), and studying an ambiguous manual called *Street Fighting for Junior Officers*'.[55] Ludovic Kennedy and his comrades 'did extensive drills, learnt the rule of the road and the meanings of flags, practised boat handling in nearby Shoreham Harbour – and one dreadful day were taken to a nearby football field to be instructed in the one form of warfare I had joined the Navy to avoid: bayonet attack... Afterwards I wondered if it was not too late to transfer to the RAF.'[56] Peter Scott found the course enjoyable and the schedule quite relaxed:

The life is not too hard – breakfast at any time after eight – Divisions nine – fifteen minutes P.T. – lectures till lunch – including heaps of parades (there are 400 of us) Lunch at twelve in the mess – lectures from one-thirty to four and then off till nine next morning with dinner in mess. Plenty of home-work, of course, which it is well to do – Morse, navigation, etc. It keeps one busy.[57]

According to Ewen Montagu:

From the very first day of operations in the *King Alfred* the staff of that 'ship' began, not only to train us in the skills which we would need, navigation, seamanship, gunnery and so on, but also to instill into us what was almost more important – the spirit of the Navy and its discipline.

As a result, 'my admiration for, and devotion to, the Navy became fixed and has persisted to the present day, in spite of ups and downs.'[58]

R. J. B. Walker was also on one of the first batches, after his experience in the Courtauld yacht:

We learnt a few of the Royal Navy traditions and the rudiments of drill (already acquired at the school Officer Training Corps), and after ten days were paraded and divided into sheep and goats, the sheep being those with yachtmaster tickets and goats without. My brother Ralph and his friend, Ralph Swan, both had tickets; I, then a Courtauld Institute student, had none. It did not make much difference. We were all drafted into the

Northern Patrol or Western Approaches where we found our Supplementary voyages in the North Sea invaluable.[59]

Geoffrey Willans also found that the main effect was to give a sense of responsibility and belonging:

'It is possible,' said one of our lecturers, 'that some of you may find yourselves in command of a dirty little ship dropping anchor for the night in a lonely little bay. I would suggest to you that it is worthwhile postponing your bath and your shave and seeing personally that colours are saluted at the proper time. St Vincent outside Toulon, at a period when men really did sea time, set a personal example by appearing in full dress with sword and decorations. Meridians are passed, weeks and years go by, but this custom has survived. You, too, would do well to insist on this discipline of the colours, even if your White Ensign is only the size of a pocket-handkerchief.

You felt then that you were in contact with something that had roots. It gave you a sense of responsibility.

But he was not entirely happy during the course.

Time was too short for anything but a smattering of naval background. We did squad drill, physical training, and trotted round in gas masks ... but one also encountered the tradition of the Navy in a manner that was quite accidental. At times it shone like a beacon through all the other brouhaha of calling one end of the building 'the bow'. There was an unwilling poetry about it that was immensely stimulating.[60]

In February 1940, Winston Churchill told the House of Commons that 400 men had already been passed through the period of training. By the end of February, 900 had been called up, and it was expected that a further 600 or 700 would be needed. By May 1940, 1,700 had passed through successfully.[61] But the direct entry scheme could not last for ever. Only a limited number of men were suitable for it, with the right age, experience and attitudes, for an almost instant commission in the Royal Navy. Early in 1940 the Admiralty outlined its future policy for *King Alfred*.

At present officers being sent for training consist of the gentlemen whose names appear in the list of the R.N.V.S.R., together with nominations from certain other sources such as the Joint University Recruiting Boards. The establishment will, however, be subsequently used for the training of R.N.V.R., R.N.S.R., and Hostilities Only ratings, who have been recommended for commissions.[62]

The new group of trainees, known as cadet-ratings and still wearing the uniform of the lower deck, began to arrive at *King Alfred* for a much longer course and the first group passed out by May 1940.

At the end of that month, the officers under training and cadet-ratings were enjoying the usual guest night and entertainment on the evening of Thursday 29th. Most of them kept up with the news and were well aware of the British army's retreat in France. Perhaps they had some inkling of what was being asked for when Commander Frai stood up between turns and took the microphone almost apologetically. He asked for anyone with knowledge of internal combustion engines to go to one of the classrooms. A large number of officers and cadets went, expecting something important, and the room was packed to overflowing as Commander Head picked out sixteen officers and the same number of cadet-ratings – he had been asked for 30, but presumably he wanted to allow some spares. The chosen men shook hands with their comrades and asked them to look after their guests. The rest withdrew back to the concert.

Around 10 p.m. Commander Head 'said "au-revoir" to the bus loads of Trainees who had volunteered for Dunkirk and who had sworn solemnly that they knew all there was to know about the insides of motor-boat engines and how to run them. It was not for me to doubt their word; my only desire was to be one of them.'[63] After a five-hour journey along unlit roads, they arrived in a hotel at Dover. An hour later, ten officers and ten ratings were called out, including Sub-Lieutenant R. F. N. Bass. They reported to the Senior Naval Officer, Dover, and Bass was put into the Dutch cargo vessel *Hilda*, commanded by Captain Pim, RNVR, taking time off from running Churchill's Map Room in Downing Street. They steamed a short distance along the coast to Deal, where they picked up six motorboats and two lifeboats. Meanwhile Cadet-Ratings Price and Foster were put into a small motorboat called the *Skylark* with a stoker to run the engine. The popular phrase 'Any more for the *Skylark*?' was some indication of the popularity of the name for seaside trip boats, and she was one of nine that took part in the subsequent operation. Price and Foster got very seasick as they were towed across the English Channel by the minesweeping trawler *Fyldea*.

The Admiralty's request for men with experience of the internal combustion engine was quite deliberate, for engine breakdowns were to bedevil the operations off Dunkirk. This is not surprising, as most boats were being pushed well beyond their usual limits, while the crews often had to work with unfamiliar engines or steering and control systems. There was a ready supply of stokers in the naval barracks, but, as their title implies, they were more familiar with the steam engine than with petrol or diesel. Even the highly skilled and experienced chief engine room artificer in the motorboat *Triton* was found to be 'utterly useless'.[64] Only about one person in twenty owned a car before the war, but they might well include most of the middle-class young men at *King Alfred*, not to mention their experience with yacht engines. Sub-Lieutenant Marwood J. B. Yeatman of *King Alfred* overhauled the engine of another *Skylark* before she was towed over to Dunkirk. Sub-Lieutenant T. W. Betts took command of the river launch *Empress* at Sheerness but soon found that the clutch of the starboard engine was giving trouble and failed even to make Ramsgate without a tow. It was hastily repaired, but off Dunkirk it refused to go into astern or even neutral gear as the boat headed for the beach, so she ran aground and was abandoned.[65]

Bass arrived off Dunkirk in the *Hilda* at eight in the evening of 30 May, less than 24 hours after volunteering at *King Alfred*. An aerial dogfight was in progress as he watched five Allied aircraft fight fifteen Germans. An hour later he was off the beach at La Panne in Belgium, watching heavy artillery directed at the destroyers and sloops that were taking British and French troops off. There is no record that he came across Commodore Sir Gilbert Stephenson, who was in charge of the beach there, but Sub-Lieutenant S. C. Allen of the rather inappropriately named yacht *Frightened Lady* met an 'Admiral with side whiskers' in the company of the army commander-in-chief, Lord Gort, and helped him to construct a jetty of abandoned vehicles. Lieutenant Irvine of the RNR first encountered Stephenson when he brought the motorboat *Triton* alongside a destroyer and an officer in a sodden lambskin coat called out, 'Well done, motor boat, wait for me.' Irvine was never quite sure of the commodore's name, even though he spent some time ferrying him around the beaches and found out about his capacity for extreme praise or blame.

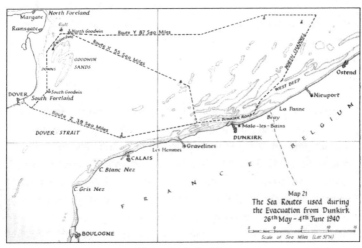

The routes to Dunkirk.

He said I had done good work, but could not allow me to rest, too much remained to be done. I might say that the Commodore said I was 'A good fellow', and on other occasions said I was 'a bloody fool'. It is not my place to pass remarks about Senior Officers, but this officer, without cap, soaked through, without food, was a great example to me. He helped me to steer, to pass lines, to haul drowning soldiers aboard, and very often would say, 'Come on the Army'. 'Where have I seen you before, you are so good looking, I'm sure I know you.' Other times he cursed the lot as stupid.[66]

RNR and RNVR officers would see much more of Commodore Stephenson during the rest of the war.

The motorboats towed by *Hilda* were sent to pick men up from the beach, and by ten that evening she had transferred her first party to a destroyer offshore. There was heavy gunfire all night, and many of the motorboats were out of action, but work was resumed at three in the morning. Pim found it was not effective to tow lines of lifeboats out to the ships, as they were very difficult to control, but he acquired various other motorboats in the area to ferry the troops out from the beaches. He was grateful for the help of young officers and ratings from *King Alfred* and the gunnery school HMS *Excellent* to man them. He was impressed with the stoicism of the British soldier, even after two or three days hiding among the dunes awaiting rescue.

The soldiers, though obviously extremely tired, made no complaints of the delay or of the wettings which they got in wading out in the surf to get into the motor boats, and were more than thankful for the kindnesses which were shown them in the various ships. … The great majority of the troops were carrying their rifles and side-arms, and I insisted that in no case must they be thrown away. I was impressed to notice that the military padres were always amongst the last to leave the beach in their respective parties.

He also commented on the good relations between the crew and the soldiers.

> I was much impressed by the good-nature of the ship's company in handing to all those who lost their clothing or were in sad condition owing to being covered in oil, any parts of their uniform or private possessions not in use. This applied equally to the soldiers who were most generous in sharing their clothing of all sorts.[67]

Hilda went alongside the destroyer *Keith* at 7.30 in the morning of 1 June to make contact with Admiral Wake-Walker, and had only just left her when she was hit by a dive-bomber. *Hilda* picked up about 50 survivors, and half an hour later the minesweeper *Skipjack* was also sunk and 60 or 70 men were rescued. There were 'fearful scenes' when some men were pulled on board covered in fuel oil. The *Hilda* now had 530 men on board, many of them badly wounded and in critical condition as she headed back to Dover.[68]

In *Skylark*, Price and Foster towed a pleasure boat whose engines had broken down. She ran into a submerged vehicle, and the towing line became entangled around the propeller, so Foster dived in to cut it. They picked up 70 British soldiers and took them to the *Fyldea*. After returning to get the crew of the wrecked ferry *Nymph* and 60 more soldiers, they took off 70 French troops. They beached the boat each time, dropping a large kedge anchor over the stern as they did so and using it to haul the boat off the shore when it was fully loaded. On the third trip they found that *Fyldea* was aground, and their attempts to haul her off failed. The engines of *Skylark* were now overheating and the boat was 'slightly on fire'. They found the destroyer *Worcester* and went on board her with the Frenchmen.[69]

Sub-Lieutenant Long was in another party from *King Alfred*, and at Sheerness he was allocated to a Thames river boat, *Tigris One*, to take charge of a civilian crew of a coxswain, engineer and deckhand. They proceeded down the estuary with a party of motorboats, slowed down by several breakdowns. At Ramsgate they received orders to go to Dunkirk, which they reached at 0845 in the morning of 1 June, but only six of the nineteen small craft were still with them. They began using the motorboats to ferry men out to *Tigris* and then on to passenger ships, but this was far too slow, so they rigged a line to the hopper *Southampton Queen*, anchored offshore, and beached *Tigris*. At first it was difficult to persuade men to come on board, but after a while they rushed on and threatened to swamp the vessel. Heavy air attacks began, but *Tigris* took about 130 men and was hauled off the beach by *Southampton Queen*. She did six trips in this way until she was too damaged to sail any further. Her crew went on board the destroyer *Amazon*, while Long continued the work in a motorboat manned by a naval CPO.[70]

Some of *King Alfred's* former students were there too. Sub-Lieutenant John Miles had been a member of the Supplementary Reserve in Northern Ireland and was commissioned in November 1939. He was now serving in the armed yacht *Grive* under the 67-year-old veteran Captain the Honourable Lionel Lambart, who had entered the navy in 1887 and first retired in 1903, then returned to win the Distinguished Service Order as a staff officer during the evacuation from Gallipoli – which was good experience for his present task. On 30 May, *Grive* launched her four boats to pick up men from the beaches but soon found this was an inefficient method, and she took only 300 troops back to Dover. She returned next day and went alongside the East Mole at Dunkirk, where the majority of men were picked up from. She took on 400 but had to leave because of a heavy air raid. On the way out she rescued men from the sinking *Ivanhoe* and *Havant* and came back with a total of 700 on board. Not all the officers could stand the strain, and Captain Lambart put ashore Lieutenant West of the RNR who was over 60 and 'had earned a rest'. He also discharged a merchant navy engineer whose nerves were shattered after a previous sinking. They sailed again for Dunkirk, but at 2230 in the evening of 1 June there was a tremendous explosion as *Grive* apparently hit a magnetic mine and sank. Miles was the only officer saved.[71]

There was great confusion off the mole in the evening of 2 June as Sub-Lieutenant Yeatman approached in the lifeboat *Michael Stephens*, having given up *Skylark* at Dover. He was rammed by a motor torpedo boat without much damage then found a sloop, which was unable to come alongside due to 'swish of tide'. He pushed her in using his powerful lifeboat engines, then went ashore himself to find a group of disorientated French soldiers. He persuaded them to board the sloop by means of 'some forceful language and a rifle butt'. Unlike the British troops, they were being taken to an uncertain future in a foreign country, rather than home. Many of them were from inland areas and had never crossed, or even seen, the sea, whereas every British soldier had at least sailed over to France. Yeatman took 52 men in the lifeboat and set off to find a tug to transfer them to. On the way he was hit again by a fishing boat, being at 'considerably greater risk from the movements of allied craft than from Nazi shelling. There seemed to be no attempt to keep any rule of the road.' There was no tug, so he took the men all the way to Dover in six hours.[72]

On board the destroyer *Worcester* on the way back to Dover, Cadet-Rating Price was sent below to help in the boiler room, a most frightening place when they were attacked by Stukas. On deck, Foster was slightly wounded by a machine-gun bullet, the only casualty in the ship. They arrived at Dover, and Foster went to hospital, while Price set off again in *Lady Cable*. Built in 1924 and 40 feet long, she had spent her life thus far in taking holidaymakers on trips along the Devon coast and rivers.[73] She had already done one trip under her owner, Mr Gooding of Torquay. She was now commanded by an aged, retired sub-lieutenant with a weak heart. Price acted well above his rate as 'first lieutenant', and a stoker took charge of the engines. They were towed over by a tug and began ferrying troops out again on the last day of the evacuation, 3 June. Again the French were reluctant to embark, as they did not want to go without orders from their officers. Nevertheless, *Lady Cable* ferried out four loads of 40 or 50 men each to a waiting tug and destroyer. After the last trip they decided to go back, as they had promised, to get a British army officer who was directing affairs on the mole. Price landed but was told that he had already left, so they took on about twenty soldiers, knowing that the tug would have gone by now and they would have to carry them all the way across – they believed they were the last boat to leave Dunkirk in the whole evacuation.

The engine was slowly failing and they began a series of adventures as it finally gave up just outside the harbour. They spotted an abandoned War Department motor launch *Haig* with one of her engines still running in neutral, and Price managed to jump on board her. Attempts to throw a line across were not helped by the French soldiers who had no idea what was going on, and Price had to swim back with it. The Frenchmen helped pump water out of *Haig*, and she began to tow *Lady Cable* across the Channel in the growing daylight, though it took some time to find out that her two engines had separate controls. One of her engines gave up about 7.30 in the morning, but the stoker had repaired *Lady Cable's*, though it stopped and started continually. The boats proceeded, lashed together, as the French troops became increasingly panicky, led by 'a soldier (Heaven knows what rank or capacity) who looked at least sixty, having a pointed grey beard!' At last they found a French warship to take the troops off, but Price was left on board her by mistake and *Lady Cable* and *Haig* had to go on with only the officer and stokers. Price was subsequently recommended for accelerated promotion for his initiative, courage and efficiency.[74]

The little ships of Dunkirk became part of British national mythology, showing determination to go on fighting in the face of devastating attacks, and demonstrating how the people of a supposedly non-military nation could improvise in adversity. In fact their role was smaller than legend suggests. About two thirds of the 338,226 troops taken off were embarked directly onto destroyers and passenger ships from the mole. But that does not diminish the bravery and enterprise of those involved, including the officers and cadet-ratings of *King Alfred*.

Back at *King Alfred*, officers completing the course were interviewed and given a certain amount of choice as to what kind of ship they would be appointed to. The small, fast ships of coastal forces had barely begun their operations in 1940, so destroyers were considered the prize appointment. Peter Scott wrote at the time, 'I've just been earmarked for destroyers, which is an absolutely plum job. It's the thing which every Wavy Navy man dreams of getting into, and I'm so terribly cock-a-hoop about it.'[75] Ludovic Kennedy was sent to a course on barrage balloons, pending a posting to his father's ship, but *Rawalpindi* was sunk and his father died heroically before that could happen. Kennedy then went to an anti-submarine course before joining the Tribal-class destroyer *Tartar*, almost the best posting that a young officer could ask for. Geoffrey Willans was also sent on to anti-submarine warfare, in which he would be followed by many other temporary RNVR officers.

> Our course at Portland was a brave attempt to give us a working knowledge of anti-submarine devices within the space of three weeks. Most of it consisted of taking copious notes, but we would sometimes go to sea for practice attacks. Once again this proved for me more of a battle against sickness than submarines.[76]

But *King Alfred* had cause for pride in September 1940 when Sub-Lieutenant Alex Donaldson came top in the final examination in the training school HMS *Osprey*, beating a regular RN lieutenant.[77]

Not all the newly-commissioned officers went to sea. Ewen Montagu was summoned by Commander Head after the details of his legal background emerged.

> Why, he demanded, had I concealed the fact that I was a K.C.? Lots of people could do Sub's jobs and 'you're not going to have a yachting holiday at the Government's expense – you're going to a proper job where your qualifications will count.'

He had to wait for an appointment and spent time among the CPO instructors, where he 'learnt more about how the Navy really works than I could have done in any other way ...' They presented him with 'The H.M.S. *King Alfred* Long Service and Good conduct Medal'. Eventually he was posted to naval intelligence.[78]

Many new officers would go to fight in the Battle of the Atlantic. By May 1941 there were 37 British-manned destroyers, 30 corvettes and ten sloops in Western Approaches Command. The destroyers were largely officered by the regular Royal Navy, with occasional reservists in the junior ranks. The sloops had a combination of RN and RNR officers, but with two temporary lieutenants and nine temporary sub-lieutenants RNVR. The corvettes were mostly commanded by RNR officers, but they had 21 temporary lieutenants and 60 temporary sub-lieutenants, more than half the 140 officers on board. Already the temporary RNVR officers were proving their worth in one of the most important struggles in history.

2
A NOVELIST AT SEA

In August 1940, Sub-Lieutenant Nicholas Monsarrat was appointed to the new Flower-class corvette *Campanula*, the 22nd[1] of 222 ships of this type built in Britain and Canada during the first half of the war. He first saw her when she was in the fitting-out basin of Fleming & Ferguson's shipyard on the Clyde, covered with the usual clutter, a scene of apparent chaos where 'there was a stupefying row going on all the time, with everyone contributing according to his means'.[2] The ship was commissioned a few days later with little ceremony:

It was only a matter of saluting while the spotless ensign was hoisted, sending a signalman to the mast-head with the commissioning pennant, and mounting an armed sentry on the jetty alongside; but what a difference it seemed to make, that transfer from a floating shell to one of His Majesty's warships in commission. We walked differently when we were aboard, we sat in the wardroom with a sense of formal proprietorship; we even came to resent the dock workers crowding the decks, and strolling about without care or caution.[3]

She carried out trials in the Firth of Clyde, then the captain 'signed for the ship' after 'full-power trials, the working of the windlass, and the firing of every gun and depth-charge thrower carried'.[4]

In its original coastal role the corvette had been designed for a crew of 29, who would have lived in comparative luxury. But now it had to serve in the broad Atlantic. In one of the great paradoxes of naval manning, it needed far more for longer trips so that its engine room, sensors, bridge and weapons could be manned day and night on long voyages. It normally carried 60 men at this stage, in considerable discomfort. For officers it had a captain, who usually held the rank of lieutenant-commander, occasionally lieutenant, in the Royal Naval Reserve; it had a first lieutenant who was usually a full lieutenant in the RNR or the RNVR, and often two very green temporary sub-lieutenants of the RNVR.

The characters of Monsarrat's great novel *The Cruel Sea* are easily identifiable from the wardroom of *Campanula* and other ships like her. By Monsarrat's own account, Captain Ericson was not in fact R. V. E. Case of the *Campanula*; he was Captain Cuthbertson of the sister-ship *Zinnia*, 'as far as looks, achievement and reputation were concerned'. Case appears in Monsarrat's memoirs as something of a bully and was partly the model for the brutal first lieutenant, Bennett. He was a man of few words: his rare official reports were terse, and his private diary concentrated on the banal. Among his fellow officers in the escort groups, he was apparently regarded as a better seaman than a U-boat hunter, and even Monsarrat later conceded that in this respect he was 'a superb professional'.[5] Richard Case was 36 at the time. He had been educated in the training ship *Worcester* and as an apprentice with the Pacific Steam Navigation Company. He was called up as a lieutenant-commander RNR at the beginning of the war and commanded an anti-submarine force of trawlers on the east coast of England. He had already been awarded the Distinguished Service Cross twice, once for his work in escorting large ships among the fjords during the Norwegian campaign of 1940.[6]

Sub-Lieutenant Lockhart is obviously close to Monsarrat himself – a yachtsman, moderately successful writer, son of a surgeon and a highly competent officer – as Monsarrat undoubtedly was. Ferraby, the young and gauche sub-lieutenant, is the one character here who does not ring true. He is said to have gone through the same training as Monsarrat but was not a yachtsman, so he would not have been eligible in real life. Possibly such a man might have gained a commission later in the war, when the navy was desperate for officers, but then he would have had to go through a long screening process including service on the lower deck, which would have made him more mature if nothing else. Dramatically, he is needed as a foil to Lockhart, but he cannot be identified with a real person. The officer who did join with Monsarrat in August 1940 was R. F. J. Maberely, a bank manager, who was much more mature and competent.

Bennett, the Australian first lieutenant, is easier to explain. A man of his superficial self-confidence and partial experience could easily have bluffed his way through the system during a phase of rapid expansion, before suitable assessment mechanisms had been set up. The *Navy List* of 1940 shows the officer in the *Campanula* was Lieutenant Christopher Callow, Royal Australian Navy Volunteer Reserve. He joined at the right moment early in 1939, so reached the rank of lieutenant quickly. However good or bad he may have been as an officer, the only thing we can be sure about is that Monsarrat did not like him. He had transferred to a shore job by December 1940, and later he became an anti-submarine instructor in Australia, which subsequently appears in fiction. If he exaggerated his war experiences, he was not the only man to do that. He is barely described in Monsarrat's wartime book *H M Corvette* – an Australian, 'accustomed to herds of dumb animals', a former officer of a naval trawler, but no real sign of tyranny. In the autobiography, *Life is a Four Letter Word*, he appears simply as an 'Australian who was to demonstrate before he left us, a high-grade talent which could have supplied the text for a most saleable book, short-titled *The Hundred Best Ways of Being an Objectionable, Uncouth, Workshy, Snarling Sod'*. There is nothing to suggest that he was guilty of cowardice. In the novel he is a complete monster, a bully, lazy, a coward, incompetent, and 'lower class'. In the film he is even worse. Though he is no longer an Australian, for obvious commercial reasons, he is held responsible for Ferraby's breakdown as he drifts in the sea after the sinking of the *Compass Rose*.

A corvette was a short and stumpy vessel, though not unattractive. It was solidly built – Monsarrat called it his 'tin lifeboat'.[7] Externally, it had a high forecastle to meet oncoming seas (though not high enough as it turned out). Perched on a platform on top of that was its 4-inch gun, the smallest that could be expected to engage a U-boat on the surface. The forecastle ended just aft of that, and the

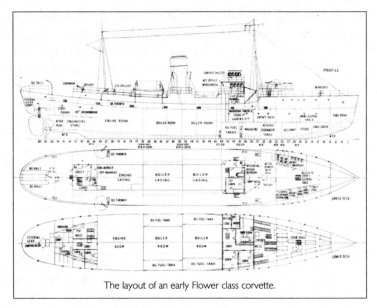

The layout of an early Flower class corvette.

sides of the ship swept down with a solid bulwark to keep the water off the upper deck – though again, not high enough. There was a mast just aft of the forecastle, soon to be fitted with a crow's nest for a lookout. Aft of that was the bridge structure, on three levels above the upper deck. On top was a square compass shelter with the main bridge around it, protected only by a rail and very exposed to the weather. Below that was the wheelhouse, which also contained the radio cabin, and under that were the captain's cabin and the officers' bathroom. A narrow deck stretched aft of the wheelhouse, covering the engine and boiler rooms. The stern of the ship rose in a steep curve and had a rounded shape, betraying the origin of the design – it had been hastily improvised just before the war, based on a type of whalecatcher. The stern was dominated by racks and throwers for its depth-charges, its only anti-submarine weapon. They could be set to explode at a certain depth, but methods of finding the submarine at close range were still inaccurate, and a large pattern of up to fourteen had to be fired at once to give a reasonable chance of a hit.

Internally, the space under the forecastle was mostly used for the seamen's accommodation, sleeping in hammocks and eating around mess tables. There were three messes on two decks so that seamen and stokers could be kept separate. Below that were store rooms for provisions and the asdic compartment, housing the echo-sounder for detecting submarines under the surface. Aft of the seamen's messes on the lower deck was the wardroom, used as a communal space and sitting room for the officers, which in a small ship included the captain. There were also cabins for the junior officers. Then came two boiler rooms and the engine room, taking up all the width and nearly half the length of the ship. The engine was a fairly simple triple-expansion type, cheap to produce and easy to maintain even in the middle of a rough ocean. At full power it could drive the ship at 16 and a half knots, faster than most merchant ships or a U-boat underwater, but slower than a U-boat on the surface. In the early days the galley was situated aft, at the end of the engine casing, an unfortunate position as meals had to be prepared on the mess decks, taken to the galley for cooking then forward again for serving. There was not much space below decks aft of the engine room, but there was a small mess for petty officers and space for some stores for provisions.

A few days after commissioning, *Campanula* sailed to the working-up base at Tobermory, where they were harassed by the legendary Commodore Stephenson, fresh from his experiences at La Panne during the Dunkirk evacuation. He was 'almost a professional Angry Man', who had a habit of arriving on board by launch on the ship's blind side and spotting any slackness. 'Daily we exercised everything, with a wild sense of crisis. We abandoned ship, we repelled boarders, we got out the kedge-anchor (an intolerable operation, this): we closed up action stations against the stop-watch, we fought fires, we prepared to tow, we put an armed boarding party ashore amid a hurricane of cheers.'[8] Captain Case, whatever his faults, was a good seaman and scored well in the final report; the despised first lieutenant was not far behind.[9]

Campanula sailed from Tobermory and arrived at Greenock on 20 September, to spend three weeks undergoing repairs. She went round the north of Scotland to join the Rosyth escort force on the east coast, but that order was quickly cancelled, and she arrived in Liverpool, Monsarrat's home town and favourite port, on 1 November. She was allocated to the Corvette Division and then became part of the Seventh Escort Group as it formed. It included the aged destroyers *Witch*, *Warwick* and *Wild Swan*, the notoriously unstable ex-American destroyers *Clare* and *Campbeltown*, and the fellow corvettes *Fleur de Lys*, *Nasturtium* and *Gardenia*. She was soon to join the titanic struggle known to history as the Battle of the Atlantic.

This was a much larger and longer affair than its title suggests. Usually a battle is taken to mean an event lasting from a few hours to a few days; this one lasted five and a three-quarter years. A battle was traditionally fought in a single place, such as Trafalgar, Waterloo, the Somme or Alamein; this one ranged even beyond the Atlantic, into the Arctic Ocean. It involved sailors of the Royal and Merchant Navies, as well as many allied fleets, airmen, shipbuilders, transport planners, dockers, and, famously, intelligence staff in the decoding of German signals.

It is no surprise to find that the extension of the meaning of 'battle' was created by Winston Churchill. At the Fall of France, he claimed that 'we have lost a battle, we have not lost a war'. He said, 'The Battle of France is over, the Battle of Britain is about to begin.' This, it turned out, was not a full-scale invasion but a series of air fights over southern England in 1940, but the use of the term was established. Churchill was also the first to use the word 'battle' to describe the war with the U-boat: 'In view of various German statements, we must assume that the Battle of the Atlantic has begun.'

At last, at nine in the morning of 24 November 1940, the Seventh Escort Group, including *Campanula*, the destroyers *Wanderer* and *Warwick* and corvette *Clematis*, put to sea with the Liverpool section of convoy OB 249. Convoys were only escorted as far as 19° West at that time, 400 miles west of Ireland, so the crews could not look forward to one of the great pleasures of a seaman's life, visits to foreign ports. There were a few nervous moments on the way north through the Irish Sea, for it was difficult to take a fix on Chicken Rock off the Isle of Man and thus avoid the hazards of the area; a trawler got in the way; then incoming convoys were met and had to be avoided. Early next morning, as the convoy passed through the North Channel between Ireland and Scotland, the wind began to increase. Dodging yet another incoming convoy, the OB 249 contingents from the Clyde and Oban were met at the appointed rendezvous, along with more escorts, including *Fleur de Lys*. They began the tedious work of arranging the 53 merchant ships into nine columns, 600 yards between each by day and 1,000 yards by night, and 400 between successive ships. About half were unladen and in ballast, 'returning the empties' as the men of the escorts put it. The rest were mostly carrying coal to help pay for the war effort. The weather got worse, and by the time the ships were in the open waters of the Atlantic a full gale was blowing from the south-west.

Monsarrat had his first taste of the Atlantic weather, and the notorious movement of the corvettes, which had been noticed early that autumn when they had their first experience of ocean conditions. After a ten-day voyage in September and October, Lieutenant-Commander Robert T. Bower of *Fleur de Lys* wrote to his superiors:

it was quite impossible to sit anywhere, all movables had to be lashed, and men off duty, all of whom were forced to take to their bunks, had great difficulty in saving themselves from being pitched out ... The seas were more than funnel-high and the rolling was quite insupportable. Immediately, things began to break loose under the impact of seas coming inboard at the break of the forecastle and sweeping aft along the waist. Thrower charges were torn from their racks, and both after Lewis-gun shields were smashed over and the mountings rendered useless. The gripes for both seaboats carried away; in the port boat, the steadying chains were torn out; in the starboard boat, the foremost block was broken by a sea hitting the boat.

... the rolling was incredible. In over twenty years in the service in every type of ship, I never encountered anything like it. Officers and men on duty became rapidly exhausted by the mere physical effort of holding on. Accurate navigation was impossible owing to the gyrations of the compass cards and the inability of helmsmen to keep the ship anywhere near her course. At times she was yawing 60 to 70 degrees.

The plight of the numerous seasick members of the crew and of some of the older men became pitiable. I am myself entirely immune from seasickness, but I must confess that I felt the strain severely from the point of view of prolonged physical effort. Under such conditions sleep, or indeed any kind of rest is impossible, as it entails considerable physical strain even to remain in a bunk.

It is impossible to escape the conclusion that these ships are unsuitable for Atlantic convoy work ... I assert with emphasis that neither ships nor men will be able to stand up to prolonged severe winter weather in the Atlantic. It is not that the men lack courage or resolution; merely that the physical strain is insupportable.

The corvettes had been designed for a coastal war, mostly in the North Sea, but the invasion of Norway and the Fall of France had changed all that. Now the U-boats could get easily out into the Atlantic and cut Britain's main supply lines. The original plan had been to man the corvettes with fishermen, but they were needed elsewhere – and anyway there were not nearly enough of them for the new, expanded navy. Whalecatchers had been manned by some of the hardiest seamen in the world; now the corvettes were crewed by hastily trained landsmen. But they had to be used, for in the winter of 1940/1 there was virtually nothing else, except trawlers and old destroyers, to fill the escort screen round each convoy. Sir

Stanley Goodall, the Director of Naval Construction, admitted: 'To say that these ships were cheap, simple to build and required only a small complement is one way of expressing the fact that they lacked much of the equipment and amenities of the normal warship, and for that they were quickly criticized.'[10]

The former yachtsmen had certain advantages in the stormy ocean. They tended to be keen on navigation, unlike regular officers who had seen too much of it their youth and regarded it as a chore. In John Fernald's novel *Destroyer from America*, an RNVR officer says, 'It was exciting, this business of navigation.'[11] In *Men Dressed as Seamen*, Gorley Putt served under 'an admirable example of the type of amateur sailor we were, as yet at a great distance, striving to emulate. He, more than any naval officer I have ever met, really did love the sea and everything about it.'[12] The Hon. Lyulph Stanley, son of Baron Sheffield, joined the Supplementary Reserve in October 1937 and became navigating officer of *Hesperus* under Commander Donald Macintyre: 'Lyulph, apart from being a splendid navigator and an utterly reliable staff officer, brought with him a charm of manner and a witty and scurrilous tongue which did much to enliven an already happy set of officers.'[13]

The new officers were also more inured to seasickness. John Fernald has the RNR chief engineer of a destroyer think, 'What lucky devils these R.N.V.R. yachtsmen were, with their insides toughened by their crazy little sailing boats. He had not dared to eat for the last forty-eight hours.'[14] Men like the engineer had probably served most of their lives in large ships, which moved much less in the sea. Regular naval officers had mostly served in battleships and cruisers in the Mediterranean and English Channel, and were not prepared for such conditions. But among the yachtsmen Peter Scott was an exception: he was very seasick on his first voyage in a destroyer and continued to feel 'poorly' for the first 36 hours of every trip. He kept it under control by either lying prone or staying on deck with a view of the horizon.

Monsarrat had his own descriptions of the corvettes, which were used many decades afterwards in training naval architects:

One measure of rough weather is domestic, but reliable. Moderate sea, the lavatory-seat falls down when it is tipped up; rough sea, the radio-set tumbles off its bracket in the wardroom.

Apart from the noise it produces, rolling has a maddening rhythm that is one of the minor tortures of rough weather. It never stops or misses a beat, it cannot be escaped anywhere. If you go through a doorway, it hits you hard; if you sit down, you fall over; you get hurt, knocked about, continuously, and it makes for extreme and childish anger. When you drink, the liquid rises towards you and slops over; at meals, the food spills off your plate, the cutlery will not stay in place. Things roll about, and bang, and slide away crazily; and then come back and *hurt* you again.

This soon led to extreme exhaustion, especially when the ship was operated in two watches.

Strain and tiredness induce a sort of hypnosis: you seem to be moving in a bad dream, pursued not by terrors but by an intolerable routine. You come off watch at midnight, soaked, twitching, your eyes raw with the wind and staring at shadows; you brew up a cup of tea in the wardroom pantry and strip off the top layer of sodden clothes; you do, say, an hour's intricate ciphering, and thereafter snatch a few hours' sleep between wet blankets, with the inflated life-belt in your ribs reminding you all the time that things happen quickly; and then, every night for seventeen nights on end, you're woken at ten to four by the bosun's mate, and you stare at the deckhead and think: My God, I *can't* go up there again in the dark and filthy rain, and stand another four hours of it. But you can, of course: it becomes automatic in the end.[15]

In fact the main problem was not rolling, which caused a great deal of exhaustion and not seasickness – it was pitching, caused by the fact that the corvettes, just 190 feet long, were simply too short to cope with the Atlantic seas. Pitching was probably felt more by the crew who lived in the bows than by the officers, who mostly lived amidships, but the up-and-down movement it created was most unpleasant. Another problem was that the forecastle was too short. It 'encouraged any green seas which came over the bow to charge over the rear end of the forecastle down on to the well deck forward: a menace to everything in its path'.[16]

Vice-Admiral (retired) F. A. Marten was serving as commodore in charge of the merchant ships of convoy OB 249 and had great difficulty in keeping his ships together in the circumstances. In fact, he did not see *Campanula* again after the rendezvous off Scotland, but that is probably because she was on the outer wing of the escort, and visibility was poor. The merchant ships were dispersed to their separate destinations. Meanwhile, convoy HX 89 had left Halifax, Nova Scotia, on the 17th and encountered fog and rough weather all the way across. It was supposed to be a fast convoy, but speed was sometimes reduced to 8 knots, sometimes to 6. The convoy was ten hours late at the mid-ocean rendezvous with the escort group, but *Fleur de Lys*, *Campanula* and *Periwinkle* found it successfully at noon on the 28th, and then *Campanula* had her first taste of action. Submarine activity was suspected, and at 1810 she dropped depth-charges astern of the convoy as a deterrent. The escorts formed a screen and the 30 deeply laden ships were escorted back to Liverpool without loss.

There, Monsarrat found a new friend in Temporary-Lieutenant Jim Harmsworth, a member of a powerful newspaper family, who joined the ship on 5 December. He was a barrister with an acid wit and served as the model for Morell in *The Cruel Sea*, though not necessarily with the same tortured private life. Callow departed around this time, leaving Monsarrat as senior lieutenant, though he does not seem to have been formally given the job of first lieutenant, who would organize the ship and deputize for the captain. In fact an RNR lieutenant, K. J. Webb, was appointed later but only served for a short time.

Meanwhile the group escorted Convoy ON 45 out to 19°. *Campanula* spent Christmas Day 1940 at sea bringing in OB 263, but it 'brought no holly, no turkey', only a message from the commodore of the convoy: 'Happy Christmas. Keep well closed up.'[17] The corvette had to return to the Clyde for repairs, but early in January the group sailed with convoy OB 270, and after some difficulty it was able to rendezvous with SL 60, 31 ships from Sierra Leone. Early in the morning of the 11th, when less than 70 miles off the Irish coast, *Campanula* signalled that two of the merchantmen, *East Wales* of 8,450 tons and *Benmohr* of 9,250 tons, had been in collision. The corvette took off most of the crew of *Benmohr*, which

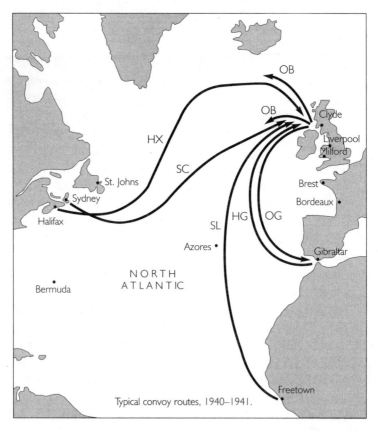

Typical convoy routes, 1940–1941.

was slowly sinking by the stern, and was given the job of escorting the stricken ships to the Clyde with the help of two rescue tugs. They arrived safely later in the day.[18] The group sailed again on 18 January to take OB 275 out and meet another inbound convoy, carrying several news photographers. *Campanula* had Ross White of the *News Chronicle*.

Convoy HX 102 had left Halifax on 11 January 1941 and soon encountered dense fog, rain and sleet. By the 15th there was a 'Fresh Westerly wind and rough sea on the port beam. Frequent heavy snow squalls.' By the 17th, the escorting destroyer *Voltaire* was rolling very heavily and manageable only by doing more revolutions on one engine than the other. By the 22nd, as the rendezvous with Monsarrat's Seventh Escort Group was approaching, even the large and stable merchant ships were 'pitching heavily and shipping seas' in the 'strong head wind and rough sea'. This was, perhaps, the scene Monsarrat had in mind when he wrote:

> In any case the rendezvous is very likely to be an impossible one: 300 miles at 15 knots in half a gale, on the off chance of finding twenty ships that have been hove to in a gale for three days in a position depending on a week-old estimate: with visibility less than two miles, and about six hours of daylight to play with. No wonder the senior officers of escort groups are men of half-humorous despair.[19]

At this time it was not unusual for an escort group to signal the Admiralty, 'Not Met', but HX 102 was found somehow at 1600 on 23 January. The seven ships of the escort took it on a new route, round the top of the Hebrides and through the Minches, to the various destinations. This was one of the first convoys to be met farther out in the Atlantic, creating an extra day's sailing for the escorts. Commander Hopkinson, in charge of the escort, pointed out to the Admiralty that they had spent eleven nights at sea. 'Officers and Men stood up to the additional watchkeeping, in poor weather conditions, admirably. It is considered however, if practicable, they should have a short period in Harbour, as hitherto, to relax, in order that a high standard of vigilence [sic] be maintained at sea.' That fell on deaf ears. The group left Liverpool again two days after its arrival.

Campanula had been joined at Liverpool by a new sub-lieutenant, which did much to relieve the strain: 'when you are working in three watches, and have eight hours off at a time, there is luxury in coming off watch: the luxury of relaxing, smoking, putting on bedroom slippers, turning on the electric heater and feeling your face thawing out and losing its stiffness; all with no sense of hurry.'[20] They left Liverpool on 1 February with the painfully slow OB 281, which was escorted as far as 25° West to avoid the U-boats. They found HX 105 on the way in from Halifax, and, as the convoy split on approaching land, *Campanula* was given the job of escorting the Milford Haven section to its destination. So far, convoy escort had been relatively uneventful, though that in itself was a source of pride. 'There is satisfaction in delivering a big convoy: a long line of laden ships that have been in company for thousands of miles, now moving slowly up river at the end of their journey, is one of the finest sights that war can offer.'[21]

White's pictures had been published by this time and filled half a page of the *News Chronicle*, not perhaps a spectacular result for eleven days at sea. They showed one of the other corvettes pitching in heavy seas, a mess deck scene and Captain Case on the bridge. There was a rather disappointing view of a depth-charge explosion and a picture of Harmsworth, Maberley and Monsarrat – lawyer, bank manager and author – looking at a chart.[22]

Campanula transferred to the Eighth Escort Group, still based in Liverpool. Her companions included the old destroyers *Vanquisher*, *Winchelsea*, *Viscount* and *Whitehall*, the ex-American *Belmont* and *Castelton*, and the corvettes *Freesia*, *Gentian*, *Hibiscus* and *Rhododendron*. Monsarrat's favourite, Captain Cuthbertson's *Zinnia*, joined the group later. Ships needed a good deal of repair because of the stresses of the Atlantic war, and it was rare for more than two-thirds of an Escort Group to serve together at once. On 23 February, *Campanula* left Liverpool with three destroyers, another corvette and the sloop *Enchantress* to escort 41 ships of OB 290.

By this time the U-boats had evolved tactics that were causing the convoys and their escorts much difficulty. Focke-Wulf Condor long-range reconnaissance aircraft were sent out from bases in France and Norway to find the convoys and direct the U-boats towards them. Boats might be ordered to form a patrol line ahead of the route, or any boat finding a convoy would shadow it and direct others towards it. It had to do this on the surface, for it could only make seven-and-a-half knots, for very short periods, when it was submerged and using its batteries. On the surface, using its diesel engines, it could do seventeen knots. A fast convoy such as HX 102 did ten knots; a slow one was supposed to do seven. U-boats would try to attack in 'wolf packs', though for the moment these tended to be small because of their shortness of numbers. They were well aware that the British asdic could detect them underwater, but on the surface they could trim down so that only the conning tower was above water as they infiltrated the convoy. This was almost impossible to see on a dark Atlantic night, and for the moment there was no radar available to defeat such a penetration. The submarine then attacked by firing its torpedoes, often from inside the convoy.

Campanula was stationed on the starboard side of the convoy, 300 miles west of the Outer Hebrides as the watches changed at midnight on the 26th. Twenty-five minutes later her lookouts spotted two white rockets being fired from the convoy. This was the signal that a ship had been torpedoed, and the 7,906-ton Belgian passenger-cargo ship *Kasongo* in the rear centre of the convoy was going down. *Campanula's* war entered a new phase as the alarm bells rang and the weary crew tumbled out of berths and hammocks to action stations. Following standard procedure, she immediately turned through 90° and increased speed to search outwards from the convoy, firing star shells to illuminate any U-boat on the surface and force her to dive. She turned back after half an hour, to be told by the destroyer *Winchelsea* that the attack was from port, the

59

other side. She was sent to search for survivors and at 0150 spotted two lifeboats in the water. Six men had died in *Kasongo*, but 28 were picked up. They did not know it, but they had been attacked by *U-47* commanded by Germany's greatest U-boat ace, Gunther Prien, who had sunk the battleship *Royal Oak* in Scapa Flow. Also in the attack was another ace, Otto Kretschmer in *U-99*.

Campanula missed subsequent attacks on the convoy, as she was detached later in the morning to escort the stricken 12,150-ton tanker *Diala*, 'with a hole like Elijah's cave in her side, into which the sea washed like surf into bay. But she was well built, and her bulkheads held: they held, in fact, for four hundred miles at three knots. On such a journey as this, you learn what patience is, and nervousness too.'[23] The ships steamed up the Clyde on the 28th.

Campanula continued with the cycle until she went in for some repairs at the end of April, and was in Liverpool for the 'May week' raids by the Luftwaffe, particularly on the night of the 3rd and 4th, when nearly 300 aircraft dropped 363 tonnes of high explosive and nearly 50,000 incendiaries. Four hundred and six people were killed that night alone. According to Monsarrat,

> One night the bonded warehouse alongside us was set ablaze, and we had to land a fire-party to help put it out, expecting all the time that the whole flaming structure, glowing scarlet like a runaway oven, would crash down on the upper deck.
>
> Since corvettes weren't built for that sort of thing, we always warped ourselves into the middle of the dock after that; it gave us, at least, an additional twenty yards' margin of safety.[24]

On 11 May, *Campanula* left Liverpool to escort convoy OB 321, made up of 40 ships sailing from Milford Haven, Liverpool, the Clyde and Oban. It had a strong escort of four destroyers and six corvettes. Naval intelligence was becoming increasingly successful at finding the movements of U-boats. They could use radio direction-finding, by which the position of a boat could be found by its own transmissions. Also, the codebreakers at Bletchley Park were becoming skilled at decoding the signals themselves. As a result, the escort of OB 321 had various warnings, starting in the afternoon of the 13th, when course was altered to avoid a U-boat. This was negated at dawn next morning when two Focke-Wulf Condor bombers appeared. They bombed the 3,015-ton *Karlander*, formerly a German tramp steamer, and damaged her so severely that *Campanula* was ordered to sink her by gunfire after her crew had been taken off by a rescue tug. Just before midday next day the escort was warned that they had been sighted by a U-boat, and then by a second one. Later that afternoon two of the destroyers had a firm contact on a submarine, but they failed to destroy it despite dropping four patterns of depth-charges. Most of the escorts were due to leave the convoy at this point, but in view of the threatening situation they were ordered to stay with it as long as possible. In any case, the homeward convoy they were supposed to meet, HG 61, was nine-and-a-half hours late. Two Tribal class destroyers, *Tartar* and *Mashona*, joined and were ordered to stay with the convoy to the limits of their endurance, while the Seventh Escort Group went off to look for HG 61.

They found it at eight o'clock in the morning of the 16th. The large number of escorts allowed a double screen in places, with *Campanula* in position D2, 12,000 yards out on the starboard side of the convoy and just ahead of it. They were attacked by enemy aircraft in the evening of the 18th, fought off a submarine early next morning, were bombed again that evening, and next day *Empire Ridge* was torpedoed. She was carrying a cargo of iron ore and sank in a minute, leaving only two survivors from a crew of 33. Later in the day the convoy was off the Northern Irish coast, and *Campanula* was given the job of escorting the Belfast section to its destination.

In view of the extension of the U-boat war over the ocean, it was now becoming normal to escort convoys all the way. In July, *Campanula* and her companions had their first chance of shore leave overseas, when they were ordered to escort convoy OG (outward, Gibraltar) 68 to its destination. *Campanula* took the

Oban portion of eight ships to the rendezvous off the Mull of Kintyre, while her 'chummy ship' *Zinnia* looked after the Clyde portion. Again the escort was a strong one, with two destroyers, six corvettes and two converted merchantmen protecting a convoy of 41 ships. With 'Ultra' intelligence, Western Approaches Command was able to steer the convoy well away from enemy activity and there was no intervention from the *Luftwaffe*. To Monsarrat it was a holiday cruise.

We passed whales and basking sharks, and once a turtle, paddling manfully westward. M[aberely] swore to having seen a flying fish in his watch: a warm breeze, imaginatively spiced with oranges, blew up from the south-east, and odd rigs were seen about the ship – bare legs, singlets, sandals, shameful tattooings.

There were problems with the food, as the *Campanula* had no refrigerator, and in any case the seamen insisted on their usual fare of tinned sausages, beans and potatoes. The destroyers left for Londonderry, due to their short range, and Case became senior officer of the escort for a while. At last after thirteen days, 'dawn broke and the Rock showed at last, and the failing lighthouse off Europa Point winked twice and then gave up in the sun'. The non-essential civilian population had been evacuated from Gibraltar for fear of a German or Spanish attack that never in fact materialized, and the Rock was a purely military base. However, it offered advantages in climate and relative freedom from air raids. Ashore, Monsarrat and his fellow officers wore tropical rig, went shopping and bathed in Rosia Bay.[25] They sailed after three days, to enter a very different experience.

On 3 August the group rendezvoused with convoy SL 81, from Freetown, Sierra Leone, to the UK. It was already being shadowed by U-boats, and that afternoon a Condor was sighted. The escort included the catapult ship *Maplin*, carrying a Hurricane fighter that could be launched to deal with such a situation. Its pilot, Lieutenant

Everett, RNVR, shot down the Condor and ditched in the sea, as was the usual practice. He was picked up and later awarded the DSO.

Meanwhile the U-boats moved in for the attack. The destroyer *Wanderer* sighted one on the surface, and she and *St Albans* launched six depth-charge attacks on her after she submerged. Asdic contact faded after that, and bubbles were seen. *Campanula* and *Hydrangea* arrived to help search the area ten or twenty miles astern of the convoy, where a second and third submarine were believed to be operating. At 2219, *Hydrangea* spotted a U-boat on the surface and fired two rounds with her 4-inch gun. The boat dived, and *Hydrangea* dropped two patterns of depth-charges. *Campanula* fired hers too, and Monsarrat gave each of the leaders of the men who reloaded the throwers half a crown (12 and a half p) each.[26] Soon in the water they found '2 sheepskin coats, 1 German seaman's collar, leather coat marked "Schmidt", 2 cushions and 3 pieces of human flesh'. *Campanula* was close by and Monsarrat commented, 'the sea, spouting and boiling, threw up what we were waiting for: oil in a spreading stain, bits of wreckage, woodwork,

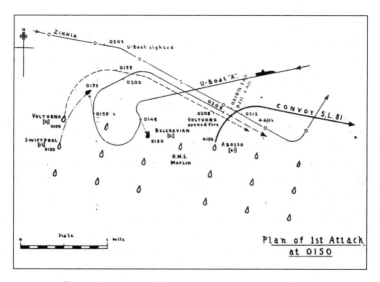

The attack on convoy SL 81, showing the action taken by *Zinnia*.

clothing, scraps of humanity … contact failed after that, and though we waited till dusk, nothing else worth collecting made its appearance. We had enough, in any case.'[27] *U-401* had been destroyed, but *Campanula* was not officially credited with a share in the killing, to the resentment of her crew. *Wanderer*, *St Albans* and *Hydrangea* were, though it was claimed that the corvette had merely 're-sunk' the same boat. Nevertheless, Western Approaches Command signalled 'Well done, continue the good work' to *Hydrangea* and *Campanula*. They felt triumphant and were congratulated by signal flags from the ships of the convoy, a moment of 'the sweetness of success'.

> We'd worked a long time for that signal: steamed thousands of miles, been bored for days and weeks on end, spent scores of nights on the alert in wet and freezing darkness, sent and received thousands of signals. Over three hundred middle watches had gone into it, weeks of eye strain, filthy weather in plenty …[28]

Another U-boat attacked on the surface early in the morning of the 5th, covered by darkness as usual. *Zinnia*, under Captain Cuthbertson, first noticed trouble at 0150, when an explosion was heard in *Belgravian*, one of the merchant ships, but it was not clear what had happened and no action was taken. Seven minutes later the corvette altered course towards the convoy to investigate, and then another merchant ship, *Swiftpool*, was torpedoed. At 0203 a U-boat was sighted on the surface 800 yards away and reported by radio. The 4-inch gun in the bows was ordered to open fire, but in the poor weather conditions the gun crew could not see the target. *Zinnia* prepared to ram, as the U-boat had still not seen her, and depth-charges were set at 50 feet in case she dived. At 5 past 2 the U-boat sighted the corvette from 300 yards and turned sharply to starboard, towards the convoy. Both vessels sailed at 16 knots. According to the report, 'The Commanding Officer decided to ignore the presence of the merchant ships at close range, and the fact that

Above: Sopwith on his yacht *Endeavour* during Cowes Week, 1935. (Hulton/Getty Images)

Below: *King Alfred* at the start of the war.

"Yes — he was a surrealist artist before the war"

Left: A typical cartoon from the pages of the *King Alfred* magazine.

Right: *Mimosa* was built at Hampton on Thames in 1935 and requisitioned by the navy. She made three trips to the beaches of Dunkirk. This picture shows her restored as she is today.

BRAY DUNES

Left: Dunkirk. Bryan de Grineau's drawing shows a collection of lifeboats, cabin cruisers, fishing smacks and other vessels taking men off the beaches of Bray Dunes and Malo les Bains, with the harbour of Dunkirk in the background. (*Illustrated London News*/Mary Evans)

Left: Lieutenant-Commander Cuthbertson of the corvette *Zinnia*.

Below: A corvette at sea, showing the strong pitching motion.

Right: The merchant ships of a convoy from the air. They are doing their best to keep in a regular formation. (IWM C 2644)

Opposite page, bottom: Nicholas Monsarrat.

Opposite page, top: A Luftwaffe reconnaissance photograph of Liverpool, with Gladstone Dock near the top. (IWM C 5518)

Opposite page, bottom: Rear-Admiral Rhoderick McGrigor finishes an inspection of the corvette *Stonecrop*, which is being fitted with an early version of Type 271 radar in its 'parrot's cage' mounting, visible at the top of the picture. (IWM A 6361)

Above: Public school boys come up against the local schoolboys while waiting for the Eton and Harrow cricket match at Lord's in 1937. (Hulton/Getty Images)

Right: A poster advertising the Y-scheme. (Royal Naval Museum)

'Y' ENTRY
INTO
THE NAVY

Boys over 17, of school certificate standard, or who have served in any of the units mentioned just below, can enrol for the Navy by the 'Y' method.

After being accepted, they train in the Sea Cadets, Home Guard, Air Training Corps or other recognised units

Then comes the day when the Admiralty calls upon them and they join the Royal Navy for service

Here they will have every chance of getting a commission as Deck Officer, as Observer or as Pilot

FOR PARTICULARS OF THE 'Y' ENTRY APPLY TO ANY COMBINED RECRUITING CENTRE OR DIRECT TO F.O.Y.E., ADMIRALTY, LONDON

Above: Boys in the training base HMS *St Vincent* drilling during cold weather in 1935. (Royal Naval Museum)

Below: Dartmouth Cadets march past the Prince of Wales in the 1920s.

survivors were known to be in the water, and the 4-inch gun was ordered to open fire, although the gun's crew could not distinguish the target.' A few minutes later another ship, *Volturno*, opened fire on the U-boat with her Bofors gun, and hits were seen on its conning tower. She crash-dived and was not seen again. *Zinnia* then dropped her depth-charges over where the U-boat was thought to be, though the asdic operator had not had a clear contact. She then carried out a thorough search of the area, and six survivors of the *Belgravian* were rescued. At daybreak a film of oil was found on the surface, but in the bad weather conditions it was not possible to get a sample to find out if it came from a U-boat. None was lost that night.

This is clearly not the same as the famous incident in *The Cruel Sea*, in which Ericson orders the dropping of depth-charges despite the survivors in the water – it took place in a homeward Freetown convoy rather than an outward Gibraltar one, it was at night rather than in daylight, and there is no evidence that anyone was killed as a result of the firing. Yet the psychological effect on the captain must have been similar, and Monsarrat later had intimate discussions with Cuthbertson. There can be little doubt that this was a large part of the inspiration for the depth-charge incident.

Convoy SL 81 arrived on 8–9 August, having lost five merchant ships out of eighteen. There was little time for rest, as the sailing of the next convoy had already been delayed. On 13 August the group left to escort OG 71, including ships from Liverpool, Milford Haven, the Clyde and Oban. *Campanula* and *Zinnia* formed part of the rear of the escort. Happy memories of the last outward trip were soon erased. The convoy was routed closer to the coast of France than originally planned. German reconnaissance aircraft soon spotted it, and the Admiralty sent telegrams warning of U-boats in the area. The first attack was on the night of 18th/19th when an escort and three merchant ships were sunk. One of them was *Aguila*, carrying the first draft of twelve Wrens to overseas service in Gibraltar. In *The Cruel Sea* Monsarrat describes how 'they had watched the girls strolling about the deck, had waved to them as they passed, had been glad of their company even at long range'. In real life they were all chief Wrens, rather more mature than Monsarrat's prose implies. All were killed instantly by a direct torpedo hit. Two destroyers then arrived as reinforcements.

The off-duty watch in *Campanula* had a sing-song in the evening of the 22nd, doing the *Lambeth Walk* to the accompaniment of a pair of harmonicas.[29] The sun was setting as they went back on watch at eight, and soon the U-boats began their second attack. Two merchant ships and a small tug were sunk. Finally, at four in the morning of this terrible night, HMS *Zinnia* was hit. Captain Cuthbertson describes it in a deadpan fashion.

I was stepping out of the bridge asdic house and facing the funnel and about 25 feet from the explosion. The asdic house collapsed and parts of the ship were thrown in the air. She immediately heeled over on to her starboard beam ends, and in five seconds had capsized through 120 degrees. The blast did not hurt me and the capsizing hurled me into the water on the starboard side abreast the bridge. Looking upwards I saw the deck of the ship coming over on top of me, when she broke in two about the funnel, and a swirl of water took me down. When I came to the surface again my lungs and stomach were filled with oil fuel, and I was partially blinded. The time was now about twelve seconds after the explosion. I could see the bows rising vertically out of the water, they disappeared within a few seconds. HMS *Zinnia* had sunk in 15 or 20 seconds. There was no wreckage.

I heard many cries for help in the water, and estimated there were about 40 men floating. I could do nothing to help them. The water was thick with oil fuel, and it was all I could do to keep my balance in the swell, and with my nose and mouth above the oil. I remained afloat for 40 minutes before finding the trunk of a body which had been blasted and was buoyant, this kept me afloat for the remaining 30 minutes. One corvette passed close without sighting me, eventually at 0530 I was picked up by a boat from another corvette, HMS *Campion*. I had to be hoisted inboard, could only crawl along the deck, and was completely blinded. I was still fully clothed.

Meanwhile *Campanula* was engaged in picking up casualties, including some of the men from *Zinnia*.

Survivors in the mess-decks, filling every available space: asleep on the deck, on benches, against bulkheads: sitting at tables with their heads between their hands, talking, shivering, wolfing food, staring at nothing. Some of them half-naked, wrapped in blankets and makeshift shoes: some with pathetic little cardboard suitcases, hugged close: puzzled black faces, pinched yellow ones, tired bleary white masks that still muster a grin. Men half-dead, men cocky as bedamned: men suffering from exposure, frost-bite, oil-fuel poisoning, cuts, gashes, broken limbs: men hanging to life by a wet thread.[30]

Some of the convoy limped into the Tagus in neutral Portugal. Seven merchant ships out of 21 had been lost, and two escorts. This was a defeat, but not a disaster. The Germans claimed a great victory, in which all the merchant ships were sunk. This was denied in the British press, and one merchant captain was quoted as saying, 'We just ran straight across the enemy's bases on the French coast. Jerry couldn't stop us.' Inside the Admiralty, one official noted on the file copy of the newspaper, 'Another example of how Huns use a propagandist multiplier.' In the Admiralty *Monthly Anti-Submarine Report*, convoy OG 71 had only a brief mention and hardly registered on the scale of disasters: 'During the month of August 1941, shipping casualties were comparatively light and so far as is known, fewer than thirty ships were torpedoed ... Taken as a whole, August was a satisfactory month.'

In *The Cruel Sea*, the horror of the Gibraltar convoy is fully conveyed and indeed overstated. It was 'by far the worst [convoy] of this or any other war' in which 14 out of 21 ships had been lost. Such exaggeration is quite acceptable in fiction, but in his autobiography, *Life is a Four Letter Word*, Monsarrat appears to have let fiction take over from fact. 'We lost fourteen merchant ships in the next five days; fourteen of our small stock of twenty-one – a percentage so appalling that the cold print seemed almost worse than the sights and sounds of action.' Oddly enough, he is closer to the German assessment of the battle than the British one.

Campanula left Gibraltar with HG 72 on 2 September, desperately hoping for a quieter trip. There was a huge escort, 13 warships for 17 merchantmen, and several diversions to avoid U-boats and Condor activity. On the 11th it merged with SL 85 from Sierra Leone, making an even larger escort of 21 warships. It was decided to risk a passage to the south of Ireland, though this brought the ships well within range of air attack. A Condor was seen on the 14th, attempting to direct U-boats on to the convoy. *Maplin* was present with her Hurricane and Sub-Lieutenant S. C. W. Walker, RNVR, was able to force the Condor to drop its bombs in the sea, though it escaped. Walker was picked up after bailing out. Another air attack took place on the evening of the 15th, and this time there was no Hurricane. The 3,854-ton *Daru*, part of SL 85 and carrying palm kernels and cocoa, was hit and sunk, but the rest arrived safely at Liverpool and the other ports on the 17th after a voyage of nearly a fortnight.

The corvette was in Liverpool for repairs between 16 September and 10 October, and Captain Case was sceptical about the prospects of being fitted with radar, remarking scornfully, '*Corvettes?* We're sucking on the hind tit.'[31] But it was clear that this was the only way of preventing U-boats from attacking on the surface at night, and the Admiralty had decided to embark on a programme of fitting it to all escort vessels. It was a second-generation version, Type 271, the first to be capable of detecting a small object like a conning tower or a lifeboat. For security reasons, Monsarrat could not describe it in wartime, but in 1970 he wrote,

I never heard anything about its arrival until I noticed that a curious, round, opaque glass cylinder, like the top third of a lighthouse, had been hoisted up and clipped to our mainmast. It had arrived under heavy guard, I learned via the galley-wireless ... and had been unpacked in strict security below decks; two scientists *in very dark clothes* had remained closeted with the Captain for over an hour while all this was going on ...

It was to work wonders for us, that precious radar set. It made station-keeping at close quarters a safe and exact science. It found lost convoys, and wandering escorts, and headlands hidden in the murk of a Hebridean summer day. It could pick up channel buoys as we went down river in a fog; and ship's boats whose survivors might otherwise have been left to die ... Best of all, it could find surfaced U-boats and, with the help of an ingenious plotting device, betray their plans.[32]

It was Monsarrat's duty to stay with the ship during the refit while most of the officers went on leave:

each morning the ship came alive again, in a way I grew to dislike even more than the night's loneliness. From 8 a.m. onwards we were invaded by an army of major and minor technicians concerned with our refit: riveters, welders, joiners, plumbers, painters, electricians, carpenters, caulkers, boiler scalers, funnel sweeps, plain crash-and-bangers, tea makers' mates ... They trooped on board in a snuffling, untidy, foot-dragging, shambling throng and took over the ship; and the ship, lately so disciplined, so taut, so keyed up to its job, began to suffer from it.[33]

Further convoys followed, until in November the ship was put into dock for a repair that would last more than two months. Monsarrat was transferred to become first lieutenant of the sloop *Guillemot* on the east coast of Britain, where the main dangers were mines and air attack rather than submarines. He understates this in *The Cruel Sea*, and Sub-Lieutenant Raikes of the *Saltash* describes the experience rather modestly. 'There's a swept channel for the convoys, with a buoy every five miles or so. If you miss one of them you probably run aground, or end up in a minefield.'

There is no doubt about Monsarrat's courage or his competence. He saw as much action as the average seaman in the Atlantic war, for only about one in ten escort vessels actually sank a U-boat. It was a war of stamina and endurance, and Monsarrat, like the vast majority of his comrades, showed both of these. Since fiction is usually an intensification of reality, it is no surprise to find that Monsarrat's own record was less active than that of his fictional characters. He arrived rather later in the war than they did. He was only on the fringes of the sinking of one U-boat, was never sunk himself, and never participated in the Arctic Convoys to Russia. He was obviously a very successful officer, and his captain in *Guillemot*, Sam Lombard-Hobson, wrote of him,

Nicholas Monsarrat was a most effective first Lieutenant. In no sense a disciplinarian, he had the respect of the crew because he was a thoughtful person, with an acute perception of the feelings of others. A real man of the world with a superb sense of humour, we all enjoyed his lively company onboard.[34]

Monsarrat was one of the first of the temporary RNVRs to command a corvette and the second to command a frigate.

Monsarrat's novel *The Cruel Sea* was published in 1951, and the film appeared two years later. It had an important effect on our awareness of the Battle of the Atlantic. Conditions were almost as horrific as on the Western Front in the First World War, and the struggle lasted even longer, though few people would suggest that it was futile. In terms of the Second World War, it received less publicity than Dunkirk, the Battle of Britain, the North African Campaign, the bombing of Germany and the invasion of Europe. The

Battle of the Atlantic was long-drawn-out, with few clear-cut victories, while serious losses could not be revealed in wartime. Because it was largely fought by temporary officers like Monsarrat, there was even a danger that the Royal Navy itself might forget about it. In 1948 one admiral said, 'I know nothing about the Battle of the Atlantic! I was never involved in it! My war experience was in completely different theatres.'[35] The campaign highlighted the role of temporary naval officers, who were to become increasingly predominant on the navy's bridges.

3
JOINING THE NAVY

As the Direct Entry scheme and the Supplementary Reserve came to their natural conclusion, the navy was already looking at ways of expanding its officer corps far beyond its normal range of recruits. It would expand more than seven-fold in wartime, and much of that would be in fields such as aviation and amphibious warfare, which required a higher proportion of officers than normal. One of the key problems was to find ways to attract and select the most suitable young men.

As with many things, the key was to be found in the education system, and behind that the class system, which was fed by it. Just as Britain traditionally had an upper class, a middle class and a working class, schools were divided into 'public', grammar or secondary, and elementary. The 'public' schools were in fact private; fees were high, and class distinction was strict. Even if one's parents could find the fees, the wrong kind of accent, occupation or family could lead to bullying and discrimination. A definition was provided by Cyril Norwood, headmaster of Harrow: 'A public school is one which has a real measure of independence, and can direct its own policy, which keeps its pupils to the full limit of age of eighteen and over, and which has a direct and regularly maintained connection with the Universities.' There were many schools that charged fees but did not come fully up to these standards – perversely, they were known as 'private schools'.

Nearly all public schoolboys had already attended private 'preparatory' schools before sitting the Common Entrance examination at the age of about thirteen, so the system was totally enclosed and had little contact with the state schools. There was no point in a boy entering the system unless his parents were confident of finding enough money to pay his fees for at least twelve or thirteen years and then support him at university or the early years of a profession after that. The system gave a good education, often with a classical bias. It gave a strong chance of entry to Oxford or Cambridge Universities, and old boys of the public schools were dominant in professions such as law, banking and politics. Stanley Baldwin was only half joking when he told his old school at Harrow that when taking office as prime minister, 'I remembered how in previous Governments there had been four, or perhaps five Harrovians, and I determined to have six.'[1]

Yet Harrow was only second on the educational tree, behind Eton. Practically every boy was aware of public schools through fiction – the comic Billy Bunter series was at its height in the thirties – but only a small proportion knew about the reality. Nicholas Monsarrat had been educated at Winchester, and he recounted the traditional story about the difference between there, Eton and Harrow. A girl comes to the room and the Etonian says, 'I say, someone ought to get her a chair!' The Winchester man gets it, and the Harrovian sits on it.[2] The older schools also included Westminster, Charterhouse, Christ's Hospital, Shrewsbury and Rugby, while newer foundations included Stowe.

The public schools were mostly boarding schools, in which the boys lived in rather spartan and strictly controlled conditions. There was usually a strong emphasis on sport, and public school boys were expected to learn leadership. They did military training using army uniforms, ranks and weapons – the very name of the organization, the Officers' Training Corps, made it clear where the peacetime army expected to find its junior officers. School uniform was insisted upon to an almost fetishistic degree. Each school had its own traditions, a private language and a rigid hierarchy, with housemasters who were rather like divisional officers in the navy, and powerful prefects chosen from among the boys. All this was good preparation for life in the navy.

Ironically however, the peacetime navy did not take much advantage of it. Most potential officers entered the Royal Naval College at Dartmouth at the age of thirteen or fourteen, just at the age their brothers or cousins were going to public school. They were nearly all from the same background as public school boys as regards family wealth and social position. They had probably started in prep school in the same way then gone on to a naval 'crammer', which specialized in passing the examinations for Dartmouth and other military colleges. William James was sent to Mr Littlejohns' establishment in Greenwich. The proprietor was 'short, rotund, irascible' and had a habit of putting offending boys on a chair and knocking them off. He was also 'a wizard at stuffing slow-witted boys with enough knowledge to pass the examination', and he 'had developed a kind of second sight which enabled him to read the thoughts of the examiners'.[3] The cadets needed nominations from figures of authority; they were carefully selected by examination and interview, and only a small proportion of those who applied were accepted. A naval background was a great advantage to acceptance, and the Royal Navy was still a family business in many ways. Once at Dartmouth, the boys were given a general education with a more technical bias than the average public school, with a certain amount of naval training, which increased in later years. It was a system which produced,

> a definite breed of fit, tough, highly trained but sketchily educated professionals, ready for instant duty, for parades or tea parties, for catastrophes, for peace or war; confident leaders, alert seamen, fair administrators, poor delegators; officers of wide interests and narrow vision, strong on tactics, weak on strategy; an able, active, cheerful, monosyllabic élite.[4]

One by-product was that naval officers knew very little about the country's educational system and had very little faith in it. They had left normal school at about 11 to go to the crammer, which was not the most rewarding educational experience.

The only other way to enter as an officer candidate in peacetime was through the Special Entry scheme, started by Churchill in 1913, partly as a way of expanding the officer corps more rapidly on the eve of war. Selected public school boys would be taken on at the age of about eighteen, to train for eighteen months instead of six or seven years before being commissioned. It was highly successful and tended to produce a good quality of officer – Terence Lewin, who joined on the eve of the war, went on to become an admiral of the fleet and chief strategist of the Falklands War of 1982. The Special Entry boys made their crucial career decision at a more mature age, had a broader general education – and they did not have time to pick up cynicism before they went to sea.

But the Special Entry scheme was not quite what the navy needed for a huge wartime expansion. Firstly, it recruited officers for a permanent career, and the navy was determined not to make the same mistake as in the last war, when it raised expectations too high, only to have them dashed when hundreds of officers were made redundant in the Geddes Axe of 1922. Ludovic Kennedy's father was one, and he described his shock: 'My service career is finished. All ambitions, all hopes, are in one moment dashed to the ground. I did not truthfully expect it, but as other good people are similarly dealt with, why should I go free? Feel just crushed to pulp.'[5] To avoid such problems this time, entry through Dartmouth and the Special Entry scheme would not be much above peacetime level.

Secondly, the Special Entry scheme was aimed at public schools. This meant that the numbers available would be far too small, and restricted to a narrow age band of seventeen to nineteen. Furthermore, it was not quite appropriate for a 'people's war'. Both as First Lord of the Admiralty and as Prime Minister, Winston Churchill was insistent on opening up the commissioned ranks to a wider social range. The Labour Party was a strong force in the wartime coalition from May 1940, and the new First Lord of the Admiralty, A. V. Alexander, was a Labour Member of Parliament. Any system which relied too openly on the public schools would not be acceptable.

In 1936 the army decided that in any future war its temporary officers would be selected from those serving in its ranks. In 1939 the navy decided to follow suit. It was a seemingly 'democratic' system, but it had a serious class bias. In the first place, the navy had no intention of promoting the regular seamen of the lower deck in large numbers. Members of the seaman branch were recruited at the age of fifteen or sixteen and underwent strict and often brutal training in shore bases. Tristan Jones was on one of the last boys' courses at HMS *Ganges*, near Harwich in 1940, and found,

Life for a boy trainee at HMS *Ganges* was one long harassment from dawn – when the bugler sounded 'Charlie' – until lights out at nine-fifteen p.m. There was hardly a minute of the waking day when we boys were not on our feet and doubling, or sat at attention in a classroom, being yelled at. Even when the 'working' day was over, our time was taken up hand-sewing our names on to our uniforms (red chain-stitches, each not longer than the rest). Some of the class were still busily engaged in this pastime, even though they had been in *Ganges* for ten weeks. There was always something to be done, and never enough time to do it. The boy who could find five minutes to sit down and write a letter home was lucky indeed.[6]

The boys at *Ganges*, and those at HM ships *Impregnable* near Plymouth, *St Vincent* near Portsmouth and later *Caledonia* in the Firth of Forth, had left school too early to have any paper qualifications. They were quite carefully selected but were not academically inclined in any sense. During the 1920s the navy had tried to form a slightly higher group, with direct entry to the 'advanced class' in the training schools and the possibility of accelerated promotion through the petty officer ranks. This had failed because the advantages offered were simply not enough to attract boys with more than a basic education. Secondary school boys were not encouraged by headmasters who saw little prestige for the school in such entries, and they spotted that even accelerated promotion was still very slow by any other standards.[7] In effect there was a wide gap between officers and men in the seaman branch of the navy. This was less true in the engineering branch, where the status of the officer was slightly less exalted, and selected young men were recruited as apprentice artificers. They could expect the rank of chief petty officer soon after qualification, with good prospects of promotion to warrant and commissioned rank. But the numbers of artificer apprentices were small compared with the RAF, which offered about ten times as many a year for the ground trades, though with far slower promotion prospects.

Promotion to commissioned rank was not impossible in the seaman branch, however. There was a slow route by which a man could be selected as a warrant officer, perhaps in his twenties, then eventually become a lieutenant. This would probably be near the end of his career, and his chances of reaching a higher rank were very small indeed. The other way was by the 'upper yardsman' scheme. Young men could be selected at the training schools or in their early days at sea. They had to improve their educational standards dramatically to qualify, and a certain amount of private study time was given to them from 1937 onwards. But lower deck solidarity did not encourage men to put themselves forward, and in any case the numbers were small. Forty-two were selected for the 1939 course but only 24 of them were recommended for commissions. The scheme continued during the war, but the numbers were never much larger than that, and it was clearly not the way to create a great expansion of the navy.

Fundamentally, naval officers did not believe that men who had joined as boys straight from the elementary schools, had been subjected to harsh discipline, employed in menial tasks and had spent several years taking in the culture of the lower deck, would ever be suitable to become naval officers. They had been 'influenced by the lower deck outlook during [their] impressionable years at sea' and were 'too old to acquire readily that breadth of outlook and spirit of service necessary in an officer'.[8] True, they might become good warrant officers, but these gentlemen had a 'narrowness of outlook' which was offset by 'the long background of service experience'. In effect the seaman branch did not have a substantial middle class, and there was a huge gulf between officers and men in almost every respect. The two groups came from widely different

77

social backgrounds, had different training, wore different uniforms, lived in very different conditions on board ship and had very different expectations from life. Of course all had to take equal risks in wartime, and the gap was narrowed on active service. As J. P. W. Mallalieu wrote, 'At sea, at all times, there was much less consciousness of the distinction between officers and ratings that here is between managers and workers in a factory.'[9]

Instead, the navy would recruit temporary wartime officers from outside its own ranks. Young conscripts and wartime volunteers might include many men of a higher educational standard than the lower deck regulars, and they could be selected for training as officers. An Admiralty Fleet Order of January 1940 demanded: 'Candidates must be of a superior standard of education in view of the shortness of the course it is possible to give in wartime.'[10] The basis of this was the CW scheme, by which men of the lower deck were picked out and observed carefully before being chosen for officer training. Even the participants in the scheme were often confused about what the letters stood for. Peter Bull speculated that it might mean 'Candidate for Wardroom.' Geoffrey Ball believed that it meant 'Wartime Commission', and the letters were reversed to avoid the abbreviation WC (though that did not stop the lower deck using that term anyway).[11] In fact the letters were the initials of the Commission and Warrant Branch in the Admiralty, responsible for the selection, training and conditions of service of commissioned and warrant officers. The candidate's progress was noted on Form CW1, hence the name.

The Admiralty made it clear to captains that it was not intended for lower deck regulars. 'While Their Lordships' policy is to obtain a high proportion of such officers by promotion from the Lower Deck … the grant of such commissions on these lines to continuous service ratings would normally result in their having to leave the service at the termination of hostilities instead of continuing the career in the Navy on which they have embarked …' A regular seaman might occasionally be selected in this way, but his hopes should not be raised.

It is not generally desirable that a long-service rating should be informed of the commencement of a C.W. Form No. 1 concerning him, although he will no doubt acquire knowledge of his prospects in the course of time without this information being definitely disclosed to him ... For permanent long-service ratings, therefore, who are candidates for permanent commissions, a suitable reticence should be maintained on the subject ...[12]

Petty Officer John Whelan thought of applying for a temporary commission later in the war, but he knew that he would be refused on the grounds that he was too valuable as an anti-submarine instructor. He took a certain perverse pleasure in his status. 'It was not until 1944 that the first H.O. [hostilities only] petty officers qualified as [submarine detector instructors]. It was possible to become a junior R.N.V.R. officer within six months of joining, but it took far longer to make an Asdic instructor.'[13]

The question was discussed in Parliament when a group of young officers wrote to Mr C. G. Ammon, MP, in 1942:

Every trainee fills in a questionnaire which is examined. Men with suitable qualifications are noted and watched. The snag is that no one who has not at least had a secondary school education is even considered, no matter what brilliance he may show while at the training establishment, thus many who might make very brilliant officers are overlooked. The official excuse for this is that without a secondary school education men cannot master the officers' training course. This, speaking from personal experience, is not true. Any intelligent man can easily master the course, while no matter how high his educational qualifications, unless they are linked with intelligence, a good officer does not result. Particularly important is the understanding which an officer has of his men, and the present insistence on education results in a gap between officers and ratings. There is no doubt that the system as at present worked

79

definitely prevents the average rating from ever being considered for a commission.[14]

In March 1943, under a great deal of political pressure, the Admiralty relented slightly on education standards and ordered,

> Recommendations of ratings should not be confined to ratings in possession of some set standard of education, such as the school certificate. Intelligent men who can quickly absorb instruction and have the required character and personality are quite capable of passing successfully through H.M.S. 'King Alfred', although their initial education has not been of a high standard. The essential qualities required are character, personality and powers of leadership.[15]

However, that was clearly aimed at intelligent but poorly educated Hostilities Only men, not at long-serving petty officers.

When commissioned, the new officers would be enrolled as temporary members of the Royal Naval Volunteer Reserve and wear their wavy stripes. But in fact they were not necessarily volunteers in any sense of the term and had not formed part of any reserve. Permanent members of the RNVR, who had put in hard service in peacetime, tended to resent this, and one suspects that the Admiralty was only using the stripes to segregate wartime officers from regulars.

The navy always believed that a good standard of education was necessary for its seaman officers, since they had to attain a good deal of technical skill in subjects like navigation. There was little time to waste in selection procedures, so again the navy looked to the education system of the country to give guidance. For the vast majority outside the public school system this was in a very slow transition. In the past it had been on two levels, beginning at the age of five when schooling became compulsory. Most children went to elementary schools and stayed there until the age of fourteen, when they usually left to go to work. Children from middle-class families mostly went to grammar schools to get a secondary education, which would take them beyond the age of fourteen. There were plans to change the system and introduce a break at eleven so that all children went to some kind of secondary school after that; but progress was slow in the financial climate between the wars, and in 1937–8 there were still more than a million and a half children over the age of 11 in elementary schools. There were 400,000 children aged eleven to eighteen in secondary schools, and the majority of them stayed on at least to the age of sixteen, if not eighteen. Overall about one in seven children stayed on beyond the minimum age.[16] Well over half of them would go on to work in the white-collar sector as professionals or clerks, about five per cent of secondary school boys went on to university in 1936–7 and a slightly larger number to other forms of higher education. Less than fifteen per cent went into manual work.[17] Much of this was decided by family circumstances and wealth – whether they could get entry to the grammar schools in the first place, and whether their families could afford to keep them on in the harsh economic climate of the 1930s. A secondary school education was almost as much based on class as a public school one.

The main aim of a secondary education (almost the sole one according to some critics) was to get the School Certificate at around the age of sixteen. This was taken in five subjects, including English, a foreign language, mathematics or a science, and one other which could be selected from 'Aesthetic and Practical Subjects', including music, art and manual work. The certificate undoubtedly influenced the curricula of the grammar schools, and it was said that it put undue pressure on the pupils at a vulnerable age; but it did provide a syllabus that was not over-specialized, and a good basis for selection. This was where the Admiralty looked for its temporary wartime officers.

Many of them were members of the new middle class that had arisen since the end of the last century and boomed in London during the last twenty years despite the depression elsewhere. The young man's father was perhaps an office worker or businessman, his mother probably ran the home with no live-in servants and a minimum of help. It was probably a small family with no more than two or three children. His parents were quietly proud of moving out of the overcrowded and unsanitary city centre during the last generation. Perhaps they were the first members of their family to be brought up in houses with inside toilets, electric light and running water. Often they lived in the new suburban houses that were springing up around the capital in districts such as Harrow, Stanmore and Pinner, and to a lesser extent in other parts of the country. In 1933, for example, a £50 deposit would secure an £850 house in the Syon Hill Estate, Osterley, Middlesex, as advertised by a local builder who apparently loved the capital letter.

The Accommodation consists of Two Reception, Three Bedrooms, Bathroom (fitted with Square-end Bath, entirely enclosed with MARB-L-COTE Plastic Paint Panel, and Chromium Plated Fitting and Taps etc.). Separate W.C.: Kitchenette (fitted with Hygena Cabinet, and Independent Boiler supplying hot water to Bathroom and Sink); Splendid Gardens. All the rooms are beautifully appointed and afford the maximum amount of Sunshine and Fresh air.[18]

All the suburbs were keen to show how healthy they were compared with the city centre, where many of the house buyers were coming from. Descriptions emphasized the height above sea level to avoid the notorious London smog, the distance from London, the frequent travel services, and the general healthiness.

A typical suburban house of 1933.

The parish of Cheam, which stands at an altitude of about 150 to 200 feet ... is one of those charming and popular residential centres which, for its healthy situation, invigorating air and bracing climatic conditions, can truly be said to be one of the most favoured localities in this respect.

It was eleven miles from the centre of London and served by 'fast electric services'. There were 'splendid and up-to-date shops' and 'The death rate of the district is much below the average'. Education came fairly low on the list of priorities, but there was passing mention of 'numerous excellent schools for boys and girls (private and otherwise)'.[19]

Home life was important, for the young man of the 1930s had no separate existence as his son might enjoy a generation later. He was expected to live with his parents at least until marriage, unless his work demanded otherwise, in which case he might find himself in a strictly-regulated boarding-house under a landlady. Though much popular music was aimed at him and his lady friends, there was no recognized category of 'teenager', and he was expected to conform to either childish or adult patterns of behaviour, with strict codes of discipline in either case.

Life in the new suburbs was very different from another Britain of extreme poverty, as seen by George Orwell in the north of England, with unemployment interrupted by spells of grinding hard work. Despite extensive building of council houses between the wars, there were many large pockets of deprivation. Housing conditions were a striking contrast to the suburbs.

'Back to back' houses are two houses built in one, each side of a house being someone's front door, so that if you walk down a row of what is apparently twelve houses you are in reality seeing not twelve houses but twenty-four. The front houses give on the street and the back ones on the yard, and there is only one way out of each house. The effect of this is obvious. The lavatories are in the yard at the back, so that if you live on the side facing the street, to get to the lavatory or the dust-bin you have to go out of the front door and walk round the end of the block – a distance that may be as much as two hundred yards ...

Conditions were no better inside, where eight or ten people might live in a three-roomed house. They often made an effort to keep the living room decent, so the overcrowding was worst in the bedrooms. 'In one family I visited there was a father and mother and a son and daughter aged round about seventeen, and only two beds for the lot of them. The father slept with the son and the mother with the daughter; it was the only arrangement that ruled out the danger of incest' – though not perhaps of child abuse, which was an unrecognized problem at the time.

This was insignificant compared with the demoralization caused by mass unemployment, whose victims were as often traumatized as the naval officers who came under the Geddes Axe.

I remember the shock and astonishment it gave me, when I first mingled with tramps and beggars, to find that a fair proportion, perhaps a quarter, of these beings whom I had been taught to regard as cynical parasites, were decent young miners and cotton-workers gazing at their destiny with the same sort of dumb amazement as an animal in a trap. They simply could not understand what was happening to them. They had been brought up to work, and behold! it seemed as if they were never going to have the chance of working again.

Those who stayed close to their roots still had a community around them, unlike those who drifted south. 'London is a sort of whirlpool which draws derelict people towards it, and is so vast that life there is solitary and anonymous ... But in the industrial towns the old communal way of life has not yet broken up, tradition is still strong and almost everyone has a family – potentially, therefore, a home.'[20]

The new middle classes in the suburbs were desperate to keep themselves and their children out of this maelstrom. They were as prosperous and stable as anyone could be in these troubled years, but constantly insecure about their social and economic position. They often bought the self-improvement books produced by publishers like Odhams and George Newnes on subjects ranging from etiquette to electric wiring. *Everybody's Best Friend* offered advice on many subjects, including etiquette, whose true purpose was 'to help the wheels of life to turn smoothly and happily'. Readers were offered 'Guiding rules for introductions', how to overcome shyness and pronounce 'awkward names' such as Cholmondeley correctly, how to receive callers, to dress for social occasions, and to use knives and forks at the dinner table. They were advised on a wide variety of types of holiday, ranging from cruising, in which the cabin steward should be tipped with 10 per cent of the passage cost, to one of the new holiday camps: 'The "atmosphere" ... is one of complete friendliness. All the campers meet on an equal level, symbolised by the fact that everyone is known only by his or her Christian name. Only the simplest clothes are required.'[21]

Schoolboys were shown the well-known map of the world with large areas coloured red and were taught that the British Empire was the greatest since the Romans. They were generally proud of it but had little personal involvement. They rarely saw people of non-European race and tended to regard them as quaint if they did. Middle-class families usually went to church occasionally, but Victorian religiosity had been badly damaged among the horrors of the last war and aroused far less enthusiasm. The middle-class boy was usually patriotic in a quiet way, and the status of the royal family was unquestioned. Only those on the extreme political left questioned these ideas, but middle-class parents tended to vote for the Conservative leader, Stanley Baldwin, with his slogan of 'Safety first'.

The middle classes might enjoy an occasional trip to the near continent, but mostly they learned about the rest of the world by BBC radio and from newspapers. Those with high aspirations might read *The Times*, which supported the appeasement of Nazi Germany, or the conservative *Daily Telegraph*, which looked similar but had a lighter style. They would probably shun the working-class *Daily Mirror* and the socialist *Daily Herald*, but they might take the *Daily Mail*, which openly supported fascism for much of the 1930s. Their favourite was Lord Beaverbrook's *Daily Express*, as classless as any newspaper could be in Britain in that decade, but with its core readership in the middle classes. It was patriotic and intensely imperialistic, but it was probably its style and its features that attracted readers more than its politics. It was relentlessly optimistic and in 1938 carried the headline, 'Britain will not be involved in a European war this year, or next year either', a view it continued to support until August 1939. The British schoolboy saw Hitler and Mussolini as joke figures, with their rasping voices and comic gestures, though the near prospect of war during the Munich Crisis of 1938 jolted them out of their sense of security and they began to realize that the last conflict had not been the 'war to end wars' that had been promised. Middle-class youths might support political movements ranging from fascism to communism, but their general mood was one of scepticism and hedonism.

The younger members of the family might read the *Boy's Own Paper*, filled with stirring tales of adventure and advice on middle-class sports such as tennis and sailing. It was proud that its editor had a BA from Balliol College, Oxford. It fostered an awareness of Britain's great empire, with many stories set on its fringes and advice on how to join the various imperial police forces. It had a large amount of information on the new medium of radio – not on listening to its programmes or appearing on it, but on the technicalities of building sets and receiving overseas messages. In sport it favoured middle-class rugby ahead of working-class football. Many of its stories were set in public schools, but it allowed space for the grammar school as well. A serial of 1929–30 was based on a rivalry between two schools, which the editor believed was valuable in 'exposing the foolishness' of such snobbery.[22] There was a good deal about the excitement of flying in its pages, not just in fighting and aerobatics but in travelling long distances quickly and seeing the world from a different point of view. The navy was also represented, and one hero of 1929–30 was a young sub-lieutenant whose early career was described in some detail – at the age of 21 he is found leading a landing party of seaman in the Gulf of Suez. Sailing was much more accessible than flying, and the *Boy's Own Paper* had its own dinghy design, 10 feet 6 inches long.

Teachers and parents were far less enthusiastic about the new *Dandy* and *Beano* which took the bold step of telling stories entirely by graphics and speech bubbles and featured the robust and slapstick adventures of classic characters such as Korky the Cat and Desperate Dan. By his late teens, a boy would have passed through the stage of reading the great (if often controversial) children's authors of the day. Enid Blyton wrote in several different styles for different ages, but her adventure stories described groups of emphatically middle-class children solving crimes and maintaining the social order. W. E. Johns offered high adventure with his Biggles stories. Richmal Crompton's *Just William* had a far less authoritarian view of life. He also came from a classic middle-class family with servants (but no public school connections). The boy and his friends, though often well meaning in their way, created havoc in their country village.

If he was of a mechanical bent, a middle-class boy might have a model train, powered by either clockwork or electricity, and a Meccano set which allowed him to build all sorts of structures and machines – 'A thousand toys in one'. Costs of kits ranged from 1/3 [6p] to 50/- [£2.50] in 1932, with all kinds of accessories to be added on. Meccano was particularly suitable for mechanical structures, and cranes were a favourite in the company's advertising at least. Special kits were available for cars and aeroplanes, but its flat plates did not adapt easily to the complex curves of a ship, while an attempt to reproduce the Eiffel Tower in miniature was far too angular. The boy might also read the *Meccano Magazine*, which described the hobby and contained many articles of technological interest. Moving into more adult fiction, young men were deeply attracted by C. S. Forester's Hornblower stories, which were fantastically popular at the time. They were set in the sailing navy during the days of Nelson, so their relevance to the modern navy was doubtful, but they did set an example of ingenuity and refusal to accept defeat, which was timeless. Detective stores, such as those written by Agatha Christie and Dorothy L. Sayers, probably appealed to an older group. Great writers like Grahame Greene, Evelyn Waugh and Robert Graves could reach a general audience.

If the middle-class newspapers were all to the political right, the most advanced elements in the book publishing industry were moving to the left. The weekly magazine *Picture Post* used a very high standard of photo-journalism to highlight the horrors of unemployment and fascism. Penguin Books made paperbacks accessible for the price of a packet of cigarettes, as its founder claimed. Victor Gollancz and his Left Book Club published left-wing authors, such as George Orwell, and made its readers aware of the Civil War in Spain and the rising menace of fascism. Later it would publish J. P. W. Mallalieu's account of naval life and Hannen Swaffer's critique of the way the lower deck was treated at the end of the war, *What Would Nelson Do?*

The young men from the new middle classes might enter various professions and trades, with differing uses to the wartime navy. Scientists, doctors and engineers were too valuable at their own professions to be retrained for anything else. The navy had a great respect for lawyers and liked to use them in intelligence, as Ewen Montague found out. School teachers had skills of discipline, command and voice projection which were not far from those needed by officers, though sometimes they were found to be insufferably arrogant with the lower deck. Office workers in banks and insurance offices had nothing in particular to offer except their general education, but there were large numbers of them available in the days before computers, and they were not essential to the war effort in their original work. Their places could be filled by keeping on older men beyond retirement age or recruiting those too young to be conscripted. Thus Brendan Maher joined the Legal and General Assurance Society in Manchester until he was taken up by the navy two-and-a-half years later.[23] As officers, young men from such occupations attracted a certain amount of resentment from both sides of the class divide. Snobbish as ever, Evelyn Waugh found that the young RNVR officers he had to deal with were 'a pathetic collection of youths straight from insurance offices ...'[24] Walter 'Stoker' Edwards, a former rating who became an MP, complained that 'people with no sea experience are selected on the experience they have had outside, which has usually been that of a bank clerk or some office worker'.[25]

The services, and particularly the navy, preferred its young men to be celibate or at least uncommitted until they had been integrated into naval culture and could choose suitable wives, but it was not in a position to insist on the point in wartime. At the bottom line, it would accept a man with an active, but not over-active or indiscreet sex life, but romances which crossed class barriers were frowned upon and any open sign of homosexuality was taboo.

If his adolescent thoughts were dominated by sex, the middle-class boy had to be discreet about it in 'respectable' society, and *Everybody's Best Friend* thought it was abnormal. 'The average boy of eighteen is far more interested in football and sports in general than in girls. It is only the precocious types who devote their spare time to romancing and love-making at this age'[26] – 'love-making' meant flirtation in those days, not the physical act. Certainly he would find nothing about it in the *Boy's Own Paper*, which had abandoned even its Victorian descriptions of the dangers of masturbation. Though the paper claimed a certain amount of female readership, the gender hardly appeared in its pages, even as mothers, sisters or friends, far less as lovers, wives or villains. Even in a story partly set in a non-boarding 'day-bug' school, there is nothing about the home lives of the boys. This was very different from the world created by Richmal Crompton, where family life looms large: William's older brother and sister have very active, if chaste, romantic lives, while the boy himself is far from immune to the charms of the right kind of girl. In any case, the middle-class boy was better placed than one in a single-sex boarding school. He might meet 'suitable' women at school or work or through tennis clubs which boomed in the suburbs. He might go to a dance, where it was quite acceptable to ask a girl to join him on the dance-floor even if they had not been introduced.

Life could be hard for a suburban boy when he was called up or volunteered for the armed services. He lived a relatively cosseted life in peacetime, usually with a full-time mother and without the separation from family that public school boys took for granted. His family probably had no military tradition except for service in the last war, which was not a happy precedent. The boy was not likely to have served in any kind of military organization at his school, though he might well be a member of a youth group such as the Boy Scouts or Boys' Brigade, which combined morality and religion with military-style drill and the outdoor life. Even in wartime his family was relatively undisturbed. Middle-aged, middle-class fathers were not liable for conscription, and his mother would probably find war work that could be fitted around the needs of the family. Young adults were not evacuated, but bombs tended to fall on city centres rather than the suburbs. He had been used to a modest standard of living, so food and clothes rationing hit him less hard than members of richer families, while there were no servants to be conscripted or go off to better-paid jobs. There was comparatively little bullying in the grammar schools. The boy probably had his own bedroom at home and was not used to the communal life of either the public school or the slums. All this would change when he went to war, especially in the navy.

The success of any policy of selecting officers from among the ratings depended on the quality of the men who could be induced to enter the navy in the first place. From the beginning of the war all young men from eighteen upwards were liable for conscription into the services, unless they were medically unfit or were in reserved occupations that were essential to the war effort. On registering for service, a young man had to fill in a form stating his preferences. He was asked if he wanted to go into the navy or the air force – he could choose only one, and if he did neither he would automatically go into the army. Even if he did tick the air force or navy box, he was far from sure of getting in, as both services were over-subscribed and both preferred men with technical qualifications or abilities. If accepted, he would be taken on for 'Hostilities Only' and could expect to be discharged as soon as practicable when the war was over.

The army was unpopular at this time, partly due to memories of the last war – practically everyone had a father, uncle or school teacher with stories of the horrors of the trenches. Military training at public schools did not always help, and J. P. W. Mallalieu was put off by it: 'My memories of the Corps at Cheltenham were still vivid; so I was not going into the army.'[27] Moreover, the army had retreated at Dunkirk, in Greece and in Crete, and had been saved largely by the navy. It had a very unattractive uniform, which made the wearer feel like a convict, according to a character in the film *The Way Ahead*. It was associated with 'ne'er do wells' in peacetime, and its wartime image was not much better. Certainly there were some young men who were happy to join the army, perhaps because of family tradition, or because they thought it might be easier to get a commission there than in the other services. But the navy had little to fear about losing the best potential officers in that way.

Anyone who was qualified to train as a naval officer was probably also suitable as a pilot in the RAF, which offered more glamour, faster promotion for the right men and needed rather less technical skill. The air force also seemed to have less class distinction than the navy. Aircrew lived dangerously, but they were free from most of the drudgery associated with military life and lived in comfortable quarters between operations – very different from the decks of a corvette in an Atlantic storm. The navy was always afraid that the best men would be tempted by what the RAF had to offer. This was certainly true after the Battle of Britain in 1940, when applicants for the RAF outnumbered those for the navy by three to one. However, the bomber offensive against Germany proved to be rather less attractive, and naval applications overtook those for the RAF at the beginning of 1942. It was two to one in the navy's favour by September 1943, and nearly three to one by the end of the war.[28]

Newspapers and radio followed the exploits of famous ships, and the public cheered when the pocket battleship *Graf Spee* was forced to scuttle herself, and the destroyer *Cossack* released prisoners from a German 'Hell-ship' with the cry, 'The Navy's here'. It laughed at the *Luftwaffe*'s repeated claims to have destroyed the aircraft carrier *Ark Royal*, until she was actually sunk by a U-boat in November 1941. It mourned the loss of *Hood*, the most famous ship in the navy, and rejoiced when her nemesis, the battleship *Bismarck*, was herself sunk a few days later – just as the army in Crete was being rescued by the navy, like a second Dunkirk. It was at precisely this point that the survey organization Mass Observation looked at public opinion on the navy. It found it was held in higher regard than the other two services, and it was believed that sailors were 'as always doing their job magnificently'. According to one observer, one seaman was 'worth six British soldiers, and three British airmen'. Another said, 'I know no sailors, but I think they are heroic.'[29] Soldiers and airmen were spread more or less evenly throughout the country, and in almost any town they could be found grumbling in pubs or cinema queues. They did not seem to take any great risks, for the bulk of the army was training in Britain for four years between Dunkirk and D-Day, while the great majority of 'airmen' in the RAF were ground crew, involved in maintenance, domestic or administrative work. Churchill complained in 1944, '...probably not one in four or five men who wear the King's uniform even hear a bullet whistle, or are likely to hear one. The vast majority run no more risk than the civil population of southern England.'[30]

The sailor, on the other hand, was rarely seen *en masse* outside a few naval ports. He was always at war, and engineers, clerks and cooks took their chances equally with gunners and torpedomen in a ship at sea. He had an exotic uniform, a mystique and a man-of-the-world air that was rarely found in soldiers and RAF ground crew – although it was different for aircrew, of course. At home on Christmas leave, officers wore uniform to parties and other ranks wore evening dress, with the exception of RAF sergeant-pilots, who were usually portrayed as heroes with attractive women on their arms.[31]

One way to attract the better kind of recruit was to sign up young men before they were old enough to volunteer or be conscripted, and start to train them in the ways and culture of the service. The RAF was highly successful at this when it formed the Air Training Corps, or ATC, in 1941. It soon attracted a fifth of all eligible boys in the age group. The only comfort for the navy was that the Corps was committed to training men for the Fleet Air Arm as well as the air force, but that was no help in finding suitable executive officers. The naval equivalent was the Sea Cadet force established 1914, run privately by the Navy League, which campaigned for a larger fleet. Its aims were,

To teach boys, between the ages of 12 and 18, habits of discipline, duty and self-respect, and to try to remedy the evil effects of street loafing in order that boys may become, by their knowledge, of practical use not only in time of peace but in time of war, and that they may be educated to believe in the British Empire and the British Navy, whereon the Empire primarily depends for its existence.

It had a rival in the form of the Sea Scouts, an arm of the Boy Scouts organization, but the Admiralty gave some encouragement to both. The Sea Cadets was taken over by the Admiralty in February 1942, and an effort was made to increase their numbers. There was a twenty per cent increase to 11,632 a year later, and 107 units were in existence, but there was a slight decline in the number of officers to train them. The Admiralty planned for 25,000 cadets, but that would still be a long way behind the ATC.[32]

The Admiralty did not worry about recruiting suitable able seamen and stokers, but it was deeply concerned about the supply of potential technicians and officers. One official commented,

... the general run of militiamen [i.e., conscripts] opting for the Navy did not contain a large enough proportion of young men of public school or secondary school education. Only a fraction had the necessary educational background to reach the technical ability and assume the responsibility required of them, and it was found that the Navy required a considerable proportion of recruits with at least secondary education.[33]

As a result it founded the Y-Scheme in May 1941, partly to influence young men of good education who might be potential officers. It was always denied that the scheme was 'officer-producing' as such, that it was equally geared to finding skilled technical ratings for the navy, including the Fleet Air Arm and Royal Marines. But mixed messages were sent out to potential recruits. The booklet *The Navy and the Y-Scheme* started by describing the career of the Coastal Forces hero Lieutenant-Commander Robert Hitchens and contained the sentence,

> a lot of other men who were boys not long ago ... have found themselves – who perhaps two years ago were bank clerks, shop assistants, motor mechanics – the captain of a landing craft on the beaches of Sicily, or the captain of a naval aircraft flying over the convoys.[34]

The selection procedures were enough to raise expectations in themselves. Candidates had to produce a School Certificate or a recommendation from a figure of authority, such as a headmaster. They went before a rather grand interview panel headed by senior officers. If successful, they were expected to join or continue with a pre-entry scheme such as the Sea Cadets or ATC (for Fleet Air Arm candidates) or perhaps to serve as amateur soldiers in the Home Guard. Also, it was reported later, 'So great ... was the demand for officers in the initial stages that a very large percentage of "Y" Scheme entrants, by virtue of their superior intelligence, was promoted to officer rank thus strengthening the misconception that the "Y" Scheme was a royal road to a commission.' This was a disappointment for many of the 2,302 men who entered the navy via the Y-Scheme in 1944–5. The navy was at full strength by that time and had much less need for new officers. Fewer than 40 per cent of them became CW candidates and potential officers, and it is quite likely that about half of these dropped out or failed at one stage or another. Another 37 per cent went to sea as ordinary seamen, with little prospect of immediate promotion, while the rest went off in small numbers to become telegraphists, supply assistants and become occupied in many other trades.[35]

It was not an up-to-date poster campaign that attracted men to the navy. In 1942, Brendan Maher visited a recruiting office:

Peacetime posters, now fading, were still in the windows. One poster portrayed sailors, in crisp white uniforms, smiling and relaxed but ready for anything. Beyond the immaculate decks of their ship rose a background of Malta, where terraced villas climbed a hill beyond the harbour ... In yet another, still-smiling seamen sat down to dinner, served apparently by white-aproned cooks. This was the life, said the posters. For all these reasons, it seemed inconceivable that anybody would want to serve other than in the Navy. At the age of eighteen, military service would be compulsory. As my own time to serve approached, the decision was obvious; join the Navy.[36]

It was the navy's public image that was its greatest asset in attracting suitable officer candidates. Newspapers were sympathetic to the service, but they were constrained by paper rationing, which often reduced them to six or eight pages, so there was little space for feature articles. Radio was practically universal, and almost all the population had access to a set, but it was not aimed at the young men who might be attracted to the navy. A set was quite expensive and formed a large item of furniture, so 'listening in' was often a family activity. Potential naval recruits were well past the age of listening to Children's Hour between five and six in the evening, and there were no specific programmes for them. The BBC operated only one domestic service with regional variations during this period, and it was still under the staid, authoritarian influence of Lord Reith (though in peacetime a more popular selection of programmes might be found by listening to Radio Normandie or Radio Luxemburg). BBC radio provided a national focus, and the whole country was glued to its sets during the funeral of King George V, the abdication which followed, the Munich Crisis of 1938, Neville Chamberlain's mournful declaration of war on Germany and Churchill's historic speeches. It could be used for practical purposes such as summoning reservists on the outbreak of war, and its popular music might be sent through the decks of a warship in a British port, but it had little immediate relevance to naval recruiting.

Film was the most important mass medium of the age – a third of the British population went to the cinema at least once a week, while another third went occasionally. This was more marked in the target groups for recruitment – nearly 80 percent of those between fourteen and seventeen went at least once a week, and more than half of those went at least twice. Among 18–40 year-olds, 43 per cent went at least once a week.[37] Shows were held in vast 'picture palaces' amid grandiose mock-Egyptian architecture. Audiences were often deeply moved and influenced by what they saw, partly by the novelty, for it was not much more than a decade since the 'talkies' had been introduced. The experience of seeing the film on a huge screen was rather different from that on a television set at home, or even in a small modern cinema. It was also a collective experience, for a cross-section of the local community might be found in the seats. Many teachers deplored the influence of films during the 1930s, and some tried to restrict cinema visits. 'If all parents exercised reasonable control over their children's visits to the cinema, it would be another matter. But so long as children are permitted to attend cinemas twice or oftener a week, and to be present at performances ending at 10 or 11 p.m. – to say nothing of the nature of the films they are allowed to witness – schools are rendering their pupils a very real service by placing cinemas out of bounds during term time.'[38]

In wartime naval ports, sailors on shore leave often formed a large and lively part of the audience, but many naval officers were as scornful as schoolteachers of the cinema's alleged vulgarity, not to mention the attention-seeking antics of film stars. More advanced officers, especially Lord Louis Mountbatten, could see that the film industry had much to offer the navy if it was handled in the right way. He was instrumental in setting up the Royal Naval Film Corporation, by which films could be hired for shipboard showing at very cheap rates.

The great majority of films shown during the war were escapist and largely American. The most popular included westerns, gangster films, Disney cartoons, love stories and musicals. British films were not highly regarded generally, for they included many 'quota quickies' made cheaply to meet government regulation. One popular strand was historical dramas produced by Gainsborough Films and usually involving spirited women. These appealed to the largely female audience left at home in wartime, and the costumes and sets provided an escape from the drabness of clothes rationing and 'utility' furniture. A small minority of films did deal with the war, and some directly with the navy. The service was not particularly well represented in the early years. *Convoy*, released in 1940, had a rather old-fashioned view of naval warfare in which officers wear spotless white uniforms with gilded epaulettes and are as much involved in love triangles as tactics. The main enemy is the battlecruiser, not the U-boat. *Ships with Wings* attempted a more modern subject, the Fleet Air Arm, but its melodramatic story, its unconvincing model work and its stereotyped Germans and Greeks did not impress the critics, though the public loved it.

The classic wartime naval film was *In Which We Serve*, made by Noel Coward and David Lean and released in 1942. Ostensibly it attempted to show men of all classes, and their wives and families, uniting in a common effort. Equality is quickly emphasized when all the principal male characters find themselves clinging to a life-raft after their ship is sunk, and the rest of the film is told in flashback. Captain Kinross, played by Noel Coward, lives in a grand house with servants even in wartime (though it was toned down from the royal background of Lord Louis Mountbatten, on whom the character was modelled). His wife is tolerant of her 'permanent and undisputed rival', her husband's ship. Chief Petty Officer Walter Hardy (Bernard Miles) is lower middle class, with a suburban house and a rather self-important manner. Ordinary Seaman 'Shorty' Blake (John Mills) is clearly working class, from a Cockney family who live in an overcrowded London flat. In reality, Hardy had presumably started on the same route through the service as Blake and is essentially Blake twenty years on, not from a different class at all. Blake marries Hardy's niece without anyone turning a hair, but it is impossible to conceive of either of them marrying one of Captain Kinross's relatives. Unwittingly perhaps, it merely confirms that the navy still had a huge gulf between officers and ratings. Though set in wartime, it deals with men who had been recruited and trained in peacetime and barely indicates the presence of Hostilities Only ratings and temporary wartime officers who were often living uncomfortably in the gap.

The film had a huge popular impact. One reader of *Filmgoer* magazine wrote,

> Here you were proud of the British Navy, no other country could feel as the British felt over this film, it was not one long weep, or one long view of fights, blood and death, but it had a little to sober you, a little to cheer you, it gave you a glimpse of the families, their home lives, it made you feel strong and proud, and what more could one ask for than that?[39]

Despite the use of Mountbatten's servant as a technical adviser, one wartime seaman connected with the film trade felt that it 'did NOT represent lower deck speech and manners', but he had to concede that, 'The average sailor loves to see patriotic stuff on the screen, although he might grumble like blazes when with his mates. Imagine the glow of pride, however, when sitting with his wife, girlfriend or 'tart wot I picked up' in the cinema. IWWS did have a real attempt at representing not only sailors at war, but families.'[40] The effect on young men awaiting conscription to the services was probably similar.

We Dive at Dawn, a submarine film also starring John Mills, treated the British class system in a slightly different way. In the first place, it employed him as an officer not long after audiences had seem him as a rating – no actor, perhaps, has played a greater range of military ranks over the years than Mills. In fact, he was the only fully developed officer character in the film. The other main character was played by Eric Portman as a leading seaman who, it was hinted, had not done as well in the service as expected – perhaps he was a failed CW candidate. The rest are mainly petty officers, including the coxswain, and a younger man who is about to get married. The film uses the private lives of the lower-deck characters less patronizingly, and both Portman and the young petty officer use heroism in battle to repair their relationships ashore. The film is an excellent portrayal of a submarine commander in action, until it descends into incredible adventure towards the end.

Went the Day Well? was set in an inland village and has only one naval character, but it says as much about public perceptions of the navy as anything else. The village is taken over by Germans disguised as British soldiers, who are soon identified by their acts of barbarity. The local Home Guard is wiped out, but the village is saved largely through the efforts of an able seaman home on leave, who wears his uniform throughout. Men in army uniform turn out to be impostors, traitors or cannon fodder, but the square collar and bell bottoms of the sailor are a symbol of trustworthiness, resource and courage.

As well as the major feature films, cinemas in those days usually filled out a long programme with a secondary 'B-feature', a newsreel and several informative shorts. This gave some chance for naval recruiting, even among those who had come to the cinema to escape from the war. *Raising Sailors* of 1940 dealt with early training. It had an inspiring script, read by the announcer C. F. Danvers Walker. It was intended to appeal to a wide range of people, either as boy entrants or adults from office and factory. It promised, 'There are many embryo officers among these HO men, for temporary commissions are available for suitable candidates,' and ended with the sailors being wished well in 'the great days that lie before you'. In *Sea Cadets of 1941*, a naval signaller, played by Bernard Miles (who was later to star in *In Which We Serve*), arrives home on leave to unqualified respect from the local community. He is approached by two seventeen-year-old boys who want to join the navy, and to no one's surprise he recommends the sea cadets, 'a kind of evening class for sailors'. They seem to have a rather old-fashioned training programme, including much flag signalling and even cutlass drill, though there is mention of the 'dye-sel' engine. *Sailors of Tomorrow* was made in 1944, also to boost the cadets. It stressed inter-service cooperation and recognized the possibility that Fleet Air Arm candidates might prefer the ATC and that those planning to enter the Royal Marines might join the Army Cadets. Indeed, the *Sea Cadets* did not look particularly appealing compared with the other organizations. The cast look rather glum when learning navigation and only brighten up when they go on board the training ship *Foudroyant*, once a French ship, which had fought at Trafalgar. But air training seems far more exciting, with flights in various aircraft and the chance to learn gliding. The film's statement that when they arrive in the service the cadets will 'need only a final polish' was not reflected in the views of naval officers, who thought that pre-entry training was of little real use.

One Company, produced by Gainsborough, was intended to attract young men to the Y-Scheme, but it is difficult to see how it could have a mass appeal. It follows the story of three boys as they approach the age for conscription. Two of them, with ambitions to fly, are at a very superior public school. The other, Martin, intends to enter as an executive officer and is able to run a powerboat despite petrol rationing – he is something of a know-all who rescues the others from a river. They go back to their school and see a Y-Scheme poster attracting the interest of a crowd of public school fiction stereotypes and are easily convinced by its arguments. The film then races through their training for their respective roles, until two of them are shot down and rescued from the sea by none other than Martin.

Almost certainly, it was the navy's well-established prestige that attracted the right kind of man to its officer corps, rather than any clever recruiting schemes. In making *In Which We Serve*, Noel Coward was influenced by his long association with the navy: 'For many years past I had been privileged to be a guest of the Royal Navy in all parts of the world, and in every type of ship, ranging from battlewagons to submarines. This will always be to me a subtle and most important honour.'[41] According to the Mass Observation report of 1941, the most common attitude to the navy was 'one of unqualified but unspecified respect'.[42]

Even if young men could be persuaded to apply for the navy, not all of them would be accepted. Standards of health were high, and seaman officers needed good eyesight without glasses. For most of the war the navy had about three times as many applicants as it needed, and could afford to pick and choose. Only in 1943–4, during the great expansion on the eve of D-Day, did it take nearly everyone who came up to the minimum standard. In the early stages of the war, it used recalled regular chief petty officers for the selection process. During a period of a few minutes, 'the Naval Recruiter concerned made his assessment of the man; obtained answers to standard questions about his willingness to be inoculated, vaccinated and so on; decided whether or not to accept him; and, if he accepted him, allocated him to a branch of the service.'[43] Spelling was considered important, and one chief was overheard to say, 'What, spell Egypt with a J? You're illegible for the navy.' Often the interviewer had little knowledge of the national education system, as John Davies found out:

'Education?' The rough, deep voice startled me.

'Oh! I took an honours degree in English at the University of London.' ...

The arbiter of my destiny gestured briefly with impatience.

'Never mind about that. Have you got the School Leaving Certificate?

'Er – yes, of course.'[44]

The actor Alec Guinness was seen by a rather reluctant chief petty officer.

He made it clear that he didn't think that I was a suitable candidate and did his best to dissuade me. ... When I answered his various questions he made little despairing shakes of the head, which were almost like a nervous tic. But I persisted. Eventually, with a gloomy sigh, as if he had caught me out, he said, 'Well, can you swim?' I answered, triumphantly, 'Yes!' He stamped a piece of paper and said, 'If the doctor passes you, you'll get your call-up, my lad. One day.'[45]

After 1942, applicants came before specially-trained Wren petty officers who used more modern psychological techniques to select men. The candidates were asked questions on 'such topics as sickness absence from civilian work, headaches, accidents, dieting, and reaction to air raids'.[46]

They would collect this information by a three-stage process, in which they would first of all get a group of candidates to fill up a simple form, rather like an extended application form, which would yield facts about the school and work record and leisure activities of each candidate. After 10 minutes or so spent on this, the group would go on to take a paper-and-pencil intelligence test (which, in order to allay apprehensions, was always referred to as an 'observation' test) lasting 20 minutes. Then, as the men trickled back one by one from the medical board which saw them on completion of the form and the test, each would be given an interview lasting about 8 minutes. The Wren's notes on her interview, and the man's score in the observation test, were to be recorded on the form he himself had initiated.

Even if he was taken into the navy as a result of these tests, even if he was a member of the Y-Scheme, the young man was far from being guaranteed a commission. He was not even a CW candidate at this stage, for these were finally selected in the training bases.

4
BECOMING A SAILOR

After his acceptance into the navy, a man might wait several months
to be called up. J. P. W. Mallalieu found the letter 'curiously polite.'

Dear Sir,
A vacancy has occurred in His Majesty's Navy for an Ordinary
Seaman. If you wish to accept it, will you notify the Naval
Centre, Edgware, and report there on February 23 at 9 a.m.
From there you will be sent to H.M.S *Frobisher*, South Down.[1]

Travel in wartime trains was often an adventure in itself for young
men who had never been away from home, and with the risk of air
raids it might take many hours, increasing the sense of separation
from home. After that the men were usually met at the station and
taken by road, or occasionally by water, to the base, where they
would spend around ten weeks learning basic naval skills and
discipline.

Like much of the British war effort, the navy's basic training bases
were improvised and originated in various ways. Some, such as HMS
Royal Arthur at Skegness, HMS *Glendower* at Pwllheli in North
Wales and HMS *Scotia* in Ayr in Scotland, were built as holiday
camps. The late jazz singer and writer George Melly found that
Royal Arthur had 'a certain architectural frivolity completely
inappropriate to a Royal Navy Shore Establishment ... The ceiling of
the lobby was painted to represent a summer sky with fluffy white
clouds passing over it. In the centre of the room, rooted in the bare
plasterboards, was a large and comparatively realistic tree ... The
serving hatch, through which a rather gloomy WREN galley rating
passed us our eating irons, was framed by mullioned windows let
into the elaborate facade of an Elizabethan inn with a sign reading
'Ye Olde Pigge and Whistle' projecting over our heads.'[2] Some, such
as *Raleigh* near Plymouth and *Collingwood* near Portsmouth, were

purpose-built very quickly on peninsulas near the naval bases. According to Alec Guinness, *Raleigh* was 'a vast parade ground, with concrete quarter-deck and rows of long wooden huts housing two-tier bunks, offices, gym, dining hall and bomb shelters'.[3]

HMS *Ganges* was the longest established of the bases, also on a peninsula where the Rivers Orwell and Stour met and close to the naval base at Harwich. It had once been an 84-gun wooden ship of the line used for training boys for the navy, until the shore base was built in 1903. It was decided to turn the base over to training Hostilities Only recruits, and the first 264 adult trainees arrived in April 1940, while the 1,500 boys moved out to HMS *St George* on the Isle of Man a month later. By June 1943 the number borne on the books of *Ganges* was 5,193, including staff. In all, it was to train 60,968 Hostilities Only ratings during the war.[4]

Adult ratings joining *Ganges* arrived at Harwich by train and were often given a cup of tea in the local YMCA before being taken across the estuary in a naval tender. On arrival, new men often had to run the gauntlet of taunts and unwanted advice from slightly more experienced men. 'Go back home while you have the chance ... You're better off in the Army ... The square bashing will murder you!' 'Take no notice, lads,' the Chief said. 'They've only been here a week themselves!'[5] At *Ganges* the first shock awaited the newcomers as they entered the annexe just outside the main base. John Davies wrote,

> To say that the Annexe was utilitarian is to cloak its extreme and depressing ugliness in as kindly a fashion as possible. Low wooden buildings, roofed with corrugated iron, enclosed a small parade-ground within a hollow square. Around three sides of the square ran a covered way, a projection of these roofs supported upon wooden uprights, and within these tin cloisters a few unwilling celibates lurked aimlessly.[6]

To John Wilson, 'Any difference between it and a concentration camp was purely coincidental.' There was no leave of any kind for two weeks and to P. Calvert, 'It was just like being in jail and the food was the worst I encountered during the whole time I was in the navy.' Geoffrey Ball agreed when he was served 'some sloppy mess that's supposed to be stew with a thick layer of grease on top, a huge block of bread and a mug of greasy cocoa'. Loudspeakers disturbed the peace with 'a queer shriek before announcing something'. There were no newspapers and nothing to read, but Ball had brought a BBC handbook and a murder novel, which became 'two of the most precious things I have ever had'. However an officer told the men that they were lucky to be at *Ganges* – all the other bases had been put up since the start of the war, whereas this one was well-established and designed for naval training.

They were allocated places in large dormitories, inoculated and given psychological tests to see what part of the navy might suit them best. Geoffrey Ball thought of becoming a writer or clerk, though later he saw the attractions of the signals branch. They settled into a routine – woken up in the cold dawn at six, breakfast at seven, dinner at 12.30, tea at 4.30 and supper at 7.30. They heard speeches by the senior officers – Ken Kimberley describes a typical captain's introduction:

> Welcome to HMS *Glendower*. I am Captain Barker, with me is my Commander and First Lieutenant. The *Glendower* will never sail away, but believe me – myself, and all my fellow officers, Chief and Petty Officers will leave no stone unturned to give you the basic RN training that the life at sea will demand of you. We have experience in peacetime and in war to make sailors of you. If we find that in the coming weeks you are not for us, we will tell you so. Likewise, if you don't like us here at *Glendower* in the next 14 days, you are free to leave. Is that clear?
>
> The training will be long, hard and vigorous, but I am sure you will find it enjoyable – to a point.[7]

New entrants to HMS *Royal Arthur* at Skegness were issued with a tiny 20-page handbook which began by describing the organization of the course, naming the commanding officer, training commander and the three divisional officers. Each division lived in chalets in a particular area of the camp and had 34 instructors, one for each class of about 50 ratings. They were told about naval ensigns and the all-important subject of naval etiquette.

> The proper answer in acknowledgement of an order from a senior officer is 'Aye, aye, Sir.' Not only are such answers as 'very good.' 'right,', 'righto,' or, worst of all, 'O.K.' forbidden, but you will soon discover that they sound unseamanlike, which is just as important a matter for potential sailors.[8]

The ratings were informed about regulations on smoking, drinking, gambling and standards of discipline – 'Obey any order given to you immediately and without question, even if it may seem to you at the time unreasonable or unjust.'[9] They were allowed leave of absence for special circumstances, and ordinary leave would normally be granted after 1630 each day, or afternoons at the weekends; money should be deposited with the paymaster, and each man should make a habit of reading the notice-board every day. Every man would be given full facilities to practise his religion.

At *Ganges*, Geoffrey Ball's group was issued with its uniforms on the second full day. It took about two hours, and he wrote, 'I didn't know there was so much stuff needed to become a sailor.' At *Glendower*,

> It was nearly dark as we filed into the long shed. We moved slowly along the counter, taking from the Wrens different items of clothing as we shuffled along. It was all done by guesswork on their part as each Wren eyed us up and down.
>
> 'No 4 size will do you,' said one, whatever No 4 size was.
>
> 'No 9s will do you fine.' Another Wren handed me a pair of boots.
>
> When I reached the end of a long counter I had collected two jumpers, two pairs of bell-bottoms to be known as No 1s and No

3s, two collars, two shirt fronts, one black ribbon, two pairs of socks, one pair of boots, one cap, one cap band, one oilskin, one overcoat, one pair of overalls, one housewife (pocket sewing outfit), one lanyard and one seaman's manual.

'That'll do for you, Jack,' the cheerful little Wren said. 'Move along the counter, find an empty spot and get your name and number marked on everything.' I found an empty spot and stamped everything with my name and number: CJX 557233.[10]

Ball's group were not allowed to put on their new uniforms until next day, because 'it needs explaining'. According to John Davies, the seaman's shirt was an 'amazing garment'. It had a square-cut neck and short sleeves, and many men had difficulty at first in finding which way to put it on. The seaman's trousers were an 'outlandish garment'.

Six buttons, three vertical and three horizontal. I struggled to find the correct buttonhole for each. The trousers gripped me tightly round the waist, but below the knees they expanded enormously. I looked down and started momentarily when I saw even the huge boots obscured by blue serge. Cautiously I moved a leg, which led to the realisation that this garment was surprisingly comfortable.

Then came the seaman's jumper, which was separate from the collar.

Getting into the jumper was an all-in struggle, no holds barred, a wild waving of arms followed finally by a condition of complete helplessness. Breathless and outwitted, I at last stood still, my shoulders and upper arms relentlessly caught in blue serge, the extremities dangling helplessly before me. Then as though in response to an intuitive feeling that all was not well, one of the white-shirted ones suddenly appeared, ducking under the screen. Without ceremony he heaved out the collar of my jumper, which had been the major cause of the stoppage, and then he tugged industriously at my waist until jumper and trousers met, and finally, with a superhuman effort, overlapped.[11]

They would soon find that a 'tiddly sailor' could find ways to modify his uniform to suit himself, and all true seamen were skilled with needle and thread.

The 'little round hat' as far from the central position as authority will permit, with the bow of its ribbon teased into a flat, symmetrical rosette. The spotless 'blue jean' collar, with its white borders gleaming. The black silk ironed to impeccable smoothness. The ribbons attaching it to the jumper are as long as possible, with swallow tail ends: by the length of these ribbons a man's taste is judged, and the longer the more dashing. And your mess-deck masher will affect a white silk scarf (not regulation, this, but allowed) tucked coyly beneath the black. The 'bell-bottoms' as wide as canny selection from 'Pusser's stores' or instructions to the ship's tailor can achieve, and for the first few moments at least bearing some trace of latitudinal folding (for trousers are stowed very carefully: first turned inside out and then folded concertina-wise lest a vertical crease appear).[12]

A seaman struggles to use the single pocket in his uniform.
(Men Dressed as Seamen)

This made an impression even on a socialist like the young James Callaghan:

109

We were taught how to tie knots and we discovered how to launder our new, dark-blue collars so that they appeared as faded and washed out as those of any veteran seaman. We risked the wrath of the chief gunner's mate by cutting the tapes of our collars so that they showed a U-front instead of the regulation V-front, and we made sure we had seven horizontal creases (no more, no less) in our bell-bottomed trousers. All these matters were important to us.[13]

The sailor's cap was notoriously uncomfortable. It was round in shape, rather than oval to follow the shape of the head, and made of rigid material. Worn properly, it put pressure on the temples, so seamen got round this by wearing it tilted to one side or perched on the back of the head, 'flat aback'. Regular officers hated this practice, and a young man who expected to get on in the service was better not to indulge in it.

The classic rating's uniform was known as 'square rig' because of the square collar. It was distinguished from 'fore-and-aft rig' (another old sailing-ship term), with jacket, collar and tie as worn in different forms by officers, petty officers and certain junior ratings such as cooks, stewards and sick-berth attendants. Square rig was enormously popular with the British public, and Tristan Jones was told on the train to *Ganges*, 'Well, matey, at least you'll be all right where crumpet's concerned. They go for the navy blokes a lot more than the army, see? Can't go wrong in your little old navy-blue suit, can you?' Many of the men loved it too, but not all, and there was much dissatisfaction by the end of the war. An able seaman wrote, 'The traditional uniform is unpleasant and unhealthy to wear and should be scrapped for the comfortable and more healthy battle-dress and beret.' A leading telegraphist said, 'I hate this uniform, which is the most idiotic and uncomfortable suit of clothes I have ever worn.' And a former serviceman wrote, 'One has only to watch an A.B. dress to have pity on him, with a uniform consisting of tapes and ribbons and bits and pieces, and a blue jean collar which another person has to hold in place while the poor chap puts his overcoat on.'[14]

The new sailor would have to get used to his dress, for now he would be in it on duty, at rest and on leave. He might discard it almost completely when he eventually reached a ship on active service, but for now he would wear it all the time, and within the confines of the training base he had little chance to modify it.

Eric Denton's first three weeks at *Ganges* were 'a dull blur of routine, discomfort and unhappiness'.[15] For most, the situation improved when they moved into the main barracks after one or two weeks. Geoffrey Ball was not impressed with the brightly coloured figureheads at the gate – 'They make the place look awful' – but he found many advantages, including a huge swimming pool, said to be the second biggest indoor one in England. There were three large gymnasia, football, rugby and hockey pitches and two NAAFI canteens, but the dominant feature was the huge parade ground surmounted by a tall mast, which was the symbol of the base and could be seen for miles around – every trainee would be expected to climb it at some time during his service, but it was not such a major feature of training as it had been for the boys who had recently moved on. Ball was advised to climb it before he was made to, in order to get some practice in.

But the dormitories were no less crowded than those in the annexe, and 70 men lived on two-tier bunks in a room designed for 30 boys. The food was a little better, though as always it conformed to the standard British taste of the era; one day Ball had beans, bacon, tea, bread and butter for breakfast. In the evening he had roast mutton, roast potatoes, cabbage and gravy with trifle for desert.

Possible CW candidates were mostly identified early in the training process, either by their standard of education or by membership of the Y-Scheme. They were interviewed by the captain, and a number were rejected at this stage as not being 'officer material'. Others were put into a separate mess, though they still trained with the others some of the time. John Wilson, son of a very distinguished doctor who was Winston Churchill's personal physician, had his first experience of meeting the urban working class *en masse*, but it was not until later, aboard ship, that he got to know them intimately. Despite his Cambridge degree, John Davies was slightly surprised to be summoned to his divisional officer and told, 'After due consideration I have decided to select you as an officer candidate. Do you want a commission?' At first he was reluctant to accept and leave his training as a telegraphist to reduce to an ordinary seaman, even for a few months. 'The Brains of the Navy no more. From now on just a poor, bloody, down-trodden, over-worked, under-paid, much abused ordinary seaman.' He was also uneasy about the way he had been chosen:

> I couldn't help feeling a little unhappy about the method of selection, for the initial choice seemed to have been based largely on paper qualifications. In my own case, for instance, I did not see how a degree in English Literature went any part of the way towards proving that I would make as leader of men. All four members of the mess who had university degrees were among the six chosen. On the other hand the irrepressible Bert, who probably had more character and vitality than the rest of us combined, was not.[16]

Sailors had to learn very quickly how to distinguish the different ranks and ratings in the service and the status attached to each. Commissioned officers, such as the CW candidates aspired to become, had the 'fore-and-aft' uniform with a distinctive cap badge and gold stripes on the arm, but they were remote figures at this stage. Midshipmen, young men training to become officers, were rarely seen in these bases. Warrant officers wore the same uniform as commissioned officers but with a single thin stripe. They were more common in the camps, and men with traditional titles like 'boatswain' and 'gunner' often supervised the training quite closely. They were mostly elderly men who had risen from the ranks. Commissioned and warrant officers all had to be saluted, and that was taken very seriously during training.

The naval salute is made by bringing up the right hand to the cap, naturally and smartly, but not hurriedly, with the thumb and fingers closed together, elbow in line with the shoulder, hand and forearm in line, with the palm of the hand turned to the left, but inclined slightly inwards.[17]

Below these were the ratings, each of whom was rated with a particular series of qualifications and skills. Chief petty officers were the highest in the service, and they too wore a fore-and-aft uniform, with three buttons on each side of the breast instead of four. They had no badges as such in ordinary dress but were distinguished by three brass buttons on the lower sleeve. Petty officers were only slightly less grand, and those of more than one year's seniority also wore the fore-and-aft rig, but with a single-breasted jacket. They were marked out by a pair of crossed anchors on the upper left sleeve. 'Unconfirmed' petty officers and leading seamen wore the same square rig as the trainees themselves, the leading seamen with a single anchor on the upper left sleeve – the anchor, and hence the man, was known as a 'killick' or 'hookey'.

Apart from the martinets in *Ganges'* annexe and the bullies among the gunnery instructors, the petty officers were usually gentle with adult trainees. When Mallalieu's CPO found the new entrants smoking without permission, he told them, 'By the way, it doesn't matter now, as this is your first day. But in the ordinary way, you mustn't smoke on the mess deck.'[18] Later he won their sympathy.

'Look 'ere. I've told you twenty times a day, ever since you came, to behave yourself when officers are about. Why don't you use your bloody loaf? If the Training Commander had seen you sucking your bloody sweets, we'd both 'ave been in the rattle. You'd have lost your bloody [leave] card and I might 'ave 'ad my pay stopped. You're a fine lot,' he went on, turning to the class. 'If I were to run you in, you'd say, "The dirty old bastard"; but if I don't run you in and then get into trouble myself, you'd only say, "The silly old runt".'[19]

Norman Hampson found that 'almost all of those in authority over us were understanding, reasonably patient and unmistakably fellow members of the human race. Even the leading seamen who did their best to bark obscenities at us when they took us for arms drill were making such an unconvincing attempt to play at sergeants that they were more amusing than intimidating.'[20] George Melly found that petty officers generally were fine people:

Long association with the sea and its ports had given them a certain tolerant sophistication, part cynical but certainly affectionately so. They had learnt to mistrust the moral imperatives of any one place because they had seen them replaced by others, often equally rigid and ridiculous, elsewhere. The [sic] made allowances too for us temporary sailors. We were there because we had to be. One day the war would be over and the Navy its old self; a machine for sailing in.[21]

The men below leading seamen had their own hierarchy, which was just as important. A man rose, almost automatically, from ordinary to able seaman after nine months or a year in the service. There were plenty of men who chose to stay as able seamen, or ABs, and wanted no further promotion. Some of the men on the staffs of their camps were distinguished by chevrons on their arms, which caused confusion among trainees who were more used to army or police ranks.

'Sergeant? Their ain't no such things in the Navy. Them three stripes on 'is arm are good conduct badges. 'E gets one after three years in the service, another after eight, and another after thirteen. 'E gets threepence a day extra for each one.'
'All right, Admiral; he's still a sergeant to me.'[22]

These were the 'three-badge ABs', men who had served at least thirteen years in the navy without taking on any extra responsibility. One of the heroes of Dunkirk was Able Seaman

Samuel Palmer, who had three Good Conduct badges and the Long Service and Good Conduct Medal. He took a 30-foot motorboat over the Channel, rescuing some French soldiers on the way. After many ferry trips to waiting craft, he coped with engine failure and lack of charts to get a group of British troops back to Ramsgate. He had passed for leading seaman in 1927 but was not promoted, perhaps because his initiative and independence did not find favour in the peacetime navy.[23]

Mallailieu tried to understand the mentality of such men:

It was strange that three-badge A.B.s ... who so obviously knew their jobs, and were in the Navy as a career and not merely out of wartime necessity, should be content to remain A.B.s instead of 'going through the hook' or even for petty officer.

But these men had all the privileges of Leading Seaman and most of the privileges of Petty Officers. They were never chivvied. Usually they were given some regular job, such as gunsweeper, which let them out of scrubbing decks, washing the paint work, or any other of the labouring jobs which were the constant lot of the ordinary seaman ... They were the elder statesmen who gave advice but were under no obligation to see that it was followed. They knew their way about. They knew to a fraction of a second when they must move unobtrusively to the port side of the ship to avoid some dirty job that was coming on the starboard side.[24]

Men like these, often recalled naval pensioners, were figures of some authority in the training camps.

Nothing was ever simple in the navy, and most experienced seamen also had a badge on the right arm showing their 'non-substantive' rating, indicating skill at a particular job in gunnery, torpedo, submarine-detecting or physical training, and largely independent of their 'substantive' ratings as able seaman, petty officer and so on. Of these, the gunnery branch was by far the most prominent in the training camps, for as well as skill at their weapons they handled the military side of naval life and were experts in parade-ground discipline.

Each group of trainees was headed by an instructor, either an aged regular or a much younger man of the 'failed CW type'. Geoffrey Ball's group had Leading Seaman Billings, a Londoner who had served in submarines in the last war. The trainees mocked his habit of speaking very slowly and pronouncing 'surely' as 'sure-leye', but he was a very good instructor, and he helped out with cleaning the mess every Saturday morning. Peter Bull's petty officer instructor was 'lazy but competent', and the class took him out for a drink on their last night.[25] A class captain was appointed for each group from among the trainees. Peter Bull made the mistake of admitting having been in the Officers' Training Corps at his public school, and to his horror he was appointed.[26] Mallalieu's CPO told them,

One of you's made leader, and his job's to march the rest to meals and see that the hut's kept clean, and so on. Redfern, you'll have that job, and Holt will help him. I'll tell you the duties in a minute. Now, the rest of you, you help the leader and his deputy as much as you can. It's a bloody job in some ways, and it's up to you to help them and do what they say.[27]

The divisional officer confirmed this.

They haven't asked for the jobs. They've been chosen for them without any pushing on their part. Maybe some of them would prefer not to be class leaders. Anyway, I want you to remember that they have the right to give you orders, and that disobeying an order in the Navy is a very serious offence indeed.[28]

John Davies found that his CW mess was run by

a formidable Yorkshireman. There was certainly no affectation about him. He was an extremely vigorous individual with a powerful voice and a mass of unruly hair. As soon as he came into the mess he roared for the cooks and drove them off up to the galley, and then bullied the others into laying the tables for dinner. I was a little surprised to learn that he was a Cambridge Ph.D.[29]

Geoffrey Ball was nominated one of eight 'cooks of the mess' from his class: 'I don't do any cooking, only fetch the stuff from the galley when it's ready.' He often had to wait for the bugle call 'cooks to the mess' to come over the camp's loudspeaker system.

At *Ganges* the day began with 'divisions' on the huge parade ground. The 3,000 men in the camp lined the edges in no particular order, then a command was given and they scrambled into the proper places, arranged by divisions, classes and watches. A group of about 70 formed one class and was lined up in six rows. They dressed by the right and stood at ease, until the instructor called them to attention and reported the class all correct. The captain then stood on his rostrum and called the parade to attention. He ordered, 'Classes left and right turn.' One watch in each class went off to train in gunnery, the other to do seamanship, and the order would be reversed next day.

Ball found that the titles were not very helpful to an outsider. The first 'seamanship' period consisted of advice on how to live in the barracks, followed by some training in the points of the compass in the afternoon. Gunnery, he found, was largely foot drill on the parade ground and around the site. Trainees learned to use rifles. Ball's group fired blank cartridges at first, until they were allowed on the range with real bullets. *Ganges* was in line for a possible German invasion attempt even in 1942, and most of the trainees were organized in platoons for local defence and mustered in full kit and pack every third night. Ball was pleased to be a stretcher bearer in the 'passive defence' section instead, to be employed for air-raid precautions. He heard a few air-raid warnings on nearby Harwich but was not disturbed from his bed because the naval base did not follow the civilian warning system.

They also trained on simulated guns, usually without firing them, including the standard modern destroyer weapon:

Most of their instruction was on the 4.7 quick firer. They were drilled in the details of the job to be done by each member of a crew: number one, the gun layer; number two, the breech worker and captain of the gun; number three, the loading number or rammer, and so on to number seven, sight setter and communication number. They were given exercises on the gun, each taking different position for each exercise until they could repeat the formulae in their sleep. They were given loading practice, not on the loading machine any more, but on the gun itself with real shells and charges filled with rubbish to the right weight. It was hard work.

Foot drill, also known to the navy as 'square-bashing' or 'gravel grinding', dominated much of the course. It was intended to weld the men into a unit and teach them to obey orders. According to the *Royal Naval Handbook of Field Training*,

The chief prop of discipline is drill, for although of itself of little fighting value, its utility as a means of exercising officers and men in instant obedience cannot be overestimated. The obedience thus enforced gradually becomes an instinct strong enough to overcome feelings of personal discomfort, and desire for self preservation even under wearisome trials, and in the face of catastrophe.'[30]

It was quite easy to organize, it was familiar to the aged petty officers among the instructors, and the bases, including the converted holiday camps, had hundreds of yards of roads that could be used for marching. Some officers questioned its value, but a group of petty officers defended it from their wartime experience.

To say that there are never any smiles or laughter during rifle training is absolute nonsense, I cannot remember one session of rifle drill passing without some amusing situation arising that is talked about for a long time afterwards. ...

The crux of the matter is that taking a bunch of raw men as new entries one must first ensure that each and every man is capable of carrying out the simplest of orders without question. It is the easiest, simplest and cheapest method to give them parade training.[31]

Even unlikely men such as the poet Roy Fuller could be won over: 'We came to enjoy squad-drill.'[32]

Physical training was hated by those who started overweight and unfit, like Peter Bull:

P.T. was, is and ever shall be my most unfavourite thing in life. To tear round a gymnasium pretending one is enjoying it is not at all my idea of fun, and I am not sufficiently masochistic to take pleasure in acting as a human pony to some great galumphing matelot. The highlight of the hour was to carry someone round the gym and change places at half time. Owing to circumstances over which I have a great deal of control, it was deemed wise for me to carry both ways. This made for complete exhaustion and careless navigation. After five weeks of this strange orgy, I fell and twisted my ankle and gave my rider quite a shock.[33]

Geoffrey Ball found that most of his PT instructors in *Ganges* were ex-boxers or professional footballers, one of whom had played for Fulham. They treated the gym as if it was a ship, with one end as the bow, the other the stern and so on, giving orders such as 'To the bows'. Their sense of humour was basic. One gave the order 'stand on your hands' and many of the men tried it, until the instructor demonstrated it by placing his hands under his feet.

Every seaman had to be able to swim, and the test at *Ganges* was to go a full length of the pool wearing a canvas duck suit, then stay afloat at the deep end for five minutes. Geoffrey Ball complained about having to rise early for the lessons: 'Think of it. Get up at six. – Wash etc; make beds, which have to be made in a special and neat way. Stow everything away that we're not using in kit-bags and be outside fully dressed (and it's a job getting these things in a hurry and fiddling about tying the scarf etc).' Life was even harder for those who were not already good swimmers, for the methods of the 'clubs' were not gentle:

> Those unfortunates who couldn't swim got no sympathy from the Clubs, the PTIs (Physical Training Instructors). First we each had to show whether we could swim or not by doing a couple of lengths up and down the pool changing to different strokes like treading water and resting types such as the breast stroke . . . The poor sods who showed they couldn't swim properly or not at all received poolside instruction from the Clubs who would be ready to assist with his boat hook but not always to let them get out when they tried to splash their way to the side. From there on they would be given personal attention until they were able to swim adequately.[34]

They saw very little of real ships during basic training. The men at *Ganges* would get a distant view of the East Coast convoy escorts that were based there and an occasional visiting cruiser, but Geoffrey Ball only had his memories of seeing warships with gleaming paintwork and polished brass during peacetime holidays in Southsea near Portsmouth.[35] Instead the trainees were shown a film, *Meet the Ship*, in which a genial CPO finds a young man waiting for the ferry across to *Ganges* and describes his own ship, a cruiser, which can be seen in the distance, in some detail. The young man is expected to visualize this in his imagination, but the viewers are allowed to see it all on film. The recruit's rather rustic civilian clothes change into naval uniform and he is taken aboard a cruiser which now appears to be in Scapa Flow. He is allowed to stand on the bridge while the CPO shows many points about the ship. He demonstrates the take-off and landing of the ship's Walrus flying boat, explains the fire-control system and tells him about the role of the Royal Marines on board – none of which was relevant for the men who would serve in smaller ships without these features. The Chief concludes on an inspiring note: 'The rest is up to you now.' His views on the Germans are drowned out by a foghorn, and the sailor is taken off in a launch, standing up among his fellows, while the chief shouts, 'See you at sea some time.'[36]

For most of the war, seamen entrants were issued with volume one of the *Manual of Seamanship*, last updated in 1932. John Davies' petty officer told him, 'You can't learn nothin' from a bleeding book', but he soon found it was 'fascinating but formidable, a book full of strange, cosmopolitan terms gleaned from the seven seas of the world'.[37] In 1943 it was due to reprint, but it was more than 450 pages long and paper was in short supply. Captain H. P. K. Oram of the Admiralty wrote,

It has been found that the Seamanship Manual, Volume I, contains too much detail and too much advanced seamanship for training of the hostilities-only seamen, with the result that the majority are unable to absorb the essential elementary knowledge required.

It was agreed to produce a new and much shorter manual, which would give new seamen 'a Pocket Book containing the seamanlike knowledge required of them during training and their first six months at sea'. It would also serve as a primer for CW Candidates. Lieutenant-Commander Crick of HMS *King Alfred* had already had plenty of experience in teaching seamanship to cadet-ratings and knew exactly what was needed. He had literary abilities as editor and contributor to the *King Alfred Magazine*, and his blackboard drawing skills were legendary. So he was given the job of producing the *Seaman's Pocket-Book*, a concise and practical distillation of what a wartime sailor needed to know about seamanship.

Crick explained that sea terms were necessary, 'because things happen too quickly at sea to allow time for long and detailed explanations. Orders must be short and snappy, and they must be instantly and exactly obeyed.' The seaman's first task was to find his way around his own ship, and he had to learn that 'abaft' meant towards the rear or stern, that 'starboard' meant right, in relation to the hull of the ship –

you can cut the hull down the middle line from end to end; along what is called the **fore-and-aft midship line**, dividing the two sides. Looking forward towards the stem, the left-hand half will be the **port** half of the hull, and the right-hand half will be the starboard half.

In both cases the line of division runs **amidships** – i.e., in the middle of the ship.[38]

Trainees learned something about the sea, and the waves which would come to dominate their lives later.

A ship steaming with her bows meeting the seas end on is said to be meeting a 'head sea.' Steaming with her stern to wind she is said to be running before a 'following sea'. In either case her bows and stern will alternately rise and fall in a **pitching** movement. With the wind abeam she has a 'beam sea', and is made to **roll**, heeling alternately from side to side.[39]

Sailors had to learn knots, more properly known as 'bends' and 'hitches'. The bowline was used to form a loop in the end of a rope, the reef knot to join two pieces of rope of roughly equal size, and the sheet bend or double sheet bend if the ropes were unequal. A round turn and two half hitches would secure a rope to a ring, a clove hitch to a rail. Hostilities Only seamen were spared the need to learn the fisherman's bend, the Blackwall hitch and the sheepshank, but they did learn a good deal about rigging and securing ropes to bollards and buoys.

CW candidates were well advised to pay attention to the sections of the *Pocket-Book* on tides, buoyage, navigation and pilotage, but they would return to them later. Everyone had to learn to take a turn at steering the ship, and that was taught in several ways. The *Pocket-Book* devoted one of its eight chapters to it. There was a steering simulator, in which turns of the wheel would move a platform while the compass moved in accordance with this.

There was also a film, in which a bulky, humourless but authoritative three-badge able seaman tells a raw hand, 'You will never be able to call yourself a sailor until you have learned how to steer.' The wheelhouse in a small ship is just under the bridge, and orders come down by voice-pipe. The young man is taught about helm orders, such as 'port 30', by which he reads the helm indicator and turns the rudder to that angle, reporting that he has done so to the bridge, as always. Normally that was the full amount of rudder used; 'hard-a-port', using the full angle of 35°, was for emergencies only. He might also receive compass orders, to steer on a particular course. The modern compass was marked in degrees, but the old fashioned system with subdivisions such as 'west by north' and 'south-south-east' was still used to indicate the direction of an object. The helmsman steered by the gyro compass but had a magnetic compass to hand in case of breakdown. He was taught how to use the helm as little as possible and to 'chase the lubber's line', a mark on the forward part of the compass that marked the direction of the ship's head. He was to bring the lubber's line on to the course, not vice versa.

Beside the helmsman were the engine-room telegraphs, one for each engine, and each manned by another seaman. Readings such as 'full ahead' and 'slow astern' were marked on a dial, and the movement of a lever rang a bell and sent the message to the engine room, where spoken messages were not easy to hear. Each telegraph could also be set to 'half speed', in which case the engine room would read the revolution indicator instead. This was cranked up by the seaman to a certain number of revolutions as ordered by the bridge.

Rowing, or 'pulling' as the navy called it, was an important skill. Many ships' boats were now powered, but a rowing boat was lighter and easier to launch in the open sea, and when rescuing survivors it was less likely to be fouled by a mass of debris in the water. Eric Denton describes the training at *Ganges*:

> There were four or five oars on each side of the boat, and one man on the tiller. After a few circles, we had to achieve a straight line, or we would never have got back ashore. Then we went in a sailing boat about twelve feet long. We learnt how to put the sails up and lower them (or did we learn?), and the philosophy of tacking, sailing against the wind – and somehow we got back ashore.[40]

Training could be exhausting, but most men found a little time for leisure. At *Ganges* local leave was allowed after the initial period in the annexe, mostly in the nearby town of Ipswich, which was served by a naval bus service. On his first leave, Geoffrey Ball spent some time checking out of the camp: 'Before leaving we had to go through a whole lot of pay-book showing, giving out station card, inspection to see if we were properly dressed and handing in little tokens to show that we were the right men to go.' In the town, they found the Sailor's Rest, listened to the wireless, had cheap snacks available only to servicemen and went to the cinema to see a film starring the popular American juvenile Andy Hardy, and *Fires Were Started*, about the London Blitz. John Wilson paid 4/6 (22½p) for a restaurant meal, went to the cinema and came back on the bus singing *Lily of Laguna* and *If You were the Only Girl in the World*. There were fortnightly dances at *Ganges*, but on most nights the sailors far outnumbered the girls. Geoffrey Ball found comfort in occasional gramophone recitals of classical music. Contact with home was entirely by letter and he apologized when he missed his daily one from *Ganges*.[41]

All trainees found themselves among a far wider cross-section of people than they had ever encountered before; Ball, for example, was the only man in his class with a secondary education. Alec Guinness had a typically disparate group of companions:

My fellow sailors, if that could be the right word for us as yet, I found agreeable and simple-hearted, with only two or three exceptions. We came from every sort of background, numbering among us butcher's assistants, a housepainter, a maker of pianos, a couple of schoolmasters (whom I thought rather intolerable, with their condescending airs), an aggressive, foul-mouthed Post Office clerk from Manchester, who could have served Hitler well, a Scottish Laird of great distinction and a dozen or so drifters from all over. Most were great swillers of beer. When in small, intimate groups, they chatted quietly of their mothers and sisters; once they were gathered in larger groups, however, the conversation, loud and hyphenated with four-letter words, was of football and the crudest sex. Nearly all wished to be taken for old salts within days of joining up.[42]

Washing clothes, or 'dhobying', was another unexpected aspect of lower deck life. It was an article of faith for the regular seaman, and Fleet Air Arm men sent to train with the RAF were so imbued with it that they resented the RAF's use of laundries. Geoffrey Ball found that it was 'absolutely essential to keep as clean as possible because we are living in very close contact'.

The new sailor had to get to know a great deal of specialized vocabulary, almost amounting to a new language. There were plenty of seamanship terms such as port and starboard, and parts of ship such as quarterdeck. Hardly anyone was known by his real name on the mess decks. Some had nicknames according to physical characteristics, such as 'Ginger', 'Lofty', or 'Stumps' for a very short man. Some had regional names, such as 'Scouser', 'Jock' or 'Geordie'. Some of the most experienced men took job titles, such as 'Guns', or 'Bunts' for signallers. There were different kinds of friendship. 'Oppo', or opposite number, was one between equals; 'wings' or 'winger' was a young man taken up by an older one (possibly, but far from certainly, with homosexual overtones). A 'party' was a girlfriend ashore.

For obvious reasons, Geoffrey Ball was coy about lower-deck swearing in his letters to his parents. He only remarked of his leading seamen instructors, 'I won't mention their language!' But everyone noticed it, especially those from middle-class backgrounds. John Wilson's gunnery instructor had an amazing flow of foul language, which he felt was almost poetic in its strange way. It was surprisingly easy to be caught up in this – 'Language deteriorated quickly. An anxiety to appear as street-wise as the next man frequently turned what should have been everyday conversation into obscene nonsense. Sanity slowly regained control over insecurity but the vocabulary of the vast majority underwent a profound change and the few who resisted the trend were regarded with suspicion.'[43] One of the main tests for a CW candidate was to avoid swearing too much, at least where officers could overhear him.

Despite his secondary school education, Geoffrey Ball was identified late as a possible CW candidate, after he got 590 marks out of 600 in seamanship and was the best in his class. He was nervous when interviewed by the captain: 'All he did was to give his advice. You know the tests told that I needed self assurance. After I had been speaking to him for about ten minutes he said, "I don't think you need as much self assurance as they made out."'

In the meantime he was involved with tests conducted by Commander Owen of the Admiralty to try to find new ways of selecting officers. This was the shape of things to come. The navy was impressed with the army system of selection boards spread over several days and combined with psychological and physical tests. The naval system was drastically reformed during 1943, and CWs were sent to special training ships in the Forth, where their behaviour was easier to assess. But the majority of temporary wartime naval officers, including those who fought in the crucial stages of the Battle of the Atlantic and in the invasions of North Africa and Europe, went through the older system.

Ball was one of two men from his watch of 39 selected as CWs; the other had been a member of the Y-Scheme. The watch was regarded as very successful, in that nearly all the men were recommended for further training in the growth areas of the navy – twelve for radar, twelve for asdic, six as anti-aircraft gunners and one as a fire-fighter. Those who were not selected in this way would go to the fleet as ordinary seamen without any 'non-substantive' badge, though they might have a chance to earn one later, perhaps in gunnery.

Ball describes the plans for the last week of his course. On Monday they would revise steering by compass then go out on a boat on the river, hoping to be given a spell at the wheel. At 5 in the afternoon there would be a preliminary kit inspection. On Tuesday they would be engaged in boat pulling all day, and he had his interview with the captain ('Hold tight'). On Wednesday the real kit inspection by the commander would take place at 10 am, followed an hour later by a medical examination and possibly leave in Ipswich ('What again!') in the afternoon. On Thursday there was the Captain's talk, a medical lecture and the Captain's final lecture, 'and of course lots of other things to do with going away'. On Friday they would return their blankets to the store, and hoped to leave for home by 9.30.

F. S. Holt of the Royal Australian Navy Volunteer Reserve did not enjoy his course: 'The training system at *Collingwood* was geared to cope with brand new recruits and by sheer necessity proceeded at the speed of those with the lowest IQ. With this background our early period in the Training Establishment was frequently boring, depressing and frustrating; in fact I cannot recall learning anything new whatsoever during at least the first six weeks.'[44]

But that was a minority view, from a man who had already done much naval training. A divisional officer in one of the training bases described what he hoped had been achieved.

F[robisher] 88, fashioned and welded together in five weeks, was returning to its individual components, but each man was taking away with him more than he brought in. Each could look after himself and his kit; whatever his category, each could swim, and pull and sail a lifeboat; each knew enough about fighting a ship not to be a nuisance at sea. And, above all, they had a sense of belonging, a rock-bottom foundation for living together, in preparation for the time when they would be locked together for months on end in a steel box far from land.[45]

5
THE CW EXPERIENCE

The selected CW candidates went on leave and were then sent to one of the naval barracks to await draft to a ship. All agreed that this was one of the lowest points of their naval career. The barracks at Chatham, Portsmouth and Plymouth had been built late in the previous century, and at the time they were a great improvement on the wooden hulks where seamen had lived between sea postings. But changing standards, poor maintenance, wartime bombings and, above all, overcrowding had turned them into slums. Three-badge ABs did not mind – they had seen enough of the sea already – and found themselves soft jobs and became 'barrack stanchions', perhaps living with their families ashore. Younger men hated the barracks on many levels. To Alec Guinness Chatham Barracks was

the nadir of my lower-deck experiences where thousands of men slept, snored, or vomited – their hammocks slung three-deep in a cavernous tunnel which served as dormitory, bomb-shelter and lavatory. Chatham, where to get a meal you had to fight your way to the food – which sometimes I refused to do. If it hadn't been for kind, tough messmates who took pity on me, I think I might have starved.[1]

CWs were often put in a separate mess, perhaps mixed with men coming back from their sea service and awaiting draft to *King Alfred*. To Peter Bull they 'seemed like gods to us with their tales of Arctic convoys, rum, peculiar leading seamen and What the Skipper Said to Them'.[2] The new CWs were given some kind of desultory training, or perhaps yet more foot drill. At last, they were called out by loudspeaker and sent on a draft to a ship.

Most went to destroyers, the smallest ships commanded by regular navy captains, who could be trusted to apply proper standards in assessing them. They were also the most active and versatile ships in the fleet. Mallalieu's group had warning of this under training, when the Chief told them, 'they're putting most of you chaps in destroyers, and it's a pretty rough life. I've 'ad good times in destroyers, even in the last war. On quiet days you sit up on your gun and watch or read or smoke in the sun. But you don't get many quiet days. Either the sea's so rough you can't stand, or you're out on some job or other and have to keep your eyes skinned. No, you'll find it hard all right.' Destroyers were even harder worked in the present war. They were the most flexible of warships, 'always on the go' according to an American naval observer.[3] They sank submarines, shot down aircraft, escorted battleships and aircraft carriers, and launched torpedo attacks. They took part in combined operations, rescued survivors and fought harder than any other ships in the war. A hundred and fifty-four were lost, more than were in commission at the beginning of the war, more than any other type of ship and more than a third of all losses of major British warships.

Some thought that destroyers were relatively free and easy compared with battleships and cruisers; some felt it was the worst of both worlds:

I don't want to serve on a destroyer. You get all the discomfort of a small ship and the pusser routine of a big one thrown in. Pusser? That means 'as per Seamanship Manual'. Rig of the day Number Threes and all that. On a submarine you can wear anything you like.

The 'torpedo-boat destroyer' had been conceived towards the end of the previous century, designed to fight off attacks by enemy boats and launch some by itself. Over the years it got bigger and more seaworthy, acquired heavier weapons and was allocated a much greater range of tasks. Paradoxically, the name was shortened to 'destroyer'. A standard layout had evolved over the years. There was a relatively short forecastle, for decks had to be kept low in midships for the torpedo tubes and in the stern for dropping depth-charges. Most had two funnels; the latest types had one. There was a definite hierarchy within the destroyer classes, with the fast, well-armed but expensive Tribals at the top, and the ex-American 'Towns' at the bottom – they broke all the rules by having flush decks and no forecastle, four funnels and a weak armament. In between were the older ones of the V and W classes, mostly used as escorts in the Battle of the Atlantic; the relatively modern A to I classes, built in the 1920s and '30s – good ships but short of anti-aircraft armament – and the J, K, L and M classes, which were essentially cut-price Tribals with a slightly reduced gun armament. Current production concentrated on the 'War Emergency' classes, which attempted to combine the virtues of all of these while keeping production costs and labour demands low. Modern destroyers, from the A to I classes onwards, were mostly armed with 4.7-inch guns. Tribals and J, K, L and M classes had them in twin turrets, while the others each had four guns in single turrets, two forward and two aft. Most had two sets of quadruple torpedo-tubes amidships; the Is had quintuple tubes, and the Tribals each had one set of quadruple tubes.

HMS *Duncan*, was already one of the most famous ships in the Battle of the Atlantic when Geoffrey Ball joined her in Londonderry after a rough ferry crossing of the Irish Sea.

'Anyone for *Duncan*?' shouted the truck driver. 'Yes! Me!' as I struggled over the tailboard while the others handed down my hammock and kitbag. The lorry drove on – the others were for different ships.

I stood there … Horrified! The ship looked a complete shambles: filthy, rusting paintwork everywhere: half-a-dozen lidless garbage bins on the deck overflowing with rotten food and vegetables: a few men in dirty blue overalls chipping away at paint on the smokestacks (funnels): a fellow sitting washing clothes in a bucket: others in various states of undress using oily rags on guard rails and depth charge racks: the relentless hum of generators and smoke drifting down to combine with the nauseating smell from the rotting rubbish. A depressing, wretched scene.[4]

Most of the seamen in a destroyer lived well forward under the forecastle. There was a large seaman's mess on the upper deck, with a smaller stokers' mess on the deck below that. The petty officers lived in the structure under the bridge in most ships, with the officers aft of the engine room. That had been the traditional position in a sailing ship, and it was not changed until the R class of 1942. There was no covered passage between the stern and the bridge area, so officers sometimes had to brave breaking seas to relieve the officer of the watch. Though modern destroyers were far larger and more seaworthy than their predecessors, their design still looked back to the days when they served mostly in the North Sea, the English Channel and the Mediterranean. Now they had to go anywhere that the war might demand, including the Atlantic and Arctic Oceans.

New arrivals were shown down to their accommodation. Unlike a training base or naval barracks, a destroyer had no room for a separate CWs' mess.

> At most, the mess deck was about 70 feet long – the length of the ship was only 300 feet. The widest place in the ship was only 27 feet. The mess deck was not at the widest place and One Mess was not at the widest part of the mess deck. It would be the only place where they could eat, sleep, read, and write, and stow their gear. It would not be comfortable.[5]

John Wilson in the cruiser *Belfast* could not find a berth for his hammock as they had all been taken up, so eventually he slung it in the capstan flat, which was quiet but very cold. Geoffrey Ball asked his leading seaman where he could sling.

> 'That's the problem. There's twice as many men as hammock places. All the normal places are taken and there's a waiting list for them when anyone leaves. I'll try to find you somewhere but you may have to sleep on the lockers for a time.'
> 'But – won't I fall off?'

'Not in harbour you won't, but at sea you'll have to go somewhere else. I'll try to help but it's a real headache.'

He did find 'a terrible place', which was 'better than nothing'.[6] It was not easy to stow gear in the lockers provided:

Williams asked him what was the best thing to do with kitbags when they were emptied.

'Best shove it in the bottom of your locker, man. You'll not be wanting it again for some time.'

'How the Hell does one get everything into the locker? It looks too damn small.' Williams's locker was already three-quarters full, although he had not emptied half his kitbag.

'You'll have to fold your things tighter than that, man. You'll get issued with any amount of stuff before we sail – warm clothing and the like. All that's got to go in too.'[7]

Toilet accommodation was no more spacious, though the dwellers in the 'back-to-back' houses described by Orwell might have felt at home:

The washroom was in the 'flat' on the other side of the ship, behind a sliding door. It was 10 feet long and 5 feet broad. It had a tiled floor. It had nine tip-up basins round the sides and at one end there was one tap and a shower. The shower did not work. It was the only washing place provided on the ship for 120 seamen, torpedo men and stokers. Farther along were five closed closets for Petty Officers, and farther along still were seven open water-closets for 170 lower-deck ratings.[8]

The CWs had already encountered the men of the lower deck in basic training. Though regulars were only present in comparatively small numbers, they dominated the dormitories, canteens and drill halls, and their culture had already made a tremendous impression. Now the CWs met the sailor in his own home, in conditions of great stress and overcrowding – and often danger. The lower deck culture was so strong, so dominant in its own environment, that it was hardly changed by its encounter with the outside world. Instead it was the HO seaman who adapted himself to the ways of the regular lower deck, even though the numbers of regulars were heavily diluted by the end of the war. As Captain H. P. K. Oram wrote of the cruiser *Hawkins*,

The Jolly Jack of peacetime was a rare bird indeed, so rare that one was tempted to pipe a tear of affection for the breed, now a practically extinct prototype. The wartime sailor, faithfully modelling himself upon his glamorous predecessor, was conscious of the ready-made aura which attached to his own interpretation of the part ... The model set for them to follow was good and by his exacting standards we were able to run our complicated machines on a very weak mixture of RN spirit! [9]

Some of the men on the lower deck were mystified by the CW scheme: 'you live on the mess deck long enough to become a pretty decent seaman, and almost fit for human society, then you go and leave. Meanwhile, you ain't one thing or the other – you ain't a rating, and you ain't an officer. You can 'ave it!'[10]

If some CWs had a poor reception when they arrived on the mess decks, that was often of their own making, Nicholas Monsarrat records that some men, 'strode into the stokers' mess deck and asked cheerily: 'Are there any other Cambridge chaps here?'[11] From a lower-deck viewpoint, John Whelan recorded CWs arriving with a cry of 'Numbah twooo mess. Six of us hev to report to numbah twooo mess, the other six are going to numbah one mess.' This was compounded by the fact that the lower deck knew that its members were being deliberately discriminated against. Walter 'Stoker' Edwards had served in the navy before being elected Member of Parliament for Stepney and he complained,

I would like to refer to the granting of commissions. This is a very sore point with the lower deck. Having served on a ship where many of the candidates get their sea training, to me there seems to be something wrong. People have been selected as candidates for commissions and put through their course of sea training, and have never been able to conduct themselves in a sailor-like way, yet they have been passed as fit to take charge of ships and men. There have been extreme cases where chief petty officers, with 20 or 30 years experience, have not been thought worth considering for commissions ...[12]

The pressures for the CW candidate on the lower deck could often be immense. First of all, there was the difficulty of entering a strange, crowded, uncomfortable and often dangerous environment. The CWs had to live amongst the seamen with no segregation of any kind. It was generally recognized that there was a huge gap between officers and men in the pre-war navy, and much of that lingered on in wartime. The CWs had to find a *modus vivendi* in the middle of this huge gulf, for six months at least, a minimum of three at sea followed by three months under training. They too, like the

Seamen on a crowded messdeck. (*Men Dressed as Seamen*)

members of the lower deck, deserve credit for what they achieved in circumstances that were not of their making.

Again, the middle-class candidates were the most anxious in many ways. Unskilled workers had no great expectations of life and were generally content with lower-deck status, if not conditions. Skilled workers were often given suitable roles and could rise quickly to petty officer grades. Public-school boys expected to be commissioned whatever service they joined, and only a few were disappointed. But those with a secondary education did not fit easily into the scheme of things and tended to feel insecure in any role. Geoffrey Ball was fearful as he joined *Duncan*: 'Not only was I a Grammar School boy but also a 'C.W. Candidate' ... Would I get all kinds of jibes, taunts and insults from the other seamen who, I assumed, would mostly be from lowly backgrounds and very anti-officer? Worse still, would I, as a future potential officer, get beaten up regularly by a gang of them?' He need not have worried. He soon acquired the nickname of 'Lucy' after the film star who shared his surname and found that the only standard was whether he pulled his weight in the mess.[13]

The CWs' reception by the lower deck was usually not unfriendly, but they had to accept that they were the lowest creatures in their ship's pecking order. Peter Bull believed that the lower deck made every effort, in its own style, to accommodate the CWs but were put off by many of them.

> They were not a bad lot, with one exception, but were out of place in such a crew. To break down the ill-feeling which is bound to exist in the mind of the average matelot towards the favoured few is not a very difficult job. But so many would-be officers conducted themselves in such a ludicrous way that the barrier was never removed. It was their constant washing and airing their knowledge that got the permanent residents down.[14]

CWs were easy enough to mock, especially by seamen with the gift of tongues, who could switch between the speech patterns of the lower deck and those of the CWs. Mallalieu apologized for using the term 'flicking', 'which no seaman would ever deign to use', instead of a more robust word that was unprintable in those days. But some of his anecdotes are better as he intended to write them. A swear box on the mess deck had only a limited effect on the vocabulary:

'Which of you fucking bastards had pinched my fucking sea-boots. All right, all right, that's only threepennorth so far. Come on, you fuckers, or I'll knock the ears back on your bastard heads, Sixpence. O.K?' Then, putting on his C.W. accent, he went on: 'should be most grateful of one of you gentlemen, perchance, peradventure, should inform me where-the-fucking-hell-my-bloody-bastard-sea-boots-are.'[15]

But sometimes even the most unlikely public schoolboys could be helpful: 'We had lice at school, you know. We rubbed pepper and sand on them. The pepper made them sneeze and they banged their jolly old heads on the grains of sand. Unconscious, they were easy game.'[16]

Messing was another problem, for all ships of destroyer size and less used the antiquated Standard Ration and Messing Allowance system, by which each mess had to provide two 'cooks' in rotation. They actually had to prepare food rather than fetch it, as in the camps. Most men had received no training for this, though those at HMS *Ganges* were given a booklet on it.

The mess caterer will decide what the mess will have to eat. You, when cook of the mess, will prepare the food – on the mess table – and take it to the galley to be cooked – after which you will hear what your messmates think about it as a **MEAL**.

They were recommended to learn how to make pastry and dumplings, and to prepare different kinds of vegetables. They were given simple recipes such as cottage pie, apple dumplings and suet puddings.[17] It was easy enough for the regulars, who had

had years to build up a collection of recipes, but harder for the HOs and especially the CWs. Most learned to cope, but many sailors had other things on their mind in wartime, and there was always the man who forgot to salt the potatoes, or did not know how much tea should be put in the urn for a good cup. Geoffrey Ball found that punctuality was the main issue by which his messmates judged him: 'did you get the food prepared quickly – to the galley for cooking and later collected so that it was HOT and on the mess table ON TIME? I excelled at this, even at sea, having always been a slave to punctuality – thus I often got that particular job.'[18]

CWs soon came to understand the ship hierarchy. The captain was a remote figure unless one became his servant like Charles McAra in *Cottesmore* or was taken up by him like Peter Bull in *Hesperus*. 'He seemed to like to talk to someone who had no particular axe to grind, and I for my part gained much useful knowledge and naturally did not abuse my privilege.'[19] The first lieutenant, 'Jimmy the one' or just 'Jimmy', was seen far more about the decks. Even in peacetime in the 1930s, his job was hard work.

> The First Lieutenant must be constantly supervising during working hours, which means that he must do nearly all his paper work – and make out his next day's programme – during the comparative calm of the Dog Watches; such problems as analyses must be deferred to even later in the day. After the first six months you will find the ship begins to 'run herself'.[20]

The junior officers in a destroyer were mostly regular RN until well into the war, with a sprinkling of RNR and RNVR. They were encountered as officer of the watch, as divisional officer for welfare purposes, and in charge of some of the weapons at action stations. The senior rating, the coxswain, was generally a benign figure and a very experienced seaman. The chief boatswain's mate, the 'chief buffer', was often more fearsome, not at all like the kindly but slightly ridiculous figure portrayed by Bernard Miles in *In Which We*

Serve. Mallalieu discerned, 'The first lesson learned by any seaman was to avoid the Buffer. The second was to avoid the Jimmie.'[21]

The CWs were part of the seaman branch and saw comparatively little of the others groups on board the ship, who were often fierce rivals. There were no marines on destroyers, so the stokers were the most numerous, apart from the seamen themselves. In peacetime they were recruited as young adults, so they did not go through the same rigorous training as the seaman boys, but they too wore the square-rig uniform. The title 'stoker' was outdated – they did not have to stoke boilers now that nearly all ships were fuelled by oil – but the image of a muscular, ignorant brute remained, at least among the seaman branch. The two branches messed separately in all but the smallest ships, for the seaman and the stoker had very different standards of discipline and cleanliness. In fact the stoker needed a good deal of skill, though not as much as the artificers who had mostly trained by apprenticeship and had the status of chief petty officers. The signallers, whether by radio or by flag, lamp and semaphore, also wore square rig but regarded themselves as a cut above the seamen. The men of the administrative, domestic and medical branches – writers or clerks, stewards, cooks and sick-berth attendants – wore the fore-and-aft rig and were invariably messed separately from the seamen and stokers.

The senior leading hand of each mess was in charge. Younger men might find their influence undermined by the three-badge ABs, and new officers were warned, 'You must always bear in mind that the young higher ratings, and particularly the Leading Seamen, have a difficult job. They find themselves in charge of men older than themselves, some of whom endeavour to trip them up.'[22] But Mallalieu's leading hand knew how to assert his authority when one man's dinner disappeared:

Now, this is the last time. If such a thing as this ever happens again, it's pusser's routine for the lot of ye. Ye'll fall in on the Iron Deck. No-one will be allowed in the mess except the cooks. Then ye'll be marched in and the other messes will laugh at ye.

The issue of the crew's rum was an important part of the daily routine, and an essential feature of lower deck culture. It was issued to the leading hand of the mess and brought down below to accompany the meal. Each man was supposed to drink his own 'tot', but in reality it was a kind of currency in the mess decks. A small favour might be rewarded by 'sippers', a small draught from each tot in the mess. A larger one would earn 'gulpers', and an exceptional debt might be paid by 'downers' or 'grounders' in which a whole tot was given up. John Whelan and his messmates were shocked when a group of CWs began to drink them one sip at a time: "'Knock them blasted tots back,' growled guns, 'The messdeck's taking on the atmosphere of a blasted cocktail party.'"[23]

Seamen had sentimental views about home, even if they were constantly undermined by their messmates.

'I wish I was at home,' said Jackie Low one night. 'I wish I was at home sitting in the armchair, by the fire, with my carpet slippers on and the missus handing me a cup of tea and the nipper squitting all over the floor just to make it home-like; and the *News of the* flicking *World* and the *Daily Mirror* every day, up to date, and not three bastard weeks late as it is up here. Coo!'

'Home!' said Jock. 'Ah know what home is like for you married men. Ye comes home on a Friday night with your pay packets and your wife sweeps the kids off the easy-chair and says, "Sit down, *dear*," and brings you a cup of tea. But when it's Monday it's "Get out of that chair," she says; "Ah wants to sit down."'[24]

No seaman ever dared to volunteer for anything in front of his messmates or show any enthusiasm for the navy, for fear he might be thought to be 'all for it'. The men were constantly complaining, or 'dripping' and, 'It was almost a convention, too, to be violent and uncivil. Instead of 'Please pass the butter' you shouted, 'Pass that flicking slide or I'll probably slash you.'[25] But paradoxically and completely unacknowledged by anyone concerned, this concealed an affection and comradeship that no landsman could hope to understand.

Through all this, mess-deck humour shone through. A sceptical seamen was confronted by another reading the Lord's Prayer.

'The Lord is my shepherd.'
'That's right. We're just a flock of flicking sheep. Wouldn't 'ave joined if we weren't.'
'I shall not want.'
'Not want? Not want? I want to go home.'
'He maketh me lie down in green pastures.'
'Wet hammocks more like.'
'He leadeth me beside the still waters.'
'STILL waters? Oh, Flicking yeah!'[26]

Most destroyers were on two watches, which could be subdivided into four when things were quiet. According to Mallalieu's CPO, 'If you're lucky you gets the Last Dog [between 6 and 8 in the evening] and then you don't have to turn out again until the Forenoon [beginning at 8 a.m.]. Last Dog and all night in. Sailor's paradise that is.' It was far worse in areas of enemy activity.

But in dangerous waters you work in two watches. That means the 'ole of one watch is on duty at a time. Port Watch takes the Middle, perhaps [Midnight to 4 a.m.]. Then Starboard Watch is up for the Forenoon. And so it goes on right round the clock. You don't get much sleep on that. Six or seven days of that, with Action Stations thrown in, and you're not fit for much.[27]

Fleet destroyers spent less time in the Atlantic where the weather was at its roughest, but life could be just as hard in the Arctic convoys to Russia.

Besides pitching and rolling, the *Marsden* had a trick which is peculiar to small ships. She would lie for a moment poised on the top of a wave and then suddenly crash into the trough. It seemed that the crash would break her back. Kettles and fannies, swinging from the deckhead, jumped off their hooks and landed with a splatter and a crash below. One man was thrown out of his hammock. All felt concussed.[28]

That was only one of the problems in bad weather.

Their spare clothes were wet, and even if they had managed to find dry ones, they could not have remained dry long. If they lay in their hammocks, water might pour in on them through the leaky deckhead. Or else there would be drips from the condensation. The air in the mess deck was foul, but the deckhead plates were cold. Drops of water formed on them and fell onto the hammocks under the vibration of the ship. If the men tried to sleep on the lockers, there were still the drips. Worse, they might be hurled, whenever the ship lurched, onto the sticky mess that covered the deck below.[29]

Doctors often commented that the overheated and under-ventilated atmosphere was unhealthy. The surgeon of a frigate found that the men had

unhealthy disrespect, that seems to be traditional among seamen, for fresh air on the mess decks. Punkah louvres were often closed, flaps closed down over exhaust trunks although the latter was justified to some extent as some cases are on record where considerable quantities of ocean found their way to the mess decks via these passages.[30]

Such complaints usually fell on deaf ears. The seaman was coming down from a cold, wet watch; he needed to dry himself and warm up as quickly as possible in his limited hours off duty; and anyway he got plenty of fresh air on deck.

For all the faults of mess-deck culture as seen by his officers, it produced the disregard for danger for which seamen were famous. No sailor wanted to show any fear in front of his messmates, and this was a key factor in British naval success. An official report of December 1942 summed up his attitude: 'I am a British Sailor. The British Sailor has always been the best seaman, the finest fighter, the hero of the people. Therefore, I am a hero.'[31]

CWs carried out most of the duties of ordinary seamen – cleaning decks, standing lookouts, rowing boats, taking a turn as cook of the mess, chipping paint and serving as junior members of gun- or depth-charge crews. In addition they might be given a certain amount of training for their future life. Charles McAra was made captain's servant, which he says, 'gave me the opportunity of observing the etiquette and conventions of life at the top in a destroyer. I could see at first hand how the captain handled the ship, how he gave helm orders, how he and other officers comported themselves and one of the lessons I learned was the importance of giving orders in a calm, confident, unruffled tone of voice.'[32] Gorley Putt was trained in navigation by an enthusiastic RNVR officer: 'He watched our improving efforts at chartwork with all the infectious zeal of a born teacher.'[33] Eric Denton assisted with pilotage: 'When we were about to leave Lock [sic] Ewe, the Captain called me over when I was bridge lookout, and told me to give him a course to get out of harbour. The shock was a bit sudden but I succeeded in producing one, and then told him when to alter course again to clear the estuary.'[34]

The CW's dilemma was to adapt to life in the mess while still keeping his distance from the lower deck – as well as learning something about sea life, CWs were being tested for their loyalty to the ideals of the navy as seen by the officers rather than their current companions. Mallalieu tells the story of a CW put on guard duty just before a ship sails and finding one of his messmates trying to get back on board before he is missed: 'Turn your back a minute, old cock, or go on your beat up the jetty a bit while I jump aboard.' The CW refuses and becomes very unpopular on the messdeck, while the offender is punished severely.[35] Whether it was literally true or not, it is a good illustration of an essential problem. Another test was to avoid swearing, at least as profusely as most of the lower deck. Only one of the CW candidates in John Whelan's ship failed to be sent on to the next stage, and that was because he had become too closely integrated. A petty officer told him, 'You forgot yer plum from Gieves. You've proved such a good lower deck seaman they won't give you a commission.'[36]

John Wilson was unexpectedly happy in HMS *Belfast* and wrote to his father, Churchill's doctor, 'This is a wonderful life. I was completely lost at first, but I'm beginning to pick it all up now, and enjoying it enormously.' Much depended on the ship. Peter Bull was thoroughly miserable in the ex-American destroyer he called 'HMS *Thing*'. Beside the usual design faults of the type, the bottom leaked, there were no spare lockers or cutlery, and there was an atmosphere in which the crew seemed 'soured and lethargic'. The other CW candidates had lost hope of passing or of getting off the ship, and the officers seemed indifferent. By a stroke of fortune Bull took passage in the crack destroyer *Hesperus* and found a different world. He spent the first few days on board 'in a dream' and found the officers and crew were friendly. 'I had not dreamed that this kind of destroyer existed ...' He contrived to have himself transferred permanently to complete his CW time and was even tempted to stay on when that was finished.[37]

Geoffrey Ball felt rather differently. He took part in several transatlantic voyages in *Duncan* but they were uneventful, the U-boats having withdrawn from mid-Atlantic, largely because of the efforts of *Duncan*'s own B7 Escort Group. He thought he had finished as the ship approached Londonderry, and he was summoned to the captain's cabin. Commander Gretton was hardly visible in the darkness, and Ball was deeply disappointed to be told that he had to do one more trip. 'I staggered out of the cabin in a kind of daze. One more trip – another "trip" as he called it, in this goddamned ship.' He later found that Gretton had persuaded the Admiralty to use his group in a support rather than an escorting role, and *Duncan* needed all the men she could get as the group raced from one beleaguered convoy to another. The sailing of the group on 13 October coincided with the U-boats' return to the Atlantic, with new weapons and new tactics. This meant that each man had to work even harder:

> Thus ensued an epic 25 days continuously at sea hunting and attacking U-Boats which had come back in force into the Atlantic. Action stations more ON than OFF – refuelling 5-6 times in heavy seas: stopping (not recommended) to pick up 2 survivors from a U-Boat and attacking with new weapons called 'hedgehogs' which projected small bombs ahead of the ship.
>
> My enduring memory of that time is of feeling so very tired even at age 18. Gretton drove everyone week after week in his relentless pursuit of U-Boats. He got the medals (Bar to his D.S.O.) … we, the seamen, did all the hard work.[38]

They sank two U-boats, but from Gretton's point of view it was all in vain. The group included several corvettes, which were too slow to dash from convoy to convoy as the job demanded, and *Duncan* was relegated to escort duties again. Ball finally left the ship in November, to go on to *King Alfred*.

John Wilson was hastily trained to work in the port air defence position in *Belfast*, immediately behind the bridge and under the orders of a midshipman. He followed a pointer and looked at dials to control the movement of the anti-aircraft guns. On Boxing Day 1943, after he had spent only three weeks on board, the ship was off northern Norway when he found himself in action against the German battlecruiser *Scharnhorst*, the last great surface action ever fought by the British fleet, and he had a good view from his action station. It began with the order 'Starshell, commence, commence, commence', which he passed on to the guns, terrified of making some dreadful mistake. These were the first shots of the action, but soon the cruiser *Norfolk* came up in support with its 8-inch guns. He watched as the German shells hit her turret and sent out a cloud of black smoke. *Belfast* was alone for a time against a far more powerful ship, but he was blissfully unaware of the risk. She went into action and fired four broadsides from her 6-inch guns, until the battleship *Duke of York* arrived in support. There were great flashes of red as her 14-inch guns opened fire. Her shells were visible in the air up to the top of their trajectory when the tracer burned out. *Belfast* and *Norfolk* rejoined the action, then the ship's commander announced that the fleet destroyers were going into the attack. Wilson gave a running commentary to the gunners as the flotillas moved into position and then raced towards the target. It all seemed like a dream until a German starshell burst overhead, reminding them that it was a real battle. *Scharnhorst*, the last of the German capital ships to have any effect on the war, was sunk, and Wilson wrote to his father, 'A naval battle at night (daylight is very fleeting here) is pretty unintelligible, but it is very impressive.' His father marked it up for his patient, the Prime Minister, to see.[39]

There is no greater test of character than life in a wartime destroyer, but the problem was in assessing the results. Captains were not given any particular guidance on this, and most of them had too much to do in any case, so they tended to pass men unless they had some very obvious fault. In John Whelan's ship they all passed (except the one man who adopted lower deck swearing habits), including one who washed his dark clothes with the rest of the men's whites, and was told by a petty officer, 'There are three kinds of officer, and you won't make none of them ... Bear that in mind when you're an officer, and remember to wash your socks in your own water. And God help you if you comes aboard any ship I'm on!' In the cruiser *Cardiff*, two out of eighteen men in Brendan Maher's draft were 'judged unsuitable for officer rank', another was discharged as physically unfit after sleeping in his hammock in an unconventional fashion. Rather chillingly, Monsarrat hints that men might have been passed simply because they were no use as seamen: 'To keep him in the ship as an A.B. is to keep so much dead wood: the status of officer might just enable him to pull his weight. But is promotion to be on these lines?'[40] It seems that the great majority of men passed this stage and were sent on for interview.

On coming to the Admiralty in 1943, Captain H. P. K. Oram found that up to 30 per cent of CWs were failing the training course at *King Alfred* by that time, and he put this down to faults in the selection system. He instituted selection tests on army lines, while three old ships were deployed in the Firth of Forth specifically for CW training. They would no longer live among the men of the lower deck, so that ended the true CW era, but not before many thousands of men had passed through the system. Even if it was not totally successful as a method of assessment, it did at least produce officer trainees who had seen a good deal of the navy from the bottom up, many of whom had seen action and knew all about the stresses of combat, and their own limitations.

CWs were sent on leave after sea service. John Wilson had the unique experience of being flown out to Marrakech where his father was tending the Prime Minister through a bout of pneumonia. Churchill listened with rapt attention as the ordinary seaman told him of the battle with the *Scharnhorst*. Then the CWs went back to the naval barracks, where they were now the 'gods' that Peter Bull had once listened to. They would be drafted to HMS *King Alfred* as vacancies occurred.

One side effect of the CW scheme was to expose the rich and exotic culture of the lower deck to a large number of articulate and well-educated people, and to produce a small but significant body of literature on the seaman's life. All these books adopted standard naval phrases as titles. John Davies produced *Stone Frigate* on basic training, and *Lower Deck* on destroyer life; Gorley Putt wrote *Men Dressed as Seamen* with illustrations by the great stage designer Roger Furse; but none achieved such fame or made as much money as *The Cruel Sea*. It is a pity that Monsarrat did not go through the CW scheme himself – it might have added yet more depth to his writing and increased his understanding of the lower deck characters.

The most successful of the 'CW' books was Mallalieu's *Very Ordinary Seaman*. He came back from sea service in the Arctic convoys and asked the training commander at Portsmouth barracks for permission to write it. He was given ten days' leave and then:

> When I got back I found that I had been appointed Commander's Messenger which meant that for eight hours a day, five days a week, I sat in Commander Reid's office, facing a blank wall and typing myself dry. There was no question of hanging about waiting for inspiration. There were no pauses for artistic temperament. I was under 'naval discipline'. I wrote.[41]

At first Commander Reid felt that Mallalieu had not kept his promise to show the navy in a positive light, but he was soon converted – 'Sorry. I've read it all again and think it's fine.' It is perhaps a measure of the book's subtlety that it can be seen in several ways. Mallalieu was always slightly ambiguous about how much was fact, how much fiction. His publishers referred to it as a 'novel' and *The Times Literary Supplement* placed it at the top of its fiction list, but the author himself often just called it his 'book'. He begins with the statement that, 'The main events round which this novel is written have really happened, though not necessarily to me and not necessarily in the manner or sequence in which they are here described.' He also adds caveats about identifying real people among his characters, about swearing and about wartime censorship – at one stage a destroyer fires blindly into a cloud of smoke and eventually hits an enemy ship, and one suspects that he was prevented from mentioning radar at this point.[42] In other words, the book is not to be considered reliable on events or personalities, but there is every reason to believe it is a very accurate picture of lower deck life in a wartime destroyer.

Very Ordinary Seaman sold 64,000 copies in hardback and remained in print for many years. Mallalieu's friend journalist and politician Michael Foot considered it was 'a masterpiece' which would be read 'as long as English seamen sail the seas'.[43] Mallalieu himself failed to qualify as a sea officer due to substandard eyesight, 'although throughout my sea time just ended it had been good enough to let me act efficiently as a lookout on the bridge.'[44] Instead he went to *King Alfred* to qualify as a non-seagoing 'green striper' of the special branch of the RNVR and wrote a manual for naval instructors.

6
KING ALFRED

After their sea service, the potential officers entered a new and equally intense phase of their naval career. Literally they followed in the footsteps of the Supplementary Reserve men who had gone before, in that they too were trained in *King Alfred* at Hove. Figuratively the route was rather different, though it ended up at the same place, as a temporary sub-lieutenant in the Royal Naval Volunteer Reserve.

From Portsmouth Barracks they were sent to Mowden School. It had been was founded in Essex in 1896, and its headmasters all came from the Snell family until 2002, when it became part of Lancing College. It was a small preparatory school for 45 boys aged from eight or nine to about thirteen. Since 1912 it had been in the Droveway on the outskirts of Hove, but the boys were evacuated inland to Market Harborough in 1940, and the building was taken over and renamed *King Alfred II*, or *King Alfred (M)*. The first cadets arrived on 8 July that year for a two-week stay. It was a small establishment, and they spent the fortnight billeted out to local landladies. Peter Bull enjoyed his brief spell with a family, even if their young daughter had to be bribed not to play *The Teddy Bears' Picnic* on the piano too often.[1] F. S. Holt had an elderly, slight 'bird-like', bespectacled landlady who greeted her tenants with a homely smile and was impervious to the horrors of enemy action – 'Would you care to join me in a cup of tea? We always have one after these raids.'[2]

There was a certain amount of training, including the old stand-by of foot drill, but Peter Bull found that work at Mowden was 'slight, and mainly consisted of interminable lectures on gas-masks delivered by an over-enthusiastic R.N.V.R. officer'.[3] The main purpose was a final assessment before beginning the officers' course proper, another nerve-racking event: 'The waiting room resembled that of a dentist. Some candidates were calm and at ease; some paced the floor, up and down, up and down; while others were busy on last-minute cramming with naval manuals, muttering to themselves all the time.'[4] Brendan Maher came before the board:

> The interview was quite brief and informal. The board already had my fitness report from the *Cardiff*. All that I can remember about the questions was that I gave a stupid answer to one of them. Asked to comment on the tidal pattern around the Island of Arran in the Clyde, where the *Cardiff* had operated, I mumbled something about noticing that high tide seemed always to come in the afternoon. My answer provoked audible amusement, and I left the interview feeling sure that I had failed.

He had not, and moved on to the next stage. Successful trainees went to Lancing College, a distinguished boarding-school six miles from Hove. It was one of a series set up by Nathaniel Woodard in the middle of the previous century, offering a Church of England education without the snobbery attached to the public schools. His promotional book, *A Plea for the Middle Classes*, was perhaps strangely relevant in the school's new circumstances. It had an imposing site and its architecture offered 'some atonement for the many heaps of ugliness which the [nineteenth century] unloaded blindly on to the English landscape'. The dominant feature was the chapel, which was 'Splendid at a distance, but close up the detail has none of the mature restraint and true originality of the rest.'[5] Its boys had been evacuated to Shropshire, and in January 1941 it opened for the training of cadets, as *King Alfred III* or more commonly *King Alfred (L)*. It was headed by Commander Hugh MacLean, who had been an instructor with the Ulster Division of the RNVR before the war.

After the rigours of sea service, the horrors of the naval barracks and the homely experiences with local landladies at Mowden, the arrival was a dramatic moment. Peter Bull found that 'several of my comrades, on issuing forth at Lancing College, were so overawed by

their surroundings that they never behaved normally again'.[6]
Another candidate reported it was 'one of the greatest surprises of
our lives':

> I stood dwarfed in the great doorway and looked down the long
> dining hall. I saw the stained glass windows, the oak panelling,
> the officers' tables and the bright red rope. I saw long tables
> stretched from one end of the room to the other; there were
> tablecloths! glasses! real knives and forks! Waitresses hurried to
> and fro with entrée dishes: cadet ratings in green gaiters and
> clean collars took their seats at the tables. Somehow I felt
> proud that I had been honoured to sit with them.[7]

Even the sleeping accommodation at Lancing was a cut above what
they had been used to, although it was not exactly comfortable. 'We
were housed in dormitories that had been modified into austerity by
removing all furniture and replacing it with iron-frame bunk beds
and metal lockers. No hammocks were used here.'[8]

Cadets were welcomed to Lancing by an excessive number of
officers, one after another. 'The Captain, the Commander-in-Charge,
the Training Commander's Assistant, the Junior Chaplain, the
Sports Officer, the Liaison Theatrical & Amenities Officer and the
Divisional Chief Petty Officer, known as the Warden, – not to
mention the Chief Medical Officer', all 'giving forth' in a short space
of time.'[9] One cadet describes listening to Captain Pelly:

> At 1400 the Division – we were called that now – assembled in
> the drill hall and we had our first opportunity of meeting our
> new Captain. There, in true naval tradition, in a deep, clear,
> determined and yet kindly voice, we listened in silence to the
> Captain reading the Articles of War. They sounded grim, severe.
> But his words also stressed that all important duty of an officer
> – to pay 'attention to detail.'[10]

The former CWs were now known as 'cadet ratings', even though their official status was no higher than when they were on board ship. Most were still ordinary seaman, though a few who had served a long time as CWs might have qualified as able seamen, or even been promoted to leading seaman. Despite Admiralty discouragement, there were a few long-service regular ratings in the courses, and some of them wore the uniform of petty officer or leading seaman, perhaps with good-conduct stripes on their sleeves. Candidates for the accountant branch also had 'fore-and-aft-rig' with a collar and tie. Apart from that, the cadets were still in the 'square-rig' uniform of the lower deck – failure rates were quite high, and there was no point in providing expensive officers' uniforms when clothing was in short supply and tightly rationed. Cadet ratings were simply issued with two white bands to be fitted round their caps to show their new status. They were popularly known as 'purity bands' and caused confusion. Some thought they were to mark out sailors being treated for venereal diseases, while in the early days of the scheme the *Lancing Magazine* carried a cartoon of two locals talking about a passing cadet rating:

Does the white band mean he's been wounded, dad?

Yes son. He comes from that convalescent home on the sea-front.[11]

Cadets did not like the bands, which marked them out as 'neither fish nor fowl' – not officers and not true members of the lower deck. Many of them removed them when on leave and well away from the base.

According to F. S. Holt, 'at Lancing there was no time devoted to mere "spit and polish".' But according to the handbook of 'General Information' issued to trainees from 1941, 'The King's Regulations as to saluting are to be strictly observed.' All the evidence suggests that this order was carried out, sometimes to the point of absurdity and to the distress of newly commissioned sub-lieutenants.

Captain Pelly was rarely seen by the cadets, but he made a point of meeting each one personally during his training. 'Holt, the way I see it is this. We are all on the steps of a ladder, the ladder of promotion. There are many rungs; I'm on one, you're just starting to climb. Rung by rung we can both climb the ladder of promotion together.'[12]

Norman Hampson found a class distinction among the instructors. 'The more abstract subjects, like pilotage and navigation, were taught by officers who lectured to us as though we were undergraduates. The more technical side of things – gunnery, signalling, mines and torpedoes – was left to petty officers, who tended to do things by rote.'[13]

This 'ere's the trigger. You put your finger on the trigger and you squeeze 'er. Finger thinks 'Oi've been squeezed, Oi ave,' and 'e presses the little old trigger. Little old trigger thinks, 'Oi've been pulled by little old finger, Oi'd better move.' So 'e moves and 'e 'it's little old spring.

Chief, I didn't quite get what the little old detonator said to the little old cartridge. Could you repeat it?[14]

A group of about 100 or more cadet-ratings arrived every week and this was known as a 'division', each named after a famous admiral from the past, such as Benbow, Anson, Cochrane, Jellicoe, Nelson and Rodney. It was headed by a divisional officer, who was instructed to keep a close eye on his men:

It is important that Divisional Officers should practice the art of observation in connection with the assessment of their ratings and it is equally important that they should impress upon their Divisions how necessary it is that every good Officer should be observant. Divisional Officers should find ways and means of cultivating, and subsequently testing, the powers of observation of men under training.[15]

Though he was a very grand figure and perhaps somewhat remote, it was felt that he should be of the highest calibre, 'for a trainee tends to model himself on his Divisional Officer, and it is very desirable that the Divisional Officer should have no physical or mental weakness. The mental side is much more important than the physical.'[16]

Chief petty officers featured prominently at this stage in the training. According to the handbook of 1941, 'Cadet-Ratings will be in the general charge of a Divisional C.P.O. who will act as Warden and in all matters of question or doubt they will refer to their Divisional Officer through him.'[17] Each division was subdivided into classes of about 25 men, headed by a class captain in the same way as the groups of officers under training. The class captain would take command when they were mustered or assembled together in classes. He would be 'generally responsible to the Divisional Officer for the good order of the class, and that any absentees from his class are reported'.[18] Brendan Maher's division was split into four platoons, A, B, C and Y, the last referring to 'youth, for it was made up of men who were too young to be commissioned as sub-lieutenants at the end of the course and would become midshipmen'.[19]

Sickness was quite common during the course, because of stress and because many of the men had recently come back from the sea and were subject to infection. In the early days, Peter Scott suffered from colds and bronchitis, though he never knew whether it was 'the dampness of the underground garage or the unaccustomed morning P.T. or the generally germ-laden atmosphere ...'[20] As the medical officer wrote later,

the trainees, having been to sea for three months or more, appear to have lost their immunity to catarrhal infections, and when they come ashore in the somewhat crowded establishment, they appear to be more than usually susceptible to colds, catarrh, and bronchitis, and from the reports these trainees give us, it is evident they are much healthier at sea than ashore.[21]

Men could be transferred to the Royal Naval Sick Quarters, where, according to a poet in the *Magazine*,

No 'Wakey, wakey, rise and shine,'
  Is heard in R.N.S.Q.
'Come get up dear, it's nearly nine'
  Is the call that wakens you.

Those who had periods of sickness were usually fitted into a later class so that their studies could resume at roughly the same point. Brendan Maher injured himself in the swimming pool at Lancing and spent two days in the sick bay. As a result he had to transfer to the following week's division.[22]

Captain Pelly outlined the aims of the course.

"King Alfred" must, within ten weeks, instill in every man the alertness, enthusiasm, sense of responsibility, conscience and good humour (as well as a basic knowledge of technical subjects) which centuries of Service experience have shown to be necessary if a Naval Officer is to carry out his normal duties.

The syllabus has been prepared in order to introduce to those who aspire to be officers, the science of Sea Warfare in a manner that builds up a picture and links up each fact assimilated. The sequence of instruction should enable every man to secure a firm grasp of fundamental principles in correct perspective, unfettered by unnecessary trimmings which so often obscure the target.[23]

Nothing was fixed in a fast-changing war, and 'owing to a change in the syllabus' became something of a catch phrase among the instructors. In the early years the course was run mostly by retired naval and reserve officers, and there was virtually nothing about radar, air cooperation or amphibious warfare, which would exercise most of the cadets once they got to sea. In command of a landing craft, Peter Bull slowly began to realize 'how much of the course [at King Alfred] had been totally wasted on us'.[24] However, there was a change in the middle of 1942 – new instructors were brought in, fresh from the modern sea war. Paul Lund did not get on with them.

He found they had been sent there after 'nerve shattering experiences at sea' and were often of 'uncertain temper'. There was 'one normally quiet-voiced little lieutenant who would, if provoked, fly into a fury, stamp his feet and even rush up to a cadet-rating and shake him violently by the shoulders'.[25]

It was decided to drop 'extremely elementary lessons in antique technicalities and procedure for the most part relevant to big ships only'. The new syllabus was 'more rationally balanced, unfettered by inessentials, and founded on definite principles calculated to develop in the short time available, those characteristics of alertness and versatility of mind which form an indispensable part of sound leadership'.[26] Subjects like seamanship and discipline, however, were perennial, and Lieutenant-Commander Crick continued to amuse the cadets with his drawings for the rest of the war, while CPO Vass continued to harass them as he had done from the beginning.

The normal week included around 26 hours of instruction, although that was not all that had to be done. Cadet ratings were offered extra tuition in the dog watches between 1630 and 1800 in the evening: 'Duty Seamanship, Gunnery, Torpedo and Signal Chief Petty Officer Instructors are available during this period … Two Instructor Officers will also be on duty between 1700 and 1800 to assist in Navigational Studies.'[27] Despite the use of the word 'voluntary', it was assumed that the all cadets would be 'taxing their brains with "dog-watch" studies'. One wrote:

if you didn't go to the Dog Watch lectures, if you didn't do navigation for at least two hours after dinner together with a rub-up of pilotage, and also read thoroughly your notes every night – well you were just for the 'high jump'.[28]

Lectures began in the first week with a rather old-fashioned description of the ships of the navy. The battleship was 'the floating fort, hard hitter', which may have seemed rather ironic to those whose course coincided with the sinking of *Hood*, *Barham*, *Prince of Wales* or *Repulse*. The aircraft carrier was for 'scouting and protection', although the events at Taranto in 1940, Pearl Harbor in 1941 and Midway in 1942 were beginning to suggest a much broader role. Cadet ratings were given a summary of the numerous smaller craft that they were most likely to be posted to – 'Coastal Forces: S.G.B.s [steam gunboats], M.T.B.s [motor torpedo boats] Q. boats, M.L.s [motor launches] H.D.M.L.s [harbour defence motor launches], M.A/S. Bs [motor anti-submarine boats] – state of sea limits their use.' There was only a cursory mention of the escort vessels and landing craft that would absorb the majority of new officers. The week continued with lectures on ships' fittings, ropes, knots and anchoring.[29]

Appointed as a lecturer in 'world affairs' late in the war, Lieutenant B. G. Mitchell found that he had a rewarding audience:

Naval discipline meant that audiences had no alternative but to attend lectures, which in practice meant that we had no alternative but to be entertaining. In this we were helped by the fact that they were for the most part highly intelligent men and were happy to enjoy a week's intellectual stimulation which they were not to be examined on.[30]

'Anti-gas' featured prominently in the syllabus because of fears that the Germans might employ chemical warfare, though they never did in this war. CPO Vass was particularly associated with such training and called for frequent drill with gas masks on. One cadet wrote:

His lungs were bursting, his eyes were blood-shot and starting out of his head, the heavy clothes he was wearing clung to him now like wet silk ... but he still had to run, his back aching and his loins as weak as water ... but he was too far gone to see or know ...

'All right, remove face pieces,' said C.P.O.[31]

Towards the end of the six weeks at Lancing, each division was expected to produce an entertainment, which meant one every Thursday evening. One example was assessed as a 'grand performance' and considered good enough to be published in the *King Alfred Magazine*, began with the lines,

> We are C.W. candidates
> With accents so refined
> We are the quaintest shipmates
> That you will ever find.

In 1945 the audience was encouraged to 'express its feelings without restraint' during a production of the Victorian melodrama *Maria Martin in the Red Barn*. 'Cheers and boos, sighs duly followed as required and, when the old mother came on there was a slight pause then the audience shouted "sympathy, sympathy" with one voice.'[32]

Putting on the show was no problem for the actor Peter Bull, who took charge of the Anson Division concert. He had some talent at his disposal and was careful to avoid the standard pattern, which involved 'innumerable satires on the staff and mild pornography'. Nevertheless, his own striptease was what he called 'the lowlight of the show', and he believed that it got him through his finals, despite low marks in torpedo. For often the show could be make or break for those who took part in it: both cadets and staff could be impressed by actors, despite affecting to despise them, as Alec Guinness found at his interview. The word went out that any satire of Captain Pelly and his habit of saying, 'Rung by rung we can both climb the ladder of promotion together' was out of bounds. 'Officer-like qualities' or OLQs were considered sacrosanct by the staff, though a group which produced a song based on the repetition of 'Negative OLQ chaps, negative OLQ' seemed to get away with it until one of them later failed the course.[33] But still some cadets went too far. One night oranges were issued on the scale of one per officer, and one between two cadets. Later in the evening they sang a song with the chorus 'Half an officer, half an orange.' This was considered beyond the pale, and they were quickly sent away for lack of OLQs.[34] Perhaps the lyrics included too much complaining or 'dripping', and smacked of 'lower deck attitudes'.

The transfer to Hove after six weeks brought a completely new atmosphere and a change of pace. Lancing was academic; Hove was like 'bees in a beehive', according to F. S. Holt. Cadet-ratings took their tea in the ante-room but had their other meals in a special part of the officers' mess, partitioned off by red ropes. Unlike officers under training, they were fed out of public funds and did not have to pay any subscription.[35] The dormitories at Hove were something of a disappointment after the splendours of Lancing. Cadet-ratings were not normally billeted out but lived in the former underground car park attached to the leisure centre. It was cold, and noise reverberated. They slept on two-tier iron-framed bunks.

Compared with the almost monastic isolation of Lancing, the site at Hove was close to Brighton and its pleasures, though as an Australian, F. S. Holt was not impressed with the shingle beach. The whole conurbation had a population of nearly 200,000 and was 'a little London by the sea', according to a popular guidebook. It had bars and restaurants, but these were segregated by rank, and the cadet-ratings were not allowed to go to the superior ones until they were commissioned. It had many theatres, and even in wartime star turns could be lured down there and perhaps even put on a special show for the cadets. But the town had a shady reputation – John Wilson called it 'raffish' – that had started with its foundation by the Prince Regent, who built the famous pavilion early in the previous century. It continued as a centre for adultery, whether genuine or faked for the purposes of divorce. Eventually the Admiralty regretted its choice of venue for the courses – Hove was 'undoubtedly a bad selection'. Apart from having a large water area for training and a large parade ground, an ideal site would have been remote from any town or city.[36]

There was only one hour of formal acedemic lectures per week at Lancing, and four during the first three weeks at Hove. After that the

above: The film *Ships with Wings*, showing formally dressed officers on the bridge. (BFI)

below: *In Which We Serve* presents a far more realistic picture of modern war, with Noël Coward as Captain Kinross clinging to a liferaft, and John Mills as an Ordinary Seaman behind him. (BFI)

Above: A parade at HMS *Collingwood* in August 1943, seen from the air. (IWM A 18929)

Opposite page, top: A gunnery class at HMS *Raleigh.* (IWM A 3144)

Right: Sailors training in boats in the outdoor swimming pool lake at HMS *King Alfred*. (IWM D 24888)

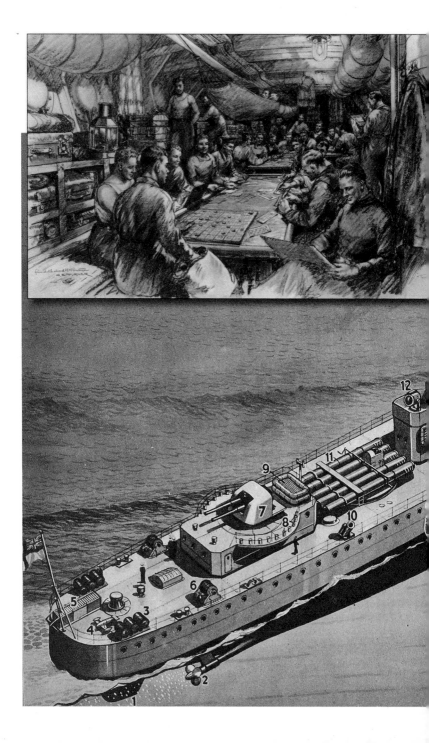

opposite page: Sailors relaxing with a game of tombola (similar to bingo) on the forward _essdeck of a destroyer in 1940. (*Illustrated London News*/Mary Evans)

elow: A cutaway view of a J-class destroyer. The crew's quarters are not shown, but _ey were under the forecastle, between numbers 19 and 28 on the drawing. The officers' _uarters were aft, between the engines and the stern.

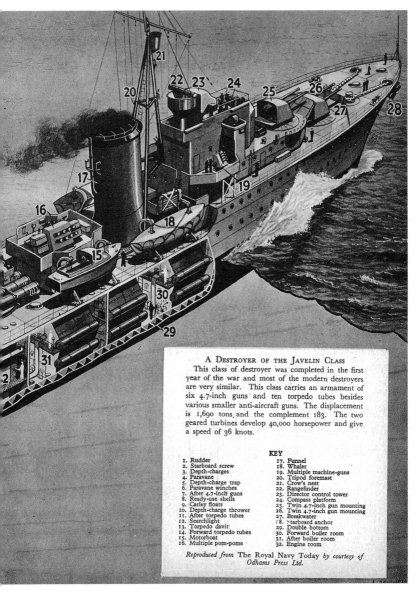

A DESTROYER OF THE JAVELIN CLASS

This class of destroyer was completed in the first year of the war and most of the modern destroyers are very similar. This class carries an armament of six 4.7-inch guns and ten torpedo tubes besides various smaller anti-aircraft guns. The displacement is 1,690 tons and the complement 183. The two geared turbines develop 40,000 horsepower and give a speed of 36 knots.

KEY

1. Rudder	17. Funnel
2. Starboard screw	18. Whaler
3. Depth-charges	19. Multiple machine-guns
4. Paravane	20. Tripod foremast
5. Depth-charge trap	21. Crow's nest
6. Paravane winches	22. Rangefinder
7. After 4.7-inch guns	23. Director control tower
8. Ready-use shells	24. Compass platform
9. Carley floats	25. Twin 4.7-inch gun mounting
10. Depth-charge thrower	26. Twin 4.7-inch gun mounting
11. After torpedo tubes	27. Breakwater
12. Searchlight	28. Starboard anchor
13. Torpedo davit	29. Double bottom
14. Forward torpedo tubes	30. Forward boiler room
15. Motorboat	31. After boiler room
16. Multiple pom-poms	32. Engine room

Reproduced from The Royal Navy Today *by courtesy of Odhams Press Ltd.*

Right: The *Scharnhorst* action. Star shells light up the sky as the battleship *Duke of York* comes up and destroyers attack on the right. (NMM BHC 0684)

Below: Lancing today. Note the Second World War pill-box in the foreground.

Opposite page, bottom: Divisions at Lancing. (IWM A 16409)

Above: A party of cadets is briefed by an officer before training on a boat at Portslade. (IWM A 16426)

Below: Cadet Rating Jack Boulton goes for his final interview. (IWM A 16437)

intellectual pace quickened, and there were eight hours in the ninth week and seven in the tenth, mostly on leadership and ship administration. Trainees were not encouraged to take notes at some periods, as it was felt that they would interfere with the value of the instruction.[37] But not all instructors agreed with this, and in 1941 Charles McAra

> listened respectfully to the lectures on Gunnery, took notes and made drawings but all with a sense of disbelief. I couldn't visualise myself on board a great floating fortress like HMS *Nelson* ... On the other hand it struck me that if I were lucky enough to be sent as a watch-keeping officer to a small ship the more I knew about navigation, signals and communication the better and I applied myself to these and to general seamanship.[38]

John Munday, who attended the course in 1943, wrote down much on the promotion rosters at the port divisions, on dental hygiene, chemical warfare and on physical and recreational training.[39]

Leadership was not often taught in those days, and Roderick Macdonald, who entered via the Special Entry Scheme, wrote that, 'Public school boys were for some reason assumed to have absorbed Leadership at school since it was not taught or alluded to in the training cruiser.'[40] But some time was devoted to the subject during the ninth week of the course at Hove. There were lectures on 'The purpose of a Commission', leadership, the ship's company, King's Regulations, discipline and punishment. To help cadets with this, in September 1943 Captain Pelly issued a booklet, the *Officers' Aide Memoire*. He acknowledged that the section on Leadership came from 'various sources'. In fact, most of it is taken almost word for word from the instructions issued to newly joined officers in HMS *Hood*, which had been written by Captain (later Vice-Admiral Sir) Francis Pridham and was in its second edition by January 1938. At first sight, it seems strange that a document intended for regular officers in the biggest warship in the world should be adapted so easily for temporary officers in landing craft, escorts, minesweepers and MTBs. But the navy was facing a crisis with its petty officers in 1938, as in 1943, with large numbers of older men reaching retirement age, just as the navy underwent its first expansion programme for twenty years.

The *Aide Memoire* also included much detail on ship administration and a thumbnail sketch of the principles of navigation. It included many references to paragraphs in the King's *Regulations and Admiralty Instructions*, for it was found in wartime that 'K.R. and A.I. is too comprehensive a volume and its relevant passages too difficult to find ...'[41] The *Aide Memoire* forms a remarkably concise distillation of 30 years' experience as a naval officer, combined with three years of running intensive training courses. According to a post-war report,

> This little booklet was designed to enable an officer, who might be confronted with an administrative problem, to find the answer quickly by looking up the relevant reference to the governing regulation or authority. This *'Officer's Aide Memoire'* proved extremely popular to Officers serving at sea, judging by the number of requests for copies from Commanding Officers.[42]

Leadership involved 'power of command', the ability to project one's voice when giving an order. This was no problem for certain professions, and Alec Guinness was at an advantage as an actor. During his preliminary medical examination, the elderly doctor 'ran a tape-measure round my chest; he told me to breathe out and then breathe in. He looked puzzled, as if he had miscalculated, and repeated his measurement.'

> 'Chest expansion over four inches. How do you account for that?'
> 'I'm an actor. It's part of the job to use your lungs.'[43]

A teacher like B. G. Mitchell also had an advantage: 'Having a strong voice and being used to performing in public, I developed a good 'power of command.'[44]

A good officer, according to the *Aide Memoire*, had to steer between the limits of becoming 'popularity Jack' and neglecting his men. He was urged to get to know their names and interests, to remember that loyalty 'can only start at the top and grow downwards', to encourage the best men without showing undue favouritism and to set a good example of smartness and confidence:

Your demeanour should be cheerful and enthusiastic – it is your business to inspire enthusiasm and pride of ship and Service. Never appear bored or fed up, however irksome the work may be. The British have a capacity for cheerfulness in adversity. Give it a chance; it is infectious.[45]

Elementary seamanship should already have been learned at the basic training camp and at sea, but it was often found that the men's knowledge was deficient, so experienced instructors like Lieutenant-Commander Crick were employed to rectify it.

Ship-handling was a higher level of seamanship, practised by officers rather than ratings. D. P. Scarle took extensive notes on the subject. In coming to a buoy, destroyers and larger ships launched a ship's boat, smaller ships had a buoy jumper who would lower himself on to the buoy in question. The ship would sail into the tide, moving slowly towards the object. A ship with twin screws had much greater manoeuvrability and would keep the buoy to windward. With a single screw, the stern of the ship would kick either to left or right as the engine was put into reverse to slow down, so a right-handed-screw ship would keep the buoy to starboard. When coming alongside in a tight berth, it was best to reverse into it. Care had to be taken when anchoring:

Anchor drags because (a) insufficient cable on bottom (b) bad holding ground (c) foul anchor. To stop dragging – veer to extent of cables and anchors – inform captain – also engine to get power on deck and main engine to weigh anchor and rebirth [sic] if necessary.[46]

Candidates spent two days on the canal at Portslade, a mile or so from *King Alfred*, where up to six motor launches were based. They were fitted with bridges, like those of larger ships, with voice-pipes and a proper wheelhouse, and an alarmingly large row of rubber tyres along each side.

The nautical 'Rule of the Road' was an important feature of seamanship, especially as war anchorages became extremely crowded with warships and merchantmen. The rights of sailing ships were largely irrelevant in the European war, but it was necessary to learn that steamships passed port to port in narrow channels, that the one with the other on its right gave way in the open sea, and that an overtaking vessel kept clear of the other until the operation was over. The teaching was not universally successful, and in 1943 one officer commented,

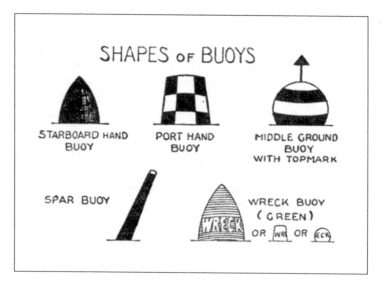

The English system of buoyage. (*Seaman's Pocket-Book*)

If you see any small craft in wartime approaching you flying the White Ensign do not assume that he knows the Rule of the Road. Assume that he MAY know the Rule of the Road, but in the other hand he MAY have hydrophobia. It is the only way to avoid collisions, in days when small craft officers have so little training.[47]

Trainees learned pilotage, which was rather like the younger brother of navigation. Twenty hours were allotted for the teaching of it, mostly during the period at Lancing. It involved finding the way while in sight of land, either in making passages along the coast, or in rivers and estuaries. The trainees had probably seen charts already during basic training or in CW service, but now they had to master them. They learned that the marks along the sea area of the chart represented fathoms of six-feet depth and that the letters alongside them represented the type of bottom, for use in anchoring: for example 'g' meant gravel, 's' meant sand. Lighthouses and buoys had their own symbols, which had to be learned, and shore features such as church steeples and water towers were marked to help in taking fixes.

It was important to know the flow of the tide over a route if the ship was to find its destination and not to be swept into minefields and other hazards. The tidal information for a particular spot was usually to be found on diamonds shapes marked on the Admiralty chart, and figures were given for the rate and direction at a particular time before or after high water at a major port in the area. All this required a good deal of interpretation, and the Admiralty advised caution, as it was more difficult to predict the rate of a tide than its height.

As well as an understanding of the tides, a knowledge of buoys was essential. In the standard English system, a conical red buoy marked the starboard side of the channel, a flat one with black-and-white check marked the port side. A round one with black-and-white horizontal stripes marked the middle ground; a red one showed a submarine cable, and a black one was for a telegraph line. The system was different in Scotland and Ireland. In a world war, the potential officers might find themselves almost anywhere and with yet another system of buoyage, so they had to be flexible.

After we had practised navigation on chart tables, we concluded that part of the course with a navigation exercise conducted in a large field. The field was dotted with scaled-down buoys, a miniature lighthouse, a church steeple, and a small rock or two. The whole thing looked rather like one of those putting golf courses found in amusement parks. Working in pairs, we were provided with a chart of this 'ocean' and an ice cream vendor's tricycle, the top of the freezer box being fitted out as a chart table with a bearing compass, dividers, parallel rule, and binoculars. Each pair was given a task, such as 'Plot course from point A to point B', these points being defined by bearings from the lighthouse or steeple. Not much was learned from this otherwise totally enjoyable and ludicrous exercise, given the facts, in addition to our ignorance, that the all-steel frame of the tricycles rendered the compasses nearly totally ineffective and that we were continually trying to avoid colliding with each other in the available space.[48]

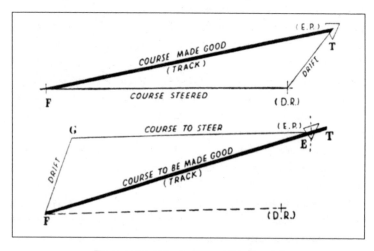

The navigational triangle. (*Officers' Aide-Memoire*)

It was also essential to learn how to find the ship's position by taking compass bearings from at least two points on land – more important than ever in wartime, when the normal hazards of submerged sandbanks and rocks were supplemented by wrecks and minefields. The bearing lines were plotted on the chart, but rarely did all lines in a three-point bearing coincide exactly. The size of the resulting 'cocked hat' gave some indication of the accuracy of the bearing.

Navigation was perhaps the most important single subject at *King Alfred*, absorbing 52 hours of formal instruction out of 235 and being worth 130 marks out of 1000 in the examination, more than any other subject. Unlike the former yachtsmen, the cadet-ratings could not be assumed to have any previous knowledge of the subject, and some found it difficult. They were introduced to the two main problems of any navigator – to establish exactly where he was at that moment, and to find the most efficient route to his destination. They quickly discovered that the sea was a fluid medium, so the ship would hardly ever travel in the same direction as the bow was pointing; that it had far fewer marks than the land; and that dangers were not always visible because they might be a few feet under the surface.

The cadets already knew how to steer by

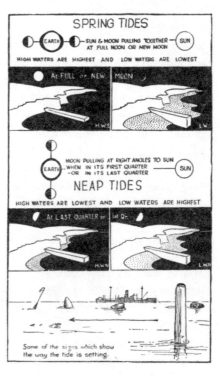

The effect of the tides, as drawn by Edward Crick.
(*Seaman's Pocket-Book*)

the compass, but a navigator or an officer of the watch had to be able to give a course to the helmsman. This was rarely simple, especially in British waters with their strong tides. When out of sight of land, he could find the compass course by joining two points on the chart, but he had to allow for variation, the difference between magnetic and true north in the part of the world he was in. Then he had to make calculations for deviation, which was caused by ferrous materials within the ship itself. That might vary according to the compass course. Then he calculated the effect of any tides or currents on his passage. This was particularly important if he was crossing a channel with strong tides that might push him from side to side. These varied throughout the day, and he had to calculate the net effect during each hour of the passage. He then produced the navigational triangle, in which the starting-point and the intended destination were joined by a line to mark the course to be made good, or the track over the ground. He calculated the effect of the tides during the period in question and drew out the direction and distance on the beginning track. Joining the end of that line to the finish point would give the course to steer to counteract the effect of the tides and currents.

If celestial navigation were not available because of bad weather or other factors, the seaman relied on dead reckoning. This was the reverse of the process used to calculate a course in a tideway. The course steered by compass was marked on the chart, and the distance travelled, say in one hour, was measured along it. The movement of the tide during the same hour was added to the end of that line, and the course made good could be plotted by connecting the starting point with the end of the tidal line. This gave the estimated position, or EP, and was marked in pencil with a triangle on the chart.

An understanding of the tides was important for another reason – their rise and fall might affect the amount of water under the ship, with potentially disastrous results, as described by one of the instructors:

Another 'classic' was the unfolding story of a young officer who thought he had found the ideal spot to anchor his craft overnight but had quite overlooked the local rise and fall of the tide. He is awakened from his sleep below decks by a scratching sound on the boat's hull; arrives on the upper deck to find the boat high and dry with a little boy scraping off periwinkles with his penknife; quickly followed by the local populace to 'see the big ship aground'. The illustrator added further touches as the crowd increased, including an ice cream man keen to ply his trade, and finally a policeman to keep everyone in order.[49]

If they had studied their *Seamanship Manual* or *Pocket-Book* as they should have done, they already knew that the tides were controlled by the effects of the sun and, more especially, the moon. There was a certain amount of theory, but F. S. Holt found it too difficult and largely irrelevant.[50] More practically, they had to be able to calculate the tidal stream at any given moment in any given place, and the rise and fall of the tide, especially near harbour entrances, anchorages and sandbanks.

Celestial navigation, the finding of position by means of heavenly bodies, was considered the peak of the navigator's art, but very little of it was taught at *King Alfred*. 'Contrary to the impression held by many outsiders, the navigation as taught in "King Alfred" really amounted to nothing more than coastal navigation, closely allied to pilotage. It consisted primarily of chart plotting exercises involving fixes, together with certain problems in connection with tides, compass errors, enemy reports, etc.'[51] The early editions of *King Alfred Magazine* had a cover picture showing an officer under training and a cadet-rating using sextants, but F. S. Holt confirms that he only learned to use it for measuring the angle between objects on the surface to get a fix. Pelly provided a 'Guide to working a sun sight' in his *Aide Memoire*, but that was the simplest of tasks in astral navigation, used to plot the latitude of the ship at noon each day. Newly commissioned officers who were considered suitable might come back to *King Alfred* for a short course in celestial navigation, as Holt did, spending long hours with the sextant in order to get the maximum number of star sights. But most of them would not need it very much in the jobs they were posted to. In convoy escort, the main problem was keeping in station off a convoy while zigzagging in fog, or finding it again after a U-boat hunt. Coastal forces needed pilotage, while minesweepers needed precise fixes, mostly from objects on shore, to establish which areas had been swept. Landing craft officers needed a special variety of pilotage to find the right spot on the right beach under fire and in chaotic conditions.

The subjects of gunnery, torpedo and signalling were even more specialized and technical. The cadets had to learn 'the essential basic principles governing Gunnery Control, including Sights and Sighting, the care of ammunition, and a detailed knowledge of certain representative short range weapons ...' The gunnery branch of the navy was well equipped with teaching aids:

An important feature of the instructional technique was the efforts on the part of the Gunnery Instructional Staff to interest their classes in a subject which so often bores so many. No pains were spared to live up to the adage 'seeing is believing' and thus voluminous sets of diagrams and film strips were used with great success, in conjunction with the actual instructional models of the weapons themselves.[52]

'Torpedo' included electricity in the navy and was taught largely by petty officers known as 'torpedo gunner's mates'. It was considered 'an essential part of an Officer's intellectual equipment' but too vast to study in detail, and 'only an outline of this great field could be taught with justification'. It was intended that an officer should be able to have 'an intelligent conversation on those matters, and have sufficient knowledge to avoid being bluffed by the experts'.[53]

Signalling was 'the only part of the syllabus in which it was considered imperative to make candidates absolutely proficient'.[54]

Marks of 75 per cent were demanded in the examination. Cadets had to understand 'Colours and meanings of Flags, Morse and Semaphore at 6 and 8 words a minute respectively, simple signals procedure, the understanding of elementary forming and disposing signals, together with an elementary theoretical knowledge of the working and uses of radar ...'[55]

Despite a strong technical bias, the syllabus said virtually nothing about marine engineering, and it occurred nowhere in a temporary officer's training. It was assumed that the navy's own engineering branch would keep the engines running, although in ocean-going corvettes, for example, the chief engineer was an engine room artificer with only the status of a chief petty officer.

Perhaps the most important aim of all was the development of 'officer-like qualities', OLQs or 'oily Qs' – rarely defined but often mentioned. Generally they meant leadership, initiative and a sense of responsibility, but it was never quite clear how far the authorities regarded them as innate and how far they could be taught. Roderick Macdonald wrote, 'Officer-like Qualities were somewhat vaguely stipulated as the aim pre W.W. II rather than Leadership'[56]

Lower deck attitudes, the opposite of OLQs, were fatal to the prospects of a commission. According to the cadets, the staff snooped around trying to find examples of inappropriate behaviour or lack of decorum, manners or etiquette: 'legends were handed down from division to division of conditions and eccentricities. Certain officers, for instance, were reported to hide between pillars and take down particulars in note-books of every small breach of behaviour.' It was believed, for example, that it was considered offensive to light one's cigarette from another without using a match. Meals became unnecessarily formal experiences, as cadet ratings indulged in orgies of politeness. 'Could I trouble you for the Salt?' and 'Would it be asking too much for you to pass the saccharine?'[57] It was a strong and perhaps deliberate contrast to customs on the messdeck.

There is no evidence that the staff really carried out such spying on their men, and if they did they were not necessarily looking for breaches of etiquette. 'Lower deck attitudes' was no better defined that OLQs, but it tended to refer to the grumbling, suspicious, unambitious mindset that regular officers attributed to the ordinary sailor, especially the peacetime regular. Captain Pridham had identified this in HMS *Hood* just before the war. He warned his officers not to trust 'three-badge ABs'. They were also made aware that the peacetime lower deck did not trust accelerated promotion: 'Trade Unionism and an innate fidelity to their own kind limit their aim to one of general security, i.e., equal opportunity to rise steadily on a pay scale.'[58]

John Wilson found the course competitive and disagreeable after his egalitarian and unpretentious life on the lower deck. It was certainly very stressful, and, according to F. S. Holt, it 'called for maximum concentration while at the same time being immensely practical'.[59] He recalled, 'the great majority of Cadet-ratings suffer from over anxiety that they may fail. This is not unnatural when one considers the stakes involved:– Commissioned rank or return to the lower deck.'[60] Failures would not go home to consider a new career; they would spend the rest of the war on the lower deck, constantly reminded of their failure and commanded by men just like those they had served with in *King Alfred*.

By the later weeks at Hove, the remaining cadets were far enough advanced to buy their officers' uniforms, though they were still not certain to pass. They were allowed a grant of £40 for this and given sufficient clothing coupons. A host of tailors with naval links set up shops in Hove:

Down to KA came the smooth, softly-spoken, reassuring naval outfitters from firms like Gieves, Moss Bros, Hope Brothers, Hector Powe, Austin Reed, all eager to measure us for two suits, number one and number three, bridge coat, cap, shirts, collars, ties, shoes, gloves, all at a total price which did not exceed the Admiralty Uniform Allowance.[61]

Most of them advertised their wares in the *King Alfred Magazine*, where Hector Powe's was perhaps the most informative and persuasive.

> Officer's uniform should automatically make a man look quietly well dressed. There is nothing obtrusive about it but in keeping with the tradition of the silent service, it is a silent expression of efficiency.
>
> To achieve this, three main factors are necessary – good cloth, good craftsmanship and good taste. Therefore make sure you deal with a house of sound repute which cannot afford to jeopardise its good reputation ...
>
> Remember, the cap is the most important. It can make or mar your appearance. Invest in a good one, it will repay you by keeping its shape and style throughout a long life.[62]

In the early days, cadets were assessed in a final examination in the last week at Hove, and each had to get 500 marks out of 1000 over all subjects. Despite his happiness on the lower deck of *Hesperus* and his regret at leaving the ship, Peter Bull became as anxious as anyone about passing at *King Alfred*: 'there was an accumulation of things to be enjoyed, like the splendiferous uniform already ordered and the prospect of indefinite leave.' He totally failed the torpedo section but somehow scraped 553 marks and passed overall.[63]

By the end of 1941, the system had changed. Weekly tests were introduced to avoid what Pelly called 'examinationitis', the very stressful period at the end of the course. It was decreed that a cadet must be adequate in each subject, rather than have 500 out of 1000 overall. He needed 50 per cent in each subject, and 75 per cent in signalling.[64] By 1943 the authorities had relented slightly on this.

> If a cadet rating fails by a small margin to obtain passing out marks in one subject but has marked officer-like abilities otherwise, he may be passed by the Board provided that his Instructor Officers and Divisional Officer can assure the Board

that for some reason his examination results are not a true measure of his knowledge and that they are sure he will make a good officer.

But an officer should never be allowed to take charge of a ship at sea 'unless the Commanding Officer is satisfied that he has a thorough knowledge of the Regulations for Preventing Collisions at Sea and a sufficient knowledge of Navigation and Pilotage to prevent the ship running into navigational dangers.'[65]

Some who failed in certain subjects or were not quite up to the medical standard were commissioned in the Special Branch of the RNVR. This meant that they wore green stripes between the gold and would never go to sea. But there was a fear that this might become a soft option and some cadets would not try to master all the syllabus. In 1943 it was decided that such men must 'have some special qualifications or are of outstanding character' in order to 'avoid any impression among cadet ratings that lack of effort will merely result in transfer to the Special Branch or prolongation of the *King Alfred* course'.[66]

Towards the end, each class had a final dinner as a 'pre-interview nerve tonic'. Establishments such as the Old Ship Hotel in Brighton, the St James's Restaurant or 'Jimmy's' and the Princes Hotel in Hove competed for custom and offered special rates for groups.[67]

When Alec Guinness went for his final interview, he was ushered in by the stage designer Roger Furse, now an RNVR lieutenant. 'Nothing to worry about, just *act* the part', he was told. He came before several aged admirals who noted, 'Navigation not too good ... Mathematics very poor, I see. Gunnery marks are appalling. You don't like guns?' The senior officer asked questions about a mediocre actor he seemed to like, then said, 'Drill, good; Smartness, yes.'

I thought, with pride, of the exquisite trouble I had taken with my black silk ribbon, collar, boots and tiddly suit. I was dismissed curtly, but I had the impression that the dear frog face watched my exit keenly. Roger collected the papers with their penciled comments and afterwards told me that scrawled across my paper by the senior Admiral were the words, 'Probably more to him than meets the eye.'[68]

The method of giving out the results was quite cruel, as the men were paraded and the names of those who had passed were read out.

[August] 21st and the announcement of our examination results. We were lined up and the results read out, starting at the back end. I stood and waited, the swine got to 18 before he called out my name. Phew! If name not called out, back to sea.[69]

Each of the rejects went off to become the 'most abject of creatures, a failed CW candidate'. Paul Lund failed, he thought, because he had not been able to hear one of his divisional officer's orders.

Uniforms were cancelled; white capbands were immediately removed. The rejects had to mess separately from the other cadet-ratings and were generally declared 'unclean'. Then came the depressing journey back to barracks. The arrival there was like receiving a bucket of icy water full in the face. The cadet-rating chrysalis had been on the point of bursting into the officer butterfly when it had been rudely stamped upon. Now one had to revert in a flash to the manner, habits and thoughts of a rating.[70]

Meanwhile the new officers said goodbye to the eccentricities of the square-rig uniform and emerged, butterfly-like, from the tailors.

The inspection over, the failures departed. The rest of us, dressed as ratings, crossed the road and changed into our best doeskin uniforms. A uniform with a single gold stripe. I was now an Acting Temporary Probationary Sub-Lieutenant in the

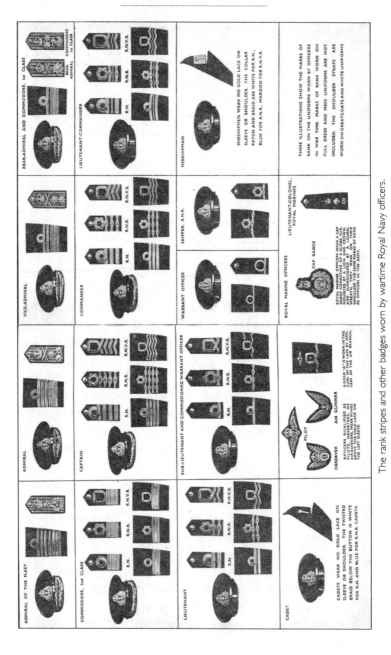

The rank stripes and other badges worn by wartime Royal Navy officers.

R.N.V.R. Bill and I walked back across the road. At the door, the sentry clattered to attention and gave us a butt salute. It was the first of many salutes but quite terrifying. It was the first time in the war that I had wanted to turn and run.[71]

Peter Bull and his companion 'spent some delirious hours trying on our new clothes'.[72] His friend Alec Guinness wrote, 'I look terrifically dandy in my uniform. And nearly faint with excitement and pride when saluted in the streets ... It's a pity I don't know anything about the sea.'[73] Like the direct-entry officers before them, they continued to wear grey flannels, gaiters and white scarves in the daytime, and full uniform in the evening.

There was much praise for *King Alfred*'s work in training officers under great pressure. Admiral H. R. Stark of the US Navy called it 'Britain's greatest experiment in democracy'. In 1942 Sir P. Harris, MP, described it as, 'one of the best bits of work the Admiralty have done during the last two years'.[74] One of the trainees, Ronald Gellatly, wrote that it was, 'without doubt the most efficiently run establishment that I met during my Naval career'.[75] But towards the later stages of the war, as the supply of experienced and able men began to dry up and cadets were perhaps rushed through too quickly, there were problems with some of the new officers. By the end of 1943 it was noticed that failures were becoming far more common.

The Captain at *King Alfred* reasoned that the failure rate was so high because the material sent to him was not up to the minimum standard required in three main areas: firstly, many of those sent to him had not got the necessary mental capacity to absorb the basic navigational requirements for an officer; secondly, they were often too confused by the sudden and dramatic change in their lives brought about by joining the Navy to display any powers of leadership which they might possess and, thirdly, quite a large proportion of them seemed to have no desire to become officers and showed no ambition to pass out successfully from the course.[76]

In command of an escort group in 1944, Derek Rayner 'could make neither top nor tail' of young men who were 'terribly serious' and obsessed with form-filling. 'Responsibility sat rather heavily on shoulders not yet broad enough to bear the weight.' But he admitted that 'the fault may well have lain equally with myself, for already I was beginning to look backwards to a time when I imagined that things had been better'.[77] In all, 22,500 officers were commissioned from the school before it closed in 1945.[78] It is difficult to see how the Second World War could have been won without them

King Alfred was not the end of the story for most of the newly-commissioned officers: they were sent to the Royal Naval College at Greenwich for another two weeks of training. As a site this was considerably grander even than Lancing. Sir Christopher Wren's buildings beside the Thames are only a few miles from central London and were also populated by Wren officers under training. The towers, colonnades and pathways form one of the finest ranges of buildings in Europe, and the Painted Hall, used by trainee officers for lunch, is, if anything, more impressive still. It was also used by members of the Board of Admiralty to entertain dignitaries, so it was a very different world from the former swimming pool at Hove. Norman Hanson recalled,

> We attended a host of lectures, mainly on naval and general British history, naval traditions and the wartime role of warships of every category. Professor Michael Lewis, probably the most celebrated naval historian of our age, captivated us completely with his charm and consummate knowledge of his subject. We were taught unarmed combat and gaily threw one another around the spacious lawns. An instructor warned us darkly of the perils of gas and bacteriological warfare.[79]

It was known as the 'knife and fork course', and naval manners and etiquette certainly played a prominent part in it. There was also a chance for further ship-handling on the River Thames. Now the new officers had to get used to operating in tidal waters, spending two days on board a motor cruiser. However, the Admiralty later concluded that the Greenwich course was not a success. 'The academic slow tempo training atmosphere of Greenwich was too much of an anti-climax for the "King Alfred" Officers, the majority of whom quite openly looked upon it as a welcome rest at the conclusion of their labours, and quite naturally found themselves inclined to relax their efforts.'[80]

Officers were given a certain amount of choice in their future appointments, though this was always subject to the requirements of the service. In peacetime the Admiralty would try to give each officer a balanced career, with time in different kinds of ship and in staff posts, but this was not possible in wartime. A temporary RNVR officer would find himself posted to a particular type of ship, and he was likely to stay in the same type for the rest of the war, since there was no time for retraining. By this time the officers knew that the navy could be divided into several different forces, each with its own ships, tactics, traditions and demands. The 'big-ship navy' of battleships and cruisers was not a growth area during the war, and new building only just covered wartime losses. It was also the last to take on temporary RNVR officers in large numbers, so only a small minority of them were posted there. Regular naval officers expected to spend some time in battleships and found it useful in making contacts with senior officers, necessary to advance a career, but that was irrelevant to temporary RNVR officers. They were likely to be just very junior members of a battleship's wardroom, with no prospect of rising to command. They would live among about 80 other officers, including surgeons, paymasters, engineers and marines. Commissioned ranks varied from captain to sub-lieutenant, with a large number of warrant officers and midshipman in addition, living in separate messes. Very few RNVR officers wanted to enter this milieu.

Nevertheless, in 1942 the Admiralty ordered that it was 'essential to extend the existing arrangements for the replacement of R.N. Officers by Reserve officers to all major war vessels not already affected'. The principles had changed. 'With the expansion of the Naval forces that has taken place within the last two years, the Fleet must be manned with Reserve officers with a leavening of Active Service officers, and not manned by R.N. Officers diluted with Reserve officers.' An RNVR officer was to be appointed to shadow a regular officer for one to three months in each ship, then the latter would be transferred out, this process continuing until there were only three regular officers left, apart from the captain, executive officer and specialist officers. In the event, this was never fully applied, and in April 1945 the battleship *Duke of York* had seven non-specualist regular RN commissioned officers including the captain, commander and first lieutenant. Twelve out of fourteen seaman midshipmen were regulars and two were RNR. There were three regular specialist officers of the gunnery, torpedo and navigation branches, plus two from the reserves. All ten engineers were regular RN, and there were 23 RNVR officers in ranks up to lieutenant-commander.[81] Temporary officers, however, even began to penetrate some of the more exclusive specialist branches. One cruiser captain saw the wavy stripes on the sleeves of his newly-appointed gunnery officer and exclaimed, 'Good God ... No!' but became reconciled to the situation.[82]

This was also to apply in cruisers and aircraft carriers, until only two regular non-specialist officers were left. In aircraft carriers, the pilots and observers of the Fleet Air Arm were trained separately, but there was some room for *King Alfred* graduates as deck officers. This was not very attractive. Not only was there no prospect of rising to a command, the aircrew rather than the deck officers were the 'heroes' and at the centre of the ship's existence.

Destroyers were considered part of the regular 'big-ship navy' at first, and only those with good connections, such as Ludovic Kennedy and Peter Scott, were likely to be posted to them. This began to change as more destroyers were built and their roles expanded. In August 1941 the Admiralty decreed that more temporary officers should be appointed to them. They

> should be trained to undertake the quarter bill duties of only one of the normal complement of Executive Lieutenants, and in addition to take charge of a watch at sea. It is not intended that they shall be fully trained for all types of executive duties, but it is hoped that many will be able to do so in due course.[83]

Submarines were also dominated by regular officers, but Edward Young was taken out of *King Alfred* early in 1940 with two others to become the first RNVR officers trained in submarines. He later got his own command. By the end of the war more than half of submarine officers were RNVR. Twelve submarines were commanded by them, with seven more under dominion Volunteer Reserve officers.[84] Edward Young's boat, however, had only one other RNVR officer against four regulars, while Arthur Hezlet's famous *Trenchant* had an RN captain, first lieutenant and engineering officer, an RNR junior officer and RNVR navigating and torpedo officers. The service did not create a huge demand for officers because it remained quite small throughout the war, with only 7,817 ratings in September 1944.[85]

Coastal forces became seen as one of the most glamorous parts of the service by 1942, with their fast, rakish craft and the chance of quick promotion to command one's own boat. They offered a life almost as exciting as a fighter pilot in the RAF, and the navy used this as a recruiting attraction. The booklet on the Y-Scheme suggested:

> A sub-lieutenant R.N.V.R. who was at school two years ago may captain an M.G.B; a lieutenant may lead the patrol. They are lucky to have one of the most exciting jobs in the Navy, for they get the chance from time to time of fighting the kind of action which every sailor seeks.[86]

But coastal forces were also quite a small part of the navy, taking up less than 24,000 men out of 739,000 in 1944, and it is difficult to argue that they had a major effect on the war compared with minesweepers, escort vessels and landing craft, for example.

Peter Bull was undecided about his own choice.

> I had no emphatic inclinations in any direction, and having been asked the question, I replied, 'Coastal Craft,' as it was at that time the chic thing to be in.
>
> 'Too old,' was the blunt reply. (I was twenty-nine.)
>
> 'Then destroyers.'
>
> 'Too old.'
>
> I was now quite at a loss, as obviously ferrying across the Styx or some similar job was the only choice left.

He left it up to the commander, and to his surprise and horror found himself posted to landing craft.

Some officers, such as Eric Denton, preferred small craft:

> I realized that if I went on a destroyer or something of that size I would be likely to see only the major ports around the British Isles, and not see quite so much of the country as I would like. If I was in Coastal Forces I would get into all sorts of smaller harbours and places where I would get a varied interest and would get a chance to see some life away from the strict rigours of the Navy.[87]

He was delighted to be posted to the training course at Fort William, where coastal forces officers learned their trade before taking a warship to sea.

Minesweepers were another important category for the temporary RNVR, though far less glamorous than some. In the previous war and at the beginning of this one, much of the work had been done by fishing-boat skippers recruited into the RNR, but new devices such as the magnetic mine required a far more scientific approach as well as the kind of discipline that was alien to the fishermen. By the end of the war the RNVR made up 63 per cent of minesweeping officers, compared with six per cent from RNR skippers and 28 per cent from the rest of the RNR.[88] Charles McAra realized that minesweepers had none of the glamour of other branches, but nevertheless he felt that there was nowhere better for a newly commissioned officer to gain experience. When he stated his choice to his superiors, there was instant approval – 'Good show! Here was a lad with no fancy notions above his station like wanting to be in a Tribal class destroyer.'[89] Brendan Maher started with the more common point of view and was disappointed to be appointed to minesweeping. Both went to the training school, HMS *Lochinvar*, in the Firth of Forth, to learn the trade.

> We streamed sweeps, set depths, changed depths, swept occasional dummy mines set there for a purpose, gave steering orders, and navigated (not difficult to do when one is in constant sight of the Forth Bridge). We also spent a few hours in the engine room and watched the stokers as they endlessly shovelled coal into the nearly blinding glare and flare of the firebox ... We rotated duties on these trawlers and gained a little experience doing each of the things that had to be done – except stoking.[90]

But the main 'growth areas' in wartime were escort vessels for the Battle of the Atlantic and landing craft for the invasions of North Africa, Italy and eventually Normandy. There were 56,000 officers and men in escort vessels in 1944, even though the worst of the Battle of the Atlantic was over; and there were more than 59,000 in landing ships and craft. These two made up the largest groups in the British navy. They were the areas where most newly commissioned temporary officers would be posted, and arguably they were the ones that made the greatest contribution to winning the war. The great majority of the 8,000 or so warships in the Royal Navy at the end of the war had at least one *King Alfred* graduate on the bridge, men who remembered Captain Pelly's habit of saying, 'Rung by rung we can both climb the ladder of promotion together', Edward Crick's blackboard drawings and CPO Vass's anti-gas exercises.

7
FIGHTING THE SUBMARINE

On arrival in his new ship, an officer would report to the captain and was expected to show him a good deal of respect. Seaman officers usually knew something about naval etiquette by this time, but ship's doctors had only a two-week course before joining a ship and had to be warned about it. 'Naval officers are extraordinarily polite', they were told, but this could be taken too far:

> Very shortly after your arrival on board, you will be presented to the Commanding Officer, who, whatever his rank, is always referred to as the Captain. Each day, on first sighting him, your 'Good morning, Sir' should be accompanied by a formal salute; thereafter you may pass him without saluting, though naturally you will salute on joining or leaving him on occasions of duty. You rise when he enters the Ward Room, and you remove your cap when you enter his cabin.[1]

If he was lucky, a naval officer might be allocated a single cabin to himself. This was particularly important for a first lieutenant, engineer officer or doctor, who might have to use it as an office. Others were likely to share, and corvettes and frigates usually had a number of two-berth cabins. If he was unlucky, a junior officer might have to sling a hammock in a corridor or in the wardroom, and this became increasingly common as more officers were appointed to each ship.

Officers also had the use of the wardroom. In a River Class frigate it was about 17 feet square, with a long table at one side, with four chairs per side and one at each end. If there were more than ten officers on board, some had to eat at a folding table on the other side of the room. That also had a settee and two more chairs. There was a sideboard, a bookcase, a radio, a safe, paper rack and several curtains. The captain would eat there most of the time, and the chair at the head of the table was reserved for him. In general, he would withdraw after the meal to allow the officers to relax.

A naval officer in an escort vessel had to be adaptable and flexible – Nicholas Monsarrat reckoned he was 'sailor, surgeon, scribe and sexton, all wrapped up in one harassed parcel tied with the tarry twine of naval discipline'.[2] Battleships and cruisers had highly trained gunnery, torpedo, navigation and paymaster officers; aircraft carriers had specialist aircrew and maintenance teams in addition. Traditionally, destroyers worked together under a leader, though that system broke down in wartime. Submarines relied on depot ships for administrative and technical support; coastal forces and minesweepers were rarely away from base for more than a few days at a time. But escort vessels might spend several weeks on the open ocean, and corvettes had no specialist officers at all. Destroyers, frigates and sloops at least had doctors and engineer officers, but other skills had to be found within their own resources.

A first lieutenant's cabin. (*Val Biro*)

Despite the training at *King Alfred*, not all officers were fully competent when they arrived on board, and often relied on petty officers to get them out of trouble. In *Clematis* in 1940, John Palmer was in charge aft as the ship left the dock. 'An order came down to get out a spring. Extraordinarily, I had absolutely no idea what the order meant and simply turned to one of the Petty Officers. I told him to get out a spring and was intrigued to watch what happened.'[3] D. A. Rayner of the regular RNVR was shocked when he had to commission *Verbena* with only three green officers.

On the morning of commissioning day the officers arrived. Two Sub-Lieutenants R.N.V.R and a Midshipman R.N.V.R. They had come straight from H.M.S. *King Alfred*, the officers' training establishment, and not one of them had a watch-keeping certificate. They had all been 'hostilities only' ratings, who had been selected from their fellows and made officers overnight. *Verbena* was the first ship they had served in as officers.[4]

All this caused a certain amount of insecurity, and the novelist Evelyn Waugh, serving as a Royal Marine officer, was contemptuous. The RNVR lieutenants and sub-lieutenants were 'dreary fellows to talk to, they were hopeless seamen … jejune, dull, poor, self-conscious, sensitive of fancied insults, with the underdog's aptitude to harbour grievances.'[5] But Waugh was heavily biased towards the officers of his own unit and was an incurable snob. Meanwhile the officers of *Verbena* quickly learned the trade and became efficient. She was the first corvette to be commanded and officered entirely by the RNVR, and she set the pattern for what was to follow.

Leaving aside Monsarrat's description of his work, the naval officer's job in an escort might be divided into several categories – watchkeeping, seamanship, navigation, 'divisional', administrative, disciplinary, and fighting.

At sea, a watch lasted four hours except for the two two-hour dog watches inserted between four and eight in the evening to vary the system from day to day. The first lieutenant might be excused watches, but most escorts were too small to allow that, and he often took one per day, perhaps the morning watch between four and eight, when he at least had the pleasure of seeing in the dawn. Other lieutenants took two watches per day in a three-watch system, and if numbers permitted each might have a second officer of the watch to assist him, either a raw sub-lieutenant or the very experienced coxswain of the ship. According to Commander Gretton, 'The Officer of the Watch is responsible for the safety of the ship. He is NOT relieved of the responsibility by the presence on the Bridge of a senior officer.'[6]

One of the first tasks for a junior officer was to earn his watchkeeping certificate – a note from the captain to show that he could be trusted to take command on the bridge in normal circumstances. ('I took damned good care of that one,'[7] wrote Monsarrat.) The Admiralty made it slightly easier by decreeing that he only had to prove himself on the type of ship and duty that he was employed on rather than be ready to serve in any kind of ship. Among other things, a watchkeeping certificate allowed promotion to full lieutenant, with a second stripe on each sleeve, provided the officer in question was over 25 (later reduced to 22 for exceptional cases), had a minimum of one year's service and a recommendation by his commanding officer. A younger officer needed two-and-a-half years' service, while a man over 30 needed only three months and could dispense with the watchkeeping certificate.[8]

Monsarrat was confident, even cocky, when his first lieutenant withdrew with the words, 'I'm going inside to log that light and have a smoke. Sing out if you see anything.'

I moved to the centre of the bridge, stirred to an odd exhilaration. ... Centered thus, with fifty-odd men sleeping between decks, and the whole ship entrusted to me as a kind of intricate going concern, I felt tremendously responsible and tremendously alert too. She was all mine: from this nerve centre on the bridge – myself – could go out a pulse that would be felt from end to end of the ship. ... magic moment of authority![9]

His fictitious character, the gauche young Ferraby, was far more nervous when the captain left him alone for the first time.

He had never known such a moment in his life, and he found it difficult to accept without a twinge of near panic. The whole ship, with her weapons and her watchful look-outs and her sixty-odd men sleeping below, was now his; he could use her intricate machinery, alter her course and speed, head out for the open Atlantic or run straight on the rocks ... He felt small and alone, in spite of the bridge look-outs and the signalman and the asdic rating who shared the watch with him: he was shivering, and he heard his heart thumping, and he wondered if he could bear it if they met a convoy, or if some accident like the steering gear breaking down – brought on a sudden crisis. He wasn't really fitted for this: he was a bank clerk, he was only twenty, he'd been commissioned for exactly eight weeks. ... But the minutes of uncertainty passed, as *Compass Rose* held her steady course and nothing happened to disturb it.[10]

Probably this was the more common reaction from new officers, especially those who had not had the advantage of taking charge of a yacht before the war.

One of the most important decisions the officer of the watch had to make was when to call the captain. Should he carry on and try to prove his competence, or should he defer to the proper authority? Most captains laid down detailed instructions, but there were always 'grey areas'. Sam Lombard Hobson, Monsarrat's captain on the east coast, gave orders on when he was to be called by the officer of the watch – on sighting or hearing a suspicious aircraft, on obtaining an asdic contact, on sighting a vessel not identified as friendly or on a course that was likely to interfere with the ship's own, on sighting flares or star shells at night and on a change in the weather. He was also to be called if a navigation mark was not sighted when expected, if a ship or escort left its proper station, a ship joined the convoy, or the presence of other ships might force them from the channel that had been swept for mines. Finally he was to be called if the officer of the watch was 'in any doubt or emergency'. When Monsarrat failed to obey these rules, he was ticked off most effectively.[11] In the destroyer *Duncan*, Commander Peter Gretton preferred to be called by the officer of the watch in cases of doubt – 'any reluctance on his part to disturb me, however well meant, will be misplaced.'[12]

When in harbour, there was usually an officer of the day rather than an officer of the watch. He was responsible for the safety of the ship, the daily routine, including meals and leave, the dress of the crew and for the reception of any boats coming alongside or visitors at the gangway. At anchor, he kept a good eye on the weather in case of the anchor dragging and took bearings on objects on shore to spot any movement. He might order steam to be kept up on the capstan engine in case it was needed in an emergency.

Seamanship was a constant factor in any officer's work, but it was particularly tested in convoy escort. As officer of the watch, he was responsible for keeping the ship's station as part of the escort, despite using zigzags to avoid any torpedoes, and to spread the cover of his asdic. This could be difficult at night or in bad weather, especially in the days before radar. In *Duncan*, the officer of the watch was warned to take care if there was a change in the weather or the course, which might cause more rolling, for example. In such a case, he should be ready to have the crew lash down objects more securely and batten down hatches. He had to know the Rule of the Road intimately in case of near collision with another ship, and he was warned to take evasive action early rather than late.

Navigation was the special responsibility of one of the officers, though he too might well be temporary RNVR, and ex-yachtsmen were generally good at this. Obviously he had to find the ship's position in the middle of the ocean, and it was important for meeting convoys, directing escorting aircraft or finding one's way back to the convoy after a chase. Celestial navigation was not always available in Atlantic conditions, so much of it was done by dead reckoning.

On the domestic side, each junior officer was responsible for a part of the crew. According to Monsarrat,

a ship's company is divided into 'divisions', according to the various branches – seamen, stokers, communications, etc: each group of men has an officer to look after it, an officer specially charged with its welfare and regulation. It is to him that they look in all their difficulties, whether concerned with promotion, training for a higher rate, doubts about their pay, internal quarrels and problems, domestic complications, compassionate leave, complaints of unfairness or favouritism. This division into small groups, if conscientiously applied, makes for a high degree of confidence between officers and men.[13]

But some felt that this did not work well with hastily-trained and insecure officers:

During the late war, due to the heavy dilution, the Divisional Officers had, as a whole, not got the full confidence of the men placed under their trust. Both sides were shy of each other, and ratings were reluctant to go to their officers in times of distress, or to enquire into their hopes of future advancement.[14]

There were very few specialist administrative officers in escort vessels, so the work often devolved on the junior sub-lieutenant, without any particular training. He was, however, offered advice by Captain Pelly on various matters. There were three types of letter in the navy. The 'formal service letter' was written to acknowledge appointments, report on proceedings or make formal requests. After the usual courtesy, it might begin, 'I have the honour to submit that I am sick on shore at the above address.' The 'communication or headed sheet' was used in all other service matters. It usually had the subject matter in the heading; a single letter should only cover one subject, and all paragraphs after the first were numbered, as in the formal service letter. A private letter to a superior officer might ignore most of these rules and perhaps begin, 'I tried to 'phone you yesterday evening, but you were out, and as it wasn't very important I didn't try again – a letter will do just as well.'[15]

Officers were also told about the various forms that had to be completed to keep the ship running. For victualling alone he needed the victualling and check books, the mess book, quarterly provision accounts, abstract of soap and tobacco issued and several others. The rum issue demanded the daily issue book, the spirit issue book and the spirit stoppage book. For naval stores he had to master the demand on naval stores in base or ship; the general utility note on transfer between ships, the survey note for stores returning to the dockyard, and yet more. For leave and other matters, he had to maintain the gangway wine and spirit book, the short leave book and the registered letter book. In addition there were several non-public funds to be administered. In *Duncan*, the ship's fund, including profits from the game of tombola (now better known as bingo) was run by the first lieutenant. One sub-lieutenant and a warrant officer ran the wardroom mess fund, another ran the wardroom tobacco fund, and the ship's doctor ran the wardroom wine fund, all under the general supervision of the first lieutenant.[16]

A junior officer also had a certain role in maintaining the discipline of the ship, either as officer of the watch or of the day in harbour, or as a divisional officer. His main role was to screen offences and decide whether they had to be referred upwards to the first lieutenant or captain, who had the power to award serious punishment. Officers from *King Alfred* were trained in dealing with 'defaulters' in this way. In a case of drunkenness an officer should ask,

Is the man fit in all respects to carry on his duty? ... If, in the opinion of the O.O.W., the answer is *no*, and providing the man's condition is due to the intoxicating effect of liquor, then the man is *drunk*.

If *yes*, then he is *sober*.

NOTE. – There is no such thing in Naval Law as 'Having Drink taken'. The man is either Drunk or Sober.

Dealing with a case of disobedience, he should enquire,

(1) Was it a direct order or message?
(2) Was it properly heard?
(3) Was it properly understood?
(4) Was it deliberately disobeyed?
(5) Was it repeated?
(6) Was it a reasonable order, and given with due regard to the circumstances?[17]

New officers were given many sensible hints in Pelly's *Aide Memoire*. A drunken and violent man, for example, should be put in the charge of one of equal rating; otherwise, he might raise the stakes by assaulting a superior officer. An officer trying a case should never allow himself to be identified with the prosecution, but at the same time he had to back up his petty officers as far as possible.

The most important role of any officer came when the ship was in action. He had to set an example of coolness and resolve, and at the same time to apply his technical and tactical skill to defeating the enemy. To do this, most seaman officers specialized in one part of the ship's armament, though not to the extent of regular officers, who often spent a year or more training in the art of gunnery or torpedo. Temporary wartime officers were lucky to have a few weeks' training, but they had to get results nevertheless.

Destroyers and sloops had quite sophisticated gunnery arrangements, with directors so that all the guns could be trained and fired together, and manual computers known as fire-control tables to work out how to aim off at a distant and moving target. They also had more numerous and sometimes larger guns than corvettes – modern destroyers had at least four 4.7 inch guns, each firing a projectile 1.4 times the weight of a corvette's single one. Corvettes and frigates relied on one or two 4-inch 'pop-guns' which were barely adequate to penetrate a U-boat's hull and had to be aimed by the gunlayers at each weapon, without any mechanical aids.

Escort commanders were advised to fire quickly if a U-boat seemed to be in a position to attack with torpedoes, and gunfire could spoil its aim and force it underwater. If it was clear that the U-boat knew it had been sighted, it was also important to fire and prevent its escape. But the escort captain had to bear in mind that gunfire might dazzle his own crew and prevent other means of attack. He was also aware that, 'Experience of encounters with U-boats had shown that they can sustain many hits from [semi-armour piercing] or [high explosive] shell without receiving lethal damage.' He was to bear in mind the possibility of ramming to finish a boat off and to be ready to carry out underwater attacks if the enemy dived despite several hits by gunfire.[18]

Most escort vessels had been fitted with radar during 1941, as Monsarrat testifies. It could be used for many purposes in wartime, such as detecting enemy aircraft and ranging for guns, but the main role in convoy escort was to find U-boats trying to attack on the surface at night or in poor visibility. The usual model in the middle of the war was Type 271, which consisted of a shape like a segment of a circle and a similar receiver inside a cage-like structure usually fitted aft of the bridge. The incoming data could not be sent over any great distance, so the operator had to stay close to the aerial and worked inside the cage structure. The aerial had to be turned by hand, and its direction reversed as it could not rotate constantly though more than 360 degrees. The signal was shown on a cathode-ray tube, but in the form of a line known as the A-scan. The aerial was pointed in a particular direction and the distance of any contact could be read off on a line on the tube. The operator had a gyroscopic direction indicator so that he could follow the movement of an object without being diverted by the yawing of the ship. A series of contacts would have to be plotted by hand to show the relationship of one to another. If a U-boat were detected outside the convoy and the escorts, it would not be difficult to track, but if it was inside, only good plotting would pinpoint it among the ships of the convoy. From 1943, ships began to be fitted with the Plan Position Indicator, or PPI, which gave an overall plan of the radar picture and saved a great deal of plotting. New aerials were also devised, which could rotate constantly and did not have to be so close to the operator.

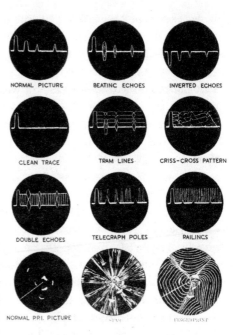

NORMAL PICTURE   BEATING ECHOES   INVERTED ECHOES

CLEAN TRACE   TRAM LINES   CRISS-CROSS PATTERN

DOUBLE ECHOES   TELEGRAPH POLES   RAILINGS

NORMAL P.P.I. PICTURE   STAR   FINGERPRINT

Radar screens, showing some of the faults that an operator has to rectify. The top three rows show the A-scan display, the bottom one has the more modern plan position indicator. (National Archives)

Many ships were also fitted with high frequency direction finding, HF/DF, or 'huff-duff'. This was used to pick up enemy signals and plot the positions of U-boats. Unlike radar, two separate readings had to be taken by different ships to get a cross-bearing, but many escort groups were able to do this by late 1942. HF/DF plotting could also be done by shore stations, but it was far less accurate because the ranges were so long. This, plus intelligence from the shore, meant that convoys were rarely attacked without warning. In 1943 the captain of the training school HMS *Osprey* went so far as to suggest that it was not necessary to keep watch on asdic unless such warnings had been received, to give the men a rest.[19]

Asdic remained the most important sensor in the escort vessel. The anti-submarine control officer, or ASCO, was intended to be a key man in an escort vessel, a final authority on any underwater contact made by asdic and able to direct the hunt for a U-boat. Sir Max Horton, Commander-in-Chief of Western Approaches, decreed in 1942 that there should be at least two such trained officers in each escort, not including the captain. But their training was short, and they had difficulty in keeping up with what was expected of them.

HMS *Osprey*, the navy's main anti-submarine establishment, was forced to evacuate its usual base at Portland on the south coast of England early in 1941 and found its wartime home on the Firth of Clyde. Dunoon could be reached by a long but beautiful car journey round the heads of several Scottish lochs; however, it was far more common to go by steamer from Glasgow or Gourock. The town was a holiday resort, at least as well known to Glaswegians as Brighton was to Londoners (though in this case the most common vice was drunkenness rather than adultery). The annual peacetime trip 'Doon the Watter' was the highlight of a working-class family's life. Now the steamers had mostly been requisitioned for the war, and the town supported various naval activities as well as hosting evacuees from the industrial towns of Clydeside.

A. H. Cherry, an American RNVR officer, was pleasantly surprised when he arrived at HMS *Osprey*. He was sent to the officers' mess in the requisitioned Glenmorag Hotel, on the hill above West Bay. 'What struck me as unusual was that all decks and stairways were carpeted. Everywhere else carpets and rugs had been removed and stored, where the military had taken over private accommodation.'[20] *Osprey* also used the biggest building in the area, the West of Scotland Convalescent Homes, twenty minutes' walk away on the other side of the town, where training took place and the petty officer instructors were also very comfortable.

I doubt whether the navy has any establishment equal to it even at the time of writing [1957]. It boasted putting and bowling greens, and tree-lined walks. I had my own private 'cabin,' fitted with H. and C., bed, wardrobe and bedside table. The petty officers' mess had been a nursery, and the walls were still covered with coloured silhouettes of animals from popular nursery rhymes. The only creature missing was one that would have been most appropriate: a pink elephant. There were billiards and table tennis, a bar – Ye Olde Seagull's Nest – and deep armchairs in an arc around a large red-brick fireplace. We ate at white clothed tables which overlooked a beech edged sward sweeping down to a stream ...[21]

There was a fine view over the Firth of Clyde from the hotel, and it had never been busier. Dunoon was too far away to hear the sound of riveting from the numerous shipyards on both sides of the Clyde, building dozens of warships and merchantmen, but they all passed the town on the way to their trials off the Island of Arran. From the heights it was possible to see across Kempock Point to the Tail of the Bank off Greenock, where convoys assembled and ships waited to load or unload, for the Clyde was second only to Liverpool as a base for the Battle of the Atlantic. The river was protected by an anti-submarine boom directly opposite the hotel, stretching across the Firth from Dunoon to the Cloch Lighthouse. Often the gate opened to let out the Clyde section of a convoy, or to let in one of the great liners bringing thousands of troops from America. Occasionally there was an even bigger shipping movement, as in the autumn of 1942, when much of the invasion force for North Africa, Operation 'Torch', sailed from the Clyde.

In the open waters of the Firth below Dunoon, every kind of naval activity was taking place. Aircraft carriers exercised and trainee pilots practised deck landing. Submarines were based just to the north, in the Holy Loch, and a few miles south in Rothesay Bay. Landing craft practised at Toward Point, just along the coast, and there were Combined Operations bases at Troon and Largs on the other side. Midget submarines trained in Loch Striven nearby for an attack on the great German battleship *Tirpitz*. In the village of Fairlie on the other side of the Firth, the Admiralty had set up its main anti-submarine research establishment, and officers looked to it for the latest techniques and tactics in the war against the U-boat.

The surroundings were charming as well as busy, but the aspiring ASCO had very little time to appreciate them. His course was only twelve days long, and he had a lot to take in. *Osprey* had a large staff, headed by Captain G. M. K. Keble-White in 1941, and Commander P. W. Burnett was in charge of training – 'probably one of the keenest minds' among the 'top flight men in anti-submarine warfare', according to Cherry.[22] In September 1943 there were eighteen anti-submarine officers on the staff, four junior officers of the RNVR special branch on technical duties, eight warrant officers, known quaintly as 'Boatswains, Anti-Submarine', and eighteen members of the schoolmaster branch, mostly for teaching technical subjects to ratings. There were also 62 petty officer submarine detector instructors, for training both officers and ratings. There were usually several dozen officers doing short and long courses at any given moment, including about forty temporary members of the RNVR. *Osprey* carried out the early stages of submarine detector rating training; hence the presence of the schoolmasters, who taught the scientific theory. The second half of that course was spent at HMS *Nimrod*, 50 miles away in Campbeltown, where sea training took place and the men lived in far less comfortable conditions.

A new officer arriving at *Osprey* might glean the most up-to-date information from the *Monthly Anti-Submarine Report*, the 'Red Book'. This was a magazine produced in the Anti-Submarine Warfare Division of the Admiralty and based on the latest intelligence. It was edited by a Welsh solicitor and RNVR lieutenant-commander, J. C. P. de Winton, and issued to all major warships. Cherry found that it gave 'straightforward accounts of enemy actions by the men who fought them, analysis of our own efforts and all sorts of interesting information gathered from confidential sources and from ships at sea.'[23] Its pages were crammed with the latest information on the U-boat war, and the cover warned recipients:

SECRET

This book is the property of H M Government.

It is intended for the use of recipients only, and for communication to such officers under them (not below commissioned officer) who may require to be acquainted with its contents in the course of their duties. The officers exercising this power will be held responsible that such information is imparted with due caution and reserve.

A typical issue, in January 1943, included regular features such as a review of the month, an account of merchant shipping losses, reports and maps on RAF Coastal Command activities, remarks on the main convoys and a record of the number of officers and men trained in anti-submarine warfare. It had special articles such as the history of *U-660*, which had just been sunk, an analysis of U-boat operations around convoy ON 144, a report on the activities of a Lockheed Hudson aircraft of RAF Coastal Command and features on the work of the United States Navy. The magazine often included intelligence reports based on the interrogation of U-boat survivors, but in general these said more about morale than about tactics and techniques. Some of the men, for example, had served terms in concentration camps for offences such as 'suspected treasonable activities'. Far more were vaguely disgruntled and it was said that some of them 'speak with loathing of their service in the U-boats, which they find very different from what they had been led by propaganda to expect. Some said that they would never have joined the U-boat arm if they had known what active service was going to be like.' The moral from such interrogations was perhaps that sailors will always grumble, the essential message was that, however bad things seem on the surface of the Atlantic, they were far worse for the U-boat men below it.

Asdic, later known as sonar, was the main means of detecting submarines underwater. It had been developed at the end of the previous war and gave the Royal Navy undue confidence that the submarine had been mastered. According to the Shipping Defence Advisory Committee in 1937,

The submarine menace will never be ... what it was before. We have means of countering a submarine which are very effective and which will normally reduce our losses from that weapon. It will never be ... a fatal menace again as it was in the last war. We have taken effective steps to prevent that.[24]

Radio was ineffective underwater, but a sound wave could be directed accurately. A transponder was mounted under the forward hull of a ship inside the so-called asdic dome, which could be retracted in ships capable of high speed, such as destroyers. It would send a 'ping' out through the water in a specific direction and measure the time taken by any echo it received. Thus both the range and bearing of any suspicious underwater object could be measured. The most common asdic set from 1941 onwards was Type 144. This differed from previous models in that it could be set to train automatically during a search or a hunt, taking some pressure off the operators. Older sets already had a range recorder, which gave a visual record of the distance of an echo over time, and an improved version was fitted on Type 144. It also had a bearing recorder, which gave a record of the target's angle in relation to the ship. It had an automatic volume control receiver that offered 'general improvements in detection, including better recording of echoes on the range recorder'.[25]

In the range recorder, a stylus moved across a piece of paper and marked a line according to the length of the asdic transmission. If there was an echo, it appeared as a darker area along the line. The paper then moved on automatically to be ready for the next transmission. Apart from their obvious value in assessing the range of any target, these traces might give an indication of its extent and whether it had clearly defined edges, all valuable information in assessing whether it was a submarine or not, its attitude in relation to the ship, and it movements.

The bearing recorder, new to the type 144, was also based on a stylus and a moving roll of paper. During a hunt, one of the operators would press a button to make a mark, either with each echo received or only with those that defined the edge of the target. Thus if the target was at constant distance, it would form two parallel lines. If the ship were closing, and the enemy took no evasive action, it would form a widening cone. If, as was more likely, the enemy was moving in one direction or another, it would show two curves gradually separating.

The signals were received and interpreted in the asdic office or hut. This was fitted in the vicinity of the bridge in most wartime ships, allowing the ASCO or officer of the watch to look at the recorder traces of any echo. In corvettes and frigates it was usually in a cramped compartment just forward of the bridge. Late in the war it was fitted down below in some ships, eventually leading to the concept of an action information centre or operations room well below decks. The standard hut for Type 144 was a little under six feet high and about the same in length, and about four feet wide, with a sloping roof. It had a table for about two-thirds of its width, with a bench on which three men could sit if required. In the centre of the table was the instrument for controlling the training of the asdic, whether automatically or by hand. The bearing recorder was mounted to the left of that, the range recorder to the right. Various instruments were mounted on the panel in front, and space was left to the right of the table for future fitting of depth-determining asdic, as soon as this became available. Often there was a small booth-like covered entrance for the ASCO to place himself and keep in communication with the bridge.

The asdic was operated by submarine detector, or SD, ratings, who were also trained at *Osprey* and *Nimrod* in large numbers. Each had a 'non-substantive' rating within the seamen branch, in the same way as gunnery ratings, torpedomen and physical-training instructors. The branch expanded hugely during the war, from 797 SDs in 1939, to nearly 6,000 at the start of 1945. Most of them were HOs and were sent to *Osprey* or *Nimrod* after basic training. The film *Meeting the U-Boat Menace* encouraged them to volunteer. It showed two trainees, one serious and one cocky, meeting a leading seaman who persuades them to volunteer for the Submarine

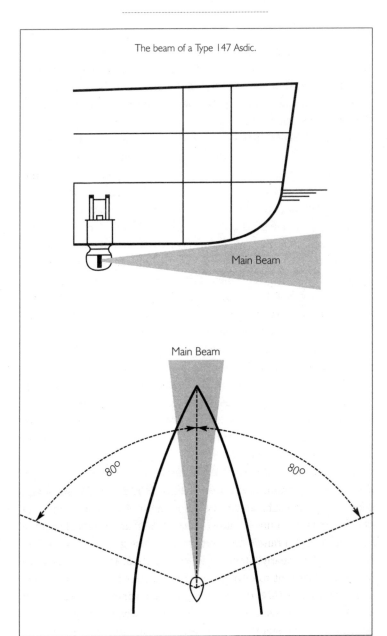

The beam of a Type 147 Asdic.

Main Beam

Main Beam

80°   80°

Detector Branch. After training, they sink a U-boat, apparently without calling out the more senior SDs on board. It ends with the two of them sitting in a pub overhearing a conversation about food supply and looking lovingly at their badges. However successful it was in attracting men, it got howls of laughter when shown at Campbeltown, especially when one of the trainees writes home, 'The girls are good and the beer is better.' Submarine detectors came in three classes. The basic SD was capable of operating an asdic set; a higher submarine-detector or HSD could take charge of a ship's team; while an instructor, or SDI, was nearly always employed on shore duties at one of the bases, instructing the ASCOs as well as the trainee SDs.

The standard asdic team in an escort vessel consisted of six men headed by a Higher Submarine Detector, who was usually a leading seaman. This allowed two men on watch at once when the ship was at three watches, with one actually operating the set. Great concentration was needed, and each operator did a twenty-minute or half-hour spell until the other took over. When not scanning, he was employed on other duties in the area and was ready to get to the set quickly if a contact was detected. Officers worried that men found it difficult to concentrate during a long convoy. Doctors suggested that the main issue was 'aural fatigue', but those who knew the situation believed that it was just normal boredom after weeks when nothing happened. One suggestion was to give an incentive by selecting men as 'Good Submarine Detectors' and to add an underclass of partly-trained men for use when there was no immediate danger. Another was to fit a 'signal injector' so that an officer could produce a spurious echo to keep the men on their toes. But in general it was recognized that this was a matter of morale, and captains and ASCOs were reminded of 'the necessity of arousing interest in the ratings on watch to keep them in the tactical picture and thus keep them alert'.[26]

By day, when a U-boat was only likely to attack submerged, each escort normally had its asdic sweeping through an arc of 160 degrees. Usually this was 80 degrees on each side of the ship, but this might be modified to take account of the positions of other escorts. A Type 144 set could be set to transmit automatically every five degrees, and the operator only had to reverse its direction at the end of every sweep. He was able to concentrate on the range recorder for any sign of an echo.

At night-time or in poor visibility, when U-boats were more likely to attack on the surface, the escort group commander might continue to use the same sweeping method, or he might order the asdics to go over to 'hydrophone effect'. This meant that they no longer transmitted, but the operator listened for the noise of a U-boat's propellers, engines and movements. Several types of noises might be heard. Whistle effect could be caused by fish, in which case it lasted for a second or less, and was a 'chirrup' or squeak. It lasted much longer if it came from a submarine and sounded like 'a creaking hinge or the groan of a boiler feed pump'. It might be possible to hear a ship's echo-sounding, used to determine depth of water, at some distance. It could be distinguished by its regular beat. The asdic transmissions of a submarine could be picked out aurally, but they were not likely to be using them in operational areas. Propeller noise could be far more useful, both when heard on its own and in determining whether an echo was a submarine.

Hydrophone effect (HE) was more likely to detect a boat on the surface, though that was not so important if the escorts were well equipped with radar. An arc could be swept more quickly with hydrophone effect, and a noisy U-boat could be detected at greater range. It might also be possible to hear the sounds of torpedoes being fired. Conversely, echo detection would work better if the enemy boat were moving slowly and quietly. It could be carried out when one's own ship was moving quite quickly, whereas with HE the noise of the movement would blot out any signals being received. It was also less affected by weather, but, most important of all, HE did not give any more than the vaguest indication of range.

Perhaps the most important task was the classification of an echo once it was obtained – as 'submarine', 'possible submarine' or 'non-sub'. The stakes were very high. When Mallalieu's shipmates were kept up all night because the HSD believed he had a contact, they complained about being 'fetched out of bed for a lot of bleeding mackerel'.[27] At the other extreme, the risk of underestimating a contact was even greater. Able Seaman James Hasty and Ordinary Seaman Edward Millichope of frigate *Tweed* classified an echo as 'non-sub' on 7 January 1944. The junior officer of the watch quickly queried this, claiming, 'That is a good trace.' A hydrophone effect was then heard on the same bearing, but the alarm was sounded too late – a torpedo broke the ship in half. An enquiry concluded:

> That blame for the torpedoing of H.M.S. 'TWEED' must rest with the cabinet crew … in that they did fail to report the suspicious echo in time for the officer of the watch to take effective action. These ratings were fully trained and their fault was due to negligence. It was reasonable to entrust to them the duty which they were carrying out. They are both deceased.[28]

As the official instructions suggested,

> A classification of 'Submarine' means that the contact sounds like a submarine and has all the characteristics of a submarine which are apparent to a first operator. As there are also other important clues which are not available to him, such a classification should never be treated as conclusive, and no operator should be considered incompetent or over-optimistic merely because a contact reported by him as 'Submarine' turns out to be something else.

At the same time, operators were warned not to cover themselves by reporting everything as 'possible submarine'.

An echo could represent one of many things, each with slightly different characteristics. A submarine should produce a clear and short echo, though it might be longer if the boat were end-on. Some echoes were only obtained in shallow water – a wreck on the bottom might be identified from the chart unless it was very recent; a rock or a shoal was often woolly and long-drawn out and should be marked on the chart; tidal races had large and inconstant echoes and produced an irregular trace. In deeper water, the wake of a ship was woolly and had large extent, so it could probably be checked by observation from the bridge. It had no Doppler effect – its pitch did not change as it moved through the water. The area of an explosion, such as of a depth-charge, was woolly, had no Doppler and was over quickly, but it could conceal the movements of a submarine behind it. A submarine could release a bubble target (see page 216) to confuse its pursuers, and it was not easy to identify, though it had no Doppler. Later ships with depth-finding asdic could identify it by its height, which was much greater than that of a submarine. A column of water created by a wreck that was still sinking could also be identified in this way, and also by observation of the sinking from the bridge and by plotting it. A bottom echo might be caused by part of the asdic beam being reflected downwards, and could be recognized by its constant range on the recorder.

Marine life also caused problems. In May 1943 one escort group in the middle of a great convoy battle passed through 'the Western Ocean Whales Spring Mating Ground':

Numerous fish echoes of exceptional clarity were obtained and frequently the recorder markings would show a pair of fish [sic] coming together and separating. Echoes of every varying amplitude on the R.D.F. scan gave evidence of the great beasts thrashing on the surface in amorous ecstasy. Before the situation was appreciated JED interrupted one romance with a ten-charge Minol pattern. I myself have witnessed a pair of whales once performing the procreative act. It is a rare and impressive sight but I can only conclude that it was the illusion of privacy fostered by the fog coupled with the unwonted spring heat that gave rise to the surely unparalleled orgy on this occasion.[29]

The MASR (Monthly Anti-Submarine Report) showed pictures of

whales on the surface, comparing their profiles with those of U-boats. A whale could be identified by its small extent and inconstant echoes, its noises and its irregular movements, which were different from those of a U-boat. A shoal of fish might be of wide extent and variable movements, and gave a crooked, irregular edge to the trace.

The ASCO was urged to consider it 'his duty to attain competence in this work', though it could not be taken for granted by the captain, who was often the better judge. As distinct from the SDs, the officers were better placed to assess other factors that might affect the classification – objects shown on the chart, the proximity of other ships and the anti-submarine plot.

If a 'submarine' contact were identified, the SD on the bridge closed up immediately to join his colleague already on the set, and both men maintained contact with the object. The crew was called to action stations, the HSD came on duty, and the three most skilled operators took over the operation of the asdic. If any suspicious echo were heard in a dangerous position ahead of the convoy, the escort would begin a counterattack immediately, then hoist a warning signal to the convoy and begin to classify the contact. In any other position it would classify the contact first, hoist the warning signal, report by radio if it was classified as 'submarine' and drop a depth-charge in any case if it was considered doubtful.[30]

Having found a probable submarine, it was the duty of the ship to hunt it, subject to the needs of the convoy and the orders of the escort commander. This would probably take all the skill of the ASCO and the rest of the team. During a hunt, one of the SDs operated the bearing recorder, another the range recorder, and the HSD sat between them pressing the echo button, which recorded the mark on the recorder paper. They used the 'step across' method to stay in contact with the target and find its extent and movements. The asdic beam itself was several degrees wide, and a submarine also covered several degrees of bearing as it was approached – sixteen to twenty degrees if it was beam-on and at a range of 1,500 yards. It was important to find the 'cut-ons' on each side – the points where the echo ceased, marking the edges of the contact. The operator trained across the target in steps of five degrees until the echoes ceased; then he reversed the operation to sweep back in two-and-a-half-degree steps until the echoes resumed. He continued this until the echoes ceased on the other side, and the extent of the target was found. This gave some indication of whether it was beam- or stern-on, while the range recorder showed the distance away,

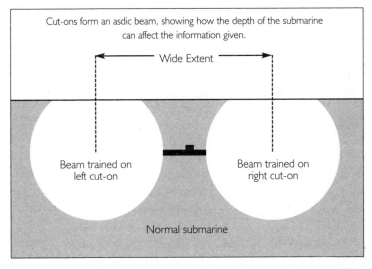

Cut-ons form an asdic beam, showing how the depth of the submarine can affect the information given.

Wide Extent

Beam trained on left cut-on

Beam trained on right cut-on

Normal submarine

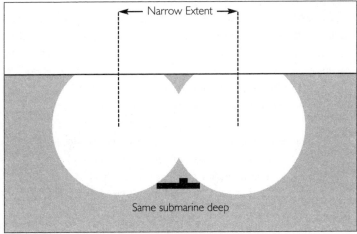

Narrow Extent

Same submarine deep

presumably narrowing as the ship closed on its target. The cut-ons had to be found constantly as the submarine manoeuvred and tried to escape, and it became more difficult as the contact became closer.

During all this, the ASCO's main job was to pass ranges and bearings to the plotting team. This was usually headed by the navigation officer and worked under cover somewhere in the structure of the bridge, according to the type of ship – in a corvette or frigate it was usually forward of the compass platform where the officer of the watch or the captain stood, alongside the asdic compartment. In a destroyer it was often in the wheelhouse. More sophisticated ships used the Admiralty Research Laboratory plotting table, which automatically recorded the ship's own movements on paper, so the plotting team only had to lay off the bearings and distance of any asdic or radar contact to trace the movements of a target. In smaller ships, the plotting team had to record their own movements and those of the target. The plot would give a good indication of the U-boat's movements, whereas the pure asdic information only showed its position in relation to the ship. It might help in classifying a contact, plus it gave some indication of what tactics the U-boat captain was using and whether he actually knew he was being chased. If contact were lost, it might give some idea where to search.

One mistake often made by inexperienced operators was to follow the wake of the submarine instead of the boat itself. This could be counteracted by looking carefully at the range trace, in which the wake was often seen as a separate mark a small distance from the true echo. Contact might be lost at some stage, in which case ASCOs and SDs were urged not to give up too easily:

Most ratings are too reluctant to start the present lost contact procedure. The report 'lost contact' is also frequently misinterpreted by the A/S Control Officer to mean that the submarine's position cannot even be estimated. It is hoped that these faults will be overcome by the initial report after losing contact being altered to 'no echoes', and by the operator being allowed to start the procedure whenever he is in doubt about his contact ... After reporting 'no echoes' the operator therefore cuts a big step of 20 degrees aft and investigates back to the last bearing. Unless contact is regained the investigation is continued through a total arc of 40 degrees, and if contact is not regained the operator then reports 'lost contact'.[31]

At a range of about 1,500 to 1,000 yards from the contact, the hunt would turn into an attack. This gave a chance to settle on a course for the final approach, while the U-boat's movements were observed and the course adjusted until the final stage at a range of 500 yards. At around this point the asdic would be set to a larger scale to show the contact in more detail. The captain had by now decided the means of attack.

The depth-charge formed the main armament of most anti-submarine vessels. It was simply a canister filled with high-explosive and fitted with a weight to sink it at a predictable rate. It had a fuze or pistol, which reacted to hydrostatic pressure and could be set to explode at a specific depth. It could be simply dropped into the water over the stern of a ship or fired a short distance away from it by means of depth-charge throwers on each side of the stern. The depth-charge armament was not under the direct supervision of the ASCO, for an escort vessel usually had a depth-charge officer as well – Nicholas Monsarrat conceded that he was 'not the skilful fellow who operated our Asdic set to decide when the depth-charges should be dropped, but the man who actually rolled them over the stern or splayed them out from the throwers ...'[32] But the ASCO needed precise knowledge of the characteristics of the depth-charge armament if he was to direct a successful attack.

The most common type of depth-charge, the Mark VII, could be set at depths of 50, 100, 150, 250 and 350 feet. The Mark VII Heavy version had extra weigh to make it sink quicker, at 16.5 feet per second instead of 10 feet, and could be set at six depths between 140 and 700 feet, with an extra-deep setting if needed. Originally they were all filled with amatol, a mixture of TNT and ammonium nitrate. Later they used minol, which added twenty per cent of ammonium powder and gave increased explosive power.

A single depth-charge was unlikely to destroy the target. As the ship got close to the U-boat it would lose the echo, and after that a good deal of guesswork was involved. It needed to maintain a certain minimum speed as it dropped its charges, to avoid its own stern being blown off. A standard Flower-class corvette firing a ten-charge pattern had to be moving at a minimum of nine knots to be safe, but one carrying the more powerful minol charges had to do at least fourteen knots. Meanwhile the submarine might well have taken evasive measures in the minutes since it was last heard on the asdic. Also, there was no easy and accurate way of determining a submarine's depth until Type 147 asdic was introduced in 1943. But the charge had to explode reasonably close, within about 25 feet, to sink a U-boat and about 100 feet to do real damage. The only answer was to saturate the area with a large number of depth-charges.

Early in the war a fourteen-charge pattern was in use, but each ship had a limited supply and could not use it too often. Moreover, with the new minol charges, it was found that one interfered with another. It was usually the captain who decided which pattern to use, based on the reliability and accuracy of the asdic contact, the tactical situation and the number of charges available. It was aimed at the 'theoretical centre' of the pattern, where the conning tower of the U-boat was expected to be. The ten-charge pattern was the most common one. To allow time for orders to be put into effect, the thrower-launched charges to travel though the air and for them to sink in the water, it was necessary to fire at least twelve seconds before passing over the target, with an allowance for any movement it might make. A four-second delay in firing would mean an error of 100 feet in the pattern. Starting at zero with the order to begin the pattern, one heavy charge would be dropped astern of the ship, from the rails. Three seconds later, a light charge would also be dropped from the rails – as it took less time to sink and would explode at almost the same time as the first charge. Two heavy charges would

A ten-charge depth charge pattern

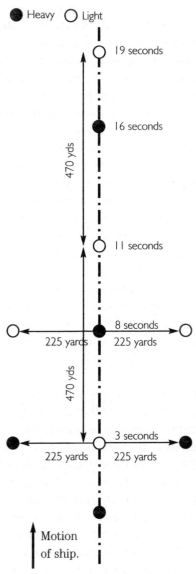

Heavy ● Light ○

○ 19 seconds

● 16 seconds

470 yds

○ 11 seconds

○ ← 225 yards ● 8 seconds 225 yards → ○

470 yds

● ← 225 yards ○ 3 seconds 225 yards → ●

●

↑ Motion of ship.

be also fired from the throwers, to land in the water about 225 feet on each side of the ship. Eight seconds into the pattern, a heavy was released from the rails, and a light was fired on each side; at eleven seconds another light was dropped from the rails, then a heavy at sixteen seconds and a light at nineteen seconds. The effect, if the ship was doing fifteen knots, was to produce two exploding diamond patterns, one above the other, 450 feet wide and 470 feet long. The explosions were dramatic when heard and felt from the surface and did as much to bolster morale in the convoy as to frighten the enemy. But they were not necessarily lethal, and only about six per cent of depth-charge attacks were successful during 1943–5. If the escort were not running out of charges and did not have to hurry to rejoin the convoy, more and more attacks could be made. Ideally a U-boat could be 'hunted to exhaustion' and forced to surface as its air ran out after perhaps 48 hours, without necessarily being damaged. But that depended on enough escorts being available, which was not the case early in the war.

A five-charge pattern could be used by some ships which did not have the full equipment or if supplies were running short or a contact was uncertain. It had the same diamond shape but on one level only. Very heavy patterns of 26 and 28 charges were developed for 'creeping attack', usually by support groups such as the famous Second Escort Group led by Captain F. J. Walker, which had no convoy of their own to tie them down and could afford to spend a long time destroying a contact.

Much of this could be learned on the Attack Teacher AS 63, a simulator 'produced to meet the training requirements for a ship's Asdic team, consisting of the Captain, A/S/C.O., plotter and one S.D. operator. In this the sound effects and plotting mechanisms were combined in a single table. The method used was ingenious and realistic.'[33] Cherry experienced it late in 1941:

> We closed up for exercise ... A quartermaster at the wheel, the A/S operator at his sound gear, Officer-of-the-Watch, who was myself, and the Captain. The operator started sweeping his arc and the drill commenced.
>
> Suddenly: 'Echo ... Green three oh,' the sound operator shouted, and the attack was one [sic], 'Range two thousand yards.'
>
> The sweep instantly narrowed down to a small arc governed by a left and right side of the U-boat caught in the sound beam. The warship altered to a collision course and went into attacking speed. Information commenced pouring in to the Officer-of-the-Watch who sifted and passed it on to the Captain: information such as the U-boat's up-to-the-minute course and speed, range and bearings; all essential for the fast approaching moment of 'Fire'.[34]

The problem of losing contact with the target as it passed under the ship could be solved by firing weapons ahead of the ship. The

Hedgehog, developed at Fairlie and put into service in 1941, was an attempt to do this. It consisted of 24 charges mounted in six rows on a base placed forward in the ship. They could be fired up to fifteen degrees to either side. On the order to fire, they would be projected forward, one after another in a fast ripple effect. They would land in a circle 30 yards in diameter, with its centre 215 yards from the ship, and sink at the rate of 25 feet per second. They were contact-charges rather than depth-charges so, except in case of misfire, there would only be an explosion if something was hit. This meant that the charges could be much smaller than depth-charges, with 35 pounds of explosive instead of 290.

Hedgehog needed rather more sophisticated aiming techniques than simply dropping a pattern of depth-charges, and unfortunately it was rushed into service ahead of rival systems without adequate training for the crews. It had to be mounted well forward in the ship, often in an exposed position, as in the case of the River-class frigates, so its delicate electrical systems were often damaged by seawater. It also lacked the moral effect of depth-charge explosions, so captains became reluctant to use it. Admiralty orders to employ it as often as possible were counterproductive in that it was often fired in unsuitable circumstances. After that, it was in danger of falling into disuse until a series of trials off Londonderry early in 1944 allowed it to find its full potential. Then it had a success rate of 28 per cent, compared with six per cent for depth-charges until a series of trials off Londonderry highlighted the faults in training and technique and allowed it to find its full potential.

A Hedgehog attack began at a range of about 1,200 yards and was carried out at a speed of eight to twelve knots, preferably the lower speed unless the U-boat was moving fast. The team in the hut consisted of the best asdic operator in the ship, who had to take frequent cut-ons as the distance narrowed; the range operator; an SD who worked the recorder; and the bearing operator, who might be an officer or an SD, reporting the centre-line bearings of the target and working out any deflection needed to counteract the submarine's movements. It was possible to set the ship to automatic

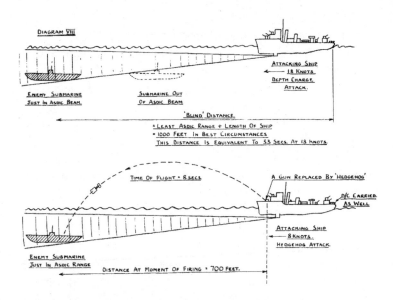

The advantages of attacking by Hedgehog. The first picture shows a depth-charge attack, in which the submarine disappears from the Asdic beam while the attacking ship passes over it. In the second picture, the Hedgehog is fired well before the submarine is reached. (National Archives)

control, so that the helmsman followed the course directly from the asdic operators, without any intervention by the captain. A second operator stood by in the crowded hut to check bearings. Another rating, the transmitter operator, sent the bearing to the Hedgehog operators. The ASCO's job was to supervise and assist all that, to pass the bearings on to the plot and receive any information it might produce on the U-boat's course and speed. The captain was free to take in the general tactical situation. The weapon was fired as soon as the range and bearing were suitable.[35]

Hedgehog's main rival was Squid, which took longer to get into service and was first used in 1944. It fired three depth-charges instead of contact-charges, and this time good care was taken to train the crews properly. It formed the main armament of the new Loch-class frigates, which replaced the Rivers in the shipyards, and

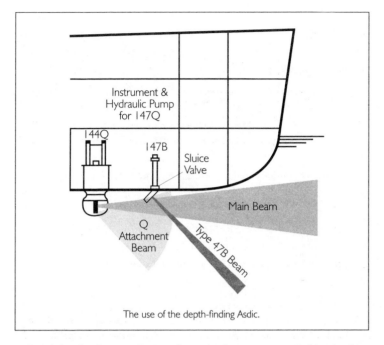

Instrument &
Hydraulic Pump
for 147Q

144Q

147B

Sluice
Valve

Main Beam

Q
Attachment
Beam

Type 47B Beam

The use of the depth-finding Asdic.

refitted Castle-class corvettes. It proved very successful in the last stages of the war, with a success rate of 30 per cent for a single mounting and 40 per cent if two were fitted side-by-side.

Captains and ASCOs had to be constantly aware of any changes in U-boat tactics, and the *Monthly Anti-Submarine Report* did its best to keep them informed. By the end of 1942 it was believed that after a torpedo attack a U-boat would probably move away at high speed on the surface – if forced to dive, he would go to a depth that depended on several factors, 'not the least important being the temperament of the Commanding Officer'. Another possibility was that he would stay close to a merchant ship he had just torpedoed and perhaps try to get to its other side to confuse his pursuers. At night he would often remain shallow, hoping to surface and either escape or resume the attack. If he were heavily hunted, either by day or night, he might go as deep as 600 feet, and at that stage British asdics had no accurate way of determining depth. It should not be assumed that he would go deep, however. A U-boat was unlikely to stay in the area after a depth-charge attack if he was still capable of movement. He could also release a submarine bubble target, a series of chemical tablets that would dissolve in the water and create a bubble that appeared very like the echo of a U-boat, lasting up to 30 minutes. ASCOs were warned how to distinguish this, as its pitch did not change.[36]

Given time and enough ammunition, officers were expected to pursue a U-boat to the end. '*A dead U-boat is dead, a damaged one may live to fight again.*'[37] If a U-boat hunt appeared to be successful, officers should find conclusive evidence – 'the only reliable proof of the destruction of a U-boat is the presence of internal wreckage or the U-boat surfacing and abandoning ship.'[38] Mallalieu's commanding officer followed this as his men searched for remains.

'Get that bit of wood. And that one. Reach for it. Reach for it. Now bring it up here. And what's that thing there? A glove? Is there a hand in it? Pity! The Admiralty would have liked a hand. Still, bring it out. What's that piece of paper? Fish 'em all out and let's have a look at them'[39]

Perhaps the most important development in the later stages of the war was the introduction of the asdic set that could determine the depth of a contact. Older sets had a beam that only projected about ten degrees downwards in the vertical plane, and any contact outside that was lost. The answer to this was to fit the Q attachment, which converted this into a very narrow beam of 45 degrees in the vertical plane. That indicated the presence of a deep U-boat, but not its precise depth. The anti-submarine branch was now aware of three main requirements for use with ahead-throwing weapons in modern conditions – information on the course to steer one's own ship, on the time to fire the charges, and the depth of the enemy. It was decided to fit an additional asdic set, the Type 147, solely to determine depth. Combined with Squid, it produced a very effective anti-U-boat system.

There was constant research at Dunoon, Campbeltown, Fairlie and in the United States on how water conditions could affect asdic performance. In November 1942 for example, the *Monthly Anti-Submarine Report* carried an article on velocity gradients, caused by differing salinity and temperatures. At that stage British ships did not operate in the Baltic or the Dardanelles, where different steams of water met, making the problem most acute. It could be a problem in the Mediterranean generally, where different layers of water were created in the summer. Lack of detailed information on the phenomenon was no excuse for failure, and the article concluded,

> Water conditions are never bad enough to warrant abandonment of asdic operations in war time. 'Bad' conditions, however, call for greater skill on the part of all concerned, not only from the operator but from the Commanding Officer and the A/S Control Officer.[40]

The course at Dunoon was very intensive. Cherry had worked hard, and found the course highly stimulating. 'I got so I could mentally carry a picture of a U-boat's under-water movements and instantly anticipate the new course to steer to place a warship in a position to attack. I had never encountered a phase of naval warfare so intensely exciting.'[41]

There was little time for leisure, and on one occasion he was invited to the cinema. 'Come, Yank ... You can explain some of the Americanisms to me.' One Sunday evening in December 1941, the officers gathered:

> Already officers were flowing into the Wardroom for the pink gin before dinner. Commander Langlands and I went to our cabins. I hurriedly washed and changed into wing collar and bow tie and went below to the spacious foyer to await

Langlands. Little groups of officers stood about in the large Wardroom, chatting over drinks. A few lounged in soft chairs and browsed through periodicals as they sipped their drinks.

The scene was interrupted when it was announced that Pearl Harbor had been attacked and America was now in the war.[42]

More than 8,000 officers were trained as ASCOs during the war, and a large majority of them were temporary RNVR. Back in his ship, the trained ASCO was a vital link in the operational chain, but sometimes a rather weak one. He had undergone twelve days' training; the submarine detectors under him had had six weeks, while the most senior one, the HSD, had probably done many voyages in the role. The SDs could concentrate on one task and were carefully protected against damage to their hearing by gunfire. Often the HSD was the real leader of the team in action. In the destroyer *Fortune*, Sub-Lieutenant Roderick Macdonald noticed, 'Our anti-submarine expertise depended entirely on the skill of the H.S.D. ... sensible, careful Leading Seaman Clark. Poor Matthews, the nominally responsible officer, knew little of the technique, and nothing of the tactics. This was the Navy's fault.'[43] The situation became even more difficult towards the end of the war, when new devices like Squid and Type 144Q asdic demanded even higher skills.[44] Like nearly all temporary officers during the war, the ASCO had to make the best of very hasty training in the unforgiving battlefield of the sea.

8
AMPHIBIOUS WARFARE

Early in 1942 Peter Bull, fresh from his course at *King Alfred*, joined his first ship as an officer. He searched the harbour at Middlesbrough for Tank Landing Craft 168 and was horrified to see that she was one of a series of steel barges in the middle of the river, looking like 'a cross between a coal shovel (large size) and an empty water trough'. Such vessels had barely been mentioned in *King Alfred*, and only in hushed whispers – Captain Pelly, Edward Crick and CPO Vass had all known a very different navy. Bull was shocked even more when one of the crew told him, 'Skipper's gone to the match with the missus. You the new Jimmy?' He thought, 'Only a few weeks ago I had viewed *In Which We Serve*, and I did not remember anyone talking to Mr Coward in that way'.[1] *Bulldozer*, the Combined Operations Magazine, quoted another example of that attitude, when a senior officer came on board and was approached by a rating. 'Want to see the skipper, sir? He's on board. Whereabouts? Oh, down in his cabin, sir. You'll find him down aft. Along that way, sir.'[2]

The problem was that the landing craft of Combined Operations were entirely new in concept and design, techniques were being rapidly developed by practical experience, and Combined Operations, even more than other branches such as minesweeping and Coastal Forces, was on the fringes of the navy.

The great majority of British wars have involved some kind of amphibious operations, though they were not in the forefront of the most recent one from 1914 to 1918. Troops had landed to seize enemy colonies dozens of times in the last few centuries, mostly rowed ashore in ships' boats, occasionally with specially designed flat-bottomed versions for landing on beaches. By 1940 the situation had changed radically. The development of modern firepower and mass armies meant that an invader was less likely to find a quiet spot to land unopposed. Moreover, he could not expect to last very long on shore without artillery, armoured vehicles, transport and the fuel and supplies needed to maintain them. Air support was essential, but it had to be very carefully directed towards precise targets on the battlefield. Most important of all, amphibious warfare was no longer something on the fringes of the main campaign. To win the war, Britain and her allies would have to re-enter the continent of Europe at some stage, against fierce resistance.

In the planning stages, the greatest burden of this fell on the navy. The air force would be fully involved in any landing, but its aircraft and men would have to carry out such tasks as photo-reconnaissance, fighter protection and bombing, which was what they did anyway. The army would provide the bulk of the personnel; they would face a very uncomfortable voyage, and they would have to learn new skills in getting themselves and their vehicles ashore. But after that, they would soon move on and fight on land as they had always done. The navy, however, had to provide thousands of specially designed ships and boats that were not much use for anything else, and tens of thousands of officers and men trained to use them.

Winston Churchill was always reluctant to get involved in a land war in Europe too soon, for he had seen the trenches in the last conflict. Though he had to be pushed into the final decision to invade Normandy in 1944, he did envisage a return to Europe in some form within days of the Dunkirk evacuation, and he set up the Combined Operations Organisation to coordinate it. Its first head was Admiral of the Fleet Sir Roger Keyes, who had led a raid on Zeebrugge in 1918 and had as much experience of amphibious warfare as anyone else. He was original and dynamic, but his insistence of flooding Churchill with unwelcome suggestions led to his replacement in October 1941. Captain Lord Louis Mountbatten was well connected with the royal family; he was a already a popular hero after his exploits in the destroyer *Kelly* earlier that year; and he was full of ideas and self confidence. He inherited an organization geared mainly for raiding the enemy coastline and began to expand and transform it into one that could mount a full-scale invasion. He was given a rapid promotion to acting vice-admiral and the right to sit in on chiefs of staffs meetings with the heads of the navy, army and air force. He was to leave in September 1943 to become commander-in-chef in Burma, and by May of that year, Combined Operations had built up from almost nothing to a strength of nearly 5,500 officers, 38,000 men, 89 landing ships, 2,600 landing craft and more than a thousand barges.[3] During the Mountbatten era the crews wore naval uniform and had naval ranks, but technically they were not part of the navy proper. This ended under Mountbatten's successor, General Laycock, they were reintegrated with the Royal Navy and came under some kind of regular discipline.

The officer situation in Combined Operations was approaching a crisis as Bull arrived early in 1942. Mountbatten had declined to take on active service regular naval officers, and instead he relied on a few retired officers as squadron commanders and a huge number of temporary RNVR. Late in 1941 the Commodore of HMS *Quebec II* complained that very few of his officers had any substantial naval background, for they had never served as officers in a ship at sea under strict naval discipline. They were 'of an age when youthful enthusiasm and esprit de corps infuse them with the necessary energy to acquire experience', but this was not what they had expected when they joined the navy. Most had not volunteered for Combined Operations, though about 40 per cent of *King Alfred* graduates were appointed to it. Their status was low during training:

He next spends his time practising – for what? operations that never seem to come off. Hope deferred and the results we know. These results are very much brought out in Combined Operations exercises and one frequently hears remarks from the Military that are anything but complimentary, and there is no doubt that the Military are justified. They have been led to expect the best of the Navy and when they are brought up against these 'amateur' sailors who hardly know how to handle their craft let alone keep her clean, smart and shipshape, they certainly cannot be filled with confidence in their sister service.[4]

The young naval officers themselves were also lacking in confidence. In February 1942 the Captain Commanding Tank Landing Craft complained of 'the general failure of Landing Craft Officers to take charge'. When they landed on a beach, an army officer would be waiting to give them further instructions, and they tended to believe that they were under the command of the army. They had 'the wrong mental attitude' – they must begin to understand 'it is the sole responsibility of the navy to collect [the soldiers] from the right place and deliver them to the right place. This responsibility cannot be shared.'[5] A few regular officers were appointed to Combined Operations after that, and perhaps it was one of them who confronted Alec Guinness on a beach during an exercise in the summer of 1942 and accused him of not wearing a tie. Guinness saluted, turned round and pulled off his scarf to show that he was correctly dressed, but there was no apology. Guinness later consoled himself by using the officer as the model for the pig-headed Admiral D'Ascoyne in *Kind Hearts and Coronets*.[6]

For a man about be commissioned, Combined Operations was less exciting than destroyers or coastal forces, but it offered the chance of quick promotion and an early command. Mountbatten found that officers at *King Alfred* were putting Combined Operations at the bottom of their list of preferences – if they selected it at all. He made a point of visiting the base from time to time to meet the cadets. Most had destroyers as their first choice, and Mountbatten had no quarrel with that, considering his exciting life with the *Kelly*, but he urged them to consider Combined Operations as well. 'The result was that almost everybody put down their first choice as destroyers and their second choice as Combined Ops. There were few vacancies for destroyers, and we scooped the rest of the cream of the officer entry.'[7]

Some officers, like Alec Guinness, had already done their lower deck service in landing craft and needed no introduction. The majority had come from destroyers or cruisers, and Combined Operations was just as strange as their first ships had been when they went to sea as CWs. In the first instance they were sent to HMS

Northney in groups ranging from twelve to 30 men. This was a series of holiday camps near Portsmouth, which also trained seamen and engineers for the new vessels. HMS *Northney* I, where they worked, was at the north end of Hayling Island, reached from the mainland by a short bridge and situated on one of the numerous arms of Chichester Harbour, which largely dried out at low water. They lived in wooden huts which were 'in great need of repair' according to the medical officer.[8] The site was rather restricted and subject to bombing, but trainee officers learned the rudiments of the new craft before being sent north.

Inveraray was the oldest of the Combined Operations bases, set up in the summer of 1940 almost as soon as the Dunkirk evacuation had finished. It was on the shores of Loch Fyne, a three-hour bus ride from Glasgow – there was no railway, but army regiments sent there for training might go by special steamer from the Firth of Clyde. It was a planned village of considerable charm and dignity, built by the Dukes of Argyll, the heads of the Clan Campbell, in the late eighteenth century. It had a peacetime population of less than 500, but it was also the county town for Argyll and had a courthouse and jail. The Duke's castle, built in the eighteenth century in mock medieval style, was half-a-mile from the town. It was set in its own park, which was now covered with huts to accommodate the army. The naval headquarters was in the town itself. The main naval camps, known as HMS *Quebec* after the combined operation under General James Wolfe which captured that city in 1759, were two-and-a half miles south-west along the shores of the loch. There were more army camps in the town itself and at the head of Loch Shira, a mile to the north-east. Rear-Admiral L. E. H. Maund wrote that it was 'as far distant as possible from attack but yet within the umbrella of some fighter organization ... Here the rains might fall almost continuously, but it gave sheltered water and was, as it were, behind the defences of the Clyde.'[9] As well as training the army to operate with the navy, Inveraray was where new landing craft crews worked up under their officers, and it was also the pool for men awaiting drafting. It was taking in a dozen officers and about 150 men every fortnight from Northney. There was a pier in the town and several slipways near the naval encampment. The loch offered no less than 64 sites where men or vehicles could be landed, though it was rarely more than two miles wide and did not offer any opportunity for large-scale exercises.

After August 1942, not all landing craft officers were trained at *King Alfred*. LCTs and LSI(L)s, in particular, needed at least two officers apiece, with ten or fifteen ratings under them. This was a far higher proportion of officers to ratings than in general service, and *King Alfred* could not keep up with the demand. Furthermore, it was becoming recognized that the full *King Alfred* training was not always needed for a landing craft officer. However, the new course was no less demanding. It was felt that, 'The standard of physical fitness required for officers in the Combined Operations organization is, if anything, higher that that required for Executive Officers in General Service.' Education was slightly less important: 'Particular attention should be given to the selection of ratings showing powers of leadership, since the majority of officers will be required to command their own craft.'[10] But Commodore de Pass of the Royal Naval Patrol Service felt that this was not followed through in practice, when some of the men he had sent on were rejected even though they were 'men of quality though not of great polish ... experienced men of character and purpose'. They had tried to help younger men but were mortified when they were failed. According to the commodore, this meant, 'Practical seamen are not required. It was a question of education and accent.'[11]

The course was held in the tiny and remote west-coast Scottish village of Lochailort, reachable only by two trains per day on the West Highland Railway. It was publicized throughout the naval side of Combined Operations, and readers of the magazine *Bulldozer* were invited to

use a little introspection and see if you find in yourself some of the qualities that are wanted, remembering that the Nation

Above: Peter Bull's class at HMS *King Alfred*. He is on the far right in the back row, next to a leading seaman of at least eight years' service who is training as a cadet.

Left: Navigational exercises at HMS *King Alfred* in 1943. (IWM A 16423)

Above: The grandeur of the Painted Hall at Greenwich. (NMM H1969)

Opposite page, top: The wardroom of the destroyer *Javelin.* (IWM A 791)

Right: The Glasgow and West of Scotland Convalescent Home at Dunoon in more peaceful times.

Above: The Asdic team in the destroyer *Anthony*, with the Anti-Submarine Control Officer talking to the operator who is inside the Asdic hut. (IWM A 22617)

Below: A depth-charge attack by the sloop *Kite* in 1944. (IWM A 21989)

above: Alec Guinness and his crew in *LCI(L) 124*. (Alec Guinness Estate)

below: A group of LCTs training in preparation for the Normandy invasion. (IWM A 23734)

posite page, top: The bridge
a destroyer, with officers
ping a sharp lookout. The seat
the officer of the watch is in
centre, with the compass just
ward of that and speaking
es beside it. (IWM A 5667)

posite page, bottom: The
w of the ex-American
stroyer *Montgomery* dressed
for a photograph, with the
cers in the middle of the
ond row. (IWM A 6343)

ove: Some of the crew of
anthus in less formal dress
er sinking a U-boat.
M A 11947)

ght: Peter Gretton before his
motion to commander.

Below: In Tobermory toda shops and restaurants line the harbour, which makes a convenient anchorage f yachts.

wants leaders and wants them now, and that it is your duty if you think you can achieve it, to give all that you have got towards the Service to which you belong and not to be content with the fact that you have done enough already.

They were warned, however, that the course was a hard one:

when you leave the train after, perhaps, a 20-hour journey, you will march into the camp and the candidates on course will tell you that you swim the Loch each morning, you climb the highest mountain before breakfast and, having dodged a couple of land mines, you work in an open lecture room for eight hours. This has a fair semblance of truth in it.

Certainly the course demanded a high degree of physical fitness, but instruction also included:

'seamanship (mostly as applied to C.O. craft), handling of craft, divisional work and elementary knowledge of paper work required in a flotilla; navigation and pilotage from a coastal point of view; elementary tides, compasses, etc; signals (morse 8 w.p.m., semaphore 12 w.p.m. and theoretical signals as used in C.O.); gunnery (parade work for power of command. Sub-machine guns, only an elementary knowledge).[12]

Opinions varied about the success of the course. Paul Lund, who did it, thought that,

As seagoing officers in major and minor landing craft they would find that all their intensive physical training had been to little purpose. Most of their time at sea would be spent standing on the bridge of an LCT or LCI or in some minor landing craft; and the strain would not be so much physical as mental – keeping awake and alert for long periods of duty and being able to go for long periods without rest or sleep.[13]

The hamlet of Lochailort did not boast any kind of shopping facilities, and the naval tailors were not lured there, so newly commissioned candidates travelled home wearing the ratings' uniform but in first-class railway compartments, which caused some consternation among the class-conscious travellers of the day. One officer bought his uniform in Glasgow from a tailor with no naval experience, to find it had 'a Chief Petty Officer's buttons around each sleeve and an Engineer Cadet's purple patch with gold buttonhole as the tab'.[14]

Meanwhile the Royal Marines began to take on some of the duties of Combined Operations. They trained as commandos to raid enemy beaches, formed part or all of the crew of Landing Craft Gun and Flak, and began to train at Northney and in North Wales as the crews of minor landing craft, under their own officers.

New officers in Combined Operations had to get used to an amazing and bewildering array of initials. There were officers known as SNOL (Senior Naval Officer, Landing), and SOASC (Senior Officer, Assault Ships and Craft), and it took time to master a paragraph such as,

> The administration of these ships will be carried out through the normal channels, i.e., H.M. Ships and all Naval craft and personnel within any group mentioned above by the C.C.O. through the S.O.A.S.C, R.F.A.s by the Admiralty through the S.O.A.S.C, and the Merchant Navy Ships by the D. of S.T. through the P.S.T.O and D.S.T.O. appointed to the staff of the S.O.A.S.C.[15]

In addition, they had to learn the names of the craft themselves – LCA, LCM, LCT, LCT (R), LSI, LCVP and many more. Their designs had been inspired by various sources – ships' boats, lifeboats, pleasure craft, fishing boats, Thames barges, oil tankers, cargo ships and many others. But there were practical ways of dividing the real craft up, by size or function.

In size, there were three main categories – ships, major landing craft and minor landing craft. Ships were mostly conversions from merchant vessels, often passenger liners or cross-channel steamers. Their main function was to carry troops, vehicles or supplies on relatively long voyages and launch minor landing craft to take them to the beaches. They were usually commanded by RN or RNR officers unless they were manned by the Merchant Navy. They included the LSI or Landing Ship, Infantry, which came in several sizes; and the Landing Ships Gantry, Dock and Stern Chute, which were intended to launch craft into the water in various ways but remained rare during the war. They were usually commanded by RN or RNR officers unless they were manned by the Merchant Navy. Temporary RNVR could find a role on board the LSIs and other ships, in charge of the flotilla of landing craft which each carried.

The Landing Ship Tank, or LST, was a special case that broke most of the rules. It was a ship rather than a craft, but it was intended to carry its load all the way from the loading port to the beach and land its vehicles though doors in the bows. It originated with Churchill's desire for a ship that could take heavy equipment anywhere, and at first it was based on tankers used in the shallow waters of inland lakes. It was taken up by the Americans, and 115 of the Mark 2 version were supplied to the Royal Navy. It could carry up to eighteen tanks or 27 lorries and needed up to fourteen officers to run it. The captains were usually RNR, the junior officers RNVR.

Next came the major landing craft, which would load up with troops or tanks at one end and disembark them on a beach at the other – 'shore to shore' craft. These were almost entirely new and typically needed a crew of two or three officers and ten to fifteen ratings. They were built in huge numbers, and these were the craft that absorbed large numbers of temporary RNVR as commanding officers and first lieutenants. Finally there were the minor landing craft, designed to be launched from a landing ship except in very short-range operations such as river crossings. Each had a crew of three to six ratings, but they were organized in flotillas under officers, who were nearly all temporary RNVR.

Combined Operations vessels could also be divided by function, again in three classes. Some were mainly for carrying personnel, some for vehicles, and a third group, known as support craft, carried out a great variety of functions. They might form headquarters for a landing (LSH), launch rockets (LCT (R)) or provide kitchen facilities for other craft (LBK). Fighter direction (FD) ships made sure that the air cover operated with maximum efficiency. Substantial numbers of craft were used to provide gun support for landings, since they could go in far closer than conventional warships and engage in the land battle. Some were equipped with artillery weapons and were known as Landing Craft, Gun and manned by the Royal Marines. Others had an anti-aircraft armament and were called Landing Craft, Flak, or LCF. Harold Goodwin, a scriptwriter for training films, jokingly suggested the LCD (Landing Craft Dental), the LBT(P) or Landing Barge Table (Pin) and the LCK(T) or Landing Craft Kinema (Talking).[16]

Of the shore-to-shore vehicle-carrying craft, the Landing Craft Tank was by far the best known. The first version was designed in Britain in the dark ages of amphibious warfare in the late 1930s, and it was the first real heavy-vehicle landing craft in the world. Already it set the pattern for what was to follow – it had a flat bottom for beach landing, a shallow draft that was greater aft than forward, an opening ramp in the bows and the engines and crew's quarters aft, leaving a large open deck for tanks and other vehicles.

The next version, the LCT(2), was two feet wider but was difficult to handle:

The Mark 2 must have been designed by a madman. It had three Scott-Paine Sealion engines, using high-octane petrol, with a home-made reverse gear which required a man on each gear lever, each pulling back with all his strength to operate a friction band which had a life of 50 hours ... Although we had three engines there were only the usual double telegraphs, so we had to use our ingenuity to rig up a telegraph for the centre engine. This was the vital one, for the craft would only steer with the slipstream from this engine on to the single rudder in the centre.[17]

The LCT(3) was lengthened by adding an extra 32-foot section amidships, making a total length of 192 feet. It drew only 3 feet 10 inches of water forward and 7 feet 10 inches aft and could make a speed of ten knots. Its sailing qualities were not good by any conventional standards:

> When under way there was no feeling of cutting through the waves; instead, these craft 'butted' their way ahead. In rough weather, they suffered a fairly high degree of juddering, while in smooth weather progress was made by a sort of straight slide ... In addition these craft were powered by engines originally designed for tanks, and had both screws turning in the same direction, which caused a bias in their movement at slow speeds. In an LCT this was noticeable when coming alongside, especially when going astern. More than once I have seen a Royal Navy officer gallantly attempting to demonstrate to a newcomer the art of coming alongside, and making a considerable pot-mess of his endeavours.[18]

The LCT(4) was built largely by shore-based structural engineers, which raised some eyebrows among naval architects. Its general structural weakness caused it to be considered expendable, to carry out one landing only, but it proved tougher than expected. The standard of officers' accommodation was improved, if only slightly:

> Things got better with the Mark 4 in the way of fittings, but there was no change in the accommodation and for two men to live together in such conditions was an art that had to be learned by experience ... they had to live, eat, sleep, wash, shave, work and play in a tiny room about ten feet by six.[19]

Running an LCT demanded a high level of skill from everyone on

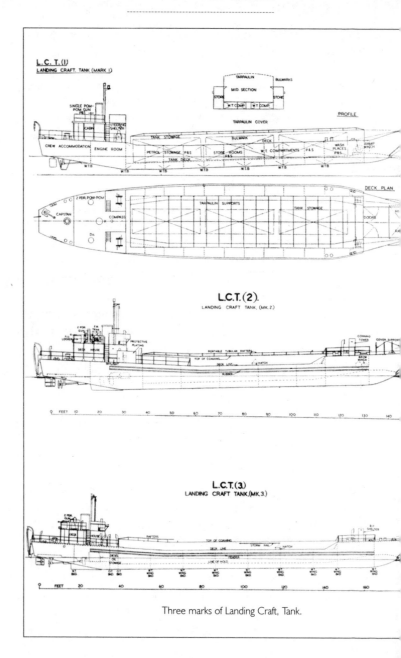

Three marks of Landing Craft, Tank.

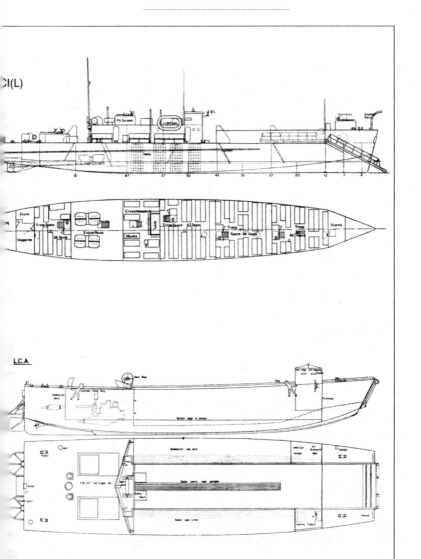

A Landing Craft, Assault for carrying a platoon of infantry.

board. It might be as large as a corvette, though with a much smaller crew, who had to be adaptable.

> Character is, perhaps, far more important in L.C.T.s than in any other craft. That is because with so small a crew in so small a space no one can adequately hide his real character as is the case in bigger ships. And the key to success and happiness in these craft is for each officer and man to aim a step higher than his rank or rating. The C.O. and First Lieut must realise they have got to be real leaders. They must continually aim at the state of mind in their crew when each man can say: 'Well, I'd follow him into any action.'
>
> Similarly coxswains are in effect doing the work of C.P.O.s: they are the 'Buffers' of L.C.T.s. If they realise that, they will make good coxswains. The way to make them feel that is to delegate more responsibility to them.
>
> Almost everybody aboard an L.C.T has to be better than he would be aboard a bigger ship.[20]

One of the greatest problems was the accommodation, for originally it had been expected that the crews would live ashore when not on operations, and they were fitted in a very Spartan manner, even by naval small-ship standards. This came as something of a shock to Peter Bull when he joined *LTC 168*, a Mark 2 vessel:

> Where I now found myself was in theory the galley, and certainly a large stove took up most of the space; but in a small alcove I espied two bunks one above another in a cubby-hole the size of a small wardrobe. Apart from two drawers under the bunks and a minute table affixed to the deckhead, this was all there was in the way of wardroom and cabins for the two officers. Separated from the galley by a blue curtain, it was still possible, as I soon discovered afterwards to my cost, to take a more than active interest in what was cooking.[21]

In the Mediterranean, the crew of *LCT 397* slung hammocks in the rear of the vehicle deck to avoid the heat of their quarters. They acquired timber to build a platform over it, and coconut matting to make it easier on their feet when they jumped out of their hammocks. The officers improved their conditions by removing the top bunk in the galley and fitting it in the wheelhouse for harbour use.[22] Later marks had slightly improved accommodation, but they were never comfortable. Operational requirements meant that the officers and men rarely had a chance to sleep ashore, but at least they were compensated by 'hard-lying money', extra pay granted for bearing gross discomfort.

After initial working up at Inveraray, LCTs were sent to the small port and peacetime holiday resort of Troon on the east bank of the Firth of Clyde. 'A full programme of day and night exercises sharpened our general performance as a unit. One black and stormy night, while anchored in the Bay of Arran, we found we were drifting and, by all-night watchfulness under near storm conditions, managed to avoid an unscheduled beaching – an uncomfortable but useful experience shared by us all'.[23] Alec Guinness was not content there. 'It's a bleakish life here and the people are dullish. My life is a routine one.' He was in limbo, 'not yet on the high seas but I'm not allowed to go home'.[24]

He was much happier when he was given command of a Landing Craft, Infantry (Large) or LCI(L) and sent across the Atlantic in the liner *Queen Mary* to commission it in Boston. He was even more pleased when, as the craft was not ready, he was able to keep his hand in as an actor by taking a role in *Flare Path* on Broadway.

The LCI(L) had originally been known as the 'giant raiding craft' and was planned for quick expeditions to enemy-held coastlines. It was first conceived by Mountbatten, who drew out a rough sketch for the American General Marshall. British shipyards had no spare capacity, so they were all built in the United States. The LCI(L) looked more like a ship that an LCT, for it had no bow doors, though it had a slab-sided superstructure above its main deck, which gave a strange appearance. There were two ramps, one on either side, by which troops would disembark. The forward part of the ship was taken up entirely by troop decks, where around 200 men could live for short periods, with mess tables and seats. The crew's quarters were near midships, with three-tier bunks in American fashion. The engine room was just aft, with eight diesel engines geared to drive two propellers. There was another troop space aft of that. The main superstructure around midships was very angular. It included a wheelhouse, a chart room and radio cabin, officers' quarters and the crew toilets. The bridge was on the deck above that. The ship was defended by a two-pounder 'pom-pom' gun on the deckhouse and Oerlikon guns on bow and stern. Instead of gears to reverse the engines, it was fitted with variable-pitch propellers. Changing the pitch from forward to reverse took some time, which a captain had to remember during manoeuvres. They were also rather delicate, which proved a problem on active service. But on the whole the LCI(L) was a very successful craft.

British officers were amazed to discover that their craft had been fitted out to American standards:

I was overcome to find that I had my own cabin, with fitted wardrobe, filing cabinet, desk, safe, and interior spring bunk complete with reading light. There were showers for both officers and ratings, and the ratings had a very spacious messdeck, quite apart from their sleeping quarters, where every man had his own bunk. The galley was beautifully equipped, with an enormous cold storage room and refrigerator adjoining.[25]

After commissioning, LCI(L)s were taken to a base in Maryland to work up, then got ready to cross the Atlantic. Alan Villiers, already well-known as a sailor and writer, commanded a group on the passage across.

They steered like tramcars with electric power and a gadget like a carman's switch; they looked like welded steel orange boxes, and their plates were so thin that in places they yielded at the tread of their sailor's feet, like sheets of thin plywood. They were mass-produced like automobiles, and women welded them together at assembly points on the east coast of the United States. They were powered with eight bus engines each, in two banks of four called quads, each quad being geared to a variable pitch propeller which was adjusted electrically. To go astern, both propellers had to be adjusted to negative pitch.

But despite his unrivalled experience in square-rigged ships, Villiers found them to be 'splendid sea boats', able to cross oceans and withstand much damage.[26]

As well as a commanding officer and a first lieutenant, an LCT had six seamen including the coxswain, who was an important figure but had little more experience than the hands under him. From November 1941 it was determined that all coxswains should be at least leading seamen, though the navy as always was reluctant to reduce standards far enough to allow sufficient men to be promoted. Many of them were chosen from among the best coxswains of minor landing craft, who up until then had the experience of running their own boat.[27] The other seamen included a few gunners for the ship's Oerlikon anti-aircraft guns, and the special non-substantive rating of Anti-Aircraft Gunner (Light Craft) was instituted for such men. Apart from seamen, each crew included a wireman who had trained as an electrician, and a motor mechanic. He had been selected from intelligent HOs of the seaman and stoker branches with experience of engines or tools and given a six-month course on the internal combustion engine. He was rated a petty officer, which usually made him senior to the coxswain. Peter Bull had a 'distinguished and erudite Petty Officer' who gave him 'a severe inferiority complex for several weeks, as he knew far more about small craft than I ...'[28] Under him were a leading stoker and a stoker, less skilled but often with considerable experience of engines. An LCI(L) had a slightly larger crew, with nine seamen and five in the engine room department.

A landing craft officer could not stand aloof from his crew, and he knew the character of each man intimately. Gavin Douglas describes the men of his LCT(4) in 1944:

> The crew of my own craft were all little more than boys: the eldest was twenty-five, and only three out of the ten hands carried were entitled to draw a rum issue, which means that only three were more than twenty. My Motor Mechanic, in charge of the craft's machinery with two assistants, was a fair-haired, boyishly smooth-faced expert of nineteen, and the First Lieutenant was a happy-go-lucky New Zealander of twenty-one. At the age of forty-five, I felt the complete horny-handed old sea-dog in such company.
>
> Only one or two of the hands had been at sea before. The coxswain had seen most of the Mediterranean landings in minor landing craft and was a fair seaman, but none of the others was much advanced from the landsman he had been not many months before.[29]

At sea, *LCT 397* operated in two watches, with an officer on the bridge, a helmsman, two men as lookouts and close to the guns, and a stoker in the engine room. During a landing the commanding officer was on the bridge with the coxswain, and the first lieutenant was forward to supervise the unloading. There were two seamen on each of the pom-pom guns, and two stokers stood by to let out the kedge anchor as the vessel beached. Two seamen let the bow door down, but it was raised by hand, and more men were needed for that. The usual procedure was for the stokers at the stern to raise the kedge anchor as the vessel sailed off with the bow doors open. Then the hard-working stokers went forward and helped to raise the doors.[30]

The most important minor landing craft was the Landing Craft, Assault or LCA, a classic British design evolved just before the war. It was just under 40 feet long, designed to carry a standard infantry platoon of 35 men and be launched from a standard passenger ship's lifeboat davits. It was nearly always sent into action by being launched from a landing ship infantry or LSI, usually a converted passenger ship. The LCA saw distinguished service in the retreats from Norway, Dunkirk, Greece and Crete before landing the first waves on Madagascar, in North Africa and Italy. An LCA was commanded by a coxswain with the rating of able or leading seaman, with a crew of two seamen and a stoker. Each group of three boats was commanded by an officer, with a flotilla officer in charge of a group of twelve craft.

Finding suitable coxswains for the minor landing craft was a task in itself, in view of the general inexperience in the early days. In December 1941 one senior officer wrote,

Take for instance the crew of the M.L.C. [i.e., landing craft, mechanized] It consists of five men all of the same standing, all probably H.O. ordinary seamen. One of them is told off as a coxswain with no substantive rate and no greater experience than his mates. How can he have power of command, sense of responsibility, initiative and knowledge of seamanship? All these he should have if he is to take charge and be a power in his craft.[31]

Eight months later the captain of the landing ship *Princess Josephine Charlotte* was equally unhappy. The crews of the ninth LCA flotilla had come on board the ship early in April, but not one of them was fit to be a coxswain of the seven boats. Three months later he had identified three men fit to take charge, but he could not see a way of going any further. 'Until the present coxswains have reached a suitable standard it is quite impracticable to train others. The result is merely two bad coxswains.' Only time and constant practice could improve the position.

Landing ships went into a position, usually about seven or eight miles off the enemy beach, where they could lower their landing craft. Getting into a minor landing craft from a ship was an ordeal in itself. For the first wave of an attack, troops had to climb into an assault landing craft suspended from davits and hanging over the side of the ship. Moreover, a soldier was top heavy and he was weighed down with his arms and equipment, so he would sink quickly if he fell in the water.

At Inveraray, officers were told about the categories of operation they might take part in. One involving a long sea voyage, such as the taking of Madagascar in 1942, was carried out by a self-contained big-ship convoy. A short sea crossing, for example in the Mediterranean, would use an advanced base such as Malta for the medium-sized craft such as LCTs and LCIs. A commando raid, such as the one on the Norwegian island of Vaasgo, might be based in landing ships, infantry. The short sea voyage, the cross-channel operation, was the one that everyone was working towards.

> This is the type of operation with which we are primarily concerned. It involves a crossing of the English Channel, which, in some places, is only 21 miles wide, in others as much as 120 miles. Some craft, in the narrower parts, could cross over direct, others on longer stretches will be taken over in L.S.I.
>
> Assaulting troops will use L.C.A. It will almost certainly be an opposed landing, although the R.A.F. and R.N. will have carried out preliminary softening. The assault will get all possible naval support, both from the cruisers and destroyer as well as the usual types of support craft. All the various types of ships and craft which have been produced as a result of experience in Combined Operations will be used in the short sea voyage.[32]

For the voyage out, a large force might be divided into three main types of convoy. A fast one could make a speed of twelve knots and was usually made up of relatively fast merchant ships converted into combined operations ships such as LSIs and landing ships, headquarters. A slow convoy went at ten knots and consisted mainly of landing ships, tank and various store ships. The craft convoy included most of the shore-to-shore carriers – older LSTs, LCTs and LCI(L)s. It could make a speed of six to eight knots. The craft convoy was formed up in several lines, with the LCTs in the centre, the support craft next and the LCIs on the outside. The whole force was protected by a screen of destroyers and cruisers. The setting off of each convoy was timed so that they would all arrive off the beaches at the same time, and the 'marriage' between the different types could be carried out.

Landing craft were notoriously difficult to handle at sea, because their shallow draught meant that they had very little grip on the water. One captain told his crew, 'They go about in a cross wind like a leaf for the same reason – nothing below the surface of the water.' He advised them, 'You ought to know that once they start turning they don't stop when you tell them to – they're floating slabs, not ordinary ships, and you've got to learn 'em.'[33] Crews did learn, and in 1943 Rear-Admiral Rhoderick McGrigor told his officers, 'I have been watching your exercises at sea and, in my opinion, experienced Royal Naval officers could not have kept better station or behaved more promisingly. I have only one request to make: when the day comes and we all go in, would you please, please *not* eat your lunches on the bridge.'[34]

Landing craft squadrons manoeuvred in obedience to flag signals, in formations which would have been familiar to the captains of battleships in the days of sail. They usually travelled in line-ahead to present the smallest front to the enemy and to pass through swept channels in minefields. An LCT squadron would travel in three columns of one flotilla each, 1,500 yards apart and with the leader 400 yards ahead. They would form line-abreast on approaching the landing beach, in order that all the craft would land simultaneously and the troops and their equipment would disembark in the right order. There were several methods of deployment, for example at night when arranged in two columns: the two central vessels would reduce speed to two-and-a-half knots and the others would increase to three, four or five knots according to the position in the line, and alter course outwards until the new line was formed. Another method was to turn parallel to the coastline, and then each would turn together to head for its appointed spot on the beach.[35]

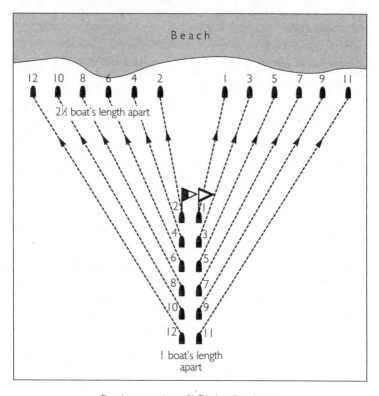

Forming a squadron of LCAs into line abreast.

Navigation was also important if the craft were to land in the right place, even in the strong tides and foul weather of the English Channel. According to the Director of Combined Training,

The chief problem with which they will have to contend is the pilotage one, of finding the right beach within 100 yards at the right time. To train an officer or a coxswain to do this with any success requires considerably more than three weeks, in view of the instruction in Beach Pilotage, and Navigational Aids, as well as ordinary Pilotage that is involved.[36]

The typical landing craft did not have the equipment or training to do this accurately in all circumstances, so specialist navigational landing craft, LCNs, were built and fitted with chart tables and navigational aids. A special navigation school, HMS *James Cook*, was established at Tighnabruaich in the Firth of Clyde. In action they might be led in by motor launches, but these high-speed craft were not always ideal for the task. A later report claimed,

> M.L.s are unsuitable for acting as navigational leaders. It is practically impossible to judge accurately their speeds when going below 8 knots. They are extremely difficult to steer at low speeds and they make less leeway than landing craft, who consequently find extreme difficulty in following them.[37]

During the landing on a beach, it was vital to drop the kedge anchor over the stern at the right moment. This could be used to haul the ship off, though that was easier than at Dunkirk, as they were arriving full and leaving empty. Just as important, it held the ship steady while it unloaded. The bow was aground, the stern was afloat and any cross-wind or tide could swing the stern round and put the ship in an impossible position. Alec Guinness's anchor cable was cut by another ship during the Sicily landings, and none of the craft present was powerful enough to haul the LCI(L) off. He had to wait there for ten days until a powerful destroyer became available.[38]

Landing craft officers had rather less room for initiative than those in other areas such as Coastal Forces, for they had to follow a detailed plan as closely as possible during a landing. However, they had much greater responsibility, not just for themselves and their crews but for the troops and equipment on board. They also had to recognize that the soldiers were in an unfamiliar environment. Major Plowden of the Royal Engineers commented,

> The soldier in battle order takes up an extraordinary amount of space ... the minimum width of any companionway or alleyway

should be about 12 feet! It has been found extremely difficult to marshal troops at their action stations as it is nearly always necessary for troops to pass through troop spaces other than their own ...

Then a most important point is sea kindliness ... one of my main worries was not that the gale would interfere with the physical act of landing, but that the troops would be in no condition to work when they got to the beaches on account of seasickness.[39]

One soldier put in a plea for better understanding between the army and the landing craft crews.

For instance, the apparent fussiness of a ship's inspection seems much more reasonable when it is thoughtfully pointed out how chaotic a troop deck containing 120 men would become if there wasn't that strictness: how spotless 'tweendecks' must be if there is to be no smell (and no flies in the tropics!). Once we grasp the idea that a sailor's ship is his home and he likes it as clean as our homes ashore we can help him 'make it so'. At present his attitude is sometimes that of the very upstage county family who find themselves with evacuees billeted on them and assume that slum conditions will automatically develop. We must make him realise we come from homes every bit as good as his.

Another thing – some of us may not even know port from starboard when we come aboard. A brief outline of the ship's routine, a 'family tree' and 'who's who' of the ship's company, their officers, their duties and their organisation is the kind of help we would appreciate.[40]

In the early days the soldiers sometimes laughed at the incompetence of the new landing craft crews, while some of their officers coveted the job themselves. The early isolation of Combined Operations from mainstream naval life, it was reported, 'plays into the hands of "amphibious-minded" soldiers, who would willingly run the naval Units concerned and have openly advocated doing so'.[41] Such problems were likely to spur the Admiralty into taking the organization more seriously.

Sometimes the officers had to assert some control over the soldiers on a long passage.

It is the responsibility of all Officers to see that the troops on board L.S.I. obey all the regulations strictly; firmness would be appreciated by the Officer Commanding troops in calling attention to men who block gangways, leave their mess decks without permission, smoke at improper times and in improper places, make a noise & C. Friendliness and hospitality should be tempered by strict discipline.

It was important to feed the troops, and in 1944 the orders for Force J demanded that, 'Men must be landed with their stomachs full, preferably with hot food' – though that did not take account of problems of seasickness on board.[42]

In the early days Evelyn Waugh remarked on the loading of landing craft, 'which the military seemed to consider an esoteric art requiring great practice'.[43] Further experience, for example in Sicily, showed that it was indeed important:

The greatest care must be taken in the stowage of ships for the assaulting force. Mistakes once made cannot be rectified afterwards. The rule 'last in first out' must be strictly adhered to and the stowage of tanks, guns, transport stores, etc., must be strictly in accordance with the *tactical* requirements of the landing. It is advisable that weapons, vehicles, stores, etc., should be evenly distributed throughout the ships of the assaulting force. Losses among ships loaded in this way would not have such a disastrous effect on the expedition as the loss of ships loaded with munitions all of a similar nature.[44]

The days of being 'nobody's baby' began to end when Force J was founded in November 1942, after the failure of the Dieppe raid. It was intended as a permanent raiding force for the English Channel area. Its headquarters were the premises of Royal Yacht Squadron on the Isle of Wight, and it was headed by Captain J. Hughes Hallet, one of the most experienced Combined Operations officers. Until then, forces for exercises were assembled *ad hoc*. It soon began to take on the role of a 'miniature Roundup', using the codename for the invasion of France as it was planned at that time. It had moorings for LCT flotillas at Southampton, Calshot, Beaulieu, Poole, Shoreham and Newhaven, with LCIs in the River Medina when they began to arrive.[45] Expansion slowed down in February 1943 when it was decided that the main effort that year should be in the Mediterranean, and Hughes Hallett complained that he barely had enough craft of the various types to carry on training. The force had around 4,500 officers and men, but it was pointed out that, 'as a result of the combination of a very high rate of dilution with an extreme shortage of officers qualified to instruct, the general efficiency of landing craft flotillas in Force "J" is actually lower to-day than was the efficiency of the Flotillas available for Channel operations this time last year.' Hughes Hallett suggested an increase of no more than ten per cent per month, to cease three months before a major operation.

By April he was in doubt about the future of his command as much of his force was taken away, but he advocated a diversionary operation, perhaps on the Dutch coast or in the Channel Islands, during 1943. This found no support because of the failure of the Dieppe raid, but Force J began to build up again in preparation for the Normandy invasion. Hughes Hallett began to train them in the three features he regarded as essential in a cross-Channel attack: precise navigation, 'working to an accurate time table, in the face of strong tidal streams and complicated hazards, such as enemy minefields, etc'; the 'ability to operate as part of a large and heterogeneous force by night and day in close company'; and the need to maintain discipline and aggressive spirit among both landing craft crews and troops.[46]

Sometimes there were quiet periods, for example on 19 January 1944 when the log of *LCT 940* recorded,

> 0630 Call Cook 0700 Call Hands 0745 Breakfast 0830 Hands to cleaning stations 1015 Stand Easy 1030 Out Pipes Hands carry on cleaning 1125 Cox'n and MM on periodical leave. 1200 Secure 1230 Dinner Mid. Thompson D.O reports to live on board. 1315 Hands turn to. 1420 Sig[naller] to instruction 1430 Stand Easy 1445 Out Pipes. 1600 Secure 1630 Tea 1700 Libertymen 2000 Supper 2300 Pipe Down.[47]

The idea of a raiding force was dropped, but the programme of exercises moved on to a larger scale: Exercise 'Westminster' in July was to demonstrate a daylight landing to a group of MPs; 'Cycle' was to practise the landing of a brigade group after the assault had already begun. Some did not involve the navy – Exercise 'Evade' was a rather jolly affair intended to practise troops in escape procedures after they had raided a 'sausage skin' factory on the Isle of Wight, 'an important link in the German sausage-producing machine'. At the same time the local Home Guard was offered a test in 'their difficult role of checking on enemy parachutists who may be disguised'. Operation 'Porpoise' in July was intended to 'carry out a trial of disembarking the vehicles of a Brigade Group, waterproofed by the asbestos compound method, under the conditions likely to prevail during the build-up phase of an operation on a flat beach'. It involved 72 landing craft tank, organized in flotillas of eight. Operation 'Etna' in September was to test the aiming of landing craft tank (rocket) with and without the use of radar. Operation 'Prince' used two flotillas of LCT and several other vessels to land 1,100 men of the RAF Regiment with 142 vehicles in 'territory not cleared of the enemy', presumably with a view to setting up an advanced airfield.

Operation 'Pirate' in October was intended to provide 'Practice by an Assault Group in leaving harbour, making a passage, dawn rendezvous, and deployment in the Assault Formation'. The ships were to make a voyage of 100 miles around the Isle of Wight to land in Studland Bay, south of Poole, supported by 'bombing and machine gun attacks from the air and by all forms of support from seaward, including bombardment by three destroyers, fire from support craft, L.C.L.(R) and L.C.A. (HR) as well as the fire of two regiments of field artillery carried in L.C.T'. Build-up forces would land on the beach later, but they were allowed to use the shorter passage through the Needles Channel 'in order to increase their turn round'. In addition, each type of craft was to have its own objectives – LCTs, for example, were to practise embarkation procedure, navigation and station-keeping, deployment and beaching, and the techniques of close support. After that exercise, the captains of the three assault groups were given a free hand to organize unit training within their groups, while exercises were held with the Canadian troops at the request of their officers.

Hughes Hallett was succeeded by Commodore George Oliver at the end of 1943 – he had been the star cadet in the Special Entry scheme in 1915, the same term as Edward Crick. More recently, he had distinguished himself leading the British naval forces in the landings at Salerno. Life continued to be busy for the individual craft, like *LCT 940* on the night of 25–25 February 1944, in waters that were familiar to pre-war yachtsmen:

1603 pass thro' Spithead Boom 1710 Anchored off Gillkicker 1841 Weighed 1903 Moored alongside 941 & 636 at buoys n Stokes Bay 2113 Slipped 2124 Beached on Hard 2126 Door Down Unloaded Army 2139 Door Up 2140 Unbeached 2157 Secured alongside 941 & 634 at buoy 2409 Slipped. Proceeded with 634 to Sailing Area – Red Bank.

0045 Secured alongside 636 and anchored in Sailing Area – Red Bank 0600 Call cook 0630 Call Hands 0700 Breakfast 0800 Slipped Proceeded (567-940-634) at G 9 to Stokes Bay, then thro' boom …[48]

The ultimate exercises were a series in May 1944 known as 'Fabius'. Each of the five major assault forces had its own exercise, and Force

J's was known as 'Fabius Three'. Landings were carried out using all arms, including army and air force, as a final preparation for a major assault. Force J at least avoided any disasters such as the one to Force U off Slapton Sands in Devon, when German torpedo-boats got among the landing craft and caused 600 casualties, raising many fears about what could happen during a real invasion.

Force J was now building up to invasion strength, with new flotillas of every kind of craft being added. Its aim was to land a full army division of around 20,000 men. It was to include three assault groups, J1, J2 and J3 to land a brigade each, with J4, which included several naval forces for landing commandos. Each of the first three groups would include five landing ship infantry and their complement of assault craft, eight landing ship tank, five flotillas of landing craft tank, one of landing ship infantry (large), three flotillas of landing craft personnel (large), two of them fitted for making smoke, a beach commando unit, a communication section, a bombardment unit and a number of support craft. The Force was exercising with the Canadian 3rd Division. By May 1944 it was almost ready to provide one of the five assault forces for the invasion of Normandy, in 'Juno' Sector. Its officers had come a long way from the amateurs that Peter Bull had joined two years earlier, but their great test was still in front of them.

BRITISH NAVY

SHOULDER BOARDS AND
SLEEVE INSIGNIA;
LINE OFFICERS

	COMMODORE, SECOND CLASS	CAPTAIN	COMMANDER	LIEUTENANT COMMANDER	LIEUTENANT	SUB-LIEUTENANT	WARRANT OFFICER

RN (ROYAL NAVY)
Made up of professional naval personnel and former professionals recalled to active duty. Higher ranks, which exist only for Royal Navy, are shown on page at left.

RNR (ROYAL NAVAL RESERVE)
Composed chiefly of men who in private life were merchant marine officers or were otherwise closely connected with maritime affairs.

RNVR (ROYAL NAVAL VOLUNTEER RESERVE)
Composed of men of varying professional backgrounds.

Naval officers ranks, showing the differences between the Royal Navy, Royal Naval Reserve and Royal Naval Volunteer Reserve stripes.

9
FIRST COMMAND

For a regular officer, taking command of a ship was the summit of his ambition, setting the seal on everything he had worked for over many years, perhaps since the age of thirteen. Peter Gretton wrote, 'I was delighted to be getting my first command, for some of my contemporaries had theirs already and I felt I was being left behind.' He was 'thrilled by the thought' and soon found, 'The day when a Captain stands on the bridge of his first ship is a memorable one in his life.'[1]

The reactions of temporary officers were much more complex, and each had his own combination of nervousness and pride. Many RNVR officers entered the navy with little or no expectation of ever commanding a ship. Even a peacetime reservist could be told by his commanding officer, 'You'll never get a command, Rayner – the Navy won't give R.N.V.R.s command of a ship, no matter how long the war lasts.'[2] Temporary officers had even less expectations, and Monsarrat wrote, 'If we had been told, as subs in HMS *Flower* [*Campanula*], that such a command would eventually come our way, it might have permanently affected our outlook – and with it our careers. It is perhaps just as well that at that stage we had no greater ambition than to earn our watchkeeping tickets and get the ciphers to come out right.'[3] But this changed rapidly as the escort force grew enormously, and reserve officers were even more dominant in coastal forces, minesweeping and landing craft. There was no time for a more general training, and temporary officers only knew one part of the navy. As Monsarrat wrote on taking command of a frigate, 'Together with ocean convoy escort, it was in point of fact the only sort of Navy I knew anything about; the ship I was going to command would be the biggest one I had ever boarded, and her job, convoy escort, had been my life for as long as I could remember.' Even so, RNVR officers would never command ships bigger than destroyers, and only a small minority would ever command escort vessels, which were mostly the preserve of the professional seamen of the RNR. It was very different in coastal forces and landing craft, where the RNVR took up nearly all the junior officer ranks.

To Monsarrat his appointment was 'the crowning piece of news', and taking command was 'this most singular honour'. On arriving on board,

> Here was I in the Captain's cabin, anyway: cigar, coffee, slippers, and all ... During the last few minutes I found I had been fingering a small rubber stamp on my desk ... Now I pressed it on the inking pad, stamped down on the signal-form in front of me, and examined the result.
>
> It said, 'Lieutenant-In-Command.'
>
> It was my favourite rubber stamp so far.[4]

Coastal Forces officers tended to be hungry for command. In G. W. Scarle's course at HMS *St Christopher* in 1940, only one was not appointed to a command, which upset him and seemed unreasonable: 'Perhaps they drew our names out of a hat for the ships available.'[5] Submarine command was a special case, where there really was some training in the form of the famous Commanding Officers' Qualifying Course, popularly known as the 'Perishers'. That however, concentrated on attack techniques rather than leadership and administration, reflecting the submarine commander's unique position in directing an attack on his own. Edward Young was delighted to be one of the first temporary RNVR officers to be sent on the course after eighteen months in the submarine service.[6]

The civil servants of the Commission and Warrant Branch of the Admiralty set policies for officer appointments and promotions, but the actual selection of potential captains was in the hands of the naval officers in the Second Sea Lord's Office for Appointments. Strictly speaking, they were appointing 'commanding officers' rather than men holding the naval rank of captain. That was reserved for officers of very long experience and considerable seniority. A commanding officer of a ship could be any rank from sub-lieutenant to full captain, according to the ship's size. Coastal forces and major landing craft were commanded by lieutenants or sub-lieutenants; corvettes and submarines by lieutenants or lieutenant-commanders; destroyers by lieutenant-commanders or above. Commanders were usually the seconds-in-command of large ships, or on staff duties, or in charge of escort groups in the North Atlantic. Full captains, or 'post captains' as they were known, commanded the largest ships, such as cruisers, battleships and aircraft carriers. Many others were on staff duties in the Admiralty, while some commanded destroyer flotillas. But every commanding officer, however junior in rank, was given the courtesy title of 'captain' even in official naval documents.

Promotion by rank was rather mechanistic and depended largely on length of service, time at sea and age, all subject to a commanding officer's recommendation. Selection for a highly responsible job like the command of a small warship was far more serious and was considered on an individual basis. The staff in the Second Sea Lord's Office consisted of 29 officers late in 1943, headed by Captain A. G. C. Madden. They came from a wide range of experience and knowledge and included Commander Humphrey Boys-Smith, RNR, who had recently commanded corvettes and frigates in the Battle of the Atlantic and brought a great deal of recent experience to bear on appointments to Western Approaches Command.[7] Commander J. G. W. Deneys was in charge of RNVR appointments. He had distinguished himself in the same class as Edward Crick in 1915; he came second overall and won the prize for seamanship, although only because the star pupil, George Oliver (later commander of Force J), was not allowed to pick up prizes in more than two subjects.[8] A. H. Cherry was interviewed by Deneys in April 1944:

He reviewed a list: vacancies varied from appointments requiring immediate filling to those in the offing, of new ships being completed, of old ships in for repairs soon to be ready for duty again. There were also openings provided by routine replacement of officers who had served their stretch on ships and were due for a change.[9]

In this case Cherry was disappointed not to be given command of a ship, but he was offered a first lieutenant's post in the famous Second Support Group under Commander 'Johnny' Walker.

The navy set great store on maturity, and eligibility for command was partly a matter of age, though the minimum was quite low for a good man. Lieutenant Thomas Fanshawe was 24, but a very experienced seaman, when he took command of the corvette *Clover* late in 1943. At the other end of the scale, Commander Mickelthwaite feared that he would be relieved of the command of the destroyer *Eskimo* at the age of 39, as 'he was getting on in years'. In fact it was stomach ulcers that removed him from the job.[10]

As well as personal knowledge of the candidates, the staff of the Second Sea Lord's office relied heavily on reports from commanding officers. Sometimes there was a difference of opinion on this. Monsarrat and the other officers of the *Campanula* had fallen foul of Captain Jack Broome when he inspected the ship. When Harmsworth was found lacking, he tried to talk his way out of it.

'Well – *faute de mieux*, sir'

'What's that?'

'Faute de mieux.'

'O ...' A suspicious glance frosted the air between them. *'Faute de mal*, I should think you mean.'[11]

Possibly this had some influence on Broome's refusal to put Monsarrat forward for a command. But Sam Lombard-Hobson had already reported that he was 'a considerate and conscientious officer and was recommended for a command of his own in due course.'[12] The Admiralty accepted this view, and Monsarrat took charge of a sloop.

The situation in Combined Operations was very different – expanding very rapidly from almost nothing, there was no established path to follow. As the Captain in charge of tank landing craft training wrote in May 1942,

> The main source of supply of commanding officers is from within the T.L.C. organisation itself, from officers drafted from *King Alfred*, given a short training course at Troon and then sent to craft as 1st Lieutenant. These officers are recommended for command of a craft by a Flotilla officer when he considers them fit and in recent weeks any officer thus recommended had immediately been given a command.[13]

Peter Bull was fearful:

> I was totally unprepared for the bombshell which fell at my feet in the interview I had. I was to commission a new T.L.C. (Type Mark 3) forthwith at Glasgow, and bring her round as soon as she was ready. I was flabbergasted, and begged Commander Bostock to reconsider his decision; I told him that I was more than content with my job and needed further experience ... But he pointed out that the shortage of officers was so acute that risks had to be taken. I saw that further resistance was useless ...[14]

Alec Guinness was more successful in his pleas when offered a command: 'I asked for it to be postponed for I don't feel quite ready yet.'[15] In minesweepers, Eric Denton had to wait some time because of his youth, but his appointment, not long before his 25th birthday brought promotion to lieutenant, which delighted him.[16]

Taking command of one's first ship was 'the greatest step that you will ever take', according to Commander Hodgkinson.[17] But there was no particular training for the role of captain in those days, despite the immense responsibilities. In a sense it was assumed that every executive officer was preparing for the job, and every part of his previous training was tending towards the moment when he first took command. There were plenty of books on ship organization, but all were out of date or designed for much larger vessels, even if Captain H. W. Biggs wanted to use extracts from them in 1944. *The Modern Officer of the Watch* had been published by Sir Reginald Plunkett in 1918. *Five Minutes to One Bell* was published by Lieutenant-Commander B. V. Sturdee just before the First World War and advocated strong military discipline on board. *Whispers from the Fleet*, was even older and was written by Captain Christopher Craddock. It contained very detailed hints but looked back to the days of sailing ships, and the short section on destroyers was the most relevant to the present day.[18] Commander W. M. James's *New Battleship Organisations* of 1916 advocated, among other things, the abolition of the ship's police, but that was never an issue in any ship a temporary officer was likely to command. A booklet, *The First Lieutenant's Handbook*, was written by Lieutenant-Commander E. A. Codrington-Ball and published by Gieves around 1932, but it does not seem to have had a wide circulation.[19] The most recent was *Running a Big Ship*, published in 1937 by Captain Rory O'Conor and based on his time as commander of HMS *Hood*. Its title signalled its irrelevance to the captain of a corvette or landing craft, but it did contain many useful hints and explained O'Conor's policy of running a ship on 'the ten commandments'. O'Conor died as captain of the cruiser *Neptune* after distinguished service, but there is no sign that his writing had much impact on the captains of corvettes or landing craft.

The idea of a booklet to be issued to new commanding officers of small ships, including coastal forces and major landing craft, first surfaced in June 1944, perhaps a little late in the day since the navy had already expanded to mount the D-Day invasion that month. It was the idea of the new Second Sea Lord. Not everyone was keen, and Lieutenant A. V. Turner, the captain of the escort destroyer *Burwell*, wrote that he would have been 'deeply offended' if he had been given such a document when taking up his first command. In any case Guy Hodgkinson, the Second Sea Lord's Naval Assistant, chaired a meeting at the Admiralty on 7 June. He was a very experienced destroyer officer, as were many of those who contributed to the booklets for temporary officers. Specialists like gunners and navigators were regarded as the 'brains' of the navy but were often too wrapped up in their subject. Fully trained anti-submarine officers were in short supply and could not be spared. Those who had served in destroyers in mid-career, however, had most of the experiences in ship-handling and leadership that were needed for the new style of warfare. Hodgkinson's regular duties included advising the Second Sea Lord on 'entries, appointments, promotions and retirements, of Executive Officers … below the rank of Captain'.[20] The other nine who attended the meeting were all experienced seaman officers and members of the unit dealing with officer appointments in the Second Sea Lord's department. They quickly decided the format and content. It was agreed that *Your Ship* would be 'a good title, as encouraging an interested approach to the book and implying the personal relationship between the commanding Officer and his ship'. It was decided to write it in three sections, entitled 'Yourself', 'Your Officers' and 'Your Men'. The members of the committee went out to collate any material already available to them and to gather more as the book should be 'the fruits of the experience of as many commanding officers as possible'. As a result, the committee collected several sets of orders, plus ideas from friends and acquaintances in the service. It was also suggested that Admiral Pridham's document for newly joined officers in *Hood* might be adapted, until the Director of Naval Training pointed out that it was already being issued to new RNVR officers as part of Pelly's *Aide-Memoire*.

In fact, little of this material was used, and the document was largely written by Hodgkinson himself. He kept to the basic structure as agreed by the committee, but there is no sign that he incorporated many of their suggestions. Great hopes were placed on an introduction by the Second Sea Lord, but he was a man of few words. According to his future son-in-law Roderick Macdonald, he was 'monosyllabic, belonging to the "Never complain, never explain" school' and who 'despised "Public relations" believing that if a policy was right it would be seen to be so'.[21] As a result, the preface was very short. The document was ready by November and was distributed in the first instance to existing commanding officers of all ships from destroyers downwards, including major landing craft and coastal forces. It would then be distributed to all new commanding officers as they took up their posts.[22]

Your Ship also applied to commanding officers of major landing craft such as LCTs. Some of the passages may have seemed a little strange to them, for example on keeping one's distance from the other officers in the wardroom, or in addressing the crew. Most of them probably followed the practice of one LCT captain as reported in the press in 1944: 'He seldom addressed them all together, but spoke to them in ones and twos, half jocularly, in the months when they were learning the technique of beaching their craft.'[23] But there was nothing that seriously jarred in the booklet, despite Hodgkinson's having had very little experience of that kind of navy. It is a measure of his success that he was able to address several different audiences.

Readers were reminded how the role of the captain differed from that of other officers:

> Firstly, you require to realise that, once appointed in command, no matter what rank you hold, you are The Captain, which means you are the ship – that when a fender is left over the side it is *your* fender left over by *your* O.O.D., that when a confidential document is mislaid by a Sub-Lieutenant it is still *your* document, that when a seaman from your crew is seen wearing his cap flat-aback ashore, that seaman is reflecting a lack of pride in *your* ship; and that when you hit the tug and not the target with your first salvo it is *your* deflection that is wrong.

Secondly, a captain needed to be aware of the example he set to officers and crew: 'Every word you say on the bridge is noted by the ship's company. Every word you say in the wardroom is marked by the officers.' Thirdly, he had to exercise a more managerial authority (in days when the word was rather less of a cliché): 'Whereas a First Lieutenant, or Specialist, orders and administers, a Captain supervises and directs.' Finally, a captain had to turn his eyes outwards towards the unit his ship was a part of. 'By all means have the smartest ship in the unit, but do so by fair means, and, when it comes to benefits bestowed, see that they are bestowed on all the unit and not only on your own ship.'[24]

Every captain had to develop his own methods in command. He was freed from the demands of watchkeeping, and he did not even have to establish the ship's daily routine, for that was the duty of the first lieutenant – though the captain would be well advised to keep an eye on it. But most had recently been first lieutenants themselves and found it difficult to let go of the role. Hodgkinson advised them not to be 'overwhelmed by the secretarial side of their duties to the detriment of the fighting and personnel side'.[25] The captain was supposed to think mainly of strategy, but not to lose sight of the detail. On delegation, Commanders Tothill and Boys-Smith were agreed that a small ship should not be a 'one-man band', that the captain should have confidence in his officers, and that he should see every message that came in, but delegate almost everything.

The captain's cabin arrangements were quite simple in a corvette. He had a very small cabin under the bridge, with a bed, table and wardrobe. When ships had their forecastles extended, this made it slightly less desirable, as Derek Rayner found out: 'the extending of the forecastle had only one disadvantage. It completely enclosed the captain's cabin below decks, and the only means of ventilation was through scuttles opening on to the covered flat outside the mess decks. I could not help hearing remarks by the men that were not intended for my ears.'[26] On later ships the cabin was a deck higher, so the problem was solved.

Destroyers had a very unsatisfactory arrangement, with the captain's cabin in the stern. As a result, in bad weather, 'To move along the upper deck was to take one's life in one's hands and it was necessary to divide the ship into two sections, those aft not being allowed to come forward and those forward having to remain there. Sometimes the after section was cut off for several days.'[27] This fault was only rectified with the R class which entered service in 1942. Meanwhile, the captain rarely saw his main cabin when at sea and lived entirely in his sea cabin under the bridge. This was quite well equipped, for example, in Peter Gretton's *Duncan*, with a settee-bunk, a table, towel rail and radiator, chest of drawers and even a folding lavatory. The position was simpler in more modern ships such as the River-class frigates. The captain had a small but adequate cabin three decks below the bridge, as described by Monsarrat: 'My own cabin, with bathroom attached, was a big one, and adequately comfortable: though here again the wartime finish was apparent – it had none of Winger's elegance in the form of polished woodwork or cushioned chairs.'[28] It was reasonably close to the bridge already, so the sea cabin was smaller, barely twice the width of the bunk fitted in it.

In Coastal Forces craft there was little privacy:

Then came the wardroom which was the officers' quarters and there was one room only which was used for eating, sleeping – everything. There were bunk beds on either side which had to be used as seats in the daytime with the blankets all being put away in lockers underneath. There was a table for meals and a couple of moveable chairs. A small wardrobe on either side and a central unit between them with drawers for clothing and so on and, luxury of luxuries, a cabinet above for keeping a few bottles of wine.[29]

A captain would find it necessary to stay fully clothed during periods in a danger area. He might be called out from a relatively warm and dry cabin to the freezing cold of the Arctic Ocean or the torrential rains of the North Atlantic. If he did undress, he had to use clothing that could be slipped in and out of easily, such as sea boots and duffel coats. Donald Macintyre describes how he coped:

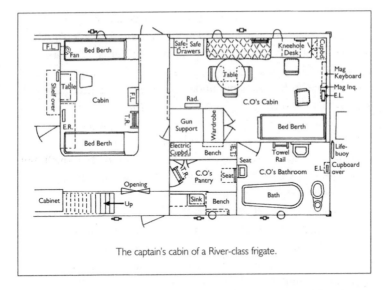

The captain's cabin of a River-class frigate.

In my sea-cabin under the bridge the endlessly repeated orders to the quartermaster at the wheel and his replies formed, with the ping of the asdic, a continuous noise background, night and day, day after day, a background which I soon ceased consciously to hear and through which I could sleep soundly only to be instantly awake should the noise pattern vary. An undertone of urgency or anxiety in the voice of the officer of the watch, or an echo to the ping, would sound an alarm in my sleeping brain, and on many occasions I found myself halfway to the bridge before the reason for my waking had penetrated my conscious thoughts.[30]

Even in the hardest days of the war, a captain would be well advised to find ways of relaxing. According to an unfavourable report, Nicholas Monsarrat was not liked by his men because, 'he was always in his cabin writing'. Sam Lombard-Hobson replied,

Bully for Nick ... how lucky, in time of war, to be able to relax in your cabin when others ... were burning themselves out, night and day on the bridge, never off duty, and causing their men, and later the Admiralty, real concern because they rarely went to their cabins to read, write, or just 'charge batteries'.[31]

Commander Mickelthwaite of *Eskimo* followed this policy, according to an American observer:

At sea the Captain was on the bridge during all maneuvers, including large changes in course. At other times he remained in his emergency cabin, a deck below the bridge, reading light literature and sleeping. He told an observer that he found out that he could not remain on the bridge all day and night and be mentally and physically alert when an emergency arose.[32]

Commander Peter Gretton went so far as to tell his officers, 'I have little to do at sea, except when in contact with the "wolfpacks".' But his orders also acknowledged the sheer exhaustion that might set in during a long convoy battle:

After a period of constant wakefulness, or disturbed rest, a man is sometimes capable of making an apparently intelligent reply without waking up. Whenever I am called by the O.O.W. it is my intention to come on the bridge unless I consider the call not to be of immediate importance, in which event I shall say so. I rely on the O.O.W. to assist me in carrying out this intention, and any reluctance on his part to disturb me, however well meant, will be misplaced.[33]

The bridge was the captain's main work station. It was usually situated about a third of the way aft in the ship and two or three decks above the forecastle. It was usually open to the elements but protected on the sides by bulwarks about four feet high, with perhaps small windscreens ahead and to the sides. The main bridge of Gretton's destroyer *Duncan* was about ten-and-a-half feet long fore and aft and fourteen feet wide. In the centre was the compass platform, roughly triangular in plan but rounded on its after part. It was made of wood, as on all ships, to reduce deviation on the compass. There was a magnetic compass in a large binnacle with a pelorus behind it, used for measuring the angle on objects ashore and at sea, and vital for station-keeping in a convoy. There were voice-pipes to the helmsman and telegraph operators in the wheelhouse below, to the director control tower for the guns, and to the captain's sea cabin. To port was a small hut used for the remote control of the guns; to starboard was a viewer to look down on the plot below. There were platforms on each side for signalling and for operating the torpedo sights. On the after bulwark were the controls for torpedo-tubes and depth-charges. Aft of the main bridge was another deck thirteen feet in the fore-and-aft direction. It formed a platform for the searchlights and the director for the guns, and later for radar. It was also used by the illumination officer to fire star shells and other illuminants in action.

Monsarrat describes it in the frigate *Ettrick*;

From the bridge, once I had it in a tight grip, command could be fittingly exercised ... It was of the authentic destroyer type: open, properly shielded by glass dodgers, with batteries of voice-pipes and telephones lining two sides of it, and a grand array of instruments – asdic repeater, log, compass, gunnery indicators, and other more discreet products – on the forward end. My chair was centrally placed, high up behind the gyro-compass: there was a solid chart-table close at hand, and a view of the plot (an instrument for recording the ship's movements as she goes along, by means of a track-chart) without walking twenty yards and turning two corners to get it. The flag-deck and signalling platform were separately sited, well clear of the main stream of activity; and there was, to finish off, a covered approach leading up from the sea-cabin.[34]

One of the most important tasks of any captain, especially in a small ship, was to form good relations with officers on the right level. On the running of the wardroom, Commander Tothill wanted as few restrictions as possible, but rigidly enforced. He would only stop an officer's wine bill as a last resort, after all else had failed to prevent him drinking too much. Captain Wise noted that criticism of a senior officer in the wardroom would soon reach other ears. Commander Tyrwhitt suggested that a small-ship captain should mess there as much as possible, to 'keep in the picture and not have to ask too many awkward questions'. But Hodgkinson advised a captain not to go too far in that direction:

Another way of 'reverting to type' is to become too much of a wardroom officer. In the smallest ships the Captain is inevitably a member of the mess and its president, but in ships like a destroyer he is an honorary member, and has a comfortable day cabin of his own in which to sit. He should normally have lunch and dinner in the wardroom as this will help him to know his officers, but his continued presence is bound to have a somewhat restricting influence, as is exemplified by the tradition that officers should stand when the Captain comes into the mess. A Captain should therefore not outstay his welcome.[35]

A captain had different relations with his specialist officers, which meant the engineer officer and the medical officer in a frigate or destroyer. The former had great responsibility under the captain and by regulation.

The Engineer Officer is to be regarded as the mechanical expert of the ship. Under the Captain's directions he may be empowered to inspect any of the mechanical fittings not in his charge and report to the Captain on their efficiency. The Engineer Officer is to have charge, and is responsible for the maintenance in a state of working order, and so far as may be, of readiness for immediate use, of all that is placed under his charge ...

He also had a special responsibility in case of 'Orders tending to injure machinery':

Whenever any order is received which, if executed, would, in the opinion of the Engineer Officer, tend to injure the machinery or boilers, or cause a useless expenditure of fuel, he is to make a representation to this effect to the Captain, but, unless the order is countermanded after his representation, he is to execute it.[36]

Corvettes and landing craft did not usually have engineer officers as such, but the same rules applied to the chief artificers or petty officers in charge of the machinery. They had a particularly great responsibility for ratings, because temporary RNVR officers had practically no training in engineering.

Medical officers were advised how to deal with the captain:

In your service contact with him, you should understand that he alone is responsible for the health of the Ship's Company, and that you are appointed as his adviser in that department. You should therefore consult him upon any change of policy, which you think desirable, and obtain his approval before putting it into force. In putting forward your ideas, try to foresee all the consequences, and have answers ready to any objections which may be raised; and remember that a complaint against some present arrangement is of very little use unless it be accompanied by a practical suggestion for a remedy.[37]

A captain had no formal disciplinary powers over his officers except, in an extreme case, by sending them on to court-martial. Any misconduct could, of course, be reflected in his reports to higher authority, and the captain could 'log' the officer concerned – the offence would be recorded in the ship's log, and possibly the Admiralty would be notified. Another way of dealing with carelessness, it was found, was to make the offender write a detailed report on his reasons for the mistake – 'for it is often the case that the more he applies his error to the light of studied reasoning in order to justify his action, the more stupid does the action appear, and the less likely he is to commit it again.'[38]

British naval officers relied heavily on their petty officers, who were mostly long-service regulars even after the rest of the crew had been diluted by HOs. Captain Pridham was aware of their limitations:

> ... the stock from which they come is that in which, perhaps for generations, the margin between sufficient food and clothing, and hunger and destitution, has been very small. As a result, their first inclination is to bid for the security of that which they now hold, rather than for an obscure possibility of what may only seem a distant prospect of improvement ...[39]

The Coxswain, the senior rating in a ship of destroyer size and less, was a very important figure, and a captain was advised to encourage him to hold 'an especial position' in the ship's company:

> There is no reason why he could not be a Second Officer of the Watch at sea. He should be a constant link between the Captain and the messdeck. He should know of any bad feeling in any mess; of any Leading Hand who is running his mess badly. If he can have an office of his own, his position is greatly enhanced. He must have the respect, but also the confidence of the ratings. He must be capable of reprimanding any of the other Petty Officers. He must have the welfare of the ship's company consistently at heart. If the junior ratings call him 'Sir', so much the better, and he should see that the other Petty Officers when on duty are addressed in a manner befitting their rate.[40]

Officers were warned about cases of petty officers with 'insufficient personality'. Such a man, it was found, was often far too lenient until he was goaded by another petty officer or reprimanded by an officer. This often caused him to 'take a man aft', to bring a charge against a rating which could have been avoided.[41]

A captain had to be familiar to, but not with, his men.

The art of command is therefore to be complete master, and yet the complete friend of every man on board; the temporal lord and yet the spiritual brother of every rating; to be detached and yet not dissociated. The basis of this art is to know your men and be known by your men. It many not be possible to know each man personally, but as soon as a man realises that you know his name he begins to feel a member of the team you captain. You should certainly know your Petty Officers.

Hodgkinson was not impressed with the style of the fictional Captain Hornblower in C. S. Forester's books, which were highly popular at the time – 'the Silent Skipper of last-century fiction, who in some way gained the devotion of his men by never uttering a word, will not be a success today.'[42] A captain had to acquire a style of command so that everyone knew exactly what was expected of him. Hodgkinson recommended three types of orders – the imperative, which must be carried out right away; the volitive, to be done at the first opportunity; and the admonitive, to be done when convenient – 'voluntary execution, disregard of which may be a little tactless'.[43]

It was generally expected that the captain would address the assembled crew on occasion, although of course the frequency depended on his personality, his ability as a public speaker and his inclinations. Lieutenant Turner of the *Burwell* thought it should be done as little as possible, only to convey general congratulations or displeasure, and it should be 'short and snappy'. Others were far more positive:

Your talks to the ship's company can also do a tremendous amount in cultivating a ship's spirit, and here your men should be taken into your confidence so far as possible, so that they may understand the vital importance of their dull and routine work. They are as interested in the ship's movement and programme as you, and any information you can safely give them should not be withheld. If necessary, shew them what would happen if they did not go to sea, so that they may understand that dull jobs pieced together spell victory.

Nicholas Monsarrat neglected the captain's address for the first few days after taking command, and was told, 'Noel Coward killed all that sort of thing stone dead, anyway ... Nowadays the troops expect too much glamour altogether ...'[44] *In Which We Serve* had reproduced verbatim Mountbatten's speech to the crew of the destroyer *Kelly*:

In my experience, I have always found that you cannot have an efficient ship unless you have a happy ship, and you cannot have a happy ship unless you have an efficient ship. That is the way I intend to start this commission, and that is the way I intend to go on – with a happy and an efficient ship.[45]

But the lines were not totally original, and already in 1938 Captain Pridham had gone further in his advice to the junior officers of HMS *Hood*. 'A ship is either efficient, smart, clean and happy, or none of these things. They go hand in hand, or not at all.' Pelly repeated the same advice in his *Aide-Memoire*.

One compulsory task was to read out the Articles of War, which had governed naval discipline since they were first drawn up under Oliver Cromwell nearly three centuries earlier. They now formed part of the Naval Discipline Act, and were 'naturally couched in old fashioned and lofty language'. Captains were recommended to explain some of the terms afterwards, for 'the crew will probably imagine the Act to be some ancient naval ceremony and will stand to attention with blank minds till it is over'.[46]

The captain of a warship, even a small one, had a huge amount of power to inflict punishments on his men – perhaps more than any other single individual in a democratic society. Courts-martial were very inconvenient in the navy, because officers from several different ships had to be assembled together and this could not be done at sea. As a result, captains were given powers to try men and give a variety of sentences. According to *Your Ship*,

As a Commanding Officer, you are an autocrat pure and simple, and you are subject to the same temptations as an autocrat. No-one in you ship can check your excesses, or point out your eccentricities; no-one can question your more downright assertions; everyone must endure your temper or any other foible you may develop. You are treated with deference and ceremony not always granted to a cabinet minister.[47]

The captain could delegate some of his powers of punishment to junior officers. Usually the officer of the watch was allowed to give a man up to two hours extra duty for one day. The first lieutenant and perhaps the engineer officer were allowed to give extra duty for up to seven days, but more serious offences had to go before the captain. He could inflict extra work or drill for up to fourteen days, stoppage of leave for up to 60 days, or deductions from pay. He could stop a man's grog or reduce him to the second class for leave, so that he would not be allowed ashore on short leaves. With the authority of an officer of commander's rank or higher, he could sentence a man to up to fourteen days in the cells; indeed he could order imprisonment for up to three months, but only with the backing of his commander-in-chief.

A small ship like a destroyer had no cells on board, and Admiral Glennie asked his captains to make sure that one was available in the depot ship at Scapa before reading out a punishment warrant.[48] Ratings were usually sentenced to 'detention' rather than 'imprisonment', as it carried less stigma and did not affect their future careers. Often, however, they served it in civilian prisons, which officers sometimes complained was not a deterrent – it was more like a rest cure after the horrors of active service.

In cases of refusal of duty, Gretton was inclined to give the man a chance to get out of it before the stakes became too high:

> If a rating is brought up for 'Refusal of Duty' he is to be told that such an offence is one of the most serious against discipline. Further, that if after five minutes consideration, he thinks better of it and obeys the order, he will only be charged with 'Not immediately obeying the order', the result of which will probably not affect his future career as would the offence of refusal of duty.

But if he persisted, he should be put under arrest.[49]

Leave-breaking was subject to severe punishments, but it had to be treated carefully. In wartime, men were often held up by bombing or late trains, and officers had to discover when such excuses were genuine.

> Many offenders will produce most eloquent reasons for being adrift. Unless they have definite proof that the misfortunes which appear to dog them were quite genuine and that they made every human effort to get on board on time and allowed a good margin to spare, the normal scale of punishment should be given.[50]

On the other hand, there was always the danger of punishing men who were otherwise blameless, and turning them into malcontents. The navy had enough of these already, and furthermore it was suggested, 'There are many ratings of an adventurous nature who like to flout the regulations for the sheer joy of it.'[51] Rayner thought that the corvette *Verbena* was fairly typical in having two ratings, a seaman and a stoker, who were constantly in trouble for arriving late when the ship was under sailing orders, though they were good hands in every other respect. Eventually he persuaded both to go for leading rates, and their behaviour improved dramatically.[52]

A captain should take an interest in the crew's recreation. He should appoint one of his officers to organize games and should encourage contests between the departments in the ship or within the flotilla. Lieutenant Turner felt that the captain should not take part himself unless he was good at the game, while Commander Tothill suggested he might take volunteers out sailing in the ship's boats – 'you will win their respect, if only through their inexperience of sailing'. All this would tend to increase the crew's team spirit, though not nearly as much as a successful action with the enemy.

A good captain would show consideration for his crew and do anything to increase their contact with home: 'it must not be forgotten that, in wartime at least, the large majority of your men feel very keenly their enforced separation from their families.' Commander Tothill suggested that the ship's postman should always be landed first on reaching a port, and officers should be ready to censor any letters the crew might want to send in reply without delay. Leave was even more important, but captains were warned not to raise expectations too high if there was any doubt. If shore leave were granted, the captain should lecture the men on any danger spots ashore and the importance of their behaviour. He should also warn about the penalties for leave breaking.

It was also suggested in the Admiralty that, 'The religious aspect should not be forgotten, and it must be realized that the higher qualities can be engendered only through a living faith and contact with religion.' But in practice the section on religion in *Your Ship* was kept quite short; it only referred to the need to hold some kind of service on board and take account of men who were not members of the Church of England.

Commander Gretton was firm on the smartness of his men: 'The tendency for small ships during this War is to grow steadily more slack in points like dress, appearance of ship, cleanliness and general smartness ... There is no need for this and I would like all officers to help in preserving a high standard.'[53] It was not only regular RN officers who felt this way, and D. A. Rayner wrote, 'it was very easy to let the men slide into slipshod ways; and once started on that road it was desperately difficult to stop. All through the war I insisted on

269

certain standards of uniform and shaving for the bridge watchkeepers and as they included the look-outs, who exchanged every two hours, it virtually meant that the whole ship's company kept themselves smart.'[54] But these were probably the exception that proved the rule, and men who slept in their clothes for nights on end could not be expected to maintain a high standard during working hours:

Normally overalls [were worn] – the blue dungaree, complete blue overalls they used to serve out in the service. Sometimes [the top part] was rolled down and the sleeves tied round the waist so you only had the bottom half on. Some used to wear grey flannels who'd come in [hostilities only crew]. Of course we didn't have any – the regulars, but they used to wear their civilian clothes, well civilian trousers. And we were always clomping around in sea boots and that sort of thing.[55]

It was equally difficult to keep the ship itself smart during hard service in rough oceans. Commander Mickelthwaite of *Eskimo* had seen Spanish ships in bad condition during their own war from 1936–9:

he said that during the recent civil war in Spain he used to see the Spanish destroyers which operated off Gibraltar. They were the dirtiest looking ships he had ever seen and he did not understand how any captain would allow a ship to get so filthy. Now he knows and would like to apologise for what he said about the Spanish ships. The guns are definitely dirty and rust very common, particularly on the close range weapons. I doubt if we [the US Navy] would permit them to fire. The gunnery officer of the destroyer said they would not do so in peacetime.[56]

The action against *Scharnhorst* on Boxing Day of 1943 caused the system of feeding crews during actions of long duration to be reconsidered. Most destroyers were fed on the antiquated Standard Ration and Messing Allowance System, which placed the onus on the individual messes. Clearly, this was difficult to use in a long action, when the men might be at their stations for hours at a time, and the mess organization would be disrupted. Chiefs and petty officers had their own messes but would be spread around the ship. Not all the stokers were needed in the engine room at the same time, and they might be deployed as a damage control party, or with gun crews. Stewards and cooks were often part of the first-aid party. Each mess tended to be jealous of its privileges and property, but Home Fleet Destroyer Orders compelled them to share some of their food, and set up an organization that cut across the traditional structures.

One of the captain's first duties on a large or medium-sized ship such as a destroyer or corvette was to draw up a set of standing orders for his officers, and to a lesser extent his crew. Usually this would be done on the basis of previous experiences. Monsarrat had been rebuked for failing to follow Lombard-Hobson's instructions to the officer of the watch on calling the captain, but he adopted them word for word for his own first command.[57]

Commander Peter Gretton was already a very experienced escort group officer by the time he wrote *Duncan's* standing orders in July 1943. He had entered the Royal Navy as a cadet in 1926 and spent most of his time in destroyers from 1938 onwards. He became senior officer of the Seventh Escort Group, based mainly at Londonderry, in November 1942 and was mostly in *Duncan*, a destroyer leader built in 1932. During the spring of 1943 he led the group through its greatest battles, escorting three convoys – HX 231 from Halifax to the United Kingdom, ONS 5 outward to the USA, and SC 130 back to Britain. Together these formed the turning-point of the Battle of the Atlantic. Admiral Doenitz specifically mentioned his defeat against SC 130 when, at the end of May, he ordered his U-boats to withdraw from the Atlantic to rearm.

Gretton's standing orders were written during a relatively quiet period after the great battles of the spring. He was prepared to listen to advice from his officers:

It may happen that as a result of experience, or change of circumstances, an order becomes redundant, or obsolete. Should this appear to any Officer to be the case, he should report the matter to me with a view to the amendment, or cancellation, of that order. An order which is in existence but which is not enforced, is a germ of slackness and inefficiency.[58]

Gretton continued to be concerned with captain's standing orders after the war. In 1961, as Flag Officer Sea Training at Portland, he was responsible for working up new ships, and he found that accidents were happening because some captains' standing orders were 'neither clear nor comprehensive' and insisted on seeing a copy of each before it was issued.[59]

Rear-Admiral Irvine Glennie, another former captain of HMS *Hood*, drew up skeleton orders for the Home Fleet destroyer force in 1943. Destroyers were originally conceived to operate in flotillas and were dependent on a slightly larger vessel for much of their infrastructure, but this quickly broke down in wartime, and most ships spent their time operating in ones or twos around the world. Roderick Macdonald observed that the old system was 'too inflexible to allow for deployment and losses in a World War'.[60] Because of the great range of their operations, they could not always rely on finding the shore support that was available to coastal craft and, in a different way, to escort vessels. Instead each destroyer had to learn to become self-reliant, which made the working-up stage particularly important.

Unlike escort vessels, landing craft and coastal forces, destroyers were mostly commanded by regular RN officers, but many of them had been promoted much faster than in peacetime, and, as the *Destroyer Orders* make clear, they were not always fully experienced in seamanship and navigation. Furthermore, they were often operating under great pressure. A large part of Glennie's document is devoted to avoiding elementary mistakes such as misreading the chart or hitting a jetty or another ship. In this respect he takes the opposite view from Pridham and Pelly – the expression

272

'safety first' is used positively. Most of his orders are only an outline, to be filled in by the officer in command with reference to the relevant King's Regulations, Admiralty Fleet Orders, official handbooks and local orders. He does not even need to cover every category mentioned: 'It will not be necessary to write orders on every subject but they must be thought over if you are to act quickly when emergencies arise.'[61] Glennie is rather more specific in the matter of signalling, because that obviously could not be left to a single ship and needed coordination within the command.

Fear of mutiny was present in many naval officers' minds during much of the war. By March 1944 the end of the European War was in sight and the new Second Sea Lord, Sir Algernon Willis, began to worry about the aftermath. He noticed that, 'We have seldom got through a major war without some breakdown of morale varying from serious mutiny down to vociferous expressions of dissension and dissatisfaction.' He was aware that naval mutinies had led to social breakdown in Russia and Germany at the end of the previous war, and even in peacetime Britain the Invergordon Mutiny of 1931 had forced the country off the gold standard and undermined the confidence of naval officers. Furthermore, there were likely to be specific problems if the war in the Pacific went on for years, as might well be expected:

some of the ingredients which go to make trouble of the type referred to seem likely to exist when the Germans are defeated and the full realisation that for the Navy this will mean an even greater effort in order to defeat Japan is brought home to the personnel. We shall no longer be fighting for our existence, the homeland will no longer be in danger, many of the other two services will be released to industry and at the same time personnel of the Navy, which must be kept at full strength, will be required to do more foreign service than ever.[62]

Willis wanted to make sure that all officers were 'mentally prepared' for such an eventuality, and a booklet was commissioned to give guidance. The result was quite alarming in places, with instructions that 'shooting to *kill* should only be resorted to as a last extremity'. Admiral Horton of Western Approaches Command objected to its tone and basic assumptions and claimed, 'no ordinary ship's company will resort to mass indiscipline unless they are labouring under grievances which a reasonable investigation will prove to be well founded.' Furthermore the pamphlet itself was dangerous:

I feel that if they are generally distributed in their present form and at the present time there is a grave danger that they will not achieve their object and may indeed help to bring about the contingencies which they are designed to prevent. We have now serving a very large number of officers, even of Commander's rank in the Reserves, with relatively short experience of the traditional principles and methods of naval discipline and leadership. I feel strongly that the effect of these instructions in their present shape on many such officers, and on the even less experienced officers to whom it is intended to be circulated, is likely to be very unsettling and to produce in them a state of anxiety and distrust which must invariably arouse similar reactions in their men.

The Admiralty took Horton's advice and the document was only circulated to very senior officers under a 'Top Secret' classification. In fact there was no great crisis, partly because the demobilization system was considered very fair, partly because the atomic bomb effectively ended the Pacific War before British naval forces were too deeply engaged. There were plenty of small mutinies in the later years of the war, mostly because, as Horton perceived, there were difficulties of leadership in individual ships. In the destroyer *Fortune*, for example, Roderick Macdonald witnessed a 'mass refusal to obey an order' which was caused by the captain's incompetence and was 'without doubt mutiny as defined in the Naval Discipline Act'. It was put down after the first lieutenant went round the mess decks reading the relevant passages from the

Articles of War.[63] A. H. Cherry had to use the threat of marines from a nearby cruiser to get the men to go back to work in the frigate *Braithwaite* in 1943. He attributed the outbreak to the men being seduced by the delights of Boston, where the ship was fitting out, and a weak coxswain.[64] But there was no general mutiny in the navy and no need to bring the harsh provisions of the Addendum to CB 3027 into play.

Even with his ship in harbour, a captain could not be totally relaxed about her safety. At anchor there was always a risk of dragging in strong forces created by wind or tide. If there was any possibility of this, he was advised to keep up some steam and have an officer of the watch taking fixes on objects on shore periodically. An experienced seaman in the bows could test the cables for vibration, which gave a good indication. Moored to a buoy, he could feel a little more secure, but there was always the possibility that part of the system might break. Furthermore, 'If lying snugly to a battleship buoy, do not imagine that you are immune from all evils. It is quite possible that another ship may drag down on you. It is therefore essential to be at short notice in dragging weather.'[65]

Gretton had problems while at anchor off Londonderry in 1943. Two very inexperienced officers were on anchor watch and were taking bearings on a distant mountain but failed to notice that much nearer objects were rushing past as the strong wind caused the anchor to drag. Gretton dashed out of his cabin and alerted the chief engine room artificer on the way. He found Ordinary Seaman Geoffrey Ball, who was doing duty as boatswain's mate, and ordered him to pipe 'action stations' on the boatswain's call. 'Everyone must have thought I'd gone mad! Action stations at anchor!' The buffer arrived to take charge on deck and a fender was got out as the ship collided with McKinney's Light, demolishing the wooden structure with a loud groan. Gretton ordered the anchor cable to be slipped as he used the engines to stop the ship going aground, and she was subsequently able to take part in her cruise as leader of a support group.[66]

Moored alongside a jetty or wharf in a tidal stream, the captain had to post men to let out or take in mooring lines with the movements of the tide. He had to be concerned about 'scend', the waves that might crash the ship against the jetty. In an enclosed dock, such as Gladstone dock, which formed the main escort base at Liverpool, he was more secure – apart from air raids and the danger of another ship crashing into him.

Notes on the Handling and Safety of Ships, one of the documents collected by Guy Hodgkinson while he was preparing the text for *Your Ship*, takes a very pessimistic view of the capabilities of amateur seamen.

If you see that a crash is inevitable, whether due to your misjudgement or some force throwing you onto a ship or jetty, see that the crash is a 'bumper' and not a 'grinder'. The 'grinder' is when you still have way on at the moment of impact. This allows the more knobbly points to grind down the other ships side, and generally come into contact with his more knobbly points.[67]

It was not just the hastily trained men of the RNVR who had difficulty in coming alongside in a strong wind, or picking up a buoy. Most regular naval officers learned seamanship in ship's boats by the age of twenty. After that they had little to do with it unless they happened to serve in destroyers in the middle years of their career. Admiral Cunningham wrote: 'the best officers to be found in big ships have come from submarines and destroyers.'[68] But other promising officers tended to specialize, and the most ambitious went in for gunnery, so that they would have little to do with seamanship until, around the age of 40, they might find themselves in command of a cruiser. *Your Ship* made it clear that the captain alone was responsible for manoeuvring the ship at close quarters – ship-handling was the sole exception to the statement that a captain would be judged 'not on what you do yourself, but on what you inspire others to do'.[69] Captain Rory O'Connor had been a highly successful commander, responsible for the administrative work of HMS *Hood*, but when promoted to take command of the cruiser *Neptune* in 1940 he found it necessary to hand over to his navigating officer when mooring up in Alexandria, saying, 'Pilot, you have done this one before; so you take the ship in, and if there is any trouble, I will take all the blame.'[70] As to *Hood* herself, Joseph Wellings of the US Navy noted that it took four hours to moor her to a buoy at Scapa Flow in December 1940, and a few days later he watched as she shifted her mooring: 'Not a very good job – cut mooring buoy.'[71] It is not surprising that the young men of the RNVR had difficulty in close-quarter seamanship, though there was little to help them as *Notes on the Handling and Safety of Ships* was not issued generally during the war. Large parts of it, including the paragraph on 'bumpers and grinders', were incorporated in the *Aide Memoire for Small Ship Captains* in 1947.

The captain's first task was to take the ship out of harbour. All elements in the ship's control system were tested beforehand, including the engine room telegraphs. After that, the engine room was sent the message 'obey telegraphs' to tell them that the test was over. The boatswain's mate piped 'special sea duty men to your stations'. The coxswain went to the wheel, and trusted men to the engine room telegraphs and to take charge of the mooring lines. On the bridge, the captain could use various techniques to get his ship out of a tight spot. If she was alongside a jetty with other ships forward and astern of her, for example, he could release all ropes except the spring leading forward from the stern. Putting the engine into astern would swing the bows out and allow him to leave the berth. Then he might have to manoeuvre out of a small dock gate or through an overcrowded anchorage.

At sea, the escort captain's main concern was to make sure that the officers of the watch kept station on the convoy, and what to do in foul weather. In this case, as a last resort the ship might have to heave to, turn slowly into the wind and head slowly forward to reduce the effect of wind and waves. If he did this, he was advised to warn the men on the mess decks first – 'This keeps the crockery bill down.'[72] In action, it was important to be able to manoeuvre his ship quickly, and here the old Flower-class had an advantage over their successors, the River-class frigates. At a speed of twelve knots, a Flower would need only 180 yards and 2 minutes 40 seconds to turn through 32 points or 360 degrees; a River would need 366 yards and 4 minutes 35 seconds.[73]

Entering a strange harbour, the captain was advised to find out as much about it as possible – navigational hazards as well as security precautions, such as booms and code-words. If anchoring, he had to choose a berth with enough room to swing through 360 degrees without hitting any obstructions, and to allow for the rise and fall of the tide. Mooring up to a buoy, he tried to approach it against the current so that he would still be able to steer the ship at slow speeds. If he was not familiar with local conditions, he might have to go over it more than once. Coming to a pier or jetty was often the most testing, especially when there were spectators. Special sea duty men were called again, including those who could throw ropes, or heave lines, with great distance and accuracy. If the wind was blowing the ship on, the captain might try to move slowly into a position opposite the berth, then gently drift in. A twin-screw ship had certain advantages in tight conditions, as the engines

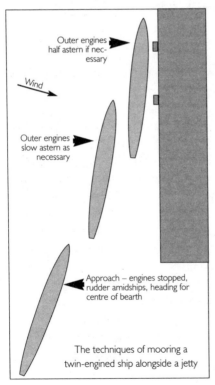

Outer engines half astern if necessary

Wind

Outer engines slow astern as necessary

Approach – engines stopped, rudder amidships, heading for centre of bearth

The techniques of mooring a twin-engined ship alongside a jetty

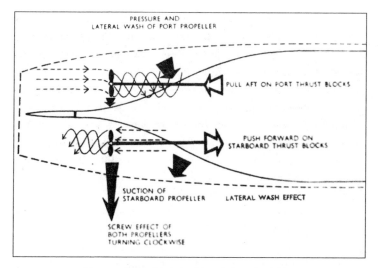

The use of propellers in berthing a twin-engined ship.
(National Archives)

could work in opposite directions to produce a high degree of manoeuvrability.

> Nearly all small twin screw warships can be placed alongside by use of headropes and screws only. Theoretically there is no need to get out any other wires until alongside. In practice, however, it is a good precaution to get a spring out forward, in case the headrope parts, but the spring should never take any weight, until finally adjusting the ship's position.
>
> The practice of hurling clusters of heaving lines out from the quarterdeck as your stern comes in is worse than useless, because it causes anxiety over the screws. In the best ships the after securing wires are handed over abreast the bollard to which they are going to be secured.
>
> Nothing looks better than a ship coming alongside in complete silence. Nothing sounds worse or is more undignified than a ship arriving alongside in a hail of heaving lines, and a tumult of shouting.[74]

Close-quarters seamanship was very poor in landing craft in the early stages, as Peter Bull testifies – 'I had five collisions in the first three days ...' He was not exaggerating, and the Captain of LCTs was pessimistic in July 1942:

It is considered that the lower standard must be accepted under the circumstances and that as a result an increase in damage through collisions must be expected. The present standard of the commanding officers is not regarded as satisfactory, and there is a tendency for it to become worse, but with the rapid expansion this appears inevitable for some months.[75]

This began to improve through many months of practice, and landing craft crews would be tested during several major landings in less than ideal conditions.

Of course battle was the supreme purpose and test of every warship, and a ship had to be as prepared as possible before leaving harbour. Destroyers had to be ready for any kind of action, and Glennie's orders give an inkling of what was involved. The crew would need to be instructed in the various degrees of readiness according to the immediacy and nature of the threat. Lookouts were briefed on their duties, and hands were trained in aircraft recognition. Control systems were set up for high- and low-angle firing, against aircraft and surface targets. There were special methods for dealing with fast targets, such as enemy torpedo-boats and dive-bombers. Crews had to be trained in the use of searchlights and star shell for night actions and the supply of different types of ammunition. They needed to know how to use depth-charges and other anti-submarine weapons, as well as torpedoes. They were trained in how to board and capture a U-boat, and how to salvage it if it was sinking.

More defensively, fire and repair parties were set up and trained, and they learned how to shore up bulkheads with wooden props. Feeding and sanitary arrangements were considered for a long action, as well as the treatment of the wounded. In case of defeat by surprise or overwhelming force, the crew had to learn how to get rid of the ship's confidential books, destroy the asdic set, abandon ship and scuttle her if necessary.[76]

Escort vessels usually had a smaller range of duties than fleet destroyers, but these were no less demanding. They were sent to the well-known base at Tobermory in the Western Isles of Scotland to prepare for the Battle of the Atlantic.

10
WESTERN ISLES

The crew of HMS *Clover* probably did not know that they were making history early in October 1944, as they headed north towards the island of Mull, off the west coast of Scotland, after finishing a refit at Belfast. The ship, a Flower-class corvette built by Fleming & Ferguson on the Clyde, had been there before, in June 1941, though with different officers and crew. Many of the officers and men had been at Tobermory too, including her captain Lieutenant T. E. Fanshawe, RNR, who had gained a great deal of action experience in his 26 years. Born in 1918, he had not long been out of the Merchant Navy training school at Pangbourne, on the banks of the River Thames, when he was called up for naval service at the beginning of the war. He was transferred out of the battleship *Royal Oak* just in time to miss her sinking by *U-47*. He went on to become first lieutenant of the corvette *Sunflower* and then to help commission *Rother*, the first of the new River-class frigates, under Monsarrat's Captain Case. Despite his youth, his experience of the Atlantic war was unrivalled. Temporary Lieutenant W. M. Baker of the RNVR was her first lieutenant, and the other officers were Temporary Sub-Lieutenants L. E. England of the RNR, and G. H. C. Evershed, H. S. Hammond and C. A. C. Chesterman of the RNVR.

The base at Tobermory had become legendary since it was set up in 1940. Originally the Admiralty had planned a joint Anglo-French operation for the working up of anti-submarine vessels, sited in the western French port of L'Orient. That was soon overtaken by events, and L'Orient became a U-boat base, so Tobermory was chosen instead. Well away from bombing and other enemy activity, it was a fine, sheltered and little-used harbour. The town, planned as a major fishing port late in the eighteenth century, had a population of less than 700 and was not likely to offer too many distractions to the crews of visiting ships, for there might be up to a dozen of them in at once with an average crew of perhaps 80, plus 200 base staff. The remoteness was not a problem from the supply point of view. Each ship would bring its own stores for a two- or three-week stay, and there was no need for rail links as enjoyed by seaside resort bases such as *Royal Arthur* and *King Alfred*. There was plenty of deep water to exercise in the Minches, between the Inner and Outer Hebrides.

Stories about *Western Isles*, the training ship at Tobermory, were well known in the navy and must have been retold in wardroom and on mess decks as the ship got closer. Most centred on the personality of her commodore, Sir Gilbert Stephenson, known as 'puggy', 'monkey brand' or 'electric whiskers', and his constant efforts to keep the crews alert and test their initiative.

Once, when he was putting a trawler through its paces, he said to a Leading Seaman, a member of a gun crew: 'You're dead, lie down.' The rating obeyed but, after a few minutes, the Commodore noticed he was on his feet at his usual station and, in his usual fierce manner, exclaimed: 'I said you're dead!' The rating's reply was: 'Dead or alive my place is at this gun.' The Commodore's reaction? 'Full marks.'[1]

They had probably heard at least one version of the most famous story:

Without any preliminaries he flung his gold-braided cap on the deck and said abruptly to the Quartermaster – 'That is a small unexploded bomb dropped by an enemy plane. What are you going to do about it?' The sailor, who had evidently heard about these unconventional tests of initiative, promptly took a step forward and kicked the cap into the sea. Everyone waited for a great roar of protest from the Commodore. But not at all. He warmly commended the lad on his presence of mind, and then, pointing to the submerged cap said: 'That's a man overboard! Jump in and save him!'[2]

Clover entered the harbour late in the afternoon of the 4th. The town's buildings had not yet acquired the brightly-coloured paint that would make them familiar to a generation of children more than half a century later, and they looked rather grey. But there was no doubting the shelter of the harbour, protected from all winds except from the north. According to the *Western Isles* syllabus, the commodore would now 'interview' the commanding officer and explain the objects of *Western Isles*. That rather understated the drama of the occasion. As the ship attempted to pick up a buoy with her raw officers and crew, Stephenson would usually arrive as dramatically as possible in his launch. Sub-Lieutenant B. G. Mitchell was mooring up his ship in the Bay as officer of the watch while the captain and first lieutenant were both below, when the commodore burst on board. 'Is everyone shaving in this ship?'[3] The arrival of *Motor Launch 559* was even more dramatic.

> The barge, very close now, seemed to disappear. Its engine cut. Where was it? Suddenly, over the flare of the bows of 559, in the centre, appeared a be-whiskered face, visible from the bridge but invisible to the Ordinary Seaman leaning on a broom, his eyes fixed on the bos'n's parties waiting, and looking puzzled, at the outer craft. He hauled himself up, straddled the guardrails, slapped the Ordinary Seaman on the back, picked up the broom he had dropped, and, holding it out in front of him like a boarding pike, charged at the bridge.
>
> As I froze into a tremendous salute, with one eye on the broom, the Commodore barked: 'I want the mincer – and your ship is on fire in the engine room!'[4]

After that Stephenson saw each captain individually, and gave them 'clearly to understand that "Western Isles" function is to help and that there should never be any hesitation on his part in asking for assistance'.[5]

The ship settled down for the night, and training began at 0845 next morning. One of Stephenson's staff officers came on board to discuss the fighting organization of the ship with the key officers and ratings – the captain, first lieutenant, gunnery, anti-submarine and depth-charge officers, the coxswain and the chief boatswain's mate. Meanwhile the *Western Isles'* gunnery officer checked over the ship's armament, 'putting in hand any repairs necessary or supplying sufficient ammunition to enable the ship to carry out the working up programme'. The engineer, electrical and radar officers also came on board from the base ship and inspected the appropriate departments.

This was over by 1130, and the crew got into the ship's boats to go over to *Western Isles* herself. This was part of the test, for Stephenson was one of the old school of officers who believed that 'a ship is known by its boats'. He often watched as they were lowered to see if there was any slackness or incompetence in that delicate operation, and he observed the crews as they rowed the cutters and whalers across the harbour. The men climbed up the side of the ship, the second to be used in the role; she had been converted from a merchant ship, formerly the Dutch *Batavier IV*, in 1941.

The crew went below and settled down in the ship's cinema to watch the film *Escort Teams at Work*. There was general agreement among the staff that it was not quite what was needed in the circumstances, but it was the best available. Amid rousing music and the dulcet tones of a newsreel commentator, it showed stock footage of convoys at sea, U-boats and British troops landing in Italy. It stressed the vital importance of protecting the convoys, and how much everyone – 'from captain to cook' – had to play his part; 'any one man who fails to pull his weight can bring disaster to the convoy.' It acknowledged that the highly secret radar, high frequency direction finding and Hedgehog each had a major role to play in the campaign. It showed engine room, asdic, radar, gun, depth-charge and Hedgehog teams at work, and the climax was the staged sinking of a U-boat. It ended with a clip of an aircraft carrier and a battleship in rough weather, almost identical to the ending of *In Which We Serve*, which had perhaps inspired some of the crew to join the navy in the first place, and with the stirring line, 'the convoys must get through'.[6]

The lights went up and most of the crew had their first good look at the commodore himself. They saw a small, highly energetic 66-year-old man with apparently uncontrollable facial hair and a brisk manner. He had entered the navy as a Dartmouth cadet in the usual way in 1892 and served in destroyers. In the First World War he led a group of trawlers in the Dardanelles and had a chance to learn about the capabilities of reserve officers. He retired from the navy in 1929 as a vice-admiral and spent part of the 1930s as secretary of the Navy League, which campaigned for a bigger fleet. He was recalled at the beginning of the war as commodore of ocean convoys and he distinguished himself at Dunkirk, where Lieutenant Irvine had noticed his black-and-white views and his capacity for inspired leadership.

Stephenson's opening words for these occasions are not recorded, but the new training school at Stornaway was modelled on his practices, and the captain there began by emphasizing the need for secrecy, and warning the men not to talk about the film or any equipment they had seen – secret weapons were not secret once they had been talked about. The working-up would consist of team training and individual training. Speed was essential in modern warfare; every member of the ship's company counted; each man must know his job and something about his neighbour's. The instruction would involve hard work and long hours; instructors would help any individual, but could not teach those unwilling to learn. The captain concluded by hoping that 'efficiency will increase, confidence in self and shipmates will ensue, thus resulting in a happy ship, to the benefit of all'. Probably Stephenson did not undermine the men's confidence by telling them what he wrote elsewhere about his philosophy: 'You take it for granted that everyone knows nothing about his job and start from rock bottom.'[7] In theory the men had been trained at their individual jobs already, but from long experience Stephenson knew better. Shore training had been rushed and oversimplified. Not everyone had been able to absorb it in the time available, and in any case it would take on a new meaning in a real ship, with a real ship's company, sailing on real seas and with the prospect of action in the Battle of the Atlantic looming ever closer.

He outlined his philosophy more generally for an article in the *Monthly Anti-Submarine Report* just after *Clover* sailed:

> To equip a major war vessel with up-to-date armament – depth charges, oerlikons, hedgehog, squid, asdics, radar and D/F – and be satisfied that part of the ship's company is sufficiently conversant with the method of operation of such equipment, does not entitle the Commanding Officer of that ship to believe that his ship is ready for all contingencies. Much more is needed before it can be claimed to constitute an efficient fighting force. The Commanding Officer has to be satisfied that every officer knows not only his own duty but that of every other officer and the whole ship's company has to be moulded into one team. This cannot be accomplished if the cook in the galley is inefficient or if there are leaks in the seamen's messdeck, if the men are undisciplined while onshore or untidy in their dress. Neither can efficiency be expected if smooth working is hampered by minor defects. Not until every man in the ship is happy in the knowledge that he knows his job and shows a carefree disposition in his mess, can a ship be considered efficient.[8]

More privately, he had decided his aims:

> my number one priority was *Spirit*: this was the first essential – determination to win. Next came *Discipline*: it's no good being the finest men in the world if you are not going to obey orders. Third – *Administration*: making sure the work of the ship was evenly divided: that meals were in the right place at the right time; that the whole organisation of the ship was both stable and elastic. Then, lastly – and this may surprise you – lastly, *Technique* – how to use the equipment. That would have been quite useless unless the spirit was right in the first place.[9]

The crew went back to their ship, and that afternoon the various teams had training in their own specialities. The fully-trained radar ratings joined with the untrained men who would assist them, and all were given instruction in the theory of radar. Some went for training as lookouts under the *Western Isles'* gunnery officer. They were taught about the different scanning techniques for anti-aircraft, far, near, fog and night lookouts, the need for concentration and the care of optical instruments. The leading members of the gun crews – the layer, trainer and sightsetter – were taught at the spotting table, which was used to record the fall of shot and whether it was 'over', 'short' or 'straddling'. The anti-submarine team went off to see a film on asdic attack, probably not for the first time. One group learned about boatwork from the physical training instructor. This was not a luxury: boats might well have to be used in the middle of the ocean to transfer men or goods from ship to ship, pick up survivors or even rescue men from one's own ship. The junior ratings went off to learn more about seamanship under the boatswain of *Western Isles*.

The ship remained in Tobermory harbour for the next five days, as yet more exercises were carried out by the various teams. Signallers trained with buzzers and flashing lights as well as semaphore, the anti-submarine team spent time on the attack teacher, and the gunnery officer conducted drill with the main armament and shooting practice with .303-inch rifles. There was a demonstration of pyrotechnics for all available officers and men, and the base accountant officer came on board to check the administrative organization. Anti-aircraft gunners saw the various parts of the *Eyeshooting film*, produced by the gunnery branch to teach them how to aim at close-range aircraft without the aid of radar or fire-control devices. Then they practised in the dome teacher, a spherical building ashore in which the movements of an aircraft were projected on to the inner surface and followed by the trainee gunner.

Meanwhile, the officers and the radar, asdic and signal ratings prepared for a communication exercise with the other ships in the harbour. The object was to test the ship's action organization, its plotting methods and communications. The captain and plotting officer of each ship in port at the moment were briefed on board *Western Isles* in the morning of the second day and given the theoretical situation of an imaginary convoy – its composition, course and speed, the state of the weather and the tactical situation. One of the captains was chosen to act as senior officer of the escort. Stephenson warned the officers not to cheat.

This exercises [sic] is designed to give you an opportunity to prove the efficiency of your Plotting and Communications Organisation before you meet the enemy. An unrealistic approach, E:G: employing additional communications numbers who would not be available in Action Plotting in any position other than that in which you would be in action, or reading up Recorder Traces beforehand in order to anticipate NON-SUBS etc: may make your plot neater and the exercise less chaotic but will achieve NOTHING towards the efficient WORKING UP of your Action organisation.

The exercise began at ten o'clock next morning when the flagship dropped a time ball to signal the start, and the teams on board each ship started their watches and plots. It involved all available executive officers of each ship, the plotting team, two submarine detector ratings, one radar operator and a number of signallers. To test the communications systems, *Western Isles* would transmit signals based on direction finding by wireless telegraphy using Morse code; radar and asdic reports by radio telephony using voice; and sighting reports visually, using lamps, semaphore or flags. Each ship would remain at anchor but might take part in imaginary chases and hunts according to the information supplied, with the captain giving courses and speeds to the plotting team. A ship would not leave her station to investigate a D/F contact unless ordered by the senior officer of the group, but with a radar contact it would be assumed to be heading to cut off the contact from the convoy. Asdic contacts were based on prepared recorder traces that would be opened on orders and would contain instructions to the operators. Ships might be detailed to pick up survivors from wrecks, in which case they would remain fifteen minutes on the task before returning. The ships would employ standard counter attacks as detailed in the Atlantic Convoy Instructions, and the sinking of a submarine by gunfire would only be counted if it was verified by control in *Western Isles*. The exercise lasted two hours, and that afternoon in the dog watches there was a post mortem in which lessons learned were assessed.[10]

Stephenson was sometimes told that his base would be cheaper and more efficient if it was on shore, perhaps in the eponymous Western Isles Hotel, which overlooked the harbour, but he defended his practice stoutly:

> the fact that the ship is moored amongst the flotilla wearing the broad pendant of the Commodore has an important bearing on the success of the base. The psychological value of being afloat cannot be over-estimated. ... Power boats transport classes back and forward and many pulling boats – whalers and skiffs – are seen approaching the gangways, all under the eyes of the Commodore and his staff officers, who are on the look-out for slackness in observing the rig of the day, or for the errors of the inexperienced oarsman or coxswain. Human nature being what it is, it is safe to say that the first impression gained on arrival at Tobermory would be considerably lessened if the introductory interview took place in a shore establishment instead of the flag ship.[11]

Stephenson directed a sophisticated operation from his office in *Western Isles*. His chief of staff at the end of the war was Commander Roy Talbot, a regular officer who survived the sinking of the cruiser *Edinburgh* on the Russian convoys in 1942 and commanded destroyers during an attack off Dieppe and at the Anzio landings. With his philosophy of 'That's life, you can't please everyone all the time', he had enough skill to handle Stephenson tactfully.[12] The commodore's secretary had an even more thankless job, and the post was held by no less than seven different officers during the war. For the moment it was Paymaster-Lieutenant-Commander C. R. Rowe, until he left in January. Reginald Palmer, the first lieutenant of *Western Isles*, had served far longer, for he was first appointed to supervise the conversion of the first *Western Isles* in 1940. He stayed with his troublesome chief until the end and Stephenson singled him out for praise: 'His skill, resource and great experience have always been forthcoming. It is difficult to picture what I would have done without him ...'[13] The ship's office also included two accountant officers and three Wrens to type out letters and training programmes. There were four staff officers who arranged and supervised the programmes. Gunnery training was conducted by two gunnery officers trained at HMS *Excellent*, two warrant gunners, four gunner's mates, a petty officer skilled in fire-control and an anti-aircraft rating. The anti-submarine branch was slightly larger, with four officers, including one to run the attack teacher, a chief and six petty officers and four AB submarine detectors. There was a substantial electrical maintenance staff, mostly for the delicate asdic and Hedgehog installations in the ships under training, as well as six petty officers and four other ratings for the repair of radar and electrical equipment. There were shipwrights, a plumber and a painter for work on the hulls, and a substantial signals staff headed by a warrant telegraphist and including eleven telegraphist and visual signal ratings, to instruct the visiting ships and help with the conduct of exercises. Also with warrant rank was the Boatswain for seamanship instruction. In the early days this post was held by Charles Fooks, a butcher's boy until he joined the navy in 1908. He qualified in gunnery and served in destroyers for most of the First World War.[14]

The engineering department was headed by a lieutenant-commander, with nine ratings at artificer, chief stoker and motor mechanic level, five petty officers and twenty below these rates. Its duties included the maintenance of *Western Isles'* own engines, though the ship rarely put to sea, except on at least one occasion just to ensure the crew's allowances of duty-free drink.[15] The department was also responsible for duties with the engines of the ships working up, though their own engine-room staffs were not hard pressed at Tobermory. They had to work as much as anyone during the sea exercises, but they had no specific training – perhaps it was assumed that they had already been exercised during the ship's trials and the voyage to Tobermory. *Western Isles'* engineers also maintained the flagship's motorboats and provided two lorry drivers for shore transport.

The medical staff consisted of a surgeon-lieutenant and a dentist, mostly operating in the disused distillery in the town and supported by four sick-berth attendants including a dental assistant and a VAD nurse. There were 49 wrens carrying out a variety of duties, living in various requisitioned buildings ashore but often working in the ship's office and cinema or in the visiting ships. They included laundry maids, shorthand typists, stewardesses, supply assistants, cooks, signallers and maintenance staff for intricate coding machines.

Western Isles had a total of six ship's boats, used for ferrying the commodore and his staff around the harbour and for taking crews to classes when their own ship's boats were not available. Stephenson's own boat's crew was carefully selected. 'In *Western Isles* we had either men old enough to be grandfathers, or young boys; the old men were so nervous that this in itself constituted a great danger, so I told the First Lieutenant to give me a crew of boys – the sort who would have a fast motor-cycle – because their dash was far less likely to be dangerous!'[16]

In addition, the command had a former Norwegian whaler, *Quest* of 214 tons, to carry water out to ships in the harbour. A 264-ton trawler, *Junco*, was used for towing practice targets, as was the much smaller *Fairy Knowe*, while *Janetha IV* served to defend the harbour against submarine attack. *Motor Launch 453* did target-towing at high speed, while the 1907 converted yacht *Clorinde*, of 147 tons, assisted with harbour defence. The largest vessel in the flotilla was the yacht *Lady Shahrazad*, of 439 tons, built in Greenock in 1904 as the *Enchantress* and now used largely for radar and asdic training. She had an RNR lieutenant-commander and an engineer-lieutenant RNR, a CPO as coxswain, ten seamen and signallers, three petty officer engineers and four stokers, a leading cook and the rather excessive number of three stewards.[17]

On 7 October part of the crew of the *Clover* went ashore for the first period of 'field training', or foot drill. Stephenson set great store on this as a way of teaching officers and petty officers to give orders – and the crew to take them. He believed firmly that, 'The great thing … is to have *one man* giving the orders.' He deflected criticism that 'the man "in charge" can utter only the approved form of words laid down in the drill book' by using his own system. 'Officers are made to give orders in detail, in their own words – not in the words of the drill book – and are made to rap out new orders every few seconds so as to keep their brains and the men alert.'[18]

At 0810 on the sixth day, the ship set sail for her first sea exercises, with the gunnery and anti-submarine officers and a radar instructor from *Western Isles* on board. No time was wasted, and by 0830 they were chasing a motor launch to learn the techniques of pursuing a surfaced U-boat, and avoiding counter attack by 'secret weapons' such as the homing torpedo or GNAT. An hour later they began a sub-calibre practice with the main guns, in which a smaller gun was attached to the side of the normal one and shots were fired at a target towed by a motor launch or drifter. The afternoon was devoted to anti-submarine exercises using a 'clockwork mouse', a training submarine based in the Clyde. They spent the night in Loch Lataich at the southern end of Mull, close to the historic island of Iona. It was a very different anchorage from Tobermory, protected from the sea but not the wind, so strong gales might disturb their sleep. They sailed again at 0900 for more anti-submarine practices and then seamanship exercises, such as taking another ship in tow, before returning to Tobermory for the evening.

By this time exhaustion was beginning to set in among the crews, though it was only a fraction of what might be expected during a bad convoy in the Atlantic. In theory they were subjected to a seven-hour day, seven days a week,[19] but the commodore was not too rigid about working hours, and in any case the men had to carry out their normal business of cleaning the ship, washing themselves, dhobying, cooking and administration. In addition, the watches on duty needed constant alertness in case of a raid or a surprise visit. Cyril Stephens of HMS *Orchis* recalled,

> Tobermory, oh my God, it was murder. We had this Commodore Stephenson, 'Monkey Brand', they nicknamed him. He used to have two little tufts on his face. And he was about seventy odd and [he and his training staff would] come aboard at any time of the night ... It was him who used to sort us out in the working up trials and he had some quite funny tricks he used to do. He'd allocate a ship to raid another ship during the night and pinch anything they could find, like the log books or gun off the bridge or something like that, and woe betide the officer next morning ... You'd come on board and you'd have exercises: 'abandon ship', 'collision at sea', 'fire in the galley', 'fire somewhere else', pipes and wires all over the place, but in the finish we knuckled down.[20]

It was even harder for officers, and according to one captain, the commodore

> concerned himself with everything and everybody and nothing was too small to escape his notice – he even questioned me thoroughly over a reported shortage of soap. On his rounds of inspection he noticed that rats were getting at some of the stores and told me to get rid of some of these pests. I did my best with wire netting and poison, but rats are cunning creatures and still the odd one managed to get in. This did not satisfy him and I remember his remark to this day: 'Walker, are you going to beat the rats or allow the rats to beat you?'[21]

Officers had to be aware of his constant tricks.

> I was disturbed by a rather casual knock at my cabin door and before I could reply, in rushed a very young RNVR officer who placed his cap on my table, sat down (without invitation) and lit a cigarette! ... Taking care to avoid a cardiac arrest I just shouted 'Get off my ship immediately and return to whoever sent you to learn manners, I have no wish ever to meet you again ...' Had I fallen for the Commodore's ruse it would have been Lieutenant Commander N. B. J. Stapleton, RD, RNR who would have been removed from his command and posted to *Western Isles* for additional training and possibly appointed to some unknown second rate shore establishment.[22]

For Stephenson had taken upon himself the responsibility for relieving officers, including captains, that he thought were not up to the job. Normally this was a very serious matter, only to be done by court-martial or on the direct authority of the Admiralty itself. Stephenson bypassed all that. 'I had a rule never to ask permission to do anything, never to ask for anything – take it and tell them to pay for it, do it and tell them I'd done it! It may sound stupid, but I knew the Admiralty – it was a big organisation; no one man could deal with a paper, it had to go the rounds, it would take *days*.'[23] As a result, many officers were retained at the base as 'officers under training' until another job could be found for them. Three hundred and seventy men had been treated in this way by September 1944, roughly one for every three ships.[24] One of the most recent ones was Sub-Lieutenant Duncan Carse, who had already gained distinction as a polar explorer but could get nothing right as an officer. Stephenson allowed him to produce plays on the ship's broadcast system until he was found more congenial work in the Admiralty Film Section in the spring of 1945. Eventually, among other things in a varied career, he became the voice of Dick Barton, the radio secret agent.

Stephenson got his way in this matter on the replacement of officers, and in other clashes with authority. In February 1943 he complained to the Admiralty that

an increasingly large number of requests are being received here for the acceptance of vessels for working up; in almost every case these vessels are Destroyers or Corvettes. Owing to the limitation imposed by the size of the anchorage, and by the size of the staff and instructional facilities, it is unfortunately necessary to turn down a number of these applications. In consequence, it is believed, the Destroyers and Corvettes turned down are compelled, in many cases, to sail for operations without that period of working up which their Commanding Officers wanted, or their Administrative Authorities considered they required.

In case anyone thought that larger ships like destroyers could operate without much training, Stephenson pointed out that 'far from needing only a little assistance, touching up or a chance to work up themselves', they were 'in many cases pathetically in need of fundamental assistance in both their A/S and gunnery organisation'. He suggested that Tobermory be reserved for destroyers, sloops, corvettes and large minesweepers and trawlers, while a new base was set up for smaller vessels. His method of communication upset his commander-in-chief, Max Horton of Western Approaches, who was just a strong a personality as Stephenson himself, and he was ordered to work through the proper channels in future. But he got his way and a new base was set up at Stornaway in the Outer Hebrides.[25]

Clover finished her second sea exercise on the thirteenth day, after firing practice at a sleeve target towed by an aircraft and a full-calibre practice of eight rounds from the main gun. There was a night exercise after dark before returning to harbour. Next day there was a second group communication exercise. *Clover* was now one of the more experienced ships, and a chance to right any faults that had emerged during last week's exercise. The ship was still a hive of activity that day, with buzzer, flashing and semaphore exercises, instruction in diving apparatus, a laying and training exercise for the gunners, a first-aid lecture and a film on identifying radar echoes.

The final assessment was a tense moment for the officers, but sometimes the commodore could get it wrong.

It appeared that numerous items in the course of Tobermory training had gone wrong with that particular ship; there was a long list of failings, from omitting to receive signals to taking up the wrong station. The commodore continued, breathless. Once or twice the Captain attempted to interrupt, only to be shut up. I stood back a few paces, feeling extremely sorry for the man. However the Commodore eventually came to the end, exhausted at such expenditure of 'steam'. He turned to go down the gangway and only then could the Captain of the frigate get out the words: 'I am afraid, sir, you have come to the wrong ship!' And so he had.[26]

Derek Rayner was more successful in *Verbena*, and Stephenson said to him, 'As far as I'm concerned you're an ocean escort now. Come and have dinner with me tonight.'[27]

Clover sailed under her young captain in the afternoon of 20 October, making history as the thousandth vessel to work up at Tobermory. She had passed all the tests, and none of her officers was taken off. Stephenson was congratulated by the Admiralty and compared with Helen of Troy, and replied in a style of wit that regular naval officers relished. 'May I say that you are the first of my friends to appreciate my face value!' The Director of Anti-submarine Warfare signalled, 'Your name has become famous in all quarters of the globe, and U-boats are not the only ones who quail at its mention.' Stephenson replied, 'It has always been our hope that if we make the escorts QUAIL they will make the U-boats DUCK.'[28]

As B. G. Mitchell left Tobermory in HMS *Genista*, he began to appreciate the reasons for the course – nothing could be worse than this, and if they could endure it they could endure anything. But that was not the full story by any means. They had learned something about survival and using their weapons, but very little about tactics, or how to work with other ships. This was not surprising, as Stephenson had very little experience of the kind of war they were about to fight in the North Atlantic.

Until late 1942, each escort group had worked out its own tactics and code-words, which caused problems when two groups had to work together. On one occasion the official report concluded, 'It is probable ... that many of them missed the old leader's voice and may on occasion have waited for an executive order which never came.'[29] Common tactics were worked out in the Tactical School at Liverpool by a team headed by Captain Gilbert Roberts. A new school was set up at Larne in Northern Ireland, where all escort vessels went on to a further stage of training as part of a group. The ships escorted a mock convoy, formed by the headquarters ship *Philante*, formerly owned by Sopwith and latterly an anti-submarine vessel on Atlantic duty – at 1,628 tons, she was bigger than a frigate.

Each escort had to be taught how to respond to submarine attack as part of a group. It had to learn every possible position in the escort screen, for it was impossible to predict how many warships would be present when the attacks happened and how many would be away on hunts or rescues. Every officer had to be able to start the procedure on a given signal because it might take time for the captain to get on the bridge. For a sudden attack by night, the 'Raspberry' was devised at the Tactical School, so called because the staff considered it was blowing a rude noise to Hitler. The object was to fire off illuminants and make the U-boat dive, while at the same time allowing for the possibility of the submarine staying on the surface and hunting it by radar. It was started by using the code word 'Raspberry', or by firing two white rockets. Escorts ahead of the convoy would stay in position and fire star shells. If one was in position S astern of the convoy, it would increase speed and zigzag across the rear while keeping its original distance. Escorts on the wings would also increase speed, turn to head for the rear of the

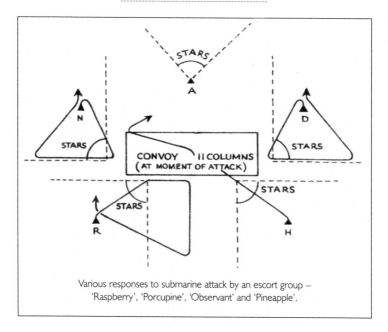

Various responses to submarine attack by an escort group –
'Raspberry', 'Porcupine', 'Observant' and 'Pineapple'.

convoy, then sweep in a triangular pattern around the area for about half an hour. If it was suspected that there were several boats in the area and a further attack was likely, the escort commander might order a 'half raspberry'. This was a shorter version, and it was also suitable for escort groups in which most of the ships could not make fifteen knots.

'Raspberry' set the fashion for fruit names, and by 1943 it was largely being replaced by 'Pineapple' and 'Banana' for dealing with night attacks. On a ship in the convoy being torpedoed at night, the escort commander would order 'Pineapple' if he had reason to believe that more than one U-boat was in the area. All escorts would transmit on their asdics, and accelerate to the maximum speed at which they could operate them. They would carry out very broad zigzags firing star shells and illuminants. If it was believed there was only one submarine, the commander would order 'Banana', in which the escorts carried out more complex operations including zigzags, triangular searches and U-turns.

In the case of a daytime attack, it could generally be assumed that the U-boat was underwater and therefore operating at slow speed. The code-word 'Artichoke' would be given, and the escort at position S at the rear of the convoy would head for the torpedoed ship, seeking as much information as he could get about the direction of the attack. If he was certain which side the torpedo had come from, he would radio that to the commander. Meanwhile the ships ahead of the convoy would turn on reciprocal courses and head just outside its wings, or through its columns. Those on the wings would stay on their course until the sweeping ships drew level with them, then they would join the sweep, forming a single line sweeping through and astern of the convoy. Once they arrived at a point 6,000 yards astern of the torpedoed ship, they would receive a signal to turn back together and sweep again towards the convoy. If there was definite information on which side the attack came from, the hunt would be concentrated in that area. The sweeps, according to the *Atlantic Convoy Instructions*, were 'designed to cover as far as possible the area in which the U-boat is likely to be, paying particular attention to the quarters of the convoy on the sweep astern, and to the convoy's wake on the return sweep …'[30]

'Porcupine' was used if intelligence sources suggested an attack was imminent although no U-boat had yet been detected. On hearing the code-word, escorts towards the head of the convoy would steam ahead at fifteen knots, then turn back after fifteen minutes. Those on the quarter would steam outwards on a diagonal course, then back again. 'Observant' was a search pattern to be used if contact with a U-boat had been lost in a particular area. A datum point would be chosen where a ship had been torpedoed, or at the last known position of a U-boat. The first escort to arrive would drop a marker then follow the estimated course of the U-boat. After a mile he would begin to search a square with sides two miles long, followed by any other escorts that could be spared for the hunt taking position in the square as far as possible from the first escort.

When the frigate *Lagan* was severely damaged in September 1943, another new technique was added. The attacking weapon was soon identified as a homing torpedo, known to the British as the German Naval Acoustic Torpedo or GNAT. It could only operate against ships making speeds between ten and eighteen knots, so an escort carrying out an attack was particularly vulnerable. They learned to do the 'step-aside' procedure, altering course violently during the approach to bring the U-boat on the opposite bow and reduce the acoustic signal.

Escorts were also taught to attack submarine contacts in pairs and small groups. They learned 'baiting tactics' in which they would confuse the U-boat by approaching slowly from astern, where its listening devices would be least effective and confusing it with signals from another escort. They were taught the creeping attack, in which one ship directed another slowly over the target, so that the enemy had no warning of what was about to take place. They also learned the creeping barrage attack, carried out by at least three vessels in a line 100 yards apart, with the centre one heading for the U-boat. When the moment came, all three would combine in a devastating attack. These tactics became increasingly useful as more escorts came into service and some could be spared from the convoys to carry out long hunts. Moreover, support groups were now in service to come to the aid of beleaguered convoys

Constant training was the key to success in the Atlantic war, and the exercises were repeated between convoys, as Commander Gretton observed:

Before leaving on each escort duty, two or three days and nights were spent exercising off the entrance to the River Foyle, working with submarines, firing at targets and carrying out the multitude of jobs which might fall to a convoy escort. In fact, the men sometimes complained that they felt more tired after the pre-convoy exercises than after the convoy itself![31]

11
CONVOY

Convoy SC 94 left Sydney on Cape Breton Island on 31 July 1942 with 30 merchant ships. The commodore, retired Vice-Admiral D. E. Moir, DSO, was in the 8,775-ton tramp steamer *Trehata*, which took the centre of the formation. As soon as they were in the open sea, they formed up in nine lines abreast of each other 600 yards apart and began to steer on a course of 028 degrees, or approximately north-east, as prescribed by the routeing instructions issued by Naval Control of Shipping. They were headed for the United Kingdom, deeply loaded and bringing the foodstuffs and oil that would keep the country in the war, as well as much-needed military supplies from the United States. Most of the ships were armed; they carried a few naval gunners, and some of their crews had been trained to use the weapons. *Anneberg*, for example, had a twelve-pounder anti-aircraft gun and four machine guns, and *Empire Reindeer* had four quick-firing four-inch guns and ten smaller weapons. But the thousand merchant seamen operating the ships knew that these would be little use against their main enemy, the U-boat. The convoy was a slow one, with a steady speed of seven knots, so they would take two weeks to cross the ocean, constantly under threat of attack. They relied on the Royal Navy and the Royal Canadian Navy to protect them against this.

SC 94 was escorted by a local group of warships for its first 500 miles or so, while the main escort force prepared in the harbour in St Johns, Newfoundland. This was a group of British and Canadian ships known as Task Unit 24.1.11, part of the Newfoundland Escort Force, which had specialized in escort duties in these waters since 1941. The senior officer was Lieutenant-Commander Ayre of the RNR in the corvette *Primrose* – rather a low rank and small ship for the task, which usually went to a full commander in a destroyer. The group did include the Canadian destroyer, *Assiniboine*, one of the best ships in her country's young navy. It also had the Canadian corvettes *Chilliwack* and *Orillia*, and the British *Nasturtium* and *Dianthus*. The three British corvettes had been together, on and off, since early 1941 when they formed part of the Seventh Escort Group based in Liverpool. In June they were transferred to the new St Johns Escort Force based in Newfoundland in support of the Royal Canadian Navy in its Atlantic escort work. They were soon in action together supporting convoy OB 318 out of Liverpool. It was not a happy occasion, and the convoy had to be dispersed off Greenland after a succession of heavy U-boat attacks sank five ships. Sometimes they served separately, and *Nasturtium* was with convoy HX 133 in August. She held an asdic contact on a target for more than five hours and played a leading role in the sinking of *U-336*.

SC 94 had a weak escort in many ways – its senior officer was rather inexperienced; it had only one fast ship capable of carrying out a U-boat hunt and getting back to the convoy afterwards; it had not exercised together enough, and most Canadian crews lacked training and experience at this stage of the war.

As they prepared to sail, the officers of the escorts had a chance to study the 'Bible' of the command, the *Western Approaches Convoy Instructions*. It was a large volume bound together, in British public service fashion, by screws with numerous amendments stuck in as the technology and tactics of the U-boat war kept changing. Old orders were cancelled and crossed out, new pages were supplied and inserted, smaller amendments were pasted on to the pages or single words or short phrases were crossed out and replaced by handwritten amendments. All this was the job of the junior officers, and they had been trained in it at *King Alfred* and Greenwich. The tattered, heavily amended volumes were on every bridge and charthouse. They described the dispositions of escorts round a convoy, but it was accepted that no escort of that day could make a U-boat-proof ring. If SC 94 had its full quota of six escorts in station by day, they would mostly be spread forward of the convoy and on each side. The U-boats were likely to be submerged in contact with the enemy in daytime. Attack from astern was unlikely, as a submerged U-boat could not keep up, but one ship was always kept in the rear to act as 'whipper-in' for any merchant ship stragglers, and to carry out rescues and attack retreating U-boats. The escorts would be stationed at a distance of 2,000 to 4,000 yards from the convoy, so they would be about 4,500 yards apart. The maximum range of asdic was 3,000 yards in ideal conditions, and 2,500 on an average day, so a determined U-boat could probably penetrate the screen. At night they were likely to attack on the surface, and the escorts were then re-arranged to cover the rear more effectively and spaced fairly evenly round the convoy. Radar was the most obvious defence when they attacked on the surface, but as yet not all escorts were equipped with it. The three British corvettes all had versions of Type 271, the main anti-U-boat radar. The Canadians often complained that they were at the end of the queue for the latest equipment, and *Assiniboine* had Type 286, which had a fixed aerial and was already obsolete; the corvette *Orillia* had an obsolete Canadian version, while *Chilliwack* had none.[1]

The officers also had a chance to reflect in the situation in the North Atlantic. They had the June issue of the *Monthly Anti Submarine Report*, where the review of the U-boat offensive began with the worrying statement, 'During June the number of U-boats operating in the Atlantic is estimated to have risen gradually to a total of 60–65 ...' and continued with statistics on the latest losses. More than 700,000 tons had been sunk during the last month, the second highest total of the war. Section 2, on countermeasures, was slightly out of date in that it suggested the enemy offensive on the East Coast and Caribbean was continuing. There was an account of the work of the RAF's Coastal Command, including the introduction of the Leigh light searchlight, which had been used to sight seven U-boats and attack five of them – 'a very promising beginning'. Section 3 had a very detailed plan of various U-boat attacks between December 1940 and January 1942, which summed up much of the experience of the war so far and was used by Cherry to devise his own tactical ideas.[2] It had a much more detailed description of the attack on convoy SL 109 from Britain to Sierra Leone, in which one merchant ship was lost. Section 4 contained various narratives of encounters with the enemy and a dramatic photograph of a surfaced U-boat under attack by a Sunderland aircraft. There was a description of the sinking of the battleship *Barham* the previous year, in which a U-boat had been able to penetrate the destroyer screen due to the negligence of the asdic operator and the officer of the watch on one ship. Section 5 on 'Miscellaneous Information' described the trials of HMS *Graph*, a captured U-boat. It included detailed reports on her speed and endurance, her diving and manoeuvrability and her turning-circle, which could all be useful to an attacking vessel. This was followed by a discussion about how deep U-boats could dive, and the authorities were gradually coming around to the view, first discovered by eavesdropping on prisoners of war, that they often went below 500 feet to escape. A report on an exercise to test the anti-submarine defences of the Firth of Clyde showed that the shore-based operators had not been very attentive, and this had lessons for their counterparts at sea. The magazine concluded with a report of the latest U-boats believed to have been sunk, bringing the confirmed total up to 74, the 'probables' to thirteen, not counting the Italian boats that had been sunk.[3]

The officers knew that the U-boats were about to change tactics. For six months after the dramatic United States entry to the war in December 1941, the Germans had enjoyed free rein off the east coast of America, where there was no convoy system and the shore lights were still in operation. That 'happy time' (as the Germans called it) had ended in May as the Americans introduced convoys, and the submarines were about to switch back to the mid-Atlantic. In contrast, SC convoys, and their faster counterparts in the HX series, had enjoyed almost compete immunity and had not lost a ship since February. There was every reason to believe that was about to change.

The task unit sailed and by 1500 on 2 August it formed up round SC 94, so the local escort could leave. Already there was confusion as the convoy was twenty miles behind schedule due to thick fog on the Grand Banks off Newfoundland. The Canadian corvette

Battleford was supposed to join them with three more merchant ships from St Johns but could not find them. Radio silence had to be broken to establish contact, which was done early in the morning of the 3rd. The convoy now had 33 ships and was escorted by seven warships.

The escorts began to fall into the usual convoy routine. On a long voyage like this, one of the main problems was boredom among the lookouts and the asdic and radar operators, especially if the convoys on this route had not suffered for some time. Officers had to consider whether to transmit the noise of the asdic through the ship's loudspeakers so that everyone would hear it and keep the operators on their toes, or perhaps switch off transmissions and listen for 'hydrophone effect', the noises emitted by the submarines. They were also urged to get the men fully involved in the operation, to explain the need for vigilance and perhaps tell them something of the tactical situation. Ships usually went on to a three-watch routine, with four hours on and eight hours off, but most of the corvettes in the escort had only three officers under the captain, each of them having subsidiary duties that had to be carried out off-watch. And it was likely to be seriously broken into if the ships were attacked and the men had to spend long hours at action stations. This was more than a theoretical possibility with SC 94.

The fog continued as the convoy headed north-east throughout the 3rd. At 6 p.m. it was due to alter course to conform to its routeing instructions, and the commodore's ship made a sound signal with its foghorn to order this. Unfortunately six ships on the port side of the convoy did not hear it, nor did the escorts *Orillia* and *Nasturtium*. They continued on 028 degrees, as the rest took a more easterly course of 054 degrees. When the weather cleared next morning their absence was noticed and at 1020 the corvette *Dianthus* was sent to look for them. Commanded by Lieutenant-Commander C. E. Bridgman of the RNR, who had been brought out of retirement, she was officered entirely from the reserves. The first lieutenant, B. J. Howick, had a permanent RNVR commission. Temporary Sub-Lieutenants M. Newington and P. T. Hickman were both recent graduates of *King Alfred*; they were depth-charge control officer and anti-submarine control officer respectively. *Dianthus* probably had the best-trained crew in the group for the task in hand, for she had made many passages with the Newfoundland force. She had an acting petty officer in charge of her asdic, while most ships had to make do with leading seamen or even ABs. She had an experienced gunner in the person of Petty Officer James Darlington and an enthusiastic Leading Cook in George White. Her engine-room crew were all rather junior in rank, for corvettes rarely carried commissioned engineer officers. Engine Room Artificer 2nd Class Clarence Metcalfe was in overall charge, and Acting Leading Stoker Thomas Barwell headed the team in the boiler room.

But the *Dianthus* soon suffered from one serious defect, which was to dog her throughout the voyage – her Type 271 radar became unserviceable. She returned to the convoy at 1300 that afternoon, then went out again in the evening with *Chilliwack*, leaving the convoy with only three ships in its escort, but came back at 2240 without success. That was 2040 local time, and darkness was

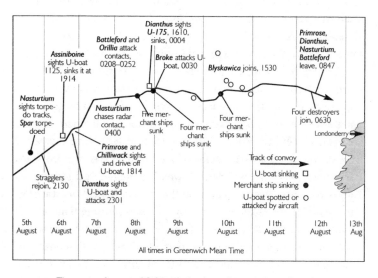

The route of convoy SC 94 showing the various attacks made on it.

coming down, which would cover any U-boat attack. Finally at 1230 on the 5th *Primrose* sent out a radio signal and *Orillia* answered, reporting the position of the missing ships as 33 miles to port of the convoy. The destroyer *Assiniboine* was sent to shepherd them in while the convoy altered course to converge with them.

The destroyer sighted the missing ships more than six miles away at about 1630. *Orillia* had managed to form the merchant ships into two columns, though *Radchurch* lagged five miles astern. The Canadian corvette stationed herself ahead and to starboard, while *Nasturtium* was astern and to port. Now the U-boat situation was moving from vague menace to specific threat. Just after two o'clock that afternoon the Admiralty direction-finding service had identified a U-boat signal in the vicinity, followed by another at 1520. The convoy was informed immediately. Then at 1649, the 4,900-ton Dutch cargo ship *Spar*, carrying fruit, timber, pulp and motor cars, was hit by a torpedo on the fore part of the boiler room. It had been fired by *U-593*, and it flooded the engine room, killing all three men on watch.[4] There was no loud explosion, but *Orillia* noticed the crew lowering boats as the ship slowly sank, damaged on the starboard side of her engine room. The corvette turned towards the stricken ship and obtained a very doubtful asdic contact, which on reflection was almost certainly 'non-sub'. Nevertheless she dropped a ten-charge pattern on the site. The lookouts in *Nasturtium* spotted another torpedo heading towards the convoy and tried to guess where it was coming from. There was no echo on the asdic, but the corvette dropped three depth-charges, which her captain believed 'discouraged the submarine from making a further attack which he could easily have done'. He scoured an area to the west of the convoy, then stopped to pick up 36 men and a dog from the *Spar's* lifeboats. *Assiniboine* sped towards the scene and carried out a search for eight miles around the wreck. At one point a large splash of water was seen, which might have been the submarine surfacing and then crash-diving as she spotted the destroyer; but nothing was found. *Orillia* took charge of the remaining merchantmen and altered course towards the convoy, rejoining at

2130. *Assiniboine* rejoined an hour later and reported worryingly that its smoke could be seen 30 miles away, a beacon for any U-boats in the area.

The reunited convoy got through that night safely, and the weather was clear but overcast next morning, with visibility of eight miles. The seven warships were arranged around the broad formation of the convoy, with *Primrose* ahead carrying the senior officer, the three Canadian ships covering the starboard side, and *Dianthus* on the port bow, *Orillia* on the port beam and *Nasturtium* on the port quarter.

Life in the corvettes was not as harsh as it had been when they first encountered the Atlantic two years ago. They had been modified in the shipyards, with bilge keels, which helped reduce rolling, and longer forecastles, which offered more accommodation and shelter for the crew. The August weather was kinder (apart from the fogs) and the crews were more experienced and used to the rolling motion. But there was no rest. The aptly-named U-boat group *Wolf* of nine boats was in the area, having already tried to attack convoys ON 113 and ON 115. The German High Command had warning of SC 94's sailing, and ordered *Wolf* to form a patrol line 400 miles north-east of Newfoundland. *U-593* at the northern end of the line sighted the convoy, and the other U-boats, from 200 to 400 miles away, were ordered to close in. More boats on passage to the Caribbean were also instructed to look out for it.[5]

By 0117 in the morning of the 6th the Admiralty had identified several U-boats in the area and sent out warnings, so all the crews were on full alert. At 1125 the lookouts on *Assiniboine* sighted an object on the horizon almost ahead and she began to chase it at a speed of 22 knots. It was soon identified as a conning tower and the destroyer's gunfire forced the submarine to dive. *Dianthus* was sent to assist her, and as she approached she found and then lost an asdic echo. *Assiniboine* soon picked it up, and *Dianthus* signalled generously, 'As it is your find and you have GA/SO [Group Anti-Submarine Officer] on board will you please take charge.'[6] The destroyer carried out two depth-charge attacks and then directed

Dianthus on to the target to drop a 'D for Duff' pattern of ten depth-charges set to explode at 100 and 225 feet. But the technique had not yet been perfected – it had probably been dropped too soon and on the wake of the submarine rather than the vessel itself. Captain Bridgman acknowledged there was 'No positive indication of success'.

The two ships continued to search for several hours. At last, at 1716, *Assiniboine* sighted the conning tower of *U-210*, which was stopped in the water on the fringes of the convoy assessing the situation. She was a new boat which had sailed from Kiel less than three weeks previously. Captain Lemcke was popular because he had once suffered for showing mercy to a man who fell asleep on watch, and because he was frank with his crew. The first lieutenant was out of his depth, the engineer officer was competent and popular, but the crew was inexperienced – not more than a dozen of them had served in U-boats before, and the ship had not yet fired a shot or torpedo in anger.[7] Lemcke decided to stay on the surface to fight it out by gunfire, which was unwise as the *Assiniboine*, out of all the ships in the escort, had a vastly superior armament of four 4.7-inch guns. The two ships twisted and turned as Lemcke tried to get his boat under the guns of the destroyer. The range was close enough for Captain Stubbs of the *Assiniboine* to see him directing operations on his conning tower. The submarine's machine-guns did some damage, and the destroyer's bridge was riddled with bullets and set on fire, killing one man and wounding thirteen. But Lemcke was killed when two shells hit his conning tower, and after 25 minutes Captain Stubbs managed to ram *U-210* twice.

By this time the fog had come down again. *Dianthus* was attacking an asdic contact and dropped a pattern on a submarine, which had probably gone deep, before she abandoned the attack for fear that in the poor visibility she might damage *Assiniboine*. With no radar, she could only steer towards the sound of the gunfire – 'a most thrilling situation', as Captain Bridgman put it. She sighted the Canadian at 1916, just in time to see the U-boat sinking. With typical generosity her crew shared in the elation, and Captain Stubbs reported, 'The yell that went up from both ships must have frightened U-boats for about ten miles in the vicinity.'[8] *Dianthus* remained to pick up 21 survivors and send seven more on board *Assiniboine*.

The destroyer's bows had been seriously damaged in the ramming and it was decided that she should go back to St Johns. *Dianthus* was to return to the convoy, which for the moment had an escort of only five corvettes, none faster than a surfaced U-boat. She set off on a course of 60 degrees, but at 2301 she sighted yet another U-boat between 800 and a thousand yards away, dead ahead and following the same course. Captain Bridgman ordered the wheel put hard to starboard and rang down for full speed. The four-inch gun fired a shot towards the enemy, but the ship had not been issued with flashless ammunition and the result was so blinding that the captain ordered it to cease firing. The submarine dived, and *Dianthus* prepared for yet another depth-charge attack. The captain sighted the swirl of water where the boat had dived and, remembering that he had fired too soon that afternoon, he waited for two minutes then ordered the firing of a ten-charge pattern set to 50 feet. Unfortunately he had not been told that Petty Officer John Kelly, the senior asdic rating, was still in contact. 'I realized as soon as the charges fired that I had been far too impatient in firing and that had I waited 15 secs. we should have secured a kill.'[9]

Asdic contact was still maintained sporadically, and *Dianthus* stayed to carry out five more attacks into the early hours, but the submarine had almost certainly gone deep. *Dianthus* stayed in the area for nearly seven hours more, carrying out a search by means of ever-increasing squares in the hope that the target might be tempted to come up. At 0735 in the morning of the 7th, the captain gave up and resumed course back to the convoy.

Things had not been quiet for the rest of the escort during the 6th. The convoy made an emergency turn to starboard at 1135 after the *Assiniboine*'s sighting was reported, then resumed course half an hour later. The Admiralty sent out another warning in the afternoon and a 40-degree turn to port was made to put off any pursuers or evade any patrol line ahead. At 1814 both *Primrose* and *Chilliwack* sighted a conning tower seven miles from the convoy and gave chase, with no results, the U-boat escaping when the fog came down yet again. At 2115 *Orillia* saw a U-boat two or three miles away through a clear patch, apparently stopped waiting for the convoy to come closer. She dived and the corvette dropped several patterns of charges, but one set to explode shallow knocked the alternator switches out of position and put the asdic out of action for a time. Further attacks were made on a vague echo with no result. Meanwhile *Nasturtium* had pursued a radar echo astern of the convoy and a torpedo missed her, but no U-boat was found.

At midnight the convoy went back to its original course of 028 degrees, and throughout the day the five remaining escorts kept watch. That night *Primrose* was stationed on the starboard bow, while *Nasturtium* with a highly effective Type 271 radar set kept watch on the starboard beam – as an attack might be expected from there in the prevailing light conditions – with *Chilliwack* astern of her on the starboard quarter. The port side was protected only by *Battleford* on the quarter, with *Orillia* covering both the bow and beam positions. The Admiralty direction-finding service found a U-boat close to the convoy at 0833 in the morning of the 7th, but no attack developed. The convoy and escort had their quietest day so far.

There was more activity early in the morning of the 8th as *Battleford* and *Orillia* both chased contacts, which were probably spurious. At 0400 *Nasturtium* picked up a radar contact at two miles' range on her starboard side, away from the convoy. There was some doubt at first, but the contact remained steady as the corvette approached it, drawing constantly to the left and apparently trying to get ahead of the escort. At 0428 the crew was roused to action stations as a wake was sighted, and ten minutes later star shell was fired to illuminate the area. Gunnery was very difficult as the ship sheared about in a rough sea, and things did not go very well. The first round was to starboard of the target, but at least it forced the submarine to dive; the second failed to explode, and the third fell in the water. Due to the crew's 'extreme excitement', three more ineffectual rounds were fired after the captain ordered a cease-fire. *Nasturtium* signalled *Primrose* as the submarine was seen to dive and a 'Raspberry' was ordered, in which all ships were to fire star shells to force the submarine underwater then carry out asdic searches in prescribed patterns. But this did not happen, because the message had not got through to the other escorts.

Nasturtium went on to carry out a series of deliberate attacks on the submerged U-boat. She dropped a five-charge pattern at 0448, and the crews struggled to reload the throwers in the heaving seas. Captain Donald Macintyre describes such a procedure on the decks of *Hesperus*:

> As the ship lurched and rolled, the 750-lb. canisters seemed to take savage and vindictive life. Swinging on their tackles they were as they were hoisted up into the throwers they could crush and mangle an unwary handler. With the ship under helm, seas came curling over the side and the struggling men were up to their waists in icy, swirling water.[10]

Nasturtium's drill was good enough, for they were ready for a ten-charge pattern seven minutes after the first, but still there was no evidence of any damage to the enemy as the submarine drifted in and out of asdic contact after each attack:

> After this attack contact was regained at 0501 to be lost at 0504. Carrying out a sweep, contact was regained at 0538, but lost again at 0541 at 400 yards. Contact gained at 0543 and lost at 0545. It was again picked up again [sic] at 0550, lost at 0552 at 950 yards. A single depth charge was fired at 0554 set to 550 ft. Contact gained at 0558 and again lost at 0600.[11]

At 0632 her crew stepped down from action stations, and the ship set course to rejoin the convoy. But seventeen minutes later there was another asdic contact 2,400 yards away, and, after a few minutes checking the validity of the echo, *Nasturtium* altered course towards it. She was over the top of what appeared to be a stopped submarine at 0705, when a four-charge pattern was dropped, set to 150 feet. Four more attacks were launched in the next hour-and-three-quarters, concluding with a ten-charge pattern at 0845. Captain Smith believed that both targets were the same boat, which had tried to escape on the surface, and that he must have sustained some damage after eight attacks and the expenditure of no less than 51 charges:

> I beg to submit that this submarine was either badly damaged or sunk. Contact was perfect and easy to hold and pick up again after each attack. Until just previous to the last attack the submarine appeared to be deep but now definitely came much nearer to the surface as we ran in for this attack and afterwards was deep again and faded out.[12]

But no U-boat was sunk. The official analysts considered it unlikely – in fact, it was believed that the second group was not fired against by a submarine at all. *Nasturtium* was now very short of depth-charges.

By the early afternoon of the 8th, there seemed to be some cause for satisfaction. The convoy had completed more than half its voyage and was still intact, having lost only one ship when it was away from the main force. It had definitely sunk one U-boat and caused an unknown amount of damage to several others. Most of the enemy attacks had been driven off. It was now broad daylight, when U-boats rarely attacked, and most merchant ship captains looked forward to an afternoon nap. But the convoy was now very weakly escorted, with *Nasturtium* and *Dianthus* still on the way back, and there was further evidence of enemy activity. Just after *Orillia*'s attack, a signal was intercepted suggesting that the position of the convoy had been discovered. And as *Nasturtium* carried out her attacks during the four hours that followed, there was evidence that at least one other U-boat was in close contact.

Even so, it was a surprise at 1325 when the commodore's ship, *Trehata*, was hit by a torpedo on the port side and sank quickly with the loss of 28 crew, the commodore and his staff. The U-boats had been waiting for a chance for days but had been constantly frustrated by fog or by the counterattacks of the escorts. The improvement in the visibility was in their favour – as *Assiniboine* had predicted, the smoke of the convoy could be seen from miles away. Now it seemed that two U-boats had worked themselves into position for a perfectly coordinated attack, one each side of the convoy, aided by the weakness of the escort screen. Leading Seaman Jeffery, one of the naval gunners on *Trehata*, watched the U-boat's periscope pass between the columns but was unable to train his gun low enough to fire before his ship had to be abandoned. *Kelso*, a 4,000-ton cargo ship belonging to the Ellerman's Wilson Line of Hull, was just behind *Trehata* when she was hit. Her helm was quickly put over to starboard, and her crew saw two torpedo tracks, one passing ahead and one astern – but a third struck her immediately afterwards and she sank as quickly as *Trehata*. The American ship *Kaimoku*, two columns away from the commodore and third ship in the column, was hit next. Carrying a cargo of ammunition, she exploded in a sheet of flame. *Anneberg*, the last ship in the column between *Trehata* and *Kaimoku*, was hit twice on her starboard side, but her cargo of wood pulp was far less inflammable and she stayed afloat for now. Her British crew of 28 all took to the lifeboats. The Greek *Mount Kassion* was astern of *Trehata* and *Kelso* and her crew watched in horror:

> Two torpedoes then struck the 'Mount Kassion' in the Engine and Boiler Room, it is thought on the starboard side and deep down, the ship was drawing 30 feet. Steam pipes were broken and Engines stopped through loss of steam. The ship began to settle down by the stern and list to starboard, and the Master gave orders to abandon ship. Lifeboats were lowered and 54 members of the crew embarked in the lifeboats.[13]

Primrose was the only escort close to the direction of the attack. She dropped depth-charges until a far greater explosion rent the air, shaking ships at both ends of the convoy. Almost certainly it was the rest of *Kaimoku's* cargo exploding. *Cape Race* in column six had her propeller shaft damaged, while the crews of *Empire Moonbeam* in column three, *Empire Antelope* in column seven and *Radchurch* in column eight began an 'inexcusable' rush to abandon ship. The first two crews were persuaded to return after it was clear that they had not been hit after all. The master of *Radchurch* remained on board but his crew flatly refused to return and she was abandoned.

The escort's response to the onslaught was weak and ill-coordinated. *Primrose's* depth-charge attack was carried out on a firm contact a thousand yards on the port bow of the convoy, but there was a breakdown in communication with the depth-charge throwers and the rails jammed so that only four charges were dropped. Contact was lost, and she went on to pick up survivors from the merchant ships. *Nasturtium* was still several miles away on her return route but screened the rear of the convoy from further attack. *Battleford* picked up more survivors while *Orillia* screened her, and *Chilliwack* remained in her position to the rear. By 1415 she had restored some kind of order to the convoy. Thirty-eight men had died, mostly in *Trehata*.

Dianthus finally arrived back at the convoy that afternoon after a long chase to catch up and took up station 3,000 yards off the port bow. At 1910 her coxswain was aft talking to the man guarding the depth-charges when he spotted a conning tower just before it was obscured by a rain squall. Captain Bridgman trusted his senior rating enough to set out in pursuit, but he warned *Primrose* that it might be a false alarm. Persistence was rewarded after an hour, when the lookout in the crow's nest spotted a conning tower eight miles away, but it was soon lost in another squall. *Dianthus* still had no radar, and nothing more was seen for more than half an hour, when two U-boats were spotted six miles away. Bridgman chose the left hand target. Petty Officer Darlington on the four-inch gun was ordered to open fire and after twelve rounds he was getting close to the target,

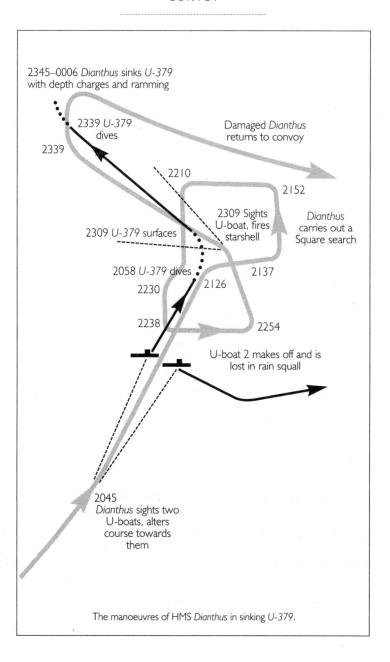

2345–0006 *Dianthus* sinks *U-379*
with depth charges and ramming

2339 *U-379* dives

2339

Damaged *Dianthus* returns to convoy

2210

2152

2309 Sights U-boat, fires starshell

Dianthus carries out a Square search

2309 *U-379* surfaces

2058 *U-379* dives

2230

2126

2137

2238

2254

U-boat 2 makes off and is lost in rain squall

2045
Dianthus sights two U-boats, alters course towards them

The manoeuvres of HMS *Dianthus* in sinking *U-379*.

though spotting was extremely difficult at long range and in bad weather. Darlington's fire forced the boat to dive, and the asdic team under Temporary Sub-Lieutenant Hickman and Acting Petty Officer Kelly came into action. *Dianthus* began yet another square search, but Captain Bridgman was feeling very gloomy when *Chilliwack* arrived to help with it. He sent the Canadian ship back to rejoin the escort but continued himself. Eventually at 2309 Signalman Ronald Kennedy spotted a dark object bearing 300 degrees and the chase was on again. The asdic team began a long-range sweep until 2139 when AB John Kirwin, on watch on the set, detected a very slight echo at the extreme range of 3,000 yards. The ship turned fifteen degrees to starboard towards it and the asdic set was switched from search to attack mode, with the recorder traces in use. By 2340 the range was down to 1,700 yards and the bearing steady. Speed was increased to the maximum of sixteen knots, and the range was quickly closed to 600 yards. By 2345 the echo was moving slowly left and soon there was an instantaneous echo, indicating that the submarine was very close. Bridgman had learned from previous failures and he waited half an echo's width longer before giving the order to drop a five-charge shallow pattern over the stern.

The target, *U-379*, was commanded by Rudolf Kettner, a rather eccentric captain who, according to his crew, did not believe in attacking on a Friday and was 'the only man who ever tried to make life in a U-boat tolerably comfortable' by washing regularly, sleeping long hours and listening to the radio. They considered him 'lazy and inefficient' and now, as his command faced the crisis of her short career, they appeared to suspect that he was all too ready to surface under depth-charge attack. *Dianthus*'s pattern burst close to port, deafening most of the crew, shattering gauges and putting the lights out of action, but no water had entered when Kettner ordered the tanks to be blown.[14]

Captain Bridgman was taking no chances as his opponent broke surface: 'Wheel put hard a port. Ordered all weapons to open fire when on target, switched on searchlight, set 5 charge pattern at 50 feet and stood by for ramming.' There was a huge crash as

Dianthus hit the U-boat just forward of the conning tower at an angle of 60 degrees; but U-boats were tough and the corvette's speed of 14 knots was not enough to sink her. Instead she rode over her, forcing her underwater, rather than breaking her in half. Bridgman dropped his pattern of five depth charges as the stern was over her, but decided to keep his five remaining charges for later and to continue ramming until he got a result. Seven rounds of four-inch ammunition were fired at her, with several belts from the Hotchkiss machine guns and about 100 rounds of pom-pom, which proved highly effective. After nineteen minutes on the surface and four more ramming attacks, *U-379* finally began to sink by the stern and was last seen sticking vertically out of the water with her bow rubbing against *Dianthus*'s forecastle; even in the darkness and confusion, the crew had time to notice that the guns of the U-boat were very highly polished. They had triumphed after the frustrations of the last few days – the breakdown of the radar, just missing on *Assiniboine*'s kill and the disappointing hunt that night. The sinking, according to Bridgman, 'gave our crew the opportunity which during the whole commission they had strived so hard'.[15]

There was still some chivalry in the Atlantic war. It was only a few days since a U-boat had torpedoed the merchant ship *Richmond Castle*, sailing alone, then surfaced and asked if anyone was seriously injured and if he should send a distress message. The crew of *Dianthus* were just as loyal to the unwritten laws of the sea, and they stopped to pick up survivors despite the damage to their own bows and the presence of at least one other submarine in the area. One of the survivors of *U-210* was brought up to the bridge and used a loud hailer to guide his countrymen to the ship. Apparently they suspected a trap, for only five could be picked up, so *Dianthus* dropped one of her Carley floats in the water, filled with supplies, and the Germans were told to swim towards it. Captain Kettner was last seen in the water, inefficient to the last, demanding to know who had taken his life-jacket. On board *Dianthus*, Leading Cook George White had spent the night with the depth-charge crews and was now put in charge of guarding the prisoners until 0530. After he was relieved in that duty he 'turned to and prepared and cooked a large hot meal, in a spirit of cheerfulness which was an example to everyone'.[16] It was a good example of Monkey Stephenson's training at *Western Isles*.

But *Dianthus* had problems of her own, for ramming was often as dangerous to the rammer as the rammed. Lieutenant Bowick went forward with ERA Metcalfe to survey the damage. They found:

> Stem badly buckled and turned at forefoot plating fractured.
> Several small holes and loose rivets on port side in forward lower mess deck.
> Large hole starboard side upper mess deck
> Following compartments flooded:–
> Fore Peak, A/S Compartment, Chain locker, Lower forward mess
> FW tank, Nos. 2 and 4, Reserve Fuel tank, oil fuel tank.[17]

In fact, the damage was not as bad as it might have been, and less than what *Assiniboine* had sustained. The bow was buckled rather than stove in, as often happened with ramming. The bottom plating was fractured, creating several leaks that were causing the trouble. The bilge keels on both sides had been crumpled by passing over the boat, and the sudden rise of her bow during the submarine's final descent had damaged the corvette's starboard side near the forecastle deck.

But the leaks were serious enough, and *Dianthus* signalled to the senior officer, 'Badly damaged ... I will try to rejoin you at slow speed.' They shored up the hull as much as they could and set off at eight-and-a half knots, but the water in the mess deck began to rise and they had to reduce to six-and-a-half. Bridgman allowed the off-watch seamen a small amount of rest for four hours, though it cannot have been easy with four feet of water making the main sleeping accommodation uninhabitable. Then at daybreak he called all hands to redistribute weight in the ship in the hope of lifting the bow out of the water. The anchor cables were dragged aft slowly and

Above: HMS *Western Isles* in Tobermory Harbour. (NMM N6739)

Below: Training exercises at *Western Isles*: getting injured survivors on board. (IWM D 20277)

Left: Towing with an anchor chain. (IWM D 20286)

Below: The officers of *Dianthus*, with Lieute[nant] Commander Bridgman (with pipe) second fro[m] right. (IWM A 11945)

Opposite page, top: *U-210* as seen from the decks of HMCS *Assiniboine*. (Nationa[l] Archives of Canada)

Opposite page, botton[m] *Dianthus'* crew reloac[ing] depth-charges – rathe[r] easier in the calm of Liverpool docks. (IWM A 11948)

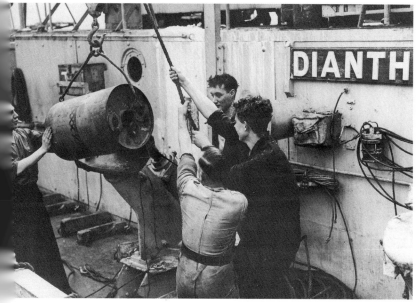

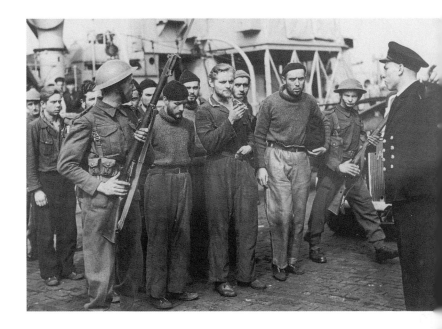

Above and opposite page, top: Back in Liverpool, *Dianthus* lands the U-boat prisoners and the merchant ship survivors. (IWM A 11939 and IWM A 11942)

Right: Some of the damage to the side of *Dianthus*. (IWM A 11949)

Above: Troops landing from an LCA during the invasion of Sicily in July 1943. (IWM A 17960)

Below: Alec Guinness's *LCI(L) 124*, to the left, is aground off the coast of Sicily, with a landing craft, tank to the right. (IWM A 17921)

Opposite page, top: A landing craft, ta loaded with AVREs, including a Churc tank fitted with a fascine to fill ditches a bridgelayer behind. (IWM H 35473)

Opposite page, below: The view from landing craft approaching 'Sword' Bea 6 June, with flail tanks and armoured bulldozers landing. (IWM B 5111)

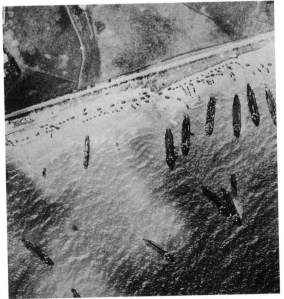

Top: Beach obstacles are inspected after the tide ha. gone out. (IWM A 23992)

Above: Troops landing from an LCA, among much larger landing craft, tank. (IWM B 5246)

Left: 'Nan White' Beach from the air, showing mainly landing craft, tank and a traffic jam building on the beach as the tide comes in. (US National Archives)

noisily, followed by the ammunition for the forward weapons. ERA Metcalfe closed down No 1 boiler and emptied it of water, transferring all remaining fuel to Nos 5 and 6 tanks farther aft. A bucket chain was organized to remove water from the mess deck, and it was reduced to two feet as the bow lifted out of the water. Some of the leaks were plugged up and *Chilliwack* arrived as an escort. It took nearly ten hours to get back to the convoy, when a shipwright and an electric pump were put on board. But *Dianthus* was now useless as an escort – she had very few depth-charges, and in any case her asdic and radar were out of operation. She was in danger of sinking and could barely make convoy speed, so she was put among the ships of the convoy,

Meanwhile the destroyer *Broke* had arrived at the convoy, having sailed from Liverpool on the orders of Western Approaches Command. Lieutenant-Commander A. F. C. Layard was to take over as senior officer of the escort, and his ship would provide at least one vessel that was faster than a corvette. He joined at 2230 on the 8th, while *Dianthus* was chasing her prey, and found a convoy in a very vulnerable position. Only *Primrose* was there – *Nasturtium*, *Dianthus*, *Battleford*, *Orillia* and *Chilliwack* were all on chases, and it was not clear when they would return. U-boats were known to be about fifteen miles away, darkness was falling, and the night screen was very thin. He put *Primrose* on the port bow of the convoy and his own ship on the starboard bow. At nightfall he ordered the convoy to execute two successive turns of fifteen degrees, to a course of 100 degrees, to confuse the enemy.

But *Broke* had recently re-commissioned with a new crew and was not experienced in convoy work. The officer of the watch allowed the ship to get well out of station during the night. It was difficult to see this in the pitch darkness, but at half past midnight the ship was found to be steering south across the face of the convoy, which was three or four thousand yards away. Almost immediately, torpedo tracks were spotted astern of the destroyer, and the wake of a possible submarine was seen passing ahead, towards the convoy. The submarine was detected by hydrophone effect on the asdic, while *Primrose*, which was alarmingly close, blew six blasts on her horn. *Broke* turned to starboard and approached the submarine, which had submerged by now. Rich in depth-charges, she fired a maximum fourteen-charge pattern, but Layard had to admit that the attack had been too hurried and was almost certainly unsuccessful: the boat was driven under the convoy and harassed by *Chilliwack* in the rear. Nevertheless, the attack of at least one U-boat was forestalled. Fortunately there were no further attacks during that night, and by 0300 all the remaining escorts had rejoined except *Dianthus*. At daybreak the escorts were put into positions in Escort Diagram D6, for six escorts in daytime, and Layard felt confident enough to detach *Chilliwack* to help *Dianthus*. The two ships arrived back at three in the afternoon. By that time the first of several shore-based Liberator aircraft had been seen after being directed on to the convoy, so air cover was now available. The Polish destroyer *Blyskawica* joined at 1530, and for the first time it seemed that the convoy had an adequate escort by sea and air.

But the agony of SC 94 was not over. The night of the 9th to the 10th passed uneventfully, but at daybreak it was found that *Blyskawica* was missing from her station. She had become separated because of a gyro compass failure, but for the moment there were fears she might have been sunk. Then at 0525 a direction-finding signal was obtained astern of the convoy, showing a U-boat less than 30 miles away. This posed Layard the classic escort commander's dilemma – how much to send ships off on chases and rescues, how much to keep the screen intact. The *Convoy Instructions* were not particularly helpful on the point – they only stated that, 'Ships should not lose touch with the convoy when hunting a contact, unless there is some very good reason for suspecting the presence of a U-boat.'[18] Moreover, neither of Layard's two fast ships was available for the hunt – *Blyskawica* was missing and his own ship had to stay with the convoy. He had to detach the corvette *Primrose*, followed by *Battleford*, in the knowledge that they might take a long time to get back again. With *Dianthus* out of action, he adopted the usual four-escort day formation, with *Broke* ahead, *Orillia* on the starboard beam, *Nasturtium* to port and *Chilliwack* astern as usual. The convoy was not in particularly good order, and some ships later admitted to being several hundred yards out of station, while the escorts were zigzagging to protect themselves and to increase the area of cover by their asdics. *Broke* was on the port leg of hers at 1023 when the men on the foredeck spotted torpedo tracks but failed to report them to the bridge.

In the third column of the convoy, the first torpedo took the 4,439-ton *Condylis* by surprise, as it hit on the starboard side between Nos 1 and 2 holds. The ship swung violently to starboard through 140 degrees, only to be hit by another torpedo on the other side. Three columns away, the 6,259-ton *Empire Reindeer* was also hit on the starboard side between 1 and 2 hatches, and some of the cargo was blown out by the explosion. In column five, the crew of the 6,008-ton *Oregon* saw a torpedo approaching on a bearing of 270 degrees but had no time to do anything before she was hit forward of the bridge. Just aft of the sinking *Empire Reindeer*, the crew of the 3,807-ton *Cape Race* saw a torpedo break surface twenty feet from the ship before she too was hit on the starboard side just forward of the bridge.

The commodore ordered an emergency turn to port, but the ships in the 7th, 8th and 9th columns sheered off to starboard by mistake. Meanwhile the attacking U-boat was passing through the convoy, making hunting it difficult. *Broke* tried to chase and got an asdic echo as she emerged from the other side, but it was found to be 'non-sub'. *Chilliwack* and *Orillia* swept independently down the starboard side of the convoy, and *Nasturtium* and *Dianthus* went to pick up survivors from the four torpedoed ships – *Dianthus* alone picked up 117 from four ships and her decks were very crowded with casualties from both sides in the battle. By 1115 it was decided to abandon the search for the U-boats and the escorts rejoined the reminder of the convoy.

At last the air escort was becoming effective. Late in the morning a US Navy Catalina flying boat sighted a U-boat near to the convoy and attacked it with depth-charges. Liberators and a Catalina from

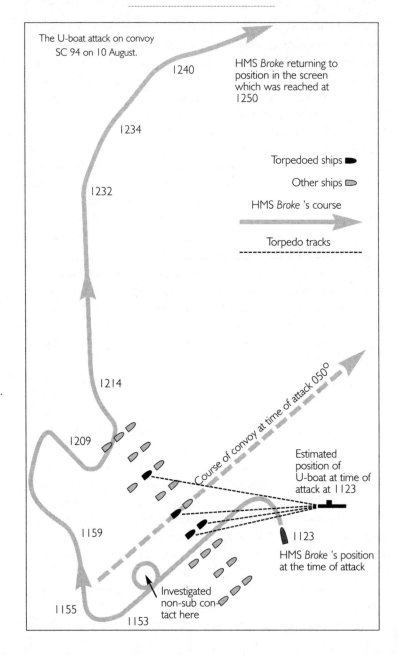

The U-boat attack on convoy
SC 94 on 10 August.

1240

HMS *Broke* returning to
position in the screen
which was reached at
1250

1234

1232

Torpedoed ships ▬

Other ships ◖

HMS *Broke* 's course

Torpedo tracks
- -

1214

1209

Course of convoy at time of attack 050°

Estimated
position of
U-boat at time of
attack at 1123

1159

1123

HMS *Broke* 's position
at the time of attack

1155

1153

Investigated
non-sub con-
tact here

324

Iceland provided almost continuous cover for more than ten hours between midday and nightfall, forcing four boats to dive during the afternoon. Two more U-boats were identified by direction finding that evening and a night attack was expected, so the exhausted crews had to stay on full alert – but nothing materialized. The Liberators were back on station early in the morning of the 11th, and the warships, now short of fuel, could concentrate on close escort. There followed another anxious night, but at 0630 in the morning of the 12th four destroyers, *Skate*, *Scimitar*, *Sabre* and *Shikari* joined from Liverpool. The corvettes could now be discharged, and *Dianthus*, *Nasturtium* and *Primrose* were able to head directly for Liverpool. It is difficult to imagine the exhaustion and strain of *Dianthus*'s crew after several nights of U-boat hunting, the loss of several fine ships, the ramming of the U-boat and the damage to the bows, and a slow voyage home crammed with more than 140 survivors. The ship needed two-and-a-half weeks in dry dock to repair her bows. It is not recorded how much rest the men needed, but it is certain that they got far less than that.

Both sides claimed some kind of victory. The Germans were happy to sink a third of the convoy, and commented that, 'All except one of the U-boat commanders involved were inexperienced, and the fact that they succeeded against heavy opposition seemed to give promise for future operations.'[19] The British were surprised that the U-boats had twice attacked in broad daylight but took comfort that they had been successfully driven off by a rather weak escort except on two main occasions, and that two U-boats had been sunk. A post-mortem in Western Approaches Command showed that there had been bad drill in *Broke* when the torpedo track was not reported on the 10th. *Nasturtium* was criticised for not using her gun early in the morning of the 8th, but there was nothing but praise for the officers and crew of *Dianthus*. Lieutenant-Commander Bridgman was awarded the Distinguished Service Order for 'skill, determination and leadership in action …' Hickman, now promoted to lieutenant, got the Distinguished Service Cross for playing 'a most prominent part' as ASCO, while Sub-Lieutenant Newington, the depth-charge officer, was mentioned in dispatches – 'His splendid work in the past in training his crew was responsible for the efficiency displayed on this occasion.' Seven ratings were also decorated for the action.

SC 94 was only one of 177 slow SC convoys that crossed the Atlantic during the war. Twenty-nine of them were attacked, making them twice as vulnerable as the faster HX convoys, and 145 ships out of 6,806 were lost. SC 94 was untypical in some ways, in that the main U-boat attack came in daylight, but it was the forerunner of the terrible winter and spring of 1942/3. The worst moments came in March 1943 when convoys HX 229 and SC 122 were attacked and lost 21 ships between them. The turning-point came very quickly after that, as new measures came into use. The air gap was closed by the use of long-range aircraft and small escort aircraft carriers sailing with the convoys. Radar was now almost universal in escorts. New ships such as the River-class frigates offered greater stability and longer range in the Atlantic war. More escorts were available, and support groups were formed to go to the aid of beleaguered convoys. Escort group B7, under Commander Gretton, protected three convoys during May, each of which was historic in its own way. HX 231 was attacked by a total of seventeen U-boats. Two of them were sunk for the loss of three merchant ships with the convoy, and three stragglers. ONS 5 fought its way through one of the greatest concentrations of U-boats to lose eleven ships out of 41, but five U-boats were sunk in its vicinity; and SC 130 got through intact against the loss of five U-boats. Doenitz withdrew the U-boats from the Atlantic for a time, and the way was clear for the great Allied build-up in Britain. It was not the end of the submarine threat and they returned to the attack later, but never again would they seriously threaten to cut off Britain from the rest of the world. Troops and supplies crossed the ocean on an unprecedented scale, to prepare for the invasion of Europe.

12
LANDINGS

By 1943 the British had gained a good deal of experience of amphibious warfare in many forms. In the Norwegian campaign of 1940 they had learned the advantages of surprise and the need for strong air cover. They had used ships and boats to withdraw from Dunkirk, Greece and Crete – and in some ways the problems were greater during a retreat, for there was no planning, the enemy knew where to concentrate his fire, and it was more difficult to get off the beach with a loaded boat than with an empty one.

The first attempt at offensive action by sea, on the French colony of Dakar in West Africa, was soon abandoned without any real action. It did provide a few lessons, including the need for specialized headquarters ships, which would not be distracted from their tasks by having to carry out another role. The Vichy French colony of Madagascar was taken in May 1942, and the needs for beach organization and plenty of minor landing craft were established. Meanwhile there were numerous commando raids on enemy-held coastlines, but the attempt in August 1942 to carry out one on a much larger scale, on the French port of Dieppe, was a disastrous failure. Later that year the North African landings, Operation 'Torch', were the first on a massive scale. The amount of resistance varied in the Vichy-held territories but was not sustained anywhere. The landings confirmed the need for salvage and recovery organizations on the beaches and for good navigational aids. They came soon after the land battle at El Alamein in Egypt, where British and Commonwealth forces defeated the Germans and Italians, making it possible to clear North Africa from both east and west. Combined Operations officers were not slow to learn lessons and made sure that they were passed on. This contrasted with the army, which did little to educate the forces at home on the tactics used in North Africa.[1]

At the Allied Casablanca Conference in January 1943, Churchill and Roosevelt agreed that Sicily would be the next target. The original idea was that the Americans would land on the west of the island and the British the east, but General Montgomery objected to this splitting of forces, and it was agreed that the British would take the south-eastern tip around Cape Passero, while the Americans landed on the beaches just west of that. Convoys of different types of vessels would arrive from various destinations and would not come together until they were off the enemy coast. Five of them, consisting mainly of troop carriers, store ships, headquarters ships and landing ships tank and infantry, sailed from the Clyde from 20 June onwards. Others assembled locally in Alexandria, Sfax, Tripoli, Bizerta, Oran and Tunis.

Peter Bull's Landing Craft Flak flotilla arrived in the Mediterranean earlier in 1943 after a hazardous but generally successful voyage from the Clyde. He was based in the North African harbour of Djidjelli, 'a Troon in tropical white clothing', which was vastly overcrowded in preparation for further invasions. He resumed his friendship with Alec Guinness when he arrived, despite fierce and sometimes violent rivalry with the LCI(L) crews.[2] Bull was assigned to support the American landings and soon had good relations with the sailors: 'They were commanded by seasoned veteran coastguards who swapped unlimited ice cream and tomato juice for our drink ration. Their craft, like all those belonging to the United States, were "dry" and as a result we had an L.C.I. alongside us most of our stay. They were grand chaps and the crew fascinated our boys.'[3]

The operation was code-named 'Husky', and reconnaissance of the beaches was meticulous. Aerial photographs were taken of the landing areas, and pictures were taken through submarine periscopes, giving views very similar to the ones that the landing craft officers would see on the way in. Combined Operations Pilotage Parties, or COPPs, were landed by canoe to make more detailed observations. One of these was COPP 6, headed by Lieutenant Ames, RNR, and Lieutenant Wild of the RNVR. They spent many days in the submarine *Unseen* off the Sicilian coast, landing for canoe reconnaissance and often being subjected to 'considerable physical and nervous strain'. They surveyed 'Bark West' and 'Bark East' beaches in the British sector and Gela and Licata, where the American landings would take place.[4] Alec Guinness and Peter Bull were among the officers shown photographs 'in a vastly long strip, about three inches deep, pinned on hessian screens. They had been taken through a periscope, from about a mile off-shore, and, understandably, were grainy and in places obscure. I was instructed to study carefully a section marked A-B ...' There was 'a small, white, pretty lighthouse' marked with the number 58, which Bull and Guinness later worked out could only be the one on Cape Passero, on the south-eastern tip of Sicily. They knew the secret of the invasion well in advance but kept quiet about it.[5]

It had been decided to gain the advantage of surprise by not mounting a preliminary bombardment or bombing the beaches. Fighter cover would be provided from airfields in Malta until local ones were captured in Sicily. The British Mediterranean Fleet was rich in capital ships and cruisers and was reinforced by six American cruisers and many destroyers. Their first job was to contain the Italian Fleet, which was still strong in ships though demoralized and lacking in training. Later the Allied ships would bombard the shore in support of the troops who had already landed.

Several new types of craft were used for the first time in the invasion. The landing craft tank, rocket or LCT(R) was an amazing weapons system, which could fire 792 projectiles, equivalent to the fire-power of 80 cruisers or 200 destroyers, but only for a single moment of glory, as it took a long time to reload. Another new type was the American 'Truck, Amphibian, 2 and a half-ton, 6x6', codenamed the DUKW and universally known as the 'Duck', which could make a speed of 6.4 miles per hour through the water and 50 on land. It was operated by the army, but it was to be used to unload landing ships moored offshore, carrying a payload of up to 5,000 pounds.

The LCI(L)s had recently crossed the Atlantic to join the force in the Mediterranean, and some of the more conventional officers in the Combined Operations base in the Middle East did not like what they saw:

Three L.C.I. (L) arrived at Kabret. The craft were dirty: their equipment was in a bad state; their guns and wires had to be refitted; discipline was poor. The officers were inexperienced and lacked authority. On one craft the coxswain was an A.B. (C.O.) of only two years standing. Officers and men had done little or no training although they had been waiting for their ships in the U.S.A. for several months.[6]

Many of the major landing craft were transferred to Malta just before the landings. Bull found the island stifling because of the big-ship navy atmosphere; Guinness, who had been there before, was saddened by the bomb damage. And pessimism seemed to pervade the high command before 'Husky'. The officers of Alec Guinness's group were addressed by an uncharismatic captain who told them, 'I shan't bother to get to know your names ... for in two or three weeks' time there will be a lot fewer of you to remember.'[7] This soon got through to the lower deck, especially in one craft where the 'the message was read out to us by our Flotilla Officer and we were informed that casualties of the order of 80 per cent were expected in the landings'.[8] This impression was partly corrected by Rear-Admiral Rhoderick McGrigor, in charge of the force, but the damage was done.

The enemy, however, was far less prepared than the Allies expected, partly because of the efforts of one of *King Alfred*'s first graduates. Ewen Montagu had joined naval intelligence, a department that took a large proportion of lawyers who were temporary members of the RNVR. He devised a plan to put a dead body in the sea, disguised as a Royal Marines major and carrying secret documents showing that the invasion would be in the Greek Islands and Sardinia, not Sicily. This trick, later a book and filmed as *The Man Who Never Was*, was enough to fool Hitler. He told his naval commander-in-chief,

The Fuehrer does not agree with the Duce that the most likely invasion point is Sicily. Furthermore, he believes that the discovered Anglo-Saxon order confirms the assumption that the planned attacks will be directed mainly against Sardinia and the Peleponnesus.[9]

At last on 9 July 1943 it was time to set off from Malta to rendezvous with the forces that had sailed from the Clyde and North Africa. Guinness opened his sealed orders, but even with his acting skills he could not feign surprise when he read that the destination was Sicily. The bad weather did nothing to improve the invaders' confidence. According to Admiral Ramsay, commanding the Eastern Task Force, the wind was increasing during the afternoon of the 9th, but there seemed to be no cause for concern. It would have been difficult to reschedule the operation in any case, as convoys from far distant places and varying speeds had been timed to arrive together.

During the afternoon, however, the wind got up steadily, and by 2000 was force 6–7. Concern was naturally felt as to how the L.C.T. convoy would fare, and indeed whether the M.L. and L.C.I (L), which by this time had joined the assault convoys, would be able to keep station.[10]

Doctors worried about the effects of seasickness on the troops. Army medical officers were experimenting with drugs to cure it, and they found that vomiting usually started after the first fifteen minutes in rough conditions, peaked after 35 to 45 minutes, and there were rarely any new cases after 90 minutes. They recommended keeping the landing craft clean and having sweets and biscuits for issue to the troops, groundsheets to keep them warm and dry, and allowing them to stand up and look at the horizon where operationally possible. It was found that the men towards the stern of a landing craft assault suffered less, so key personnel were to be seated there. But this was not enough to help the men who were rushing towards the beaches to face unknown dangers on empty stomachs and in debilitated condition.[11]

Sailors were expected to have built up immunity to seasickness, but that was not always so. In *LCI(L) 124*, Guinness was one of the few men not to be seasick, and even his trusted first lieutenant was 'too ill to do anything'. Guinness leant on the rail of his bridge, 'hearing the far-off retching of everyone else'. The ship was swung around by the wind, crockery was smashed, and conditions in the cabins were chaotic.[12]

Guinness's job in his LCI(L) was to take men off the landing ships at the lowering position offshore and transport them to 'Bark South' beach, 'just left of Cape Passero lighthouse'. Loading the men was very difficult in the heavy seas, as the craft was lifted six feet by each successive wave: 'each soldier had to wait for a wave to lift us sufficiently high and then, with gun and equipment, jump for it. It was a slow process, one at a time and long intervals. The whole operation took about three quarters of an hour longer than planned.' He then had to take the troops eight miles to the beach. He had been able to study the coastline because of Bull's insight into the route, and on the way he found a group of other craft 'which appeared to be lost, or at least in a quandary'. He hailed one of them and led them in, not knowing that the landing had been postponed for an hour, so they were among the first to arrive. They hit the coast very hard, with the kedge anchor out as was standard, but another ship hit them on the stern and severed the cable, causing the LCI to swing round to 'an unenviable angle' to the beach. The troops had to disembark by ropes on to the surf and waded ashore to scramble up the beach looking 'wet, miserable and silent'.[13] Fortunately, resistance was non-existent. The Germans were based farther inland, the Italians were demoralized, ill-equipped and wanted nothing to do with the war that Mussolini had inflicted on them. According to Guinness, 'It was as if the Italians wanted us to come, and only made a little resistance to avoid being clouted by their German brothers.'[14] But *LCI(L) 124* spent ten days on the beach. Attempts at rescue failed until the powerful engines of a destroyer became available to haul her off.

Peter Bull's job was to provide anti-aircraft cover for the landings in the American sector. His group got separated in the passage across due to the weather, but this was slightly better by the time of the landings, partly because there was shelter from the coast. The enemy mounted some successful air attacks in this sector:

> We lay a few hundred yards off the beach and watched the unloading. It was progressing efficiently and rapidly and by the afternoon we were feeling relieved. But air activity suddenly started up, and until the local airfields were captured we were continuously closed up. This occurred the evening of the second day: a good deal of damage was done in the meantime and several ammunition dumps and a small local train were blown up. Close to us an American L.S.T (super tank landing ship with lifts and platforms many times the size of the L.C.T.s) was hit and many casualties resulted. She lay there, a burned-out hulk, and cast a deep gloom during our stay.[15]

More than 17,000 men were put ashore on the 'Bark' beaches in the British sector alone on the first day, over half the men that would eventually land there. Four hundred and fifty vehicles also landed that day, with 700 the following day and 690 the day after that. This was the peak of vehicle landing, but eventually 4,364 were brought ashore, largely on 'Bark South', which Admiral Ramsay found was superior to the other beaches. Build-up of stores was slower, with only 160 tons in the first day, increasing to more than 5,000 tons on D+11, to a total of 38,000 tons.[16]

There was no doubt about the success of the DUKWs, which were of 'immense value' during the build-up, and 125 of them were used to land the stores on the 'Bark' beaches. The LCI(L) was also a success, though it was reported,

> The craft are not assault craft. They ground in too deep water, and appear to catch fire easily when hit, under which conditions they are death traps. The brows have too steep an angle of descent and are too slippery for quick disembarkation of men in hobnailed boots. The first man off each ramp should be a sailor stripped to swim who takes a line in and secures it

ashore. This gives the loaded soldier something to hang on to if he loses his feet; it also enables the depth between the ramp and shore to be ascertained.[17]

It was generally agreed that the rocket craft had been useful, and Mountbatten heard 'nothing but praise' for them, though they had only been tested against almost non-existent beach defences. It was reported that, 'a large number of rockets had fallen in the target area and had obviously caused consternation among the defenders judging by the obvious hurry with which they had abandoned their huts and pill-boxes.' But practically no material damage was caused, mainly because, 'This area was hardly worthy of the name of defended area and consequently all the rounds had fallen on dunes, vines or tomatoes.'[18] They had caused the Italians to retreat, but would they work against more determined Germans? It was clear that the invasion was not a real test of the capabilities of the assault forces. After 'Torch' and 'Husky', Mountbatten concluded, 'caution must be exercised lest the success of these two assaults may tend to engender an easy optimism unjustified by future possibilities.'[19]

Sicily was conquered in just over a month, and Mussolini was driven from power. Allied troops crossed to the toe of Italy with strong gunfire support from the Sicilian shore, but there they were cut off in a very narrow peninsula. Further landings along the coast of Italy were necessary, and Mountbatten's predictions came to pass. The landing at Salerno in September was the first to be strongly opposed, and the outcome hung in the balance for several days. It proved more difficult than expected to use fighters from escort carriers, and the army moved inland before its flank was secure and suffered heavy casualties. At Anzio farther up the coast in January 1944, the opposite mistake was made: the initial landing was successful, but the army delayed too long, and the Germans were able to bring up reinforcements. Although Italy had surrendered in September 1943, the Germans continued to fight on doggedly. The war in Italy did not prove as easy as Churchill had hoped, but in August 1943 at Quebec he finally agreed to a full-scale assault on northern France. All the Allied experience of opposed landings on a large scale would be needed to achieve this.

The plan for the Allied invasion of northern Europe was code-named 'Overlord', the naval part being 'Neptune'. Landsmen like Hitler tended to assume that the Allies would use the shortest sea crossing, at the Straits of Dover, which would also bring them closer to the frontier of Germany. Seamen knew that shipping would have to be massed in many ports far from the scene, so the short crossing was irrelevant. The coast of Normandy had many more suitable beaches and the Cotentin peninsula afforded a certain amount of shelter from the westerly winds, and it was still within the range of Allied air cover from England.

No one expected this landing to be easy. The Germans were building their much vaunted 'Atlantic Wall' along the coast of France, using huge resources of military and forced labour. They built bunkers and blocked beach exits with concrete, and placed obstacles on the beaches. Admittedly Field Marshal Rommel was horrified with the lack of progress on the wall when he inspected it at the end of 1943, but he soon injected energy into its construction, and it would cause the invaders many difficulties, for the invasion of France was no 'Husky'. There was far less room for things to go wrong. Each beach suitable for landing was covered with several different types of obstacles. 'Element C' was a series of gate-like structures nine feet square, fitted on rollers and joined by cables and placed in estuaries and on open beaches. 'Hedgehogs' were made of seven-foot girders riveted together with points outwards, arranged so that if the device was upset, another point would come up to impale any craft hitting it. There were 'tetrahedra', which were six feet high and weighed nearly a ton, and ramps on stakes. Many of these were linked to explosives known as Teller mines. Every two kilometres or so along the coast was a Wiederstandnester, or 'resistance nest', equipped with 50mm anti-tank guns, mortars and six to ten machine guns, with larger concrete bunkers at key points.

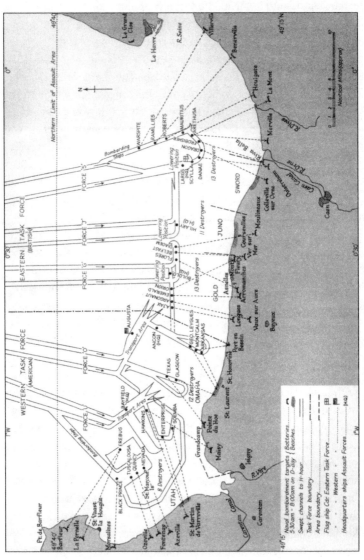

The overall plan of the Normandy invasion, showing the forces for the various beaches.

Meanwhile the Allied forces were devoting their full range of resources to the problem. Every kind of deception was used to encourage the Germans in their belief that the invasion would come across the short sea route. Air and sea superiority were achieved to protect the landings. Numerous inventions, some more successful than others, were developed in an atmosphere of great creativity. The seaborne forces would bring the great majority of the men, vehicles and supplies for the army and were perhaps the most important element in the plan, but there were many others. Air power was needed to bomb vital points such as railway junctions before the assault and to support the armies in greater detail after they had landed, both by keeping enemy aircraft away from the beaches and by attacking enemy tanks and strongpoints. Paratroops and gliders would be landed the night before to protect both flanks. Detailed reconnaissance would take place using any means available – pre-war holiday snaps, aerial photography and landings by canoeists on the beaches. To help in the build-up of forces after the initial invasion, two mobile ports, the 'Mulberries', were to be created. A pipeline, PLUTO, or 'pipeline under the ocean', was to be laid to ensure fuel supplies for the advance into Germany. Every kind of British and American ingenuity was deployed to produce numerous inventions, some successful, some not.

The invasion area was divided into five sectors, two American, two British, and one to be invaded by Canadian troops. At sea, however, the Royal Navy would be the predominant force. Landing craft were manned almost equally between the two main navies, with 32,880 British and 30,009 American personnel in them. But the Royal Navy provided more than 78,000 men for the covering warships, compared with 20,000 Americans and just under 5,000 from other Allied navies. It provided more than two-thirds of the naval crews on that day. In addition, there were around 25,000 Allied merchant seamen.[20]

The essence of the plan was that the first elements of the force would arrive off the beaches soon after dawn on a low, but rising, tide. This would expose the obstacles the Germans were placing on the beaches in increasing numbers. The first wave in each sector would consist of about twenty swimming or 'DD' tanks launched from LCTs ten minutes before H-Hour. These had canvas screens, which allowed them to float for a few miles, and they could be propelled by their own engines. Once ashore, they would pick a way through the exposed beach obstacles while engaging enemy shore batteries. Meanwhile more LCTs would approach carrying several devices for defeating the beach obstacles and defences. They included adapted tanks known as AVREs, or Armoured Vehicles, Royal Engineers. These were the 'funnies' designed by the eccentric Major-General Sir Percy Hobart to clear the obstacles on shore. Some were equipped with chains that would flail in front of them to explode mines; others had mortars known as 'petards' to smash concrete obstacles. Some carried bridges, which could be used to create exits from the beaches over ditches or sea walls; others had tracks that would open out to fill a gap; some had 'bobbins', which could be unrolled to create a road; and yet more carried fascines, or bundles of sticks, to drop into ditches.

Also in this wave were hastily-armoured landing craft, tank carrying Centaur tanks manned by the Royal Marines, which were planned to act as self-propelled artillery and engage the shore defences both afloat and after landing. After them would come the first infantry, carried in landing craft, assault launched from the landing ships, infantry, which would be at anchor seven miles offshore. The whole assault would be covered by destroyers on each flank firing guns, by landing craft (rocket), by landing craft (flak) for air cover behind and by landing craft (gun) and (support) engaging the enemy defences at closer range.

The Canadian beach was between the two British ones known as 'Gold' and 'Sword', and it was code-named 'Juno' as the existing Force J was allocated the task of landing the troops there. Originally it was expected that the landings would touch down simultaneously at all five beaches. Planning was well advanced when it was reported (erroneously) that the water over the rocks off 'Juno' beach was only three feet deep, instead of five as had been reckoned, and this demanded drastic changes of plan. The landing on that beach would have to be slightly later to allow the tide to rise. Ramsay spent all of 23 May in meetings on the subject: 'This entirely mucking up H-Hour. Could find no satisfactory conclusion except to wildly stagger J with S and G and all with W.T.F. [the American Western Task Force]. The result on the assault is to make it more chancy.'[21] The actual day of the landing was uncertain, and it was necessary to plan for more than one, but the low tide had to be around dawn. On 'Sword' Beach for example, H-Hour would be at 0645 on the 5th, 0725 on the 6th and 0800 on the 7th. Any later than that and the approach would be in broad daylight, which would need a new plan altogether.

The 'Juno' sector, like 'Gold' and 'Omaha', was divided into two, with an assault group and an army brigade allocated to each, plus a third for the follow up. Each of these areas was further subdivided into several actual beaches where the landings would take place. Thus 'Juno' would be attacked by Assault Force J carrying the Canadian 3rd Infantry Division. Within that, Group J1 would carry the Canadian 7th Infantry Brigade to 'Mike Green' and 'Red' beaches to the east of the small port of Courseulles, and 'Nan Green' to the west of the port. Group J2 would take the 8th Brigade farther east, to 'Nan White' and 'Red' beaches. Group J4 would land commandos, including a force of Royal Marines, on the eastern flank. This was to head east and link up with the forces on 'Sword' Beach, the five miles between the two being unsuitable for landing, so it was important to fill the gap as quickly as possible. Group J3 would carry the supporting brigade later in the day.

Again, planning was meticulous. Crews were issued with instructions on how to get hold of various facilities on 'the far shore', mostly by applying to a particular ship or officer. They were told how to get petrol and oil, to get help with salvage, to get charts and navigational information and, most chillingly, how to dispose of the dead – by burying them at sea.[22] The voyage across would be protected by the full range of Allied resources. A hundred and seventy-one squadrons of fighters, nearly 2,000 aircraft, were

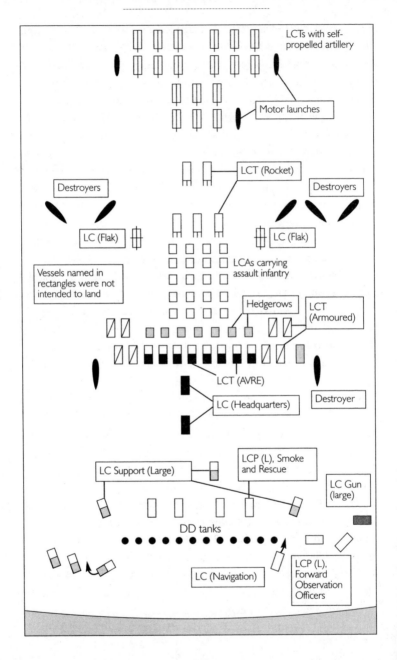

LCTs with self-propelled artillery

Motor launches

LCT (Rocket)

Destroyers

Destroyers

LC (Flak)

LC (Flak)

LCAs carrying assault infantry

Vessels named in rectangles were not intended to land

Hedgerows

LCT (Armoured)

LCT (AVRE)

LC (Headquarters)

Destroyer

LCP (L), Smoke and Rescue

LC Support (Large)

LC Gun (large)

DD tanks

LC (Navigation)

LCP (L), Forward Observation Officers

available that day. Heavier aircraft patrolled the sea routes and kept U-boats and E-boats at bay. On the sea itself, the escorts for coastal and cross-channel convoys would comprise sixteen sloops, 34 frigates, seven American destroyer escorts, 66 trawlers, 353 coastal forces vessels and 73 corvettes, including Atlantic veterans such as *Clover*, under Captain Fanshawe, *Clematis*, *Campanula* and *Dianthus*. Farther away from the invasion forces the anti-submarine screen included 63 more vessels, mainly Captain-class frigates.[23]

Although the landings would not take place before 5 June, the first movements began on 23 May in the far-away Scottish port of Oban, where some of the Corncobs, old and slow merchant ships to be sunk as breakwaters for the artificial harbours, were gathered. Other elements in the operation moved out over the next few days, timed to reach the invasion beaches at the right moment: for example, bombarding ships from the Clyde on 2 June. Troops were embarked and vehicles loaded at the southern ports, and Commodore Oliver's orders for Force J made it clear that the landing craft officer or coxswain was responsible for that, especially to ensure that the army did not overload it. One RNVR officer describes his LCT(4) as loaded for D-Day in the American sector:

My craft carried six Sherman tanks, two half-track supply trucks, and a Red Cross jeep. With this load, we carried four officers and fifty-four GIs. To accommodate these soldiers we had, officially, two small cabins and a troop space about fifteen feet by five feet. My crew were a hospitable crowd, and the Yanks were all as willing to take what came. I, the First Lieutenant, one Army Officer and the Flotilla Officer slept in the wardroom. The other officers had the cabins. The non-commissioned officers had the troop space, and the rest of the troops were given bedding on the mess-deck and engine room decks.[24]

Left: The intended order of landing on 'Sword' Beach. The reality was very different; most of the DD tanks did not arrive on the beaches, while many of the armoured LCTs and the Hedgerow craft were lost on the way.

LCT 1094, commanded by Lieutenant Surtees, RNVR, with a new sub-lieutenant as his assistant, was loaded up with her six armoured vehicles on the 4th. There was no room for proper sleeping accommodation, but the junior army officers slept on the wardroom floor while the other ranks bivouacked on the tank decks among the vehicles.[25]

But now there was a delay. The weather forecast for the 5th showed an anticyclone moving over Britain with thick cloud that would prevent accurate bombing and airborne landings, while weather fronts would bring rain and winds of force four or more, which were dangerous for the smaller landing craft. The supreme commander, General Eisenhower, outlined the consequences of further delay.

If none of the three days should prove satisfactory from the standpoint of weather, consequences would ensue that were almost terrifying to contemplate. Secrecy would be lost. Assault troops would be unloaded and crowded back into the assembly areas enclosed in barbed wire, where their original places would already have been taken by those to follow in subsequent waves. Complicated movement tables would be scrapped. Morale would drop. A wait of at least 14 days, possibly 28, would be necessary – a sort of suspended animation involving more than 2,000,000 men. The good weather period available for major campaigning would become still shorter and the enemy's defences would become still stronger![26]

The movements for 5 June were cancelled. Then there was a sign of hope as the chief weather forecaster, Group Captain Stagg of the RAF, predicted a fair period beginning early on the 5th and lasting into the morning of the 6th: 'During this interval, cloud will mainly be less than 5/10 with base 2,500-3,000 ft. Wind on the beaches in the invasion area will not exceed Force 3 in this interval and will be westerly. Visibility will be good.'[27] These conditions were marginal. There was no guarantee that they would not be worse than that on the day, for it was difficult to predict the movement of the weather system precisely, and it would certainly get worse later for the follow-up waves. The high command met at Southwick House near Portsmouth in the evening of the 4th, and Eisenhower decided to go ahead. He prepared a memo taking full responsibility if the operation failed. The landing craft would have to sail in conditions far worse than they had been designed for.

LCT 2424, commanded by Sub-Lieutenant Erwood, had loaded up with six AVRE tanks in Stanswood Bay at the entrance to Southampton Water on 3 June, then moved to a buoy for the night. The sailing next day was cancelled, but at 10 past 7 in the morning of the 5th, she slipped her mooring. The weather was still rough, and some of the 'pongoes', or soldiers, on board were seasick. On board *LCT 1094*, under Lieutenant Surtees, there was impatience with the delays, but she slipped her mooring just before midday on the 5th. She passed Fort Blockhouse at the exit from Portsmouth Harbour, and they were allowed to open their secret orders. Now they discovered that the town known as 'Poland' in the coded plans was in fact Caen, and much became clear to them.[28]

The Canadian landing ship *Prince David* raised her anchor at 2140 on 5 June. She was carrying more than 400 British and Canadian troops for 'Nan White' sector on 'Juno' Beach; they had been on board for the last three days and had spent their time exercising with the landing craft. The ship passed through the anti-submarine gate at Spithead at 2240 and sailed out under an overcast sky with the moon breaking through occasionally. Flashes could be seen on the far horizon, presumably from bombing on the opposite shore.[29]

LCT 1094 passed the Isle of Wight, and the seas instantly became rougher. She was towing a landing craft, assault, loaded with weapons known as 'Hedgerow', adapted from the anti-submarine Hedgehog. This consisted of two dozen 60-pound spigot bombs intended to destroy enemy minefields. But towing became impossible, and Lieutenant Dickinson of the Royal Engineers found that the LCA 'shimmied' in a way that reminded him of Carmen

Miranda. The crew of the LCA had to be transferred on board, to the annoyance of their officer. At nightfall, the soldiers removed the camouflage netting from their tanks – there was no need to conceal them any longer – and settled down for the night. When they awoke next morning, their stomachs caused most of them to head straight for the gunwales.[30]

Most of the 4,126 landing ships and craft in the operation, except those forming Force U for 'Utah' Beach, were to pass through Area Z, known as 'Piccadilly Circus' to the troops. This was ten miles in diameter and its centre was 25 miles south of Portsmouth, so Force J's journey to it was comparatively short. From there, each of the groups would steer south to find paths being swept through the German minefields across the wide mouth of the Baie de la Seine. There was a feeling of unreality as the huge fleet headed out into the open sea and across the Channel. Allied forces were ready for a sudden air or sea attack, but nothing materialized.

Ten channels were swept of mines on the approach through the Baie de la Seine, a fast and a slow one for each landing area. Brendan Maher, a former insurance clerk who had been commissioned from *King Alfred* in September 1943, was on board *ML 137* that night.

> Our role in the invasion had placed us as the first ship in Channel 9, one of the ten channels that were to be swept ... Our task was to sweep mines to leave a safe depth for the larger fleet sweepers of the 1st Flotilla, led by the *Harrier*. They, in turn, swept at an even greater depth and width to clear the water necessary for the larger invasion vessels coming behind them ...[31]

The ships of Force J had some difficulty finding the ends of the channels in the dark, and some blamed the crews of the harbour defence motor launches that were responsible for marking them, but it was probably because the lights did not show up well enough in the poor conditions. Group 312, carrying the AVREs for the 7th Brigade on 'Mike' and 'Nan' beaches in the 'Juno' sector, got into channel five instead of seven alongside the ships heading for 'Gold' beach. The commanders of the ships of Force G had some difficulty in getting the intruders to admit their mistake, for they 'stoutly maintained that they were in number seven, the correct channel'.[32] When the error was eventually acknowledged, they were ordered to increase speed to reach their lowering positions on time, but they were a little behind schedule, and this caused a further postponement of ten minutes to H-Hour on 'Juno' beach.[33]

The force had achieved complete surprise. The Germans thought that the weather was impossible for a landing – they did not have the benefit of accurate information on weather approaching from the Atlantic. Field Marshal Rommel, in command of the Channel defences, took the opportunity to take some leave, and his forces were not on the alert. In his minesweeper off 'Sword' beach, Brendan Maher was intrigued:

As we reached the last few hundred yards of our sweep, the German defences were clearly visible through binoculars. My initial thought was to wonder why they were not firing at us. The approaches to the beaches were packed with thousands of ships, stretching back to the horizon as far as the eye could see … It was as if the whole thing had taken this part of the defences by surprise.[34]

To establish the correct position to launch the DD tanks at the start of the assault, two midget submarines were ordered to lie off the beaches. *X-20*, under Lieutenant Hudspeth of the RANVR, was allocated to 'Juno' and arrived off the coast in the morning of the 4th carrying three officers from beach pilotage parties as well as her own captain, first lieutenant and engine room artificer. She had to wait there for an extra 24 hours because of the postponement, and conditions were extremely cramped on board the tiny craft. At last at 0345 in the morning of the 6th, she was able to surface in her allotted position and prepare a flashing green light and a radar reflector. At 0615 the sun began to rise, and the light was no longer necessary. The crews of LCTs waved as they passed her.[35]

As Lieutenant Hugh Dinwiddy guided *LCT 441* towards 'Juno' beach in the growing daylight, he became aware of the shape of a great British battleship to starboard, soon to open fire on the enemy positions.[36] The landings on 'Juno' were not, in fact, supported by any battleships, but the cruisers *Belfast* and *Diadem* were there with their 6-inch and 5.25-inch guns, along with eleven destroyers with 4.7-inch guns. The heaviest firepower in the British area was allocated to 'Sword' beach, where the battleships *Warspite* and *Ramillies* protected the flanks. The long-range fire was very impressive, but it had its limitations. It followed a relatively flat trajectory, so it was dangerous to fire over the heads of one's own forces, and, despite the presence of naval forward observation officers with the troops and spotting aircraft overhead, it was comparatively inaccurate. Six-inch guns were not allowed to fire within 500 yards of their own men, larger guns within 1,000 yards. This created a role for the landing craft (gun), which could come in much closer and engage directly with points on shore.

Lieutenant Dinwiddy was sure that the weather was too rough to launch his DD tanks and signalled this view to his flotilla commander. He was ordered to proceed and let the first one go. It sank almost immediately, with the loss of all its crew. He decided to head for the beach instead and hit a mine on the part of the craft where the tank had been, but there were no casualties and the other tanks were landed conventionally. His craft was out of action, however, not the last to suffer that fate during the morning.[37] Most of the DD launchings were cancelled all along the British and Canadian Sector, further upsetting the plans. Only the nineteen tanks of B Squadron of the 9th Armoured Regiment for 'Sword' Beach were launched as planned. Four of them were lost on passage by shell fire or being run down, one landed at another beach, and two more arrived and deflated their flotation gear, to be swamped by the rising tide; but the rest took part in the battle.[38]

Meanwhile the bad weather was beginning to affect the next part of the plan, for the second wave. This consisted of armoured LCTs carrying Centaur tanks manned by the Royal Marines, and more

LCTs carrying Hobart's 'funnies'. But the job of armouring the LCTs had been done very poorly, and most of them began to leak. Some had to slow down because their engine rooms were flooded, a few capsized and nearly all of the rest were too late at the beaches to form part of this wave.

In the AVRE-carrying craft, Lieutenant Reginald Edwards of *LCT 2436* describes what he thought went wrong off 'Juno' beach:

> We carried AVRE vehicles designed to cut through the obstacles embedded on the beaches. It had been calculated that the state of the tide at the time would enable our LCTs to touch-down with the obstacles between us and the shore defences, the AVRE vehicles would cut a way through, and the tanks, and the assault infantry who landed from LCAs alongside us would nip through the gaps created. Wonderful! The only trouble was that someone had messed up the time of the tide, so that when we went in the beach obstacles were either submerged or, like the fearsome Element C, partly submerged. Consequently we had no alternative but to ride over the lot.[39]

In fact, the AVREs were intended to clear paths inland from the high-water mark, exploding mines, demolishing obstacles and laying bridges. In the absence of most of the DD tanks, the AVREs also engaged concrete bunkers and pill-boxes on shore in support of the infantry. The heavy bombardment had not silenced the enemy bunkers, which had concrete many feet thick and gun-slits facing sideways to enfilade the landing troops rather than pointing out to sea. On 'Gold' beach, for example, three AVREs destroyed a pill-box with their petards and then crossed a wall to force the Germans to retreat while one of the flail tanks 'posted a letter' through the embrasure of a strong point to destroy it.[40]

The beach obstacles themselves were to be cleared by dismounted parties of Royal Engineers, for it was easier to attach charges to one and destroy it that way than to do it by gunfire. But because of the lateness of the hour and the rise of the tide, they were able to do very little. Underwater work was to be done by groups known as Landing Craft Obstacle Clearance Units, or LCOCUs, provided by the navy and the Royal Marines. They were equipped with primitive underwater breathing apparatus, but because of the rough weather and the wash of passing craft they too could do little. So the beach obstacles remained intact throughout the first hours of the landing. According to Lieutenant Reginald Edwards of *LCT 2436*, 'Land the Army at all costs' was the order.[41] This was echoed in Force G's orders – 'the Assault ... is to be pressed home with relentless vigour, regardless of loss or difficulty.'[42] The craft had to find ways through or over the obstacles.

On 'Nan White' beach off the small town of Bernieres, the 103rd and 106th flotillas of LCTs led the way in under Lieutenant-Commander Robinson, RNVR, carrying AVREs. It was difficult to keep station in bad weather, but they managed to maintain some sort of order in the final approach by occasional use of emergency full power on the engines. Rocket craft fired over their heads, but a little too far off to have full effect, and most of the projectiles seemed to land just above the high-water mark, missing the enemy defences on shore. They were used extensively in the Normandy landings, as described by Lieutenant R. B. Davies, RNVR, of *LCT 647*:

> A terrific 'whoosh' sounded on our starboard quarter and we saw the streaks of 500 rockets rising shorewards from one of our rocket craft ... The last mile coming up – no opposition yet noticeable – then suddenly hundreds of flashes right along the sand dunes. 'Here it comes,' I thought, 'Coast batteries opening up at the last moment.' But nothing came and I realized that the flashes were rocket explosions from those we had seen launched seconds before.[43]

But they were notoriously inaccurate, and one salvo even shot down a friendly Typhoon aircraft off 'Nan White' beach.

Robinson ordered his LCTs to increase to full power of 2200 revolutions to drive the craft as far up the beach as possible. The enemy remained quiet as two 'Hedgerow' craft came in and fired their bombs with 'great deliberation' among the beach defences. The LCTs picked their way through the partly-submerged obstacles, which were exactly as described in the operation orders, and they were able to avoid the mines. They were about 100 yards from their beaching positions when the 'Hedgerow' craft withdrew, and the enemy finally opened fire with machine guns from many points. There were several casualties, and the coxswain of the leading craft was killed by a bullet through the central aperture of the armoured wheelhouse. There was more danger as the Oerlikon gunners of one of the craft astern opened up with fire that was 'more keen than accurate', and several shells hit the quarterdeck and the after part of the bridge. The craft all beached in 3 feet 6 to 4 feet 6 inches of water. Many of the tanks had not yet started their engines or got their guns ready due to the need to prepare waterproofing, and the LCTs only had their Oerlikon guns to engage the enemy in the meantime. After a few minutes the tanks were able to open fire, and they began to land at maximum speed. They included a bridging tank, which opened up an exit from the beach into the town.

LCT 1092, commanded by Lieutenant Wigley, was planned to land on 'Sword' beach ten yards to the east of a house known as 'sad sack villa' to the troops. This was spotted from 1,200 yards out, but the craft was ordered to slow down to let the DD tanks get ahead. Two hundred yards farther on, a landing craft (rocket) discharged its salvo, and some of it was seen raining down on craft about to land. The LCT headed for the beach at full speed. The house had been obscured by the barrage but was seen again at 300 yards. Unfortunately a damaged craft was in the way, so it was decided to head for another spot. Twenty yards from touch-down, the LCT was attacked by four aircraft bearing British markings. The Oerlikons were used against them and against snipers in the houses on shore. The tank crews climbed in just as the bow doors were opening and headed for a gun just opposite, led by a flail tank clearing the way.[44]

Lieutenant Dennis Brown was a peacetime RNVR rating, commissioned after a course at *King Alfred* in the autumn of 1940.

He was a very experienced flotilla officer in the Landing Ship (Infantry) *Princess Maud* on 'Gold' beach, having served at the withdrawals from Greece and Crete as well as the landings on Sicily and at Salerno. His coxswains were also well seasoned by that time. He and his crews went to embarkation stations at 0545. The first ten LCAs were lowered twenty minutes later, followed by a second wave of five after another fifteen minutes. They formed up in two columns, each in line ahead, astern and to port of their navigational leader, *Motor Launch 594*, while a support landing craft from the ship deployed on the port flank. They had expected to be in the third or fourth wave in, but as the DD tanks were not being used, they were in the second. The motor launch turned off about a mile from the shore, and they were expected to find their own way from there on. They turned into line-abreast for the final approach, and Brown was proud that they landed together at the right time and in the right place. The shore was gently shelving, and he touched bottom about 50 yards off, in a most unpleasant surf. Having beached, disembarkation was rather slow, as some of the seasick men took time to get moving. There was machine gun fire, but he saw no casualties as his troops moved inland.[45]

Arriving off 'Queen Red' beach in the 'Sword' sector, the men on *LCT 1094* found themselves surrounded by tiny LCAs, which had been launched from their parent ships. The group of LCTs stayed in line ahead while the officers compared the skyline with photographs they had been issued with. At 0725 they formed line-abreast to head for the beach, as they had practised many times. *LCT 1094* hit a submerged obstacle and had to back off from it, with damaged craft all around. The officers saw a complete row of obstacles sticking out of the water, with Teller mines attached to them. They had hoped to land the troops dry-shod, but in fact they beached in four feet of water. The engineers began the mine clearance work which they had practised at Littlehampton, but they found it very different in rough weather, and there were more Teller mines than they had been led to expect.

Sub-Lieutenant Erwood's *LCT 2424* struck the first line of underwater obstructions, known as Element C, on the way into

'Juno' Beach, then in the confusion she ran down a landing craft assault. It was feared that all her crew were lost, but her officer was seen to swim out astern and was thrown a lifebelt. The Oerlikon guns were fired to make the Germans keep their heads down, and the tanks were launched, though some assault boats for the Royal Engineers proved too difficult to launch by hand. One was towed off by a tank, but its bottom was holed; another was towed, but the line broke, and the task was eventually accomplished with the help of an LCA.[46]

The tide was rising and arriving craft had to pick their way through the obstacles as well as they could. Lieutenant-Commander Rupert Curtis of *LCI(S) 519* reported:

> My mind concentrated on finding a path through the underwater obstructions. Fortunately at that state of the tide, the tops of many of them were still visible sprouting above the surface of the sea, many with lethal attachments.
>
> Working completely by instinct ... I felt I could discern a clear path through the menacing stakes. It looked a bit of a zig-zag but I backed my instinct and took 519 through with rapid helm orders. We emerged unscathed and I called for more power from the engine room to thrust our bows hard on to the beach to ensure as dry a landing as possible. Then we kept both engines running at half speed to hold the bows in position.[47]

Most landing craft officers and coxswains had similar experiences that morning. Sometimes the obstacles were only visible in the troughs of waves, which was one advantage of the rough weather. Sometimes the crews of small craft such as LCAs had to fend off from an obstacle using a boathook, fender or hands.

The LCAs of the 518th Flotilla led by Lieutenant Turner, RNVR, had been launched at 0635 and headed for 'Juno' beach led by a motor gunboat. They heard on the way that H-hour had been postponed by 25 minutes, and they were to land at 0830, so they reduced speed. Finally the MGB captain passed on the order to proceed, and they headed for 'Nan White'. Despite accurate fire from support craft, it was clear that several LCTs were already in difficulty on the beach. The tide was rising fast, and many of the obstacles were covered, while posts could be seen sticking out of the water – they were joined together by stretches of barbed wire, and the mines attached to them could also be seen. There was no alternative but to force a way through. The stern of *LCA 710* hit a mine as she was penetrating the third row: a stoker was killed, and the engine compartment was flooded. The troops were disembarked and waded ashore safely. *LCA 881*, carrying the divisional officer Sub-Lieutenant Dew, hit a mine on the bows before the troops were landed, but there were no casualties. *LCA 841*, under Sub-Lieutenant Parks, got through the obstacles and landed her troops but had so many holes that she had to be withdrawn from service. *LCA 650* was holed on the way in but continued to beach, and the troops got ashore. *LCA 844's* propeller shaft was bent on beaching. *LCT 835* took off the crews from some of the damaged craft but fouled a life-belt on the way out and the starboard engine seized up. As with many of the landings that morning, casualties were light among the men but high among the landing craft, mostly caused by beach obstacles and mines.[48]

Many craft had picked their way successfully through the mines and obstacles then reversed out. The crews were probably slightly less attentive by this time, and space was more restricted, so many of them hit something at this stage, and damage to engine rooms and sterns was common. On 'Juno' it was found that 25 per cent of 144 LCAs and 31 per cent of 146 LCTs were lost or damaged.[49] But they were stoutly built, and the great majority were able to land their troops even if they could not return for another party.

It was much worse for the landing craft infantry (small) that were to take 48 Commando of the Royal Marines to the eastern flank of 'Juno', where they had orders to head along the shore to meet up with men from 'Sword' beach. These craft had been designed as a smaller, mass-produced British version of the American LCI(L), but they were built in wood to a design by Fairmile, better known for fast coastal forces craft. They were not strong enough to get over the beach obstacles – eight of the 37 were lost and 75 per cent of the rest damaged:

Our motion checked sharply, and Timmermans swore as we hung rolling on the beach obstacle we had fouled; then a wave caught our stern, swung us, and carried us forward to beach at a bad angle and rolling. As we struck the obstacle, the enemy opened fire with mortars and machine guns from the esplanade, a little more than a hundred yards away. The sailors replied with crashing bursts of Oerlikon fire.[50]

This party managed to land with the aid of smoke, but many others were delayed or lost, and the Special Service Brigade was unable to achieve its objective of linking up with 'Sword' beach.

The support organization began to build up, led by the men of the beach commandos, who would control movement of ships, men and vehicles in the crowded area. On 'Nan White' in the 'Juno' sector, the naval party embarked from the landing ship, headquarters: 'After some skilful handling by the officer in charge of the LCA, in the course of which all except one of the obstructions were avoided, and the mine on this one did not explode, a landing was effected exactly at the pre-arranged position ...' Landing at H+60 minutes, the officer in charge missed the earlier confusion and thought it 'differed little from my experience during exercises'. The biggest problem, he found, was the tendency of minor landing craft crews, especially marines, to wander inland and neglect their craft after the landing.

The four craft of the 30th LCT Flotilla arrived two miles off 'Nan Red' beach in the 'Juno' sector and increased engine revolutions to 1,300 to take them in. They received a signal not to beach unless they saw an opening and manoeuvred round several obstacles to hit the beach very hard five minutes early, at H plus 85 minutes. They opened their bow doors and noticed that as the drivers of the trucks and lorries sped off as fast as they could under mortar and rifle fire they set up large waves, which swamped other vehicles. Meanwhile

LCT 707 beached without using a kedge anchor and was swept round to an angle. Her captain, Lieutenant Hollands, was unable to back her off due to obstacles astern, and she came under heavy mortar fire from a nest fifteen yards away. When a bomb landed on the deck, a leading stoker threw it overboard. A leading wireman opened fire with the port Oerlikon gun until he was killed, and the captain opened fire with his submachine-gun until he too was mortally wounded. Midshipman Fowler took command – he had never been to sea before joining the ship. He went ashore to find a bulldozer to push the craft off. The boat could not be steered as both the rudders had been lost, so a tow was arranged.[51]

Now the beaches were becoming dangerously crowded. There were many stranded landing craft, often damaged while unloading or just after. As the tide rose, the stretch of beach available to mass troops began to narrow. Often the exits from the beach were blocked or restricted. In the 'Juno' sector the engineers were delayed in preparing two exits from 'Mike Red', M1 and M2. Several landing craft were stranded, a huge traffic jam was building up, and a unit that landed at H+2 hours found 'things were chaotic; as yet there were no exits for vehicles, tracked or otherwise. The tide was in and an enormous amount of equipment was jammed in a narrow strip of sandy beach.'[52]

As the morning drew on, the main elements of the assault troops had been launched into action, and the gun emplacements and machine gun positions on the beaches were silenced, but there was no cause for complacency. Very few of the underwater obstacles had been cleared. The enemy now knew where the landings were taking place, and any counterattack by land, sea or air would be devastating. But the remnants of the *Luftwaffe* were deployed against the Allied bombing of Germany and on the Eastern Front, so their aircraft barely appeared in Normandy. Radar stations had been put out of action, and there had been no photo-reconnaissance or signal intelligence to tell them about the build-up of Allied shipping. The U-boats and surface fleet were defeated and did not interfere. On land, the armies were scattered across a wide area, and command was divided between Hitler and Rommel. Even several weeks after the landings, the German high command was convinced that the real assault would come elsewhere and did not deploy its full strength. All this gave the western Allies time to build up their forces in Normandy for a decisive land battle.

There was increased congestion again around midday on the 6th, as the inexorable rise of the tide reduced the beach to a very narrow strip. Major De l'Orme, of the Royal Engineers, was disconcerted when he first landed on 'Sword':

> The scene on the beach was indescribable – an absolute inferno, burning tanks, broken down vehicles, and very many dead and wounded lying about in a narrow strip between the sea and the wire at the back of the beach. There were shells, mortars and the occasional bomb falling, and a considerable amount of small arms fire. For a few moments I thought none of these things we had planned had come to pass. We were now nearly one and half hours late, the tide was almost high, we were all on one beach instead of spread along the whole divisional front. Our task of clearing beach obstacles was obviously hopeless ...[53]

The LSI(L)s arrived carrying infantry reinforcements – a now famous sequence of photographs shows them disembarking their men close to the Norman house on 'Juno' beach. The men struggled ashore grasping lines and carrying bicycles, which proved useless in service. Commodore Oliver worried about the flat Rhino ferries which were supposed to bring troops and tanks from the ships offshore to the beaches – would they be able to operate in these conditions? At 1120 the first group of twelve landing ships tank arrived with the good news that they had towed all their Rhinos over successfully. The minesweepers had cleared a path for the LVTs to beach, and they moved in with a welcome reinforcement of heavy vehicles through the litter of vessels and vehicles. On 'Mike Red' beach it was decided to ground as many LSTs as possible and allow them to dry out until the tide rose again. As yet there was no space to unload the Rhinos, and attempts to deploy them on 'Nan' beach were generally unsuccessful that day due to the weather. But Force L, carrying the 51st Highland Division, arrived that afternoon, and the build-up continued. Night fell, and Commodore Oliver reported:

> At dusk it was clear that the unloading of L.S.T. was badly behind the planned time-table and unless the weather and the state of beaches improved, unloading of build-up convoys expected at daylight on D+1 would not be satisfactorily completed.[54]

During the night three convoys of ferry craft and salvage and repair vessels arrived despite the rough weather, and beach clearance could begin in earnest. A landing craft repair party arrived on 'Nan White' beach at 2000 on D-Day and soon found plenty of work – over the next week it serviced and refloated 26 vessels including LCI(L)s, LCMs, and LCAs.

Despite the great problems, the landings had all been successful. At 'Utah' the Americans had landed on the wrong beach but found that it was less well defended than the one they had planned to use, so they had few casualties. On 'Omaha' beach the situation was far worse. Lieutenant Kenneth Sewell, RNVR, commanded a group of LCAs from the LSI *Prince Leopold* carrying American troops to the beach:

> As we closed Dog Red beach things started to hot up. We changed into line abreast formation and took our position with the waves of craft from other flotillas. We saw landing craft with men we had known so well disappear under a mortar explosion. We watched a mortar bomb bounce off a wave and slowly spin overhead ... it was apparent that something had gone badly wrong. There was a lot of fire coming from the beach – heavy artillery, mortars and machine gun fire, and as we made our

final run in we saw beach defences still intact including the Element C tripods of girders [sic] with mines lashed to the top – some craft in front of us blew up on these. Fortunately the obstacles had been placed just far enough apart for us to wriggle the craft through.[55]

As well as landing where a strong enemy force was waiting, the force at 'Omaha' lacked preparation. It was reported:

units became scattered on the final approach. Since the men had been briefed only for their particular areas, they were confused by the changed picture ... Debarking in water sometimes up to their necks, the troops on some sectors of the beach were met with a hail of bullets that drove some to seek shelter under the surf, others to scramble over the sides of their craft ... the first wave should have landed nine companies evenly spaced along the beach. Because of enemy fire and mislandings, however, the right wing all but disintegrated; two companies bunched in front of Les Moulins, and the remainder of the landings (elements of four companies) clustered in the Colleville sector. One company was carried so far east that it landed an hour and a half late.[56]

The American commander agreed that the landing crews were inadequately trained: they had received 'only a few days instruction' and 'they did not arrive in the theatre soon enough'.[57] But the troops rallied and eventually secured a beachhead, though they were a long way behind their objective for the day.

On 'Gold' beach, where the British attacked, the weather was perhaps at its worst, with force five winds making life very uncomfortable for the troops as they entered the LCAs. The first landings were planned for ten minutes earlier than on 'Juno' and took place on time, though the DD tanks were landed later by beaching the LCTs. The beach obstacles were particularly numerous in this sector, and there was much damage to landing craft. Port en

Bessin was not captured to link up with the Americans, but the landing was secure by nightfall.

In a sense the initial landing on 'Juno' beach was the most successful. The Canadians had succeeded in pushing up to seven miles inland, as much as any force that day, and achieved practically all their intermediate objectives, to capture a line known as 'Elm', though they did not take their final objective, 'Oak' which was three or four miles farther on. Casualties were relatively light, and the Canadian units lost only 340 men killed, many of them in the land battles after they left the beaches. The greatest losses were about 100 men from 48 Commando, partly due to their unsuitable craft. That represented the main failure in that area – the link-up with 'Sword' beach was not accomplished, and units of the German 21st Panzer Division were able to establish themselves in the gap.

On 'Sword' beach to the east of 'Juno', the expected opposition from batteries and warships at Le Havre did not materialize, and the majority of the DD tanks were launched and landed successfully, if a little late. The whole of the assault brigade was on shore by 0943, just eighteen minutes behind schedule, but resistance ahead was still strong, and they failed to reach the town of Caen that day – it would take more than a month of bloody and destructive battle to capture it.

Following their moment of making history, the landing craft crews settled down to more routine tasks of ferrying and servicing. After unloading their tanks, the LCTs were put at the disposal of beachmasters or landing-force commanders to evacuate wounded and prisoners, support the assault and land further waves of men. *LCT 2014* arrived alongside *Prince David* at 1145 and transferred a wounded soldier, who soon died. Then the troops climbed down scrambling nets on the side of the LSI and into the LCT. She slipped her mooring at 1335 and headed back to the beach.[58] After that, most of the LCTs were formed into convoys to go back to England, where they would pick up more tanks and vehicles. With *LCT 441* badly damaged on 'Juno' beach, Lieutenant Dinwiddy found a role directing traffic. One day he witnessed a visit by DUKW of King George VI and Winston Churchill, followed by one by General de Gaulle. Eventually his craft was salvaged and sent back for repair.

'Pluto' and the 'Mulberries' were less successful than had been hoped. 'Pluto' delivered only eight per cent of the fuel supplies needed for the invasion. The American 'Mulberry' harbour was put out of action by storms on 19–21 June, while the British one at Arromanches was damaged and carried less traffic than hoped for. On the other hand, the 'Gooseberries', simpler harbours created by sinking a row of blockships, were very successful. According to the official report, they 'exceeded all expectations in value for money' and remained intact during the storms. Smaller existing harbours, such as Port en Bessin proved quite useful until larger ones like Cherbourg could be captured and opened.

After many months of training and the experience of several operations, the landings were almost too efficient, in that their success was largely taken for granted by historians. The navy made it look too easy, and most accounts of the invasion concentrate on the events that befell the armies during and after the landings. The greatest danger came in the first hour or two, and this was largely over before the higher authorities were aware of it. In London, the Chief of Imperial General Staff, Sir Alan Brooke, was as anxious as anyone the night before and went through 'agonizing hours'. He wrote in his diary that morning,

By 7.30 I began to receive first news of the invasion. The airborne landings had been successful, the first waves reported as going in, opposition not too serious, batteries firing from flanks, etc. Throughout the day information has gone on coming in. On the British front the landing has gone well and the whole of 3 divisions are ashore.[59]

At home, the people were informed by radio and by the early editions of the evening newspapers. In London the *Evening News* proclaimed:

Montgomery Leads British, U.S., Canadian Force
WE WIN BEACHHEADS
4,000 Ships, 11,000 Planes in Assault on France:
'All going to Plan' – Premier

The anxieties of the morning of 6 June were largely forgotten, but it had been a brief period that stretched the temporary naval officer to the limit. With a minimum of training and very few experienced officers to guide him, he had to find his way to a beach in far worse conditions than expected, to thread his way among barely visible obstacles, maintain his calm in the face of losses and improvise in case of damage. He maintained his drive towards the objective of landing the army with minimum casualties, and there is no sign that anyone thought of turning back. It was a very different experience from the Battle of the Atlantic, which required endurance over months and years. Instead, the landing craft officers changed history in the course of a few hours in the morning of 6 June 1944, by their persistence and their skill in handling their strange craft. It too showed the products of the CW scheme and *King Alfred* at their best.

CONCLUSION

By the end of the war, most of the people whose stories are told or quoted here had risen in rank. Monsarrat describes how he was duty officer at the Admiralty when the war with Germany ended:

I was Duty Captain at the Admiralty, charged (on a strictly sub-contracting basis) with Britain's entire naval destiny, on the last night of the war.

Even inside the massive building, one could hear the tremendous noise from nearby Trafalgar Square, which, when I had come on duty at 9 p.m., was already packed with a cheering, roaring, dancing, swaying crowd: a crowd sampling the magic taste of the first evening of peace ...

On a guilty impulse I deserted my post, and climbed up the devious stone pathway to the top of Admiralty Arch ...

There was someone standing within five yards of me, also staring down at the crowds, and oblivious of close company ... The massive display of gold braid told me that he was an admiral ... In fact I suddenly recognised, he was the Admiral of the Fleet. The man in my company was the First Sea Lord and Chief of Naval staff, Admiral Cunningham. ... We had won. He had won. It must be quite a moment for him.[1]

Ludovic Kennedy was a lieutenant by that time, having served mostly in Tribal-class destroyers. Ewan Montagu worked entirely in intelligence and was an acting lieutenant-commander. Mallalieu was commissioned in the non-seagoing Special Branch and wrote a manual for naval instructors. Geoffrey Ball was younger than the others: he started as a midshipman and was commissioned in December 1944. Six months later he was serving in *Motor Launch 574*. After his failure at *King Alfred*, Paul Lund was commissioned through HMS *Lochailort* and was serving as a sub-lieutenant.

Many of the temporary officers did well after the war. James Callaghan went on to be the only person ever to hold all four of the great offices of state – Prime Minister, Chancellor of the Exchequer, Foreign Secretary and Home Secretary. J. P. W. Mallalieu also entered Parliament and served for a time as Parliamentary Under-Secretary of State for the Navy, and his wartime experience proved very useful there. Monsarrat, of course, became a highly successful novelist, but he never quite managed to shake off his image as a specialized writer of sea stories. Ludovic Kennedy had an equally famous media career and wrote several important books on naval history.

Peter Bull was a successful actor, best known perhaps as the Russian Ambassador in *Doctor Strangelove*. The career of his friend Alec Guinness is too well known to need any description here, but it is interesting to speculate how much his naval service influenced his acting. In looks he was more like the mild-mannered clerk he played in *The Lavender Hill Mob*, but he actually played a large number of navy, army and air force officers, for example in HMS *Defiant*, *Tunes of Glory* and *The Malta Story*, and most famously in *Bridge on the River Kwai*. In contrast, Peter Sellers, the other great character actor of that generation, served in the ranks of the RAF and spent some of his time impersonating officers. He played far fewer military roles, the most famous of which is Group Captain Mandrake in *Doctor Strangelove*. Sellers played him as a typical upper class buffoon, though in fact his was the only intelligent and completely sane character in the film and almost saves the world from nuclear destruction. Guinness could get inside the role of an officer, Sellers, for all his talents, could only mimic one.

Others attracted less fame but had equally successful careers in their own fields. Geoffrey Ball stayed in the naval reserves and eventually became a lieutenant-commander. He became Professor of Ophthalmics at Birmingham Aston University.

After the war, tradition reasserted itself and the navy tried to go back to its old peacetime self. Battleships were given priority again; amphibious warfare was neglected. Admirals insisted that old standards of discipline were restored, but change was on the way by the mid-fifties. The age of entry for naval officers was raised from thirteen to sixteen, then eighteen, and eventually most new entrants were university graduates in their early twenties. The last battleship was scrapped in 1960, and the navy returned to its wartime roles of anti-submarine and amphibious warfare, which the temporary wartime officers had done so much to develop. Officer ranks were opened up to the lower deck, and a large proportion of modern naval officers started as ratings. Sea training, based on the principles of 'Monkey' Stephenson, was taken more seriously, and a modern ship goes through a long and gruelling process before she goes to sea. In many ways the Royal Navy of today is closer to that of 1942 than that of 1939, or even 1950.

NOTES

1. The Yachtsmen go to War

1 Ewen Montagu, *Beyond Top Secret U*, London, 1977, p. 16

2 *Yachting World*, 13 November 1936

3 Nicholas Monsarrat, *Three Corvettes*, London, 2000, p. 5

4 Nicholas Monsarrat, *Life is a Four Letter Word*, Vol 2, London 1970, pp. 20, 3

5 *Yachting World*, YW 16/4/37

6 C. E. Tyrrell Lewis, *Coastal Cruising for Landsmen*, London, 1932, p. 2

7 Ibid. p. 5

8 Bernice Slater, *The Royal London Yacht Club*, Cowes, 1988, passim.

9 Silver of Rosneath, catalogue, 1938, pp. 10–11

10 *King Alfred Magazine*, vol 1, p. 23

11 *Royal United Services Institute Journal*, 1831

12 D. A. Rayner, *Escort, The Battle of the Atlantic*, London, 1955, p. 27

13 S. W. Roskill, *The War at Sea*, vol 1, London, 1954, p 575

14 National Archives, ADM 116/3509

15 Ibid.

16 Ibid.

17 *The Times*, 12 November 1936

18 *Yachting Monthly*, Dec 1936, p. 91

19 *Yachting World*, 30/10/36

20 *Yachting Monthly*, 6/11/36

21 *Yachting World*, YW 26/2/37

22 *Mariners Mirror*, vol 93, no 4, November 2007, p. 504

23 *Yachting Monthly*, March 1937

24 K. Adlard Coles, *Sailing Years*, St Albans, 1981, passim. Peter Scott, *The Eye of the Wind*, London, 1961. p. 268

25 National Archives, ADM 1/10054

26 F. G. C. Carr, *The Yacht Master's Guide and Coaster's Companion*, London, 1939, passim.

27 Navy List, June 1939, pp. 485-512

28 National Archives, ADM 1/9778

29 National Archives, ADM 116/3509

30 National Archives, ADM 1/9778

31 Geoffrey Willans, *One Eye on the Clock*, London, 1943, p. 13

32 Ibid. p. 8

33 *King Alfred Magazine*, vol 1, no 5, p. 2

34 Quoted in *HMS King Alfred, 1939-1945*, op. cit. p. 51

35 *Beyond Top Secret U*, op. cit. p. 19

36 Vol 1, no 1 p. 11

37 *King Alfred Magazine*, vol 1 no 4 p. 3

38 Ludovic Kennedy, *On my Way to the Club*, London, 1990, p. 93

39 Vol 1 no 11 p. 26

40 J. Lennox Kerr and Wilfred Granville, *The RNVR*, London, 1957, p. 151

41 Ewen Montagu, *Beyond Top Secret U*, London, 1977, p. 18

42 *King Alfred Magazine*, vol 1 p. 11

43 *On my Way to the Club*, op. cit. p. 93

44 *The RNVR*, op. cit. p. 151

45 General Information leaflet, Hove Library, pp. 10-11

46 *Beyond Top Secret U*, op. cit. p. 17

47 *On My Way to the Club*, op. cit. p. 92

48 Ibid. pp. 92-3

49 *King Alfred Magazine* Vol 1 no 7, p. 22

50 Ibid. vol 1, p. 11

51 Peter Scott, *The Eye of the Wind*, London, 1961, p. 277

52 *King Alfred Magazine* vol 1 no 5, p. 14

53 General Information leaflet, pp. 1, 3-5

54 *King Alfred Magazine King Alfred Magazine*, vol 1 no 3, p. 11

55 Nicholas Monsarrat, *Life is a Four Letter Word*, vol II, Breaking Out, London, 1970, p. 6

56 *On My Way to the Club*, op. cit. p. 93

57 *Eye of the Wind* p. 276

58 *Beyond Top Secret U*, op. cit. pp. 17, 19

59 *Mariners Mirror*, vol 93, no 4, November 2007, p. 504

60 Geoffrey Willans, *One*

Eye on the Clock, London, 1943, pp. 13–14

61 Hansard, 14 Feb 1940, col 741, col 2012, *King Alfred Magazine*, vol 1 no 1 p. 2

62 Admiralty Fleet Order 94/1940

63 *King Alfred Magazine*, Feb 42, p. 3

64 National Archives, ADM 199/787

65 National Archives, ADM 199/791

66 National Archives ADM 199/787

67 Ibid.

68 *King Alfred Magazine*, vol 1 no 2, pp. 28-9

69 National Archives, ADM 199/787

70 *King Alfred Magazine*, vol 1 no 4, pp. 8-9

71 National Archives, ADM 199/792

72 National Archives, ADM 199/791

73 Christian Brann, *The Little Ships of Dunkirk*, Cirencester, 1989, p. 142

74 National Archives, ADM 199/787

75 *The Eye of the Wind*, op. cit. p. 280

76 *One Eye on the Clock*, op. cit. p. 18

77 *King Alfred Magazine*, vol 1 no 5, p. 26

78 *Beyond Top Secret U*, op. cit. p. 20

2. A Novelist at Sea

1 Monsarrat calls her the 18th, presumably not counting two ex-French ships and two built in Canada by that time.

2 *Three Corvettes*, op. cit. p. 13

3 Ibid. pp. 15-6

4 Ibid. p. 18

5 Ibid. p. 5

6 Gordon Read, *A Guide to the Records of Merseyside Maritime Museum*, vol 1, Liverpool, 1995, p. 133

7 *Life is a Four Letter Word*, op. cit. p. 7

8 *Three Corvettes*, pp. 21-2

9 Ibid. p. 25

10 *British Warship Design*, London, 1983, p. 112

11 John Fernald, *Destroyer from America*, London, 1942, p. 22.

12 S. Gorley Putt, *Men Dressed as Seamen*, London, 1943, p. 85

13 Donald Macintyre, *U-Boat Killer*, London, 1956, p. 104

14 *Destroyer From America*, op. cit. p. 25

15 Nicholas Monsarrat, *Three Corvettes*, reprinted London, 2000, p. 31

16 *British Warship Design*, op. cit. p. 124

17 *Three Corvettes*, p. 35

18 National Archives, ADM 199/2119

19 *Three Corvettes*, p. 36

20 Ibid. p. 31

21 Ibid. p. 38

22 News Chronicle, 10 Feb 1941, p. 4

23 *Three Corvettes*, p. 63

24 Ibid. p. 293

25 Ibid. pp. 40-1

26 Imperial War Museum, papers of N. J. W. Bates, p. 188

27 *Three Corvettes*, p. 68

28 Ibid. p. 68

29 IWM Bates, op. cit.

30 *Three Corvettes*, p. 60

31 *Life is a Four Letter Word*, p. 75

32 *Three Corvettes*, p. 294

33 Ibid. p. 295

34 Sam Lombard Hobson, *A Sailor's War*, London, 1983, pp. 132–3

35 Navy Records Society, vol 137, 1997, *The Defeat of the Enemy Attack on Shipping*, p. xvi

3. Joining the Navy

1 Quoted in HC Barnard, *A History of English Education*, London, 1961, p. 283

2 Monsarrat, *Life is a Four Letter Word*, op. cit. p. 29

3 William James, *The Sky was Always Blue*, London, 1951 , pp. 22-3

4 Charles Owen, *No More Heroes*, London, 1975, p. 131

5 Ludovic Kennedy, *On my Way to the Club*, London, 1989, p. 33

6 Tristan Jones, *Heart of Oak*, 1984, reprinted Shrewsbury, 1997, pp. 29, 44–5

7 National Archives ED/12/245

8 National Archives, ADM 1/17944

9 J. P. W. Mallalieu, *Very Ordinary Seaman*, London, 1944, p. 122

10 Admiralty Fleet Order 276/1940

11 Peter Bull, *To Sea in a Sieve*, London, 1973, p. 13, Geoffrey Ball papers, Imperial War Museum 83/45/2

12 Admiralty Fleet Order 882/1941

13 John Whelan, *Home is the Sailor*, London, 1957 , p. 178

14 *Hansard*, vol 378, cols 1088-89

15 Admiralty Fleet Order 1163/1943

16 *Report of the Consultative Committee on Secondary Education*, HMSO,

London, 1938, Table 1

17 Ibid. Table 13

18 Frank Green and Sidney Wolf, *London and Suburbs, Old and New*, London, 1933, p. 193

19 Ibid. p. 158

20 George Orwell, *The Road to Wigan Pier*, pp. 49, 51, 71, 76

21 Harold Wheeler, ed, *Everybody's Best Friend*, London, 1938, p. 416

22 *Boys Own Annual*, ed Geoffrey R. Pocklington, London, 1930, p. 573

23 Brencan A. Maher, *A Passage to Sword Beach*, Shrewsbury, 1996, p. 7

24 *The Letters of Evelyn Waugh*, ed Mark Amory, London, 1980, p. 492

25 *Hansard*, 3/3/43, col 598

26 *Everybody's Best Friend*, op. cit. p. 9

27 J. P. W. Mallalieu, *On Larkhill*, London, 1983, p. 202

28 B. Lavery, *Hostilities Only*, London, 2004, pp. 30-2

29 University of Sussex, Mass Observation Archive, Report nos 886-7

30 Max Hastings, *Overlord*, London, 1985, p. 58

31 'Raff', *Behind the Spitfires*, London, 1941

32 National Archives ADM 1/12133

33 Admiralty, *The Navy and the Y-Scheme*, 1946, (Copy in the NMM Library) p. 1

34 Ibid. p. 5

35 Ibid. passim.

36 Brendan A. Maher, *A Passage to Sword Beach*, Shrewsbury, 1996, pp. 10-11

37 J. P. Mayer, *British*

Cinemas and their Audiences, London, 1948, p. 254

38 *Everybody's Best Friend*, op. cit. p. 350

39 *British Cinemas and their Audiences*, op. cit. p. 195

40 Quoted in Anthony Aldgate and Jeffrey Richards, *Britain Can Take It*, Oxford, 1984, p. 216

41 Noel Coward, *Future Indefinite*, London, 1954, p. 48

42 Mass Observation, Reports 886-7

43 National Archives ADM 1/21955

44 Davies, *Stone Frigate*, op. cit. p. 6

45 Alec Guinness, *Blessings in Disguise*, London, 1985, p. 152

46 National Archives ADM 1//21955

4. Becoming a Sailor

1 J. P. W. Mallalieu, *Very Ordinary Seaman*, London, 1944, p. 13

2 George Melly, *Rum, Bum and Concertina*, London, 1977, pp. 5–6

3 Alec Guinness, *Blessings in Disguise*, London, 1985, p. 154

4 D. L. Summers, *HMS Ganges*, 1866–1966, Shotley, 1966, p. 51

5 Ken Kimberley, *Heavo, Heavo, Lash up and Stow*, Kettering, 1999, p. 14

6 John Davis, *The Stone Frigate*, London, 1947, p. 24

7 *Heavo, Heavo, Lash up and Stow*, p. 14

8 HMS Royal Arthur, *Handbook*, Skegness, 1943, p. 10

9 Ibid. p. 13

10 *Heavo, Heavo, Lash up and Stow*, op. cit. p. 17

11 *The Stone Frigate*, op. cit. p. 39

12 S. Gorley Putt, *Men Dressed as Seamen*, London, 1943, pp. 34–5

13 James Callaghan, *Time and Chance*, London, 1987, p. 58

14 Hannen Swaffer, *What would Nelson Do?*, London, 1946, p. 92–3

15 Eric Denton, *My Six Wartime Years in the Royal Navy*, London, 1999 p. 17

16 *Stone Frigate*, op. cit. p. 112

17 Admrialty, *Manual of Seamanship*, London, 1937, vol 1 p. 7

18 *Very Ordinary Seaman*, op. cit. pp. 18–19

19 Ibid. p. 48

20 Norman Hampson, *Not Really What You'd Call a War*, Whittles, 2001, p. 3

21 George Melly, *Rum, Bum and Concertina*, London, 1976, p. 7

22 *Very Ordinary Seaman*, op. cit. p. 34

23 Natinal Archives, ADM 199/788A

24 *Very Ordinary Seaman*, op. cit. p. 121

25 Peter Bull, *To Sea in a Sieve*, London, 1973, p. 12

26 Ibid. p. 10

27 *Very Ordinary Seaman*, op. cit. p. 20

28 Ibid. p. 28

29 *Stone Frigate*, op. cit. p. 125

30 Admiralty, *Royal Naval Handbook of Field Training*, London, 1920, p. 19

31 *Naval Review*, January

1955, pp. 80–83, 128–29

32 Roy Fuller, *Vamp Till Ready*, London, 1982, p. 142

33 *To Sea in a Sieve*, op. cit. p. 11

34 Albert H Jones, *No Easy Choices*, Upton on Severn, 1999, pp. 22-3

35 Information supplied to the author

36 Imperial War Museum Documents, A111

37 *Stone Frigate*, op. cit. p. 127

38 Admiralty, *A Seaman's Pocket Book*, 1943, reprinted London 2006, p. 7

39 Ibid. p. 17

40 Eric Denton, *My Six Wartime Years in the Royal Navy*, London, 1999, p. 20

41 Imperial War Museum Manuscripts 83/5/1

42 *Blessings in Disguise*, op. cit. p. 155

43 Fred Kellet, *A Flower for the Sea, a Fish for the Sky*, Carlisle, 1995, p. 11

44 F. S. Holt, *A Banker All at Sea*, Newtown (Australia), 1983, p. 29

45 J. Lennox Kerr and David James, *Wavy Navy, by Some Who Served*, London, 1950, p. 194

5. The CW Experience

Quoted in Piers Paul Read, *Alec Guinness*, London, 2004, p. 135

2 Peter Bull, *To Sea in a Sieve*, London, 1973, p. 13

3 Joseph Wellings, ed John Hattendorf, *On His Majesty's Service*, Newport, Rhode Island, 1983, p. 75

4 Document communicated to the author

5 *Very Ordinary Seaman*, op. cit. p. 88

6 Communicated to author

7 *Very Ordinary Seaman*, op. cit. p. 90

8 Ibid. p. 93

9 H. P. K. Oram, *The Rogue's Yarn, London*, 1993, p. 229

10 John Davies, *Lower Deck*, London, 1945, pp. 79-80

11 *Three Corvettes*, op. cit. p. 49

12 Hansard, 3/3/43, col 598

13 Communication to the author

14 *To Sea in a Sieve*, op. cit. p. 25

15 *Very Ordinary Seaman*, op. cit. p. 166

16 *Home is the Sailor*, op. cit. p. 149

17 Noel Wright and A. C. G. Sweet, *How to Prepare Food; Tips and Wrinkles for Cooks of Messes in Standard Ration Ships*, Ipswich, 1941

18 Communication to author

19 *To Sea in a Sieve*, op. cit. p. 25

20 *A First Lieutenant's Handbook*, c 1932, NMM pamphlet collection, p. 8

21 *Very Ordinary Seaman*, op. cit. p. 87

22 Admiralty, *A Royal Navy Officer's Pocket Book*, ed Lavery, 2007, p. 25

23 *Home is the Sailor*, op. cit. p. 147

24 *Very Ordinary Seaman*, op. cit. p. 163

25 Ibid. p. 141

26 Ibid. p. 173

27 Ibid. p. 51

28 Ibid. p. 158

29 Ibid. p. 160

30 National Archives, ADM 101/623

31 National Archives, ADM 239/335

32 Charles McAra, *Mainly in Minesweepers*, London, 1991, p. 49

33 *Men Dressed as Seamen*, op. cit. p. 84

34 Eric Denton, *My Six Wartime Years in the Royal Navy*, London, 1999, p. 50

35 *Very Ordinary Seaman*, p. 110

36 *Home is the Sailor*, op. cit. pp. 146–7

37 *To Sea in a Sieve*, op. cit. pp. 18–29

38 Communication to author

39 Imperial War Museum documents, Moran papers, 92/45/1

40 *Three Corvettes*, op. cit. pp. 49–50

41 J. P. W. Mallalieu, *On Larkhill*, London, 1983, p. 203

42 *Very Ordinary Seaman*, op. cit. p. 265

43 *On Larkhill*, op. cit.

44 Ibid. p. 303

6. King Alfred

1 *To Sea in a Sieve*, op. cit. p. 34

2 F. S. Holt, *A Banker All at Sea*, Newtown (Australia), 1983, p. 101

3 *To Sea in a Sieve*, op. cit. p. 35

4 Paul Lund and Harry Ludlam, *The War of the Landing Craft*, Slough, 1976, p.71

5 Nairn and Pevsener, *The Buildings of England*, Sussex, 1965, pp. 256, 39

6 *To Sea in a Sieve*, op. cit. p. 35

7 *King Alfred Magazine*, vol 6, p. 29

8 Brendan A. Maher, *A Passage to Sword Beach*, Shrewsbury, 1996, p. 27

9 National Archives, ADM 1/18959

10 *King Alfred Magazine*

11 Ibid. Vol 1 no 6, October 1940, p. 15

12 *A Banker All at Sea*, op. cit. pp. 108–9

13 Norman Hampson, *Not Really What You'd Call a War*, Caithness, 2001, p. 29

14 *A Passage to Sword Beach*, op. cit. p. 29

15 *King Alfred* Syllabus in Hove Library

16 National Archives, ADM 1/18698

17 Syllabus, Hove Library, p. 3

18 Ibid. pp. 4–5

19 Brendan A. Maher, *A Passage to Sword Beach*, Shrewsbury, 1996, p. 27

20 Peter Scott, *The Eye of the Wind, London*, 1961, p. 280

21 National Archives, ADM 1/18698

22 *A Passage to Sword Beach*, op. cit. p. 30

23 Syllabus, Hove Library

24 *To Sea in a Sieve*, op. cit. 57

25 *The War of the Landing Craft*, op. cit. p. 74

26 National Archives, ADM ADM 1/18959

27 *General Information* leaflet, p. 4

28 *King Alfred Magazine*, vol 7, p. 29

29 Syllabus, Hove Library

30 Imperial War Museum Documents, 05/6/1

31 *King Alfred Magazine*, vol 1, no 5, p. 23

32 Imperial War Museum Documents, 05/6/1

33 *A Banker All at Sea*, op. cit. p. 109

34 *HMS King Alfred, 1939–1945*, op. cit. pp. 26–7

35 General Information leaflet, p. 17

36 National Archives, ADM 1/18959

37 Ibid.

38 *Mainly in Minesweepers*, op. cit. p. 52

39 National Maritime Museum manuscripts, BGY/M/3

40 Sir Roderick Macdonald, *The Figurehead*, Durham, 1993, p. 199

41 National Archives, ADM 234/290

42 National Archives, ADM 1/18952

43 *Blessings in Disguise*, op. cit. pp. 152–3

44 Imperial War Museum Documents 05/6/1

45 *Royal Navy Officers Pocket Book*, p. 15

46 Imperial War Museum Documents 94/43/1

47 National Archives, ADM 1/15676

48 *A Passage to Sword Beach*, op. cit. pp. 28–9

49 *A Banker All at Sea*, op. cit. p. 104

50 Ibid. p. 110

51 National Archives, ADM 1/18959

52 Ibid.

53 Ibid.

54 Ibid.

55 Ibid.

56 *The Figurehead*, op. cit. p. 199

57 *To Sea in a Sieve*, op. cit. pp. 35–6

58 National Archives, ADM 1/15676

59 *A Banker All at Sea*, op. cit. p. 103

60 Ibid. p. 103

61 *Mainly in Minesweepers*, op. cit. p. 54

62 *King Alfred Magazine*, passim.

63 *To Sea in a Sieve*, op. cit. pp. 39, 40

64 Syllabus, Hove Library

65 National Archives, ADM 1/14015

66 Ibid.

67 *King Alfred Magazine*, vol 1 no 6 p. 1 and passim.

68 *Blessings in Disguise*, op. cit. p. 160

69 King Alfred website, p. 2

70 *The War of the Landing Craft*, op. cit. p. 78

71 King Alfred website

72 *To Sea in a Sieve*, op. cit. p. 41

73 *Blessings in Disguise*, op. cit. p. —

74 *Hansard*, vol 378, p. 1090

75 *HMS King Alfred, 1939-1945*, op. cit. p. 21

76 Ibid. 233

77 *Escort*, op. cit. pp. 218-9

78 Ibid. p. 1

79 Norman Hanson, *Carrier Pilot*, Cambridge, 1979, p. 60

80 National Archives, ADM 1/18959

81 *Navy List*, April 1945, pp. 2576–77

82 J. Lennox Kerr and Wilfred Granville, *The RNVR, a Record of Achievement*, London, 1957, p. 176

83 CAFO 1615/41

84 *The RNVR, a Record of Achievement*, op. cit. p. 187

85 National Archives, ADM 116/5346

86 Admiralty, *The Navy and the Y-Scheme*, 1944, p. 18

87 Eric Denton, *My Six Wartime Years in the Royal Navy*, London, 1999, p. 61

88 Waters 186
89 MIM 56
90 *A Passage to Sword Beach*, op. cit. pp. 35, 45

7. Fighting the Submarine

1 *Notes for Medical Officers, in A Naval Officer's Pocket-Book*, ed Lavery. London, 2007, p. 47
2 *Three Corvettes*, op. cit. p. 279
3 John Palmer, *Luck on my Side*, Barnsley, 2002, p. 26
4 Escort, op. cit. p. 64
5 Evelyn Waugh, *Diaries*, ed Michael Davie, London, 1976, p. 492
6 Order no 4, quoted in *A Naval Officer's Pocket-Book*, op. cit. p. 77
7 *Life is a Four Letter Word*, op. cit. p. 19
8 Admiralty Fleet Order 489/40
9 *Three Corvettes*, op. cit. p. 20
10 *The Cruel Sea*, 1951, pp. 49–50
11 *Life is a Four Letter Word*, op. cit. pp. 154–6
12 Orders no 4, quoted in *A Naval Officer's Pocket-Book*, op. cit. p. 77
13 *Three Corvettes*, op. cit. p. 57, *HM Frigate*, op. cit. p. 14
14 National Archives, ADM 234/290, p. 41
15 *A Naval Officer's Pocket-Book*, op. cit. p. 44
16 Ibid. p. 84
17 Ibid. p. 30
18 National Archives, ADM 239/298
19 National Archives, ADM 1/13680
20 A. H. Cherry, *Yankee RN*, London, 1951, p. 148

21 John Whelan, *Home is the Sailor*, London, 1957, p. 172
22 *Yankee RN*, op. cit. p. 148
23 Ibid. p. 117
24 Navy Records Society, vol 137, 1997, *The Defeat of the Enemy Attack on Shipping*, p. 3
25 MAS, August 1942, pp. 52–3
26 National Archives, ADM 1/13680
27 *Very Ordinary Seaman*, op. cit. p. 153
28 National Archives, ADM 1/15871
29 National Archives, ADM 199/353
30 National Archives, ADM 239/344, p. 93
31 MAS, March 1941, p. 38
32 *Three Corvettes*, op. cit. p. 278
33 National Archives ADM 239/248, Training, p. 4
34 *Yankee RN*, op. cit. p. 150
35 National Archives, ADM 239/298
36 Ibid.
37 Ibid. para 174
38 Ibid. 239/298, para 169
39 *Very Ordinary Seaman*, op. cit. p. 215
40 Monthly Anti Submarine Report, November 1942, pp. 40–1
41 *Yankee RN*, p. 152
42 Ibid. p. 151
43 *The Figurehead*, op. cit. p. 43
44 National Archives ADM 239/248, pp. 8–9

8. Amphibious Warfare

1 *To Sea in A Sieve*, op. cit. pp. 42, 44
2 National Archives DEFE 2/703, *Bulldozer* magazine
3 National Archives DEFE 2/697, p. 59

4 National Archives DEFE 2/1430
5 Ibid.
6 *Blessings in Disguise*, op. cit. 164–5
7 Phillip Zeigler, *Mountbatten*, London, 1985, p. 162
8 National Archives, ADM 101/641
9 L. E. H. Maund, *Assault from the Sea*, London, 1949, p. 75
10 National Archives, DEFE 2/6
11 National Archives, ADM 1/14003
12 National Archives DEFE 2/703
13 *The War of the Landing Craft*, op. cit. p. 91
14 Ibid. p. 135
15 National Archives, DEFE 2/802
16 National Archives DEFE 2/703
17 *The War of the Landing Craft*, op. cit. p. 40
18 *Mariners Mirror*, 2002 p. 213
19 A and L p. 67
20 National Archives DEFE 2/703
21 *To Sea in A Sieve*, op. cit. p. 46
22 Imperial War Museum Documents 99/6/1
23 Mariners Mirror, op. cit. p. 214
24 Read, *Alec Guinness*, op. cit. pp. 139, 40
25 *The War of the Landing Craft*, op. cit. p. 63
26 Alan Villiers, *The Set of the Sails*, London, 1950, pp. 273-75
27 National Archives, ADM 1/14725
28 *To Sea in A Sieve*, op. cit. p. 48
29 J. Lennox Kerr, ed, *Wavy Navy*, London, 1950, p. 223

30 Imperial War Museum Documents 99/6/1

31 National Archives, DEFE 2/833

32 National Archives, DEFE 2/847

33 National Archives, ADM 7/705

34 *Blessings in Disguise*, op. cit. p. 179

35 National Archives, DEFE 2/1783

36 National Archives, DEFE 2/898

37 National Archives, ADM 179/506

38 *Blessings in Disguise*, op. cit. pp. 183–4

39 *British Warship Design*, op. cit. p. 35

40 National Archives DEFE 2/703

41 National Archives, ADM 199/943

42 National Archives, DEFE 2/730

43 *Diaries*, op. cit. p. 492

44 National Archives, DEFE 2/847

45 National Archives, ADM 179/254

46 National Archives, ADM 179/255

47 National Archives, ADM 53/119762

48 National Archives, ADM 53/119763

9. First Command

1 Peter Gretton, *Convoy Escort Commander*, London, 1964, pp. 45, 46, 48

2 *Escort*, op. cit. p. 23

3 Nicholas Monsarrat, *HM Frigate*, London, 1945, pp. 15–16

4 *Three Corvettes*, op. cit. pp. 129,130, 134

5 G. W. Searle, *At Sea Level*, Lewes, 1994, pp. 31–2

6 Edward Young, *One of Our Submarines*, London, 1982, p. 124

7 Daily Telegraph, *Book of Naval Obituaries*, London, 2004, pp. 288–91

8 W. S. Galpin, *From Public School to Navy*, Plymouth, 1919, pp. 36–42

9 *Yankee RN*, op. cit. p. 411

10 Joseph Wellings, *On His Majesty's Service*, Newport, Rhode Island, 1983, p. 65

11 *Life is a Four Letter Word*, op. cit. p. 62

12 Sam Lombard Hobson, *A Sailor's War*, London, 1983, pp. 136–7

13 National Archives DEFE 2/1430

14 *To Sea in A Sieve*, op. cit. p. 47

15 Read, *Alec Guinness*, op. cit. p. 140

16 Eric Denton, *My Six Wartime Years in the Royal Navy*, London, 1999, pp. 142, 145

17 National Archives, ADM 234/235

18 R. Plunkett-Drax, *The Modern Officer of the Watch*, Portsmouth, 1918; B V Sturdee, *Five Minutes to One Bell*, London, 1914; Christopher Craddock, *Whispers from the Fleet*, Portsmouth, 1907; W M James, *New Battleship Organisations*, Portsmouth, 1916

19 *A First Lieutenant's Handbook*, c 1932, NMM pamphlet collection

20 National Archives, ADM 116/4331, p. 39

21 *The Figurehead*, op. cit. pp. 196, 76

22 National Archives, ADM 1/15676

23 National Archives, DEFE 2/705

24 *Your Ship, in The Royal Navy Officer's Pocket Book*, op. cit. p. 90

25 Ibid. p. 92

26 *Escort*, op. cit. p. 73

27 Donald Macintyre, *U-Boat Killer*, London, 2002, p. 17

28 Monsarrat, *HM Frigate*, op. cit. p. 16

29 *My Six Wartime Years in the Royal Navy*, op. cit. p. 66

30 *U-Boat Killer*, op. cit. p. 23–4

31 *A Sailor's War*, op. cit. pp. 136–7

32 *On His Majesty's Service*, op. cit. 66

33 National Maritime Museum manuscripts, GTN/4/1

34 Monsarrat, *HM Frigate*, op. cit. p. 18

35 National Archives, ADM 231/235

36 Admiralty, BR 16, *Engineering Manual*, 1939, p. 10, para 7

37 *The Royal Navy Officer's Pocket Book*, op. cit. Notes for MOs, p. 2

38 National Archives, ADM 234/290, p. 31

39 National Archives, ADM 1/15676

40 *The Royal Navy Officer's Pocket Book*, op. cit. p. 20

41 National Archives, ADM 234/290, p. 29

42 *The Royal Navy Officer's Pocket Book*, op. cit. p. 104

43 Ibid. p. 96

44 *Three Corvettes*, op. cit. p. 146

45 Quoted in Zeigler, *Mountbatten*, op. cit. 122

46 National Archives, ADM

234/290. p. 27

47 *The Royal Navy Officer's Pocket Book*, op. cit. p. 95

48 National Maritime Museum manuscripts, GTN/4/1VII, 11

49 Ibid. no 8

50 National Archives, ADM 234/290, p. 29

51 Ibid. p. 27

52 *Escort*, op. cit. pp. 99–101

53 National Maritime Museum manuscripts, GTM/4/1 , no 18

54 *Escort*, op. cit. p. 76

55 Chris Howard Bailey, *The Battle of the Atlantic*, Stroud, 1994, p. 110

56 *On His Majesty's Service*, op. cit. p. 76

57 *Life is a Four Letter Word*, op. cit. p. 154, *Three Corvettes*, op. cit. p. 154

58 National Maritime Museum manuscripts, GTN/4/1, no 1

59 Ibid. GTN/5/7

60 *The Figurehead*, op. cit. p. 195

61 *The Royal Navy Officer's Pocket Book*, op. cit. p. 118

62 National Archives, ADM 1/22967

63 *The Figurehead*, op. cit. p. 142

64 *Yankee RN*, op. cit. pp. 386–92

65 National Archives ADM 1/15676

66 *Convoy Escort Commander*, op. cit. pp. 167–8, Ball letter to author, 5 January 2008

67 National Archives, ADM 1/15676

68 Quoted in Warmer, *Cunningham of Hyndhope*, p. 62

69 *The Royal Navy Officer's Pocket Book*, op. cit. p. 98

70 Nixie Taverner, *A Torch among Tapers*, Bramber, 2001, pp. 282–83

71 *On His Majesty's Service*, op. cit. pp. 81, 85

72 National Archives, ADM 234/290, p. 12

73 National Maritime Museum Ships' Covers, 311e

74 National Archives, ADM 1/15676

75 National Archives, DEFE 2/1430

76 National Archives ADM 1/15676

10. Western Isles

1 Richard Baker, *The Terror of Tobermory*, reprinted Edinburgh 1999, p. 112

2 Ibid. p. ix

3 Imperial War Museum manuscripts, 05/6/11

4 *The Terror of Tobermory*, op. cit. p. 104

5 MASR, October 1944, p. 15

6 This and several other films are included in IWM *Protect the Convoy* DVD

7 *Monthly Anti-Submarine Reports*, October 1944, p. 16

8 Ibid. October 1944, p. 14

9 *The Terror of Tobermory*, op. cit. p. 98

10 National Archives, ADM 199/1729

11 Admiralty, *Monthly Anti-Submarine Reports*, October 1944, p. 18

12 *Daily Telegraph, Book of Naval Obituaries*, op. cit. pp. 252–54

13 *The Terror of Tobermory*, op. cit. p. 151

14 Henry Baynham, *Men from the Dreadnoughts*, London, 1976, p. 258

15 *The Terror of Tobermory*, op. cit. p. 122

16 Ibid. p. 133

17 Manuscript in the author's possession

18 Admiralty, *Monthly Anti-Submarine Reports*, October 1944, p. 15

19 National Archives, ADM 239/248, p. 35

20 Chris Howard Bailey, *The Royal Naval Museum Book of the Battle of the Atlantic*, Stroud, 1994, pp. 12–13

21 *Naval Review*, 1979, p. 329

22 Ibid.

23 *The Terror of Tobermory*, op. cit. p. 98

24 Manuscript in the author's possession

25 National Archives, ADM 1/12817

26 *The Terror of Tobermory*, op. cit. p. 115

27 Escort, op. cit. p. 71

28 PRO ADM 199/1729

29 *Monthly Anti-Submarine Reports*, July [sic] 1941, p. 27

30 National Archives, ADM 239/344

31 Peter Gretton, *Crisis Convoy*, London, 1974, pp. 37, 170–71

11. Convoy

1 National Archives ADM 187/20

2 *Yankee RN*, op. cit. p. 277

3 National Archives ADM 199/2059

4 Richard Woodman, *The Real Cruel Sea*, London, 2004, p. 489

5 Gunter Hessler, *The U-Boat War in the Atlantic*

1939-45, London, 1989, p. 33

6 National Archives ADM 199/713

7 MASR, October 1942, pp. 34–5

8 Ibid. p. 30

9 National Archives ADM 199/713, f 205

10 *U-Boat Killer*, op. cit. p. 127

11 National Archives ADM 199/713, f 226

12 Ibid. f 224

13 Ibid. f 236

14 MASR, September 1942, p. 31

15 National Archives ADM 199/713 f 213

16 Ibid. ADM 1/12271

17 National Archives ADM 199/713 f 211

18 National Archives ADM 239/344, p. 48 article 4

19 *The U-Boat War*, op. cit. p. 33

12. Landings

1 Timothy Harrison Place, *Military Training in the British Army*, London, 2000, passim.

2 *To Sea in a Sieve*, op. cit. pp. 85–90

3 Ibid.

4 National Archives, ADM 199/947

5 *Blessings in Disguise*, op. cit. pp. 177–8

6 National Archives, ADM 199/858

7 *Blessings in Disguise*, op. cit. p. 179

8 *War of the Landing Craft*, op. cit. p. 111

9 *Fuhrer Conferences on Naval Affairs*, London, 2005, p. 327

10 National Archives, ADM 199/858

11 National Archives, ADM 199/947

12 *Daily Telegraph*, 20 August 1943

13 *Blessings in Disguise*, op. cit. pp. 183–4

14 *Daily Telegraph*, op. cit.

15 *To Sea in a Sieve*, op. cit. p. 97

16 National Archives, ADM 199/858

17 Ibid.

18 Ibid.

19 Ibid.

20 L. F. Ellis, *Victory in the West, The Battle of Normandy*, London, 1962, p. 222

21 Winston G. Ramsey, ed, *D-Day Then and Now*, vol 1, London, 1995, p. 200

22 Imperial War Museum documents, Miscellaneous 60

23 John De S. Winser, *The D-Day Ships*, Kendal, 1994, pp. 6–7, 110–15

24 J. Lennox Kerr, *Wavy Navy, by Some who Served*, London, 1950, pp. 224–25

25 Imperial War Museum documents, 87/28/1

26 *D-Day Then and Now*, vol 1, p. 57

27 Ibid. p. 166

28 Imperial War Museum documents, 87/28/1

29 National Archives, ADM 179/506

30 Imperial War Museum documents, 87/28/1

31 *A Passage to Sword Beach*, op. cit. p. 118

32 National Archives, DEFE 2/416

33 National Archives, ADM 179/506

34 *A Passage to Sword Beach*, op. cit. pp. 118–9

35 National Archives, ADM 179/506

36 *Mariners Mirror*, 2002, p. 215

37 Ibid. p. 215

38 *D-Day Then and Now*, vol 2, London, 1988, p. 475

39 *War of the Landing Craft*, op. cit. p. 158

40 R. P. Pakenham-Walsh, *History of the Corps of Royal Engineers*, vol IX, Chatham, 1958, pp. 349–50

41 *War of the Landing Craft*, op. cit. p. 158

42 National Archives, DEFE 2/400

43 *War of the Landing Craft*, op. cit. p. 160

44 Imperial War Museum documents, 87/28/1

45 Ibid. 92/45/1

46 Ibid. 99/5/1

47 Ibid. p. 177

48 National Archives, ADM 179/506

49 Ibid.

50 *D-Day Then and Now*, vol 1, p. 506

51 National Archives, ADM 179/506

52 *D-Day Then and Now*, vol 2, p. 467

53 Pakenham-Walsh, *History of the Corps of Royal Engineers*, vol IX, 1958, p. 347

54 National Archives, ADM 179/506

55 *War of the Landing Craft*, op. cit. pp. 169–70

56 Quoted in ibid. pp. 191–2

57 Ibid. p. 191

58 National Archives, ADM 179/506

59 Lord Alanbrooke, *War Diaries*, ed Danchev and Todman, London, 2001, p. 554

Conclusion

1 *Life is a Four Letter Word*, pp 146–9

BIBLIOGRAPHY

GENERAL AND SOCIAL HISTORY

Calder, Angus, *The People's War, Britain, 1939–1945,* St Albans, 1982
Mowat, Charles Loch, *Britain Between the Wars, 1918–1940,* reprinted Cambridge, 1987
Taylor, A. J. P., *English History, 1939–45,* reprinted Oxford, 1975

GENERAL NAVAL HISTORIES

Barnett, Corelli, *Engage the Enemy More Closely*, London, 1991
Potter, E. B., *The Great Sea War,* London, 1960
Roskill, S. W., *The War at Sea,* 4 vols, London, 1954–61

NAVAL AND MILITARY HISTORY, ASPECTS AND CAMPAIGNS

British Warship Design, London, 1983
Fuhrer Conferences on Naval Affairs, London, 2005
Bailey, Chris Howard, *The Battle of the Atlantic,* Stroud, 1994
Ellis, L. F., *Victory in the West, The Battle of Normandy,* London, 1962
Hessler, Gunter, *The U-Boat War in the Atlantic 1939–45,* London, 1989
Kerr, J. Lennox and Granville, Wilfred, *The RNVR,* London, 1957
Kerr, J. Lennox, ed., *Wavy Navy,* London, 1950
Lavery, B., *Churchill's Navy,* London 2006
Lund, Paul and Ludlam, Harry, *The War of the Landing Craft,* Slough, 1976
Maund, L. E. H., *Assault from the Sea,* London, 1949
Middleton, Judy, *HMS King Alfred, 1939–1945,* Brighton, 1986
Pakenham-Walsh, R. P., *History of the Corps of Royal Engineers,* vol IX, Chatham, 1958
Ramsey, Winston G., ed., *D-Day Then and Now,* 2 vols, London, 1995
Summers, D. L., *HMS Ganges, 1866-1966,* Shotley, 1966
Swaffer, Hannen, *What Would Nelson Do?,* London, 1946
Winser, John De S., *The D-Day Ships,* Kendal, 1994
Woodman, Richard, *The Real Cruel Sea,* London, 2004

PERSONAL MEMOIRS AND BIOGRAPHY, PUBLISHED

Bull, Peter, *To Sea in a Sieve,* London, 1973
Callaghan, James, *Time and Chance,* London, 1987
Cherry, A. H., *Yankee RN,* London, 1951
Fernald, John, *Destroyer from America,* London, 1942
Gretton, Peter, *Convoy Escort Commander,* London, 1964
Gretton, Peter, *Crisis Convoy,* London, 1974
Guinness, Alec, *Blessings in Disguise,* London, 1985
Read, Piers Paul, *Alec Guinness,* London, 2004
Hampson, Norman, *Not Really What You'd Call a War,* Caithness, 2001
Holt, F. S., *A Banker All at Sea,* Newtown (Australia), 1983
James, William, *The Sky was Always Blue,* London, 1951
Jones, Tristan, *Heart of Oak,* 1984, reprinted Shrewsbury, 1997
Kennedy, Ludovic, *On my Way to the Club,* London, 1990
Kimberley, Ken, *Heavo, Heavo, Lash up and Stow,* Kettering, 1999
Hobson, Sam Lombard, *A Sailor's War,* London, 1983
McAra, Charles, *Mainly in Minesweepers,* London, 1991
Macdonald, Sir Roderick, *The Figurehead,* Durham, 1993

Macintyre, Donald, *U-Boat Killer,* London, 1956
Maher, Brendan A., *A Passage to Sword Beach,* Shrewsbury, 1996
Mallalieu, J. P. W., *Very Ordinary Seaman,* London, 1944
– *On Larkhill,* London, 1983
Melly, George, *Rum, Bum and Concertina,* London, 1977
Monsarrat, Nicholas, *HM Frigate,* London, 1945
– *Three Corvettes,* London, 1953
– *Life is a Four Letter Word,* Vol 2, London 1970
Montagu, Ewen, *Beyond Top Secret U,* London, 1977
Zeigler, Phillip, *Mountbatten,* London, 1985
Taverner, Nixie, *A Torch among Tapers, (Rory O'Conor),* Bramber, 2001
Oram, H. P. K., *The Rogue's Yarn,* London, 1993
Owen, Charles, *No More Heroes,* London, 1975
Palmer, John, *Luck on my Side,* Barnsley, 2002
Putt, S. Gorley, *Men Dressed as Seamen,* London, 1943
Rayner, D. A., *Escort, The Battle of the Atlantic,* London, 1955
Scott, Peter, *The Eye of the Wind,* London, 1961
Searle, G. W., *At Sea Level,* Lewes, 1994
Baker, Richard, *The Terror of Tobermory, (Sir Gilbert Stephenson)* reprinted Edinburgh 1999
Villiers, Alan, *The Set of the Sails,* London, 1950
Waugh, Evelyn, ed Michael Davie, *Diaries,* London, 1976
Wellings, Joseph ed Hattendorf, John, *On His Majesty's Service,* Newport, Rhode Island, 1983
Whelan, John, *Home is the Sailor,* London, 1957
Willans, Geoffrey, *One Eye on the Clock,* London, 1943
Young, Edward, *One of Our Submarines,* London, 1982

PERSONAL MEMOIRS, MANUSCRIPT

Imperial War Museum;
Ball, 83/45/2
Dinwiddy, 04/31/1
Harris, 84/54/2
Jones, PP/MCR/66
Kitching, 86/11/1
Lingwood, 05/6/1
Moran, 92/45/1
Richardson, 94/43/1

OFFICIAL AND SEMI-OFFICIAL PUBLICATIONS

Technical manuals
Admiralty, *Engineering Manual for His Majesty's Fleet, BR 16,* 1939
Admiralty, *First Aid in the Royal Navy, BR 25,* 1943
Admiralty, *The Gunnery Pocket Book, BR 224/45,* 1945
Admiralty, *Machinery Handbook, BR 77,* 1941
Admiralty, *Manual of Navigation,* Vol. I, Vol. III, 1938
Admiralty, *A Seaman's Pocket Book, BR 827,* 1943
Admiralty, *A Royal Navy Officer's Pocket Book,* ed Lavery, 2007

Staff histories

Amphibious Warfare Headquarters, History of the Combined Operations Organisation 1940-1945, London, 1956
Admiralty, *The Navy and the Y-Scheme,* 1944
Waters, D. W. and Barley, F., *The Defeat of the Enemy Attack on Shipping,* Navy Records Society, 1997

Pamphlets

Wright, Noel, and Sweet, A. C. G., *How to Prepare Food; Tips and Wrinkles for Cooks of Messes in Standard Ration Ships,* Ipswich, 1941

A First Lieutenant's Handbook, c 1932, NMM pamphlet collection

OFFICIAL RECORDS

Dunkirk, National Archives;
ADM 199/786-796B

Convoy records, National Archives

There are few files for individual convoys in the early stages, and they are grouped together in various ways which can be found by means of a card index in the National Archives. Often the same convoy is to be found in several files. The ones use here are as follows;

ADM 199/50, HX 89
ADM 199/59, OB 263, HX 102
ADM 199/708, OG 71
ADM 199/713, SC 94
ADM 199/2099, HG 61, ON 27, HG 11
ADM 199/ 2110, HX 89, OB 249, OB 263
ADM 237/512, OB 275

Amphibious warfare training files are often to be found in the papers of the Ministry of Defence, DEFE, as well as the Admiralty papers, ADM, and occasionally in the War Office (WO) and Air Ministry (AIR) files. Important examples are;

DEFE 2/898, Manning of landing craft
DEFE 2/1319, Inveraray, précis of lectures
DEFE 2/1429, Training of Stoker Drivers and Coxswains
DEFE 2/1430, Training and drafting of landing craft officers and ratings

Accounts of amphibious operations, National Archives

These are best followed through the operational orders and the final reports by the naval officers in charge, which also include many accounts by junior officers;

DEFE 2/401-2, Force G orders
DEFE 2/416-7, Report by naval commander, Force G
ADM 179/335, Training and exercise programme for Force J
ADM 199/1559, Force J, orders and memoranda
ADM 179/506, Report of proceedings of Force J
ADM 199/1561, Force S, orders and memoranda
ADM 179/504, Report of proceedings of Force S

Admiralty Fleet Orders can be found in the library of the Royal Naval Museum in Portsmouth and in the National Archives in the ADM 182 series

PERIODICALS

King Alfred Magazine, complete run in Hove Public Library
Daily Telegraph, Book of Naval Obituaries, London, 2004
News Chronicle, August 1941
Mariners Mirror, Journal of the Society for Nautical Research
Naval Review
Admiralty, Monthly Anti-Submarine Report, 1939-45, in NMM library and National Archives ADM 199/2057 to 2062

FILMS

Collections of training and propaganda films are available on DVD from the Imperial War Museum, including:

The Royal Navy at War, 1940-1943, 2005, including Corvettes and Meet the Ship

Protect the Convoy, 2005, including Escort Teams at Work

The Royal Navy at War, Naval Instructional Films, 2005, including Duties of a Helmsman and Duties of a Lookout.

The Royal Navy at War – Fleet Air Arm, 2005

The Royal Navy at War – Know Your own Navy, 2005

The Royal Navy at War – Naval Instructional Films, 2005

The Royal Marines at War, 2003

Shipyards and Docks at War, 2004

FEATURE FILMS

Convoy, In Which we Serve, We Dive at Dawn and many others are available on DVD

INDEX